Spanish
Jesuit Churches
in Mexico's
Tarahumara

Tarahumaras gather for Mass at the church of San Luis Rey de Francia de Guaguevo near the edge of Barranca del Cobre.

Spanish Jesuit Churches in Mexico's Tarahumara

Paul M. Roca

UNIVERSITY OF ARIZONA PRESS

Tucson, Arizona

About the Author . . .

PAUL M. ROCA has spent most of a lifetime collecting books and manuscripts relating to Arizona and the Southwest and to the history of the Jesuits in Sonora and Chihuahua. Since the middle 1950s he has made at least one trip a year into the back country of northern Mexico investigating Spanish Jesuit churches and ruins. He is also author of *Paths of the Padres Through Sonora: An Illustrated Guide to Its Spanish Churches.*

THE UNIVERSITY OF ARIZONA PRESS

Copyright © 1979
The Arizona Board of Regents
All Rights Reserved
Manufactured in the U.S.A.

Library of Congress Cataloging in Publication Data

Roca, Paul M.
    Spanish Jesuit churches in Mexico's Tarahumara.

    Bibliography: p.
    Includes index.
    1. Architecture, Jesuit—Mexico—Chihuahua
(State) 2. Church architecture—Mexico—Chihuahua
(State) 3. Architecture, Colonial—Mexico—
Chihuahua (State) 4. Tarahumare Indians—
Architecture. 5. Indians of Mexico—Mexico—
Chihuahua (State)—Architecture. I. Title.
NA5256.C45R6   972'.1   78-14467
ISBN 0-8165-0651-5
ISBN 0-8165-0572-1 pbk.

In Reverent Homage to
Those Members of the Society of Jesus
Who Served in Tarahumara
From 1611 to 1767

and

His Excellency
Don Salvador Martínez Aguirre, S.J.,
Titular Bishop of Arca in Armenia

and

Vicar Apostolic of the Mission of the Tarahumara,
Retired

Contents

Part III. Reference Material

Illustrations

Preface

A special fascination surrounds the churches and church pueblos built by the Jesuits among the Tarahumara Indians of Mexico—or, as it was then called, New Spain—between 1611 and 1767. My friend Paul Urbano and I discovered this firsthand on a succession of excursions into the mountains of western Chihuahua from 1968 through 1976.

The three parts of this book explore various aspects of Tarahumara's Spanish Jesuit churches. The first section provides background for understanding the missions—the geography, the living style of the people and the history of Tarahumara. In Part II each chapter describes a head church and its several subordinate churches. The final section contains reference materials that supplement and reinforce the text. The Biographical Directory focuses mainly on Jesuits, but also includes key Spanish civil and military figures, as well as Tarahumara war chiefs. The Notes to the Chapters are chiefly source materials, but also provide supplementary background. Meanings for the abbreviations used for the titles of references are contained in the list preceding the Biographical Directory, while full citations occur in the Bibliography. The Glossary, to be found after this Preface, offers definitions of status titles and various other words which appear in Spanish in the text because their specialized meanings often cannot be conveyed by simple equivalent terms in English. Throughout the book I have followed the style of italicizing foreign words only upon their first appearance and have not regarded as foreign a word found in standard English dictionaries. The Index includes Spanish, English and Rarámuri (Tarahumara) names of persons and places.

The part of Chihuahua Paul Urbano and I traveled is but a portion of the old Jesuit mission area. This book deals only with the ancient homeland of the Tarahumaras, thus excluding the towns of the Jesuits established in northern Durango and in the Guadalupe y Calvo area of southern Chihuahua, which was anciently Tepehuán country, even though it later has become part Tepehuán and part Tarahumara. Similarly excluded is all of the Jesuit province of Chínipas, that mountain-locked southwestern segment of Chihuahua bounded on the east by Barranca del Cobre and on the west by the state of Sonora. Tarahumaras make their homes throughout the Chínipas region, but in the seventeenth century this was the country of the Tubares, the Guazápares, the Varohíos, the Chínipas and the Témoris, all relatives of the Tarahumaras and all similar in language and culture.

Conversely, I include within the country I call Tarahumara two large areas which are without Tarahumaras today but were within the boundaries of Tarahumara as the Jesuits knew it in the seventeenth century. The first is the entire eastern segment of the ancient Tarahumara homeland, lying east of an imaginary line from Satevó in the north, then south through San Felipe de Jesús to Huejotitlán and finally to San Pablo Balleza. The second area is the northern portion of old Tarahumara, which includes the headwaters of Río Papigóchic south and east of Ciudad Guerrero as well as the country on both sides of the river as it flows northwest toward Yepómera and Sírupa. The Indians steadily moved out of these areas in the face of Spanish and mestizo colonization and sought refuge to the west and south, always farther into the mountains and barrancas of the sierra.

To the ethnological or linguistic purist, the word Tarahumara doesn't exist, being only a bad Spanish transliteration of the word Rarámuri, which is the term the Indians use.[1] There is not even agreement as to the proper spelling of the Spanish word, and while Tarahumara with an "a" is the most prevalent, some people drop the "a" in favor of Tarahumar,[2] some spell it Tarahumare[3] and others prefer Tarahumari.[4] Strictly speaking, the term Tarahumara should probably be applied only to the Indians, although an occasional map[5] designates as Sierra Tarahumara the highest, most difficult and most inaccessible portion of the Sierra Madre Occidental, anciently the western reaches and today the center of Tarahumara country. For simplicity's sake, however, Tarahumara is used here as a shorthand place name to designate the area in which the Rarámuri lived when the Jesuits built their churches among them in the seventeenth century.

Learning about, finding and photographing those churches has been a challenge. When Paul Urbano and I started looking for Tarahumara churches in 1968, we had almost no modern information at all about the actual location of the churches nor about how to get to them; we didn't know which ones were still in existence and which were in rubble; finally, we didn't know who could give us any of the information we lacked.

We thus began our assault on the sierra on the basis of a list of all the churches reported by Father Juan Ortiz Zapata in the *Relación*[6] which resulted from his 1678 visitation. With respect to each church, I set down the meager geographical data of the *Relación*, even though in most cases there is no more than a statement that the next church is a given number of leagues northerly or westerly of the last. Because the *Relación* arranges the churches by administrative groupings, I did the same thing in my list. The basic Jesuit administrative unit was then the *partido*, or mission area, with a single *cabecera*, or headquarters church, and a number of *visitas*, or relatively nearby churches which were cared for by the priest resident at the cabecera.

Because southwestern Tarahumara had not yet been brought to Christianity in 1678, I supplemented the *Relación* with the 1765 *Demostración*, or visitation report of Bishop Pedro Tamarón,[7] adding not only the post-1678 partidos, with their cabeceras and visitas, but also the additional churches built in the older areas after the date of the Ortiz report.

Having made our lists, I tried to apply them to such modern maps as were available. Most of the larger places were relatively easy to locate—the Rarámuri place names usually hadn't changed, and if the Indian name was given by Ortiz or Tamarón, I had a good chance of finding it on a modern map. But if the old reports gave only the saint's name for the church, we had real trouble, and regardless of which name was given, we had constant problems with the small places. As to about half the churches on our list, we started out not really knowing where we were going and dependent solely on our ability to find someone who knew where the church was and could speak enough Spanish to tell us.

Thus our own investigation proceeded on the basis of the geographical arrangement of the partidos—a cabecera surrounded by visitas, the locations of which were either shown on a map or were known to someone at the cabecera. The arrangement of the chapters relating to the churches is the same arrangement, based on both the Ortiz system and on our travels.

Roads into the sierra start from either Parral or Chihuahua. While either is satisfactory, it seems more logical to start from Parral and, following the chronological order of settlement, look first at the churches in the southeastern part of ancient Tarahumara. Thus, after a preliminary look at the geography of Tarahumara, and at its people, followed by a general overview of their history, this book takes up for separate consideration each of the old partidos, starting with Parral and the oldest partido of them all, San Miguel de las Bocas.

In the course of finding, exploring and photographing the old churches I have formed opinions, not only concerning construction and ornamentation, but also concerning age, beauty and sometimes utility. In this book, all descriptions are of the churches as they were when I visited them, and all opinions, unless they are specifically attributed to someone else, are my own.

Many people have been of very great assistance to me, not only in locating churches but in the sometimes more difficult task of finding archival and manuscript records. For their interest, hospitality, and constant help of all kinds, my sincere gratitude goes to all the Jesuits of the *Misión de la Tarahumara*, but in particular to my friends Fathers Benjamín Tapia and Carlos Díaz Infante. I have had the very real assistance of those excellent Jesuit scholars Father Ernest J. Burrus and Father Charles W. Polzer, the constant help and encouragement of the preeminent Tarahumara scholar

Campbell W. Pennington, and the indispensable advice of the staffs of the Bancroft Library and the library of the University of Texas. My thanks go to all of them for making possible the necessary research, both field and archival.

Others helped in other ways and share equally in my thanks—Jeanne Willard, who did most of the typing; Margarita Terrazas Perches of Chihuahua; my cousins, Rosa Lee W. de Muñoz of México, and Ralph O. Yeager of California, all of whom helped in innumerable ways; my wife, who has been long-suffering and uncomplaining; the Reverend Paul D. Urbano, without whom there would have been no trips; and the highly professional staff of the University of Arizona Press, without whom there would have been no book. Thank you, all of you.

PAUL M. ROCA

Glossary

Acta.	Record of official proceedings.
Adelantado.	Title sometimes conferred on governor of newly conquered territory or newly established province.
Alcalde.	Town official, generally with civil, police and judicial authority.
Alcalde mayor.	Superior alcalde; an alcalde with greater or more important jurisdiction.
Alcaldía.	Territorial or other jurisdiction of an alcalde.
Audiencia.	Judicial body existing at various levels of government, with broad investigative and trial authority.
Baldaquino.	Baldachin or baldaquin. A canopy borne in ecclesiastical processions or, if fixed, supported by columns or projecting from wall; often it is placed over the altar and holds the image of a saint.

Beato.	Blessed; beatified, but not yet canonized.
Cabecera.	In a mission system, the headquarters or principal church of the district.
Campanario.	Belfry, frequently arched, added to or built in a wall in lieu of a bell tower.
Coadjutor.	Assistant ecclesiastical officer with right of succession on the death of the incumbent.
Consultor de provincia.	Advisor of the province.
Cura.	Parish priest, curate. A member of the secular clergy rather than of one of the Orders.
Cura teniente.	Temporary or substitute curate.
Ejido.	Farm, ranch or timber land held and operated in common by a group of workers organized under the Mexican Agrarian Land Law.
Estancia.	Farm, country home.
Fiscal.	Attorney general, a ministerial officer who acts for the government by which he is appointed.
Gobierno.	Government, executive power.
Hermana.	Sister; a member of a religious order for women.
Hermano.	Brother; member of a religious order for men who is not an ordained priest.
Juez.	Judge.
Juez comisario.	Judge whose jurisdiction is derived from and limited by special commission or order of appointment.
Kilómetro.	Kilometer, about .62 miles.
Licienciado.	Lawyer.

Maestre de campo.	Field master, a military rank.
Maestre general.	Military rank below a full general.
Maestre general de milicias.	Military officer in charge of militia.
Municipio	In Mexico, administrative area roughly equivalent to a U.S. county but often with rights and privileges similar to those of a city.
Nación.	Nation, race, Indian tribe.
Obispo.	Bishop.
Parroquia.	Parish, parochial church.
Partido.	In Jesuit missionary usage, term applied to area which included one cabecera, or head church, and one or more visitas, or dependent churches, all usually served by one priest.
Patrona.	Patroness, titular saint of a church.
Procurador.	Attorney, one who is in charge of another's affairs.
Profeso.	One who has taken religious vows.
Quinto.	One-fifth; a duty paid to the Spanish crown.
Ranchería.	Small band of Indians living in the same general location, or the settlement in which they live.
Real.	Royal. Also a Spanish coin worth an eighth of a silver peso. Also a mining camp.
Rectorado.	Rectorate, rectorship.
Residencia.	House where priests live.
Teniente.	Deputy, substitute, lieutenant.
Vicario.	Vicar, ecclesiastical deputy.

Visita.   In Jesuit missionary usage, church of secondary importance, generally without permanent clergy, served from headquarters or cabecera.

Visitador.   Ecclesiastical inspector with power to change missionary assignments and to enforce discipline.

Visitador general.   Visitador with jurisdiction over all the Jesuit missionary activities in New Spain.

Part I

Background

Geography

Any consideration of the Spanish Jesuit churches of Tarahumara must necessarily begin with geography. Indeed, any consideration of anything having to do with Tarahumara must begin with geography, and this is true whether the word is being used to refer to the country, to the mountains, that is to say, to the Sierra Tarahumara, or to the Indians who have lived in the high valleys of the sierra for at least 2,000 years.[1]

The Sierra Tarahumara is the highest, most rugged and the most nearly impenetrable portion of the Sierra Madre Occidental, which is Mexico's portion of the continental spine that runs from the Canadian Rockies to Central America. The sierra fills and bulges at the edges of most of western and southwestern Chihuahua, Mexico's largest state. From its heights rise the headwaters of Río Conchos, a principal tributary of Río Grande, or as the Mexicans call it, Río Bravo, which drains substantially the entire eastern slope of the sierra and all of eastern Chihuahua into the Gulf of Mexico.

Across the Continental Divide, but in the same high mountain country, are the headwaters of Río Urique, Río Batopilas, Río Verde and Río Chínipas, four mighty rivers which join near the corner common to Sonora, Sinaloa and Chihuahua to form the stream so appropriately named Río Fuerte. Again, just across the Divide and

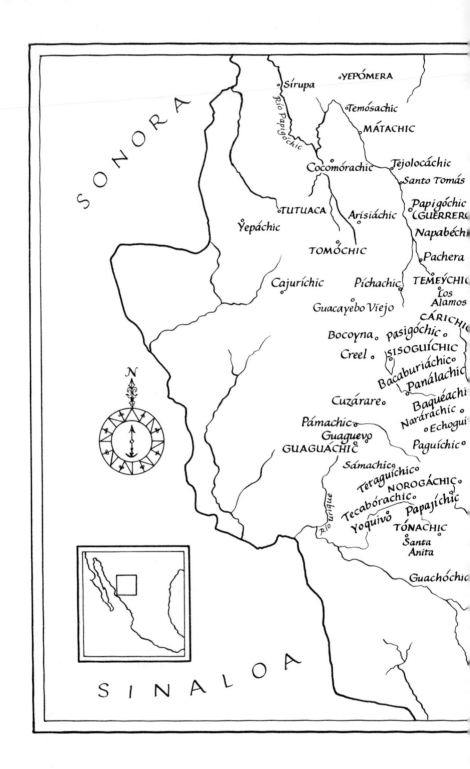

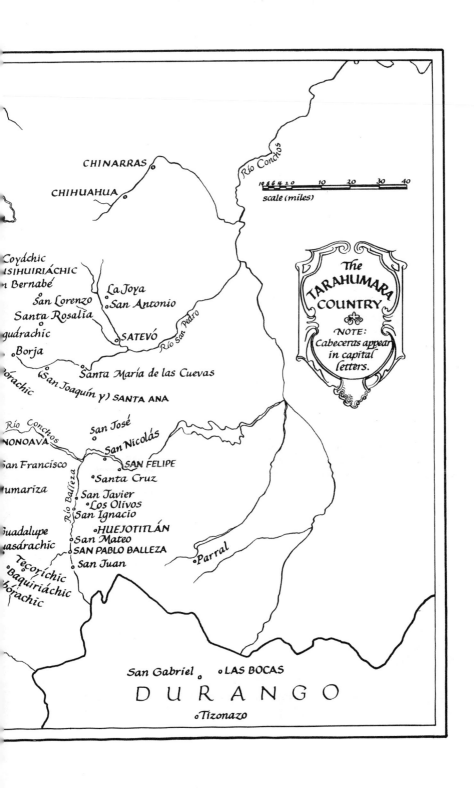

CHINARRAS

CHIHUAHUA

Río Conchos

scale (miles)

10 20 30 40

10 8 6 4 2 0

The
TARAHUMARA
COUNTRY

❧

NOTE:
*Cabeceras appear
in capital
letters.*

Coyáchic
ISIHUIRIÁCHIC
n Bernabé
San Lorenzo   La Joya
Santa Rosalía   San Antonio
gudráchic
Borja   SATEVÓ

Río San Pedro

Santa María de las Cuevas
óráchic
(San Joaquín y) SANTA ANA

Río Conchos

San José
NONOAVA
San Nicolás
San Francisco   SAN FELIPE
Santa Cruz
Iumariza   San Javier
                   Los Olivos
                   San Ignacio
Guadalupe   HUEJOTITLÁN
asdráchic   San Mateo
Tecorichic   SAN PABLO BALLEZA
Baquiriáchic   San Juan   Parral
óráchic

Río Balleza

San Gabriel   LAS BOCAS

DURANGO

Tizonazo

a little to the north are the headwaters of Río Papigóchic which flows first north, then south, then again north, and, after changing its name and looping around most of northeastern Sonora as Río Yaqui, finally reaches the Sea of Cortés, or as the gringos call it, the Gulf of California. A little farther to the southwest, but still in the same area, are the springs which feed Río Candameña and Río Moris, which join to form Río Mayo. Río Mayo in turn empties into the Gulf at Navojoa in southern Sonora, just a little north of Sinaloa's Topolobampo, where Río Fuerte meets the sea. Together, Río Fuerte, Río Mayo and Río Papigóchic (or Río Yaqui, depending on where you are) drain the entire western slope of Sierra Tarahumara, and thus the western third of Chihuahua from New Mexico to Durango, and together they also carry to the Gulf of California waters from northern Sinaloa and from all but the northwestern edge of Sonora.

The extent of the sierra, north and south, east and west, and up and down, is simply beyond any ability to describe. If you start west from the city of Chihuahua or from Parral, you are almost immediately in the sierra. Chihuahua itself is at an altitude of almost 5,000 feet and Parral at more than 6,000, but soon you will be in a country where only the lesser valleys are as low as 6,500 feet and most agriculture is carried on above 7,500 feet. The mountain ranges run largely north and south, not as a succession of individually high peaks but instead as massive outcroppings from valley floors, which themselves are at altitudes which would dwarf all but the Rockies, the Sierra Nevada and the Cascades of the United States. The peaks of the sierra are not so high as those of Central Mexico, nor even of Colorado or California, but the sierra is instead an endless succession of mountain chains which gives a total effect of much greater mass. Part of the Sierra Madre is in Sonora, but all of that part which is the Sierra Tarahumara is in Chihuahua. It extends east and west from the north-flowing Río Balleza to the border of Sonora, and from Río Papigóchic in the north to Río Verde, just above the Durango border.

The country I call Tarahumara is larger than Sierra Tarahumara because it includes the high foothill area at the eastern edge of the sierra as well as the upland plains which border Río Papigóchic. Thus Tarahumara extends from San Felipe de Jesús on middle Río

Conchos west almost to Batopilillas in the old Jesuit mission district of Chínipas, a poorly mapped,[2] poorly charted and largely untraveled distance, but at least 200 miles as the crow flies. From Nahuárachic in the north almost to Chinatú in the south would be another 300 miles if anyone should ever measure it. In the north, along the uplands at the headwaters of Río Papigóchic, there are great grassy llanos, or plains, with basic altitudes between 6,500 and 7,500 feet, which extend almost interminably to the mountains at every horizon. Similar but less magnificent plains are at the eastern boundary of Tarahumara, but there they are cut by the deep but relatively narrow gorge of Río Conchos and by the barrancas of Río Balleza, Río Nonoava and the other Conchos tributaries. At the Divide, which runs from southeast to northwest and separates the headwaters of the rivers of the Pacific from those that flow to the Gulf of Mexico, the altitude soars to above 9,000 feet, but seldom with spectacular peaks.

On the western slope of the sierra, the scenery becomes truly magnificent, for here is the famous Barranca del Cobre, a great gorge carved by Río Urique as it flows south to join Río Verde and then to form Río Fuerte. Observation trains of the Ferrocarril Chihuahua al Pacífico sometimes stop at Divisaderos on the western edge of the barranca to let the traveler view its vastness, and in 1975 a road was built from Bahuichivo (accessible only by rail) down to the settlement of Urique. But most of the canyon, to say nothing of Pámachic, Guaguáchic, Guaguevo, and the other Tarahumara settlements lying all or part way down to the river, is wholly inaccessible except by horse or mule.

The awesome Barranca del Cobre is becoming well known, but only slightly less spectacular are the similar barrancas of Río Urique's two principal tributaries, Río Batopilas and Río Verde. Unfortunately for the tourist, they are even more inaccessible.[3]

The vegetation of Tarahumara results from a combination of altitude and latitude. The oak and pine which grow in northern Arizona at 5,000 feet don't appear in the Tarahumara until 7,000 feet, the difference being the result of eight degrees of latitude. But throughout Tarahumara, wherever the altitude reaches or exceeds 8,000 feet, the pines are very large, with luxuriant foliage.[4] Sawmills, both operating and abandoned, are scattered throughout the

Breath-taking Barranca del Cobre is carved into the western slope of the Sierra Tarahumara. This view was taken from the east rim in April 1972.

sierra, and lumbering is far and away the most important industry of the high country. Oak is mixed with pine at the lower edge of the timber belt, and finally, as the altimeter drops, the forest gives way to scrub oak and brush.

The great upland llanos on both sides of Río Conchos and its tributaries and along Río Papigóchic are below the timberline, but they are heavily grassed and for the most part provide splendid rangeland. In the Mennonite area around Cuauhtémoc and south to Laguna de los Mexicanos, grainfields replace rangelands. On the upper end of Río Papigóchic, at about 7,500 feet and a latitude of 29° 30′, apple-raising has become a major industry. The varieties are numerous, the product is tasty and government-financed warehouses are everywhere. When my friend Paul Urbano and I have been in the area, we have never been able to buy apples—every generous grower, warehouser and shipper insisted on giving us all we could carry.

Most of Tarahumara is rainy much of the time. In the winter there is a rainy season which turns to snow in the highlands, and in the summer there is a rainy season which causes the rivers to flood and the roads, such as they are, to turn up mud. April usually is reasonably free of rain, and sometimes this is true of October. It is these months which we have used for travel. But I have known the summer rains to merge with the winter so that October can be the wettest month of all, and while I haven't experienced it, I am told that now and again the winter continues well into May. Except in the very high part of the sierra, summer days (if it isn't raining) are warm, and (again if it isn't raining) winter days are pleasantly brisk. The nights are cold at all times of the year; above 9,000 feet they're bitterly cold.

While the sierra may well include more unexplored, unmapped and unknown mountain country than any other North American area in the temperate zone, it is not entirely inaccessible and reasonably complete accessibility has been planned. In November 1971 the state of Chihuahua, in cooperation with the federal government, began the planning and construction of Plan Gran Visión, a tremendously ambitious and expensive program to make the sierra available to commerce and tourists by means of a system of paved toll roads. The Plan calls for a road southwest from Parral to and beyond Guadalupe y Calvo which will eventually connect with a road from Durango. Another segment is to carry traffic west from La Junta through Tomóchic to Yepáchic and the Sonora border, with a turnoff south to San Juanito, then to Creel and, in a great loop, back through Guachóchic to Balleza and Parral. But the extent to which the ambitious Plan will ever be completed is unpredictable. Some parts of it I have traveled with pleasure, but unless I specifically mention a portion of a completed or partially completed Gran Visión project, the roads I refer to in this book were built without its benefits.

From Chihuahua, an old paved road goes west more or less along the north edge of Tarahumara through Cuauhtémoc to Ciudad Guerrero, which was the ancient pueblo of Papigóchic. Then, mostly paved and uniformly passable to an ordinary passenger car, the road follows Río Papigóchic downstream, and northwest, along the La Junta-Ciudad Juárez branch of the Ferrocarril Chihuahua al Pacífico to Yepómera, which is at the very northernmost point of the Tarahumara homeland. From Guerrero south there is a passable road on which four-wheel drive is not essential. A well-sprung car, lightly loaded and with adequate clearance, can readily make it to the rail center of Creel, using for a portion of the way Gran Visión pavement. From there, a sturdier car can go south to a crossing of Río Urique, just before it begins to carve the Barranca del Cobre. From Río Urique, if you have four-wheel drive, you can go southeast to Guachóchic and, finally, east to the pavement at Parral.

With four-wheel drive, there are many more roads within the area thus circumnavigated. From a point west of Chihuahua on the Chihuahua-Guerrero highway, you can go south through Satevó, San Felipe de Jesús and Valle de Zaragoza to Parral. A little farther west another byway goes south to San Francisco Borja, from which there is a passable road to Nonoava which was extended to Humariza in 1973.

From Cuauhtémoc south there is a road, at first deceptively and enticingly smooth. One fork, the left, goes to Cusihuiriáchic and then to San Francisco Borja; the other goes to Cárichic. From Cárichic south the road is unusually bad, but a better west branch goes, somewhat tortuously, to Sisoguíchic, and on to a connection with the Guerrero-Creel carretera (the term the Mexicans use not only for a fine highway but also for any road of importance). Still another road from Rochéachic (a stopping place about two hours west of Guachóchic) goes north to Norogáchic, and there are poorer roads both northwest and northeast from there. One can go from Mátachic southwest to Tutuaca and Yepáchic, and from Yepáchic a few people have driven across the Sonora frontier to Maicoba and Yécora. Gran Visión has planned to carry its La Junta-Basaséachic road to Yepáchic and then on to Sonora.

These four-wheel drive roads, almost always bad, are wholly in addition to a haphazard system of forest roads which have been built, or have sprung up, to serve the lumber industry. There is a steady stream, throughout as well as to and from the sierra, of ten-wheeled trucks uniformly piled with logs four and five feet in diameter, cut to a length which, when laid across the truck bed, precisely fills the full width of the road. The forest roads go to (but almost never beyond) sawmills, operating or abandoned, but, like all other roads, they are frustratingly naked of signs or markers.

Since 1961 it has been possible to enter and to cross the sierra by train, for that year saw the completion of the Ferrocarril Chihuahua al Pacífico[5] from Creel south and southwest past the Barranca del Cobre to and then along Río Fuerte to Los Mochis in Sinaloa. Until Gran Visión is extended to Yepáchic and then to Maicoba, the area will remain accessible from Sonora only through the Carretas pass at the north end of the Sierra Madre between Bavispe and Janos or by going through two other states—first south to Culiacán in Sinaloa and thence across the sierra through Durango and finally north to Parral.

From Texas or New Mexico you should go first to Chihuahua, either from Ojinaga (called Presidio on the Texas side) or from El Paso. From Arizona and California the worst way is south from Douglas to Bavispe and then across the Carretas pass to Janos, but the quickest is to go south from Interstate 8 between Deming and Lordsburg to Hachita and then across the border at El Berrendo, traveling passable dirt roads to the pavement at Janos. From Janos it's an easy day's trip by way of Nuevo Casas Grandes either southeast to Chihuahua or south to Madera. People leaving from Phoenix should allow two days to get to Chihuahua even by the shortest (El Berrendo) route, for my odometer calls it 1,100 kilometers from the capital of Arizona to the capital of Chihuahua.

The People

When the first Spanish Jesuits reached Valle de San Pablo about midway downstream (north) on Río Balleza and thus first made contact with the Tarahumaras, there probably were around 40,000 Indians living in the approximately 120,000 square kilometers lying north of Río Verde, south of Sírupa and Nahuárachic at the northern margin of Río Papigóchic, west of San Pablo (the modern Balleza) and San Felipe de Jesús and east of a line drawn from the Barranca del Cobre roughly north to Yepómera.[1] In the 1970s there were probably 40,000 to 45,000 Tarahumaras living in the west half of the ancient homeland, an area of about 60,000 square kilometers.[2] The shift is the obvious result of a steady movement to the south and west.

The earliest report from which anyone can guess at population is that of Father Juan Ortiz Zapata in his visitation report of 1678.[3] He counted a total of 2,102 Christian families under mission control, and from this figure (using an average of five persons per family), Pennington[4] extrapolates 10,000 Tarahumaras under mission influence, and thus assumes a total population of somewhere between 30,000 and 40,000. In 1894 Lumholtz[5] estimated the number at 30,000. The official government census of 1930 came up with 28,000 Tarahumaras, but was admittedly inaccurate because a mule carrying an undetermined number of census sheets was lost over the edge of a barranca.[6] The government count ten years later showed 25,000 Tarahumaras,[7] but it is probably not any more reliable. What is perhaps the best modern estimate came to 44,000 in 1945.[8]

Pennington has concluded,[9] and probably correctly, that the Tarahumara population has remained reasonably static from the early seventeenth century until modern times. This constant population is the logical result of the interaction of all the factors which have influenced Tarahumara life in the 350 years since the first Jesuit "reductions," or consolidations of the Indians into settlements around the churches.

In other parts of Mexico assimilation with the white or mestizo[10] population has resulted in the very nearly complete elimination of many tribes. But not so with the Tarahumaras. They have lived alone and among themselves, shunning outside contact as though it were a plague (as indeed sometimes it was). But isolation did not work to increase the population, as it did in the case of the Navajo.

Many other factors have operated to keep the population level. The harshness of the upland and mountain country in which the Tarahumaras lived when the Spaniards came, and even more the inhospitality of the barranca area to which they fled, have undoubtedly held down any natural increase. Infant mortality has been extremely high,[11] due in large part to a diet seriously deficient in protein. While the Tarahumara revolts of the seventeenth century resulted in Spanish soldiers killing Tarahumara men on a basis which the old accounts make sound both brutal and wholesale, the actual numbers who met death in this way were really not very large, compared to the total population. Similarly, while there were reports of epidemics in both the seventeenth and eighteenth centuries,[12] the results apparently were no more than a series of temporary setbacks which balanced other influences working to increase population.

On the plus side, the Tarahumaras live in a climate which, despite the rain, is probably as healthy as that of any place in North America, and a good deal healthier than that of much of the United States. More importantly, at least in the eyes of some Tarahumaras,

A sinewy Tarahumara man stands in a field south of Cárichic. Nearer the railroad and the mestizo ranches, jeans are replacing the traditional loincloth.

is the high curative power of *tesguino*, the native corn beer which is produced throughout the sierra.[13]

Like any other people, the Tarahumaras come in a number of sizes and shapes. Typically, however, both men and women are short of stature, being seldom more than a few inches over five feet. The men are very lean and sinewy, often weighing no more than 100 pounds. The women tend to be larger, undoubtedly because of their more sedentary occupations, but seldom is an adult of either sex truly fat, at least by Pima or Pápago standards.

The Tarahumaras, particularly the men, are extremely dark-skinned. The males wear their straight black hair long, most commonly held by a sweatband around the forehead and sometimes also braided. The women's hair is always long. The men are largely without facial hair.

Tarahumara men are surprisingly strong. Again and again I have seen them carry over very long distances burdens which must quite certainly greatly exceed their own weight. If a load is being carried any distance, it is ordinarily held in a blanket or otherwise attached firmly to a strap across the forehead, with the weight resting almost entirely on the back, which is bent at a 45° angle. With this kind of a rig, a Tarahumara man will carry lumber for miles without any appearance of getting tired. I have seen a Tarahumara man who could not conceivably weigh more than 100 pounds pick up with apparent ease a sackful of grain so large and so heavy that anywhere in the United States the task would routinely have been assigned to no fewer than four men.

The Tarahumaras have tremendous endurance and are famous for running great distances with little or no obvious effort. If he is carrying a substantial burden, a Tarahumara will walk, but if he is without heavy equipment or has something he can carry in his hand, he would prefer to run, moving effortlessly at a pace which eats up the miles. The standard Tarahumara method of hunting is to run down a deer or rabbit, and it is said to be not at all uncommon for a Tarahumara who is following a deer to catch up to him, exhausted and dying, after a chase which has lasted two or three days.[14]

The exceptional Tarahumara ability at running great distances is related, not surprisingly, to the relatively universal game called *carrera de bola,* or kickball, involving a race between opposing teams. The members of each team kick a wooden ball with great rapidity over a prescribed and usually very long course, with victory going to the team whose ball first covers the full distance. Carrera de bola is engaged in both by prearrangement and casually, is often accompanied by relatively substantial betting and is frequently an incident of a tesguino festival.[15]

Both culturally[16] and linguistically[17] the Tarahumaras are related to the Pimas and to the other tribal groups of the southwestern United States and northwestern Mexico which belong to the Uto-Aztecan language family.[18] Almost as soon as they entered Tarahumara, the Jesuits undertook to master the language, and most of the Spanish Jesuits before the expulsion were able to preach and to teach in Rarámuri or, as the Spanish-speaking Tarahumara more frequently says today, *la idioma.* A number of the Jesuits wrote vocabularies for their own use, transliterating the Rarámuri sounds into Spanish, and in 1826 the Franciscans published a Rarámuri grammar.[19]

K. Simon Hilton, an American resident of Sámachic, has published a Rarámuri vocabulary and a translation of the New Testament.[20] Additionally, a Rarámuri-English dictionary has become available,[21] and in 1953 Father David Brambila, the Jesuit priest then at Cerocahui, published his scholarly and authorative *Gramática Rarámuri,*[22] with complete rules for number and gender, the declension of nouns, the conjugation of regular and irregular verbs, the classification of tenses, and numerous other grammatical nuances.

In common with most of the non-Indians who deal with the Tarahumaras, my own knowledge of the language goes only slightly beyond "Kwire-vá," the universal greeting. But in that and other Rarámuri words which have crept into this book, I have followed the lead of the Jesuit writers and transliterated into Spanish, using a stress accent where appropriate to show a departure from the standard Spanish accent system. Indeed, in this respect, Rarámuri appears to be similar to many other members of its language family—polysyllabic words tend to carry an accent at least one syllable ahead of what would be more common in Spanish.

Unless he has worked in the mestizo towns or ranches, the average Tarahumara knows very little Spanish. But the percentage who are at least partially bilingual is higher than in past generations. The coming of the railroad has meant employment for many Tarahumaras who live within a walk (or run) of only a day or two of the right-of-way and have thus been able to seek employment, necessarily involving Spanish.[23] More and more Indians have had other dealings with the Spanish-speaking population because of increased lumbering activity, the opening of new mines, the building of roads and employment opportunities on mestizo ranches at the edges of Tarahumara.

The percentage of Spanish-speaking Tarahumaras should grow, both because the government has been pursuing a more aggressive program of education and because the Jesuits have been working hard at teaching throughout Tarahumara. The government effort is twofold. As in the rest of the Republic, since the 1930s there has been a tremendous increase in public educational facilities. Schools are being built in all but the most remote areas of Tarahumara. For quite a few years, the government has been attempting to train native teachers at a special academy in Guachóchic.

The Jesuits have carried on a somewhat different program. In Sisoguíchic they have built a radio station to make daily broadcasts throughout Tarahumara, giving four hours of instruction in Spanish and four hours in Rarámuri. At remote places the priests have built small boarding schools presided over not by teachers but by a reliable man and woman who take care of the physical needs of the students and maintain order while the student, provided with books, listens to his lessons on the radio.

Tarahumara dress is distinctive. The women uniformly wear brightly colored, long billowing skirts and long-sleeved full blouses with bandana-type headdresses. In the nineteenth century Lumholtz reported that many of the women went bare breasted at home or in the barranca,[24] but I have no corroborating experience.

Near the railroad and on the edges of Tarahumara, many men have adopted Levi's and conventional shirts, but we found that the typical male costume in the interior still consists of thong sandals, a loose-fitting loincloth in lieu of pants, a long-sleeved loose shirt tied at the wrists and gathered at the waist, a sash around the middle like a belt, and a band around the forehead to hold the long hair. Ordinarily the shirt and loincloth are white, but the headband may be any color, and red is frequently seen. Thus dressed, a Tarahumara man will run without tiring all day at altitudes approaching 10,000 feet and at night, if he has no blanket, he will spend the entire night standing beside a small fire. Children are dressed precisely as adults, but on a smaller scale.

Living conditions among the Tarahumaras remain at almost the same primitive level as in the seventeenth century. A very large number live in caves, not because they are cave dwellers in the prehistoric sense, but because a cave is a most convenient dwelling.[25] There are already three sides and a roof—a front wall is all that is needed to build a house which is often a good deal more comfortable than a conventional building. Cooking utensils are fire-hardened ollas and wooden spoons—corn is ground with a stone mano on a stone metate in exactly the same way it was ground 400 years ago. A principal Tarahumara food is *atole*, a gruel made by boiling ground cornmeal to a watery consistency.

In all the Tarahumara cornfields I have never seen a metal-plow—the usual arrangement is a wooden plow pushed by one man. Occasionally I have seen a cow, and less frequently a horse, pulling a plow in front of the man; a few times I have seen a woman pulling; and once I saw a triple play—a horse pulling, a woman guiding from behind and a man standing on top as ballast to force the wooden blade deeper into the soil. Most Tarahumara farmers have a metal hoe and a metal axe, but other metal tools are unusual.

The Tarahumaras are an agricultural people, but their principal and usually their only crop is corn. The incidence of nutritional deficiency from a low protein diet, particularly in children, is predictably very high. But Tarahumaras change habits slowly. They were growing corn in the *ciénagas*, or marshy meadows, in the high valleys of the sierra when the Spaniards came, and ever since they have continued to grow corn in the same fields, and in other fields even more remote from European civilization. Modern efforts, by government agents and by the Jesuits, to encourage crop rotation and a greater variety, have been courteously but effectively rebuffed.[26] Few Tarahumaras have cattle or horses, and where they are found they are not raised for food but as beasts of burden and draft animals. There are a few sheep and many goats, although again the goat is principally raised for its coat and is not prized for either milk or meat.

Photo by Paul D. Urbano

A Tarahumara man ploughs his field near Paguichic with the
aid of two steers.

The Tarahumaras are largely unassimilated, and they have apparently wanted it this way. Their steady retreat to the southwest,
farther and farther into the sierra, the higher mesas and ciénagas,
farther down the barrancas, has been a retreat from European civilization and thus from the possibilities of assimilation. Usually
gently, sometimes fiercely, but always resolutely, they have wanted
to be alone. Indeed, except for the Jesuits who have sought to
minister to them, both Spaniards and mestizos have left them
largely alone for three and a half centuries.

History

In 1611, only 71 years after Pope Paul III recognized the existence of the fledgling order,[1] the Society of Jesus began its assault on the harsh barrancas of Tarahumara and its work of teaching the hands and minds of the Indians while converting their souls to Christianity.

Four years earlier, in 1607, Father Juan Font, then a missionary to the Tepehuán, made the first Jesuit contact with the Tarahumaras. He went only to Valle de San Pablo, the site of the modern Balleza, but there he met Tarahumaras who invited him to go farther inland. He returned then to the south, but in 1608 he went to Guadiana, the modern Durango,[2] to seek permission to settle permanently as a missionary to the Tarahumaras. It took two years for the permission to come, but by early January of 1611, he was again at Valle de San Pablo, and this time, with Tarahumaras showing the way, he went much farther to the north and west, possibly as far as Nonoava.[3] In the back country he was able to induce several hundred Tarahumaras to go to the south and to settle at the town which he founded in the Valle de San Pablo, on what is now known as Río Balleza.

In 1611 Valle de San Pablo was the ultimate frontier. To the north and west lay the whole vast and almost totally unexplored[4] Sierra Tarahumara. Across the mountains to the east was the raw mining town of Santa Bárbara,[5] the only European settlement in what is now the state of Chihuahua and the jumping-off place from which Juan de Oñate, only 13 years before, had started his long march to found and settle New Mexico. To the southwest was Guadiana, the capital of Nueva Vizcaya, the frontier province founded fewer than 50 years before. Guadiana was days away, but many weeks away was México, the capital of New Spain which itself had seen Europeans for only 90 years. From 1611 until their expulsion in 1767, the Jesuits who followed Juan Font looked not back toward those settlements but steadfastly north and west to the sierra and the barrancas, to the Tarahumaras. In the next 156 years they converted a whole people and built more than 100 churches, some rude, some exceedingly fine, but all with a single purpose. A surprisingly large number are still standing.

The Christian conquest of Tarahumara was slow and decidedly uneven. The mountain country was harsh and incredibly difficult—but the Jesuits were used to that. The Franciscans, the Dominicans and the other Orders had already taken the choice areas, and all that was left for an Order younger even than New Spain was the mountain spine running north from Guadiana, peopled first by the Tepehuán, then by the Tarahumaras and, across the Divide to the west, by the Mayos, Yaquis and Pimas in the unexplored wastelands of Sinaloa and Sonora.

In 1611 Font was able to start the Tarahumara conquest because the Tepehuán were believed to be secure for Christianity. The belief was violently shattered five years later when the Tepehuán revolt in what is now northern Durango took the lives of Juan Font and Gerónimo Moranta, who had joined him at San Pablo in 1614, along with six other Jesuits, one Dominican, one Franciscan[6] and hundreds of Spaniards. There was no revolt among the Tarahumaras, but the two Jesuits were killed when they were caught on the road between San Pablo and Zape, where they were on their way to join the Tepehuán missionaries at a fiesta.

The result not only was disaster for the Tepehuán mission, but it meant the temporary abandonment of San Pablo, which was not reoccupied until 1630, when the Jesuits started all over again. But during the 14 years San Pablo was without a resident priest, there had been some Jesuit contact with the Tarahumaras. Not long after Font's death, Sanguesa and Nicolás Estrada had gone back to San Pablo and spent a few months. A few years later José Lomas, the missionary to the Tepehuán at Guanaceví, visited San Pablo, and in 1623 Martín Larios induced a large number of Tarahumaras from San Pablo to move with him south to Río Florido, where he may have begun the new town of San Miguel de las Bocas, with a mixed Tarahumara and Tepehuán population. The experiment was probably not very successful, but a second try, in 1630, resulted not only in a permanent Tarahumara settlement at Las Bocas, but soon thereafter in two more nearby establishments, San Gabriel and Tizonazo. The 1630 effort followed an *entrada* by Captain Juan Barraza and the Jesuit Juan Heredía, who went as far northwest as Nonoava, from which they brought back 400 Tarahumara settlers for San Miguel de las Bocas.

But the Jesuits didn't make a frontal attack on Tarahumara until 1639, eight years after the discovery of the mines at Parral[7] brought a thin trickle of Spanish settlers into southern Chihuahua. The pioneers of 1639, José Pascual and Gerónimo Figueroa, pushed beyond the frontier of European civilization, represented by an east-west line between San Pablo, Santa Bárbara and Parral, and penetrated to Río Conchos, founding churches throughout what came to be called Tarahumara Baja, or Tarahumara Antigua, and building the towns of San Felipe de Jesús, San Gerónimo de Huejotitlán, San Francisco Javier de Satevó and San Francisco Borja.

Nine years later, by 1648, there were five principal Jesuit establishments serving Tarahumara: San Miguel de las Bocas on Río Florido, San Pablo on Río Balleza, San Gerónimo de Huejotitlán between Río Balleza and Río Conchos, San Felipe de Jesús on Río Conchos, and San Francisco Javier de Satevó, a little north of Río Conchos. Each had a resident priest and each had two or three visitas. Christianity seemed well settled in the foothills of Sierra Tarahumara between Río Florido and Río Conchos.

But appearances were deceiving. The year 1648 marked the first of the Tarahumara revolts. The causes were many: the *hechizeros,* or medicine men of the Tarahumaras, resented the Jesuit missionaries and the spread of Christianity; despite the royal prohibition from distant Madrid, too many of the Indians were forced to work in the mines at Parral and Santa Bárbara; often the Spanish soldiers, settlers and merchants in the two towns were arrogant, domineering and demanding.

The revolt was not as devastating as the earlier uprising of the Tepehuán. Rebel Tarahumaras attacked the mission herds along the Conchos, but no priests lost their lives, and only one church, the visita at San Francisco Borja, was destroyed. After some pillaging and not a great deal of damage, the rebels retired farther west into the mountains as if to escape the Spaniards rather than to attempt the futile job of stamping them out. The Spanish military took the field in a punitive expedition to search out the Tarahumaras in their mountain fastnesses, with the standard notion that those who could be subdued and returned to Christianity were good Indians and those who could not should be safely and quickly killed. An "army," consisting of 40 Spanish soldiers and 300 Indian allies under Juan Barraza (now a General), left Parral and chased the Tarahumaras effectively as far as Cárichic and beyond. In January 1649, Barraza was joined by the new governor of Nueva Vizcaya, Diego Guajardo Fajardo, with another 40 soldiers and several hundred Indians. Barraza and Guajardo crisscrossed most of Tarahumara, killing what Indians they could catch and accepting the submission of the scattered bands which chose surrender.

By the spring of 1649, the revolt was over, and the governor returned to Parral, but not before he had laid plans to build a new presidio, town and missionary settlement across the Divide along the upper reaches of Río Papigóchic. Purísima Concepción de Papigóchic and Villa Aguilar were established side by side at the site of the modern Ciudad Guerrero, and thus began the Christianization of Tarahumara Alta, the term applied to the valley of Río Papigóchic and the mountain areas south and west of that stream.

Peace was illusory. In 1650, less than a year after the establishment of Villa Aguilar, the Tarahumaras revolted again, killing Father Cornelio Beudín, the priest at Papigóchic, burning his church and the Spanish farms in the immediate vicinity but avoiding a direct attack on the presidio at Villa Aguilar. General Barraza was sent again from Parral, this time with General Juan Fernández Morales. The second time around, the Tarahumaras made better use of geography, and several hundred retired to a natural fortress on a *peñol*, an inaccessible rocky mesa from which they could not be dislodged.

After the troops drew back, the greatly superior force of Indians attacked the Spanish camp and ultimately forced the soldiers to leave in the night. New troops led by Governor Guajardo arrived and took up the attack on the mesa, from which many Indians had now drifted off. After heavy losses, the remaining Tarahumaras left under cover of night, and the Spaniards had a hollow victory. Guajardo chased the rebels into the trackless canyons southwest of Papigóchic, but after a time, wounded and exhausted, he returned to Villa Aguilar.

An uneasy peace was restored after a few months, but in March 1652, the truce was shattered with a furious attack on Temeýchic, Papigóchic and Villa Aguilar, which cost the lives of most of the Europeans in the valley of Río Papigóchic, including that of the priest who had taken Beudín's place, Father Giacomo Antonio Basilio.

Guajardo again took the field, and again a large body of Tarahumaras retired to an inaccessible peñol, this time near Píchachic. But, as before, instead of holding out indefinitely, the Indians slipped away in the night. Ultimately Captain Cristóbal Narváez, his troops joined by many loyal Indians, surrounded the main body of Tarahumaras. A surrender was arranged, and the leader of the revolt, one Tepóraca, was turned over to the Spaniards. He was summarily hanged on a convenient tree, and his body, filled with arrows by the repentant Tarahumaras, was allowed to rot.

Thus peace came after the third Tarahumara revolt, but Papigóchic and Villa Aguilar, as well as the other European settlements of Tarahumara Alta, had been devastated. All were now abandoned, and the Christianization of the area was not again attempted for 21 years.

In the two decades which followed the destruction of Papigóchic, the missions of Tarahumara Baja prospered, although not spectacularly. More visitas were established downstream or north on Río Balleza, and on both sides of Río Conchos upstream or west from San Felipe. But it was not until 1673 that a determined reconquest of Tarahumara Alta was initiated. In that year the new governor of Nueva Vizcaya, José García Salcedo, called a great strategy session at Parral, a meeting of priests, soldiers, miners, settlers and Indians. The Jesuits were led by Gerónimo Figueroa, who by now had been 34 years among the Tarahumaras and was the superior of all of the Tarahumara Baja churches.

Within a month of the Parral gathering, two Jesuits new to the area, Fernando Barrionuevo and Juan Manuel Gamboa, left for the north to begin rebuilding beyond Río Conchos and along the Papigóchic. Barrionuevo was soon replaced by José Tardá and Gamboa by the even more famous Tomás Guadalajara. Together Tardá and Guadalajara did a fantastic job—they built churches, they gathered Tarahumaras into more or less settled areas around the churches, they baptized, they taught, and they exposed the Indians to at least a minimum of European civilization. By 1678 they had planted missionary settlements downstream along the Papigóchic as far as Yepómera, and by then they were being joined by a thin but steady stream of priests from all over Europe. The new Jesuits—Germans, Italians and Slavs—came as Spanish citizens because foreigners were not permitted in the mission field, and whenever they could, they translated or simply changed their names to something more Iberian than their native German or Slavic.[8]

But after an unprecedented period of mission expansion, the pattern of revolt reasserted itself, and with greater fury. All of the grievances which led to the 1648 revolt were intensified by 1690—the only difference was that by now there were more Spaniards. There had been renewed mineral exploration in the 1680s and a rush of Spanish and mestizo miners and settlers from the south[9] contributed mightily to the Indian unrest which erupted furiously in April, first at Yepómera, and then throughout Tarahumara Alta. A dozen churches were burned, and two Jesuits were killed, Manuel Sánchez in an ambush near Yepáchic[10] and Juan Ortiz Foronda at Yepómera.

Again the soldiers came from Parral and chased the Indians into the barrancas and caves. This time the troops were under new leaders, Captain Juan Fernández Retana and Governor Juan Pardiñas, but, like a familiar minuet, the action was as before. Fernández won a notable victory against heavy odds in the only pitched battle, but the governor and his troops retired in frustration when a large body of hostiles occupied, as usual, a totally unapproachable peñol. The rebels were pardoned, the Jesuits went back to their churches, or at least to most of them, and peace, again uneasy, was restored.

Quiet didn't last much longer than it had after 1648. Early in 1697 dissident Tarahumaras revolted and gathered again on a peñol near Sírupa, only to disappear in the night when besieged by the frustrated Fernández. The captain, though, had his revenge. His forces brought 60 captives to Cocomórachic, and, after all but a few had been shot, Fernández had the heads of 30 impaled on spears to line the road from Cocomórachic to Yepómera.[11] The grisly exhibition downstream from Cocomórachic didn't calm the rebels, and before the year was out the Tarahumaras had burned 15 pueblos, with their churches, and wreaked havoc throughout the area.

Father José Neumann, the best known of the black robes who served after Guadalajara, was forced to flee Sisoguíchic, and from the mountain to the east watched his church burn. The priests in the lower Río Papigóchic and to the west escaped and were safe at Villa Aguilar, and thus no Jesuits were killed in the fifth revolt. But destruction was greater than in any of the earlier uprisings. The fighting came to a head, and the tide turned in favor of the Spanish, in June, when Fernández surrounded and defeated a large force near Sisoguíchic. Again, he set up 33 spears on the hill above Sisoguíchic and placed the head of a rebel on each. This time the warning had better effect, and after a good deal more fighting, peace finally came in the spring of 1698.[12]

The Tarahumaras did not again revolt. The story of the first two-thirds of the eighteenth century is one of steady expansion of the mission settlements throughout Tarahumara, of a constant increase in the Spanish and mestizo population in the southeast and east, of an ever-mounting pressure on the Tarahumaras by the non-Indian population, and of a gradual Indian retreat deeper and deeper into the sierra and the barrancas. In 1709 Chihuahua was founded[13] and soon assumed commercial and governmental importance to eclipse Parral. By 1753, Balleza, Huejotitlán, Satevó and the other settlements in southeastern Tarahumara were adjudged to be so thoroughly Hispanized that the churches were taken from the missionaries and secularized under the bishop of Durango.

Finally, at the point of their greatest expansion, and when the Tarahumara mission was stronger than it had ever been, the Society of Jesus lost, totally and irretrievably. By order of Carlos III, the Jesuits were expelled from all of New Spain in 1767, and six years later, after intense political pressure, Clement XIV abolished and suppressed the Society.[14] In Tarahumara, when the expulsion decree of 1767 was executed, 19 Jesuits were gathered up from all over the area, brought to Chihuahua, taken south to Parral, and then ultimately to México, Veracruz and prison in Spain.[15]

Some of the churches emptied by the expulsion were reoccupied by Franciscans, and secular priests tried to serve others. But there weren't enough diocesan priests and there weren't enough Franciscans;[16] too many of the churches were necessarily wholly abandoned. Some fell down from simple neglect or were destroyed. The wonder is that so large a number are standing today.

Many churches have been kept in reasonable repair during the more than 200 years since expulsion. Any number of them still have fine oil paintings (largely without frames), which the Jesuits had brought from Spain and from México in the early years of the eighteenth century. In the long days without priests and despite the violent anticlerical feeling which accompanied and followed the Mexican Revolution, many churches and church decorations have been reverently preserved by the Tarahumaras, who continue to use the buildings as meeting places and social centers.

The Jesuits have been back in Tarahumara since 1900, but they are pitifully few[17] and terribly busy. There are as many Indians as there were in 1611, and their needs for education, medical help and the material things of modern living are greater than ever before. The modern Jesuits are not faced with revolts nor with the necessity of building new churches and converting hostiles. But their task is too great for comprehension, in part because they are so few but also because the greater needs of the twentieth century seem to keep them always a little behind schedule.

Part II

The

Churches

San Miguel de las Bocas

El Real de San José del Parral

Even though it is part of what is now the state of Durango, and south of the ancient Tarahumara homeland, the partido of San Miguel de las Bocas was part of the Jesuit Misión de la Tarahumara Baja. After the Tepehuán revolt, the Jesuits began the reconversion of the Tarahumaras, not by settling in the more northerly areas where the Indians lived, but instead by bringing Tarahumaras south to establish mixed Tepehuán-Tarahumara communities on Río Florido.

In addition to the town of San Miguel de Las Bocas (later Villa Ocampo) the San Miguel partido included San Gabriel and San José de Tizonazo as well as (sometimes) some smaller Tepehuán communities farther south. El Real de San José del Parral, to the north of Las Bocas, was never a mission town and should not, perhaps, be here considered. But Parral always was, and still is, immeasurably more important.

NOTE: As detailed in the Preface, Part II presents the churches in the administrative groupings set up by the Spanish Jesuits. Each chapter represents a partido, or mission area, consisting of a headquarters church (cabecera) and its subordinate nearby churches (visitas) which were cared for by the resident priest of the cabecera.

Parral[1] is the gateway to Las Bocas, just as it is the gateway to all the rest of Tarahumara Antigua. In the seventeenth century, Parral was a teeming, brawling, lusty frontier town—and the most important military capital north of México. Today it is a small but crowded city of narrow crooked streets that look like they were laid out by a blind miner following a drunken burro, but it retains, mixed with the trappings of modernity, some of the old frontier flavor and a good bit of the ancient colonial charm. Since you must go to Parral first if you would visit San Miguel, and since you probably will find Parral more interesting, you should know something about it.

In July 1631, silver was discovered in the sands of Río Parral. Miners, merchants, camp followers and impedimenta were drawn as though by a magnet from Santa Bárbara only 15 miles away and, soon thereafter, from Guadiana and other points much more distant. Before the year was out, Parral was a thriving pueblo of 300 Spaniards.[2] Some two years later, the governor of Nueva Vizcaya, Luis Monsalve, moved his military headquarters from Guadiana, and from then on, Parral was of equal or greater importance, with a steadily increasing population, numbering 800 in 1639,[3] toward 6,000 in 1683,[4] 5,193 in 1788,[5] 18,581 in 1930,[6] and undoubtedly more than 50,000 in 1970.[7]

In the seventeenth century, civilization, as usual, brought incidental "benefits." An insatiable demand for workers in the mines stimulated excursions to the northwest and east to impress Indian labor, and a thriving slave market was established at Parral. Blacks, brought from abroad and already enslaved for life, were worth between 300 and 400 pesos if they were male, healthy and young enough to work in the mines. Indian men—Conchos, Tarahumaras, Tobosos and even Apaches—were indentured for ten-year terms and thus, like black women and children, sold for no more than 100 to 150 pesos.[8]

But Parral was not without its redeeming features. While priests were stationed there with the soldiers from 1633 on, there was no permanent religious establishment to serve the civilian population until late in the century. In 1668 a chapel was begun by the Jesuits, and on December 3, 1669, it was dedicated to San Francisco Xavier.[9] Earlier, in 1651, at the request of the governor, the Jesuit provincial had been authorized to open a residential boys' school called a *colegio*, or college,* for the benefit of the Spaniards and the Tarahumaras who worked in the mines,[10] and a license for the establishment was issued on December 31, 1677.[11]

Nothing much really happened about the college until the gifted Tomás Guadalajara, worn out and ill from his years on the northern Tarahumara frontier, got to Parral in the fall of 1684.[12] The following year Luis Simois, a rich Portuguese, was induced to endow the school, and Father Guadalajara became its first rector, serving until 1690.[13]

Except for Ortiz Foronda, who was procurador of the colegio in 1687,[14] the names of very few of the Jesuits who helped Guadalajara run the school appear in those records which have survived. Francisco Medrano came no earlier than 1692, but he stayed at least until 1699, and perhaps much longer. Nicolás Grisoni, who had been briefly at Mátachic, was at Parral in 1696, and probably had come about three years before. How long he stayed isn't recorded, except that he couldn't have been there in 1703.

The extent to which the school may have had early prosperity is not apparent, but it seems quite evident that it was not flourishing by the middle of the next century. In 1732 Juan Manuel del Hierro, longtime missionary from the Yepómera-Temósachic area and many times visitador, came to serve as rector, but stayed only a year before going back to the Tarahumaras of upper Río Papigóchic. In 1744, Father Ignacio Sugasti, who had been at Parral for many years, left for Durango, and only two Jesuits remained, Miguel Castillo, the superior, and Lázaro Franco, who taught grammar.

Some time after 1751, the church and college (apparently a single structure) were destroyed by fire, but under the direction of the last superior, José Pastrana, the building was rebuilt before 1761.[15] Pastrana, who may have succeeded Gaspar Trujillo some time after 1750, was still there at the expulsion, when he and his assistant, Vicente Guerra, were arrested and transported to Spain.[16]

---

*Throughout this book the term *colegio* has been frequently translated *college*. Institutions referred to by this term vary from small rural boarding schools to large urban training centers, but in the area and period covered by this book, such institutions bore little resemblance to modern colleges.

In Hidalgo del Parral, at the back of what was once the oldest
educational institution in Chihuahua, a bas-relief cross can still
be discerned. April 1970.

When I was first at Parral I found that a substantial portion of
the building which was once the college was still standing. Father
Dunne reported that the site was occupied by the hardware store of
Jorge Pérez on (appropriately) the Calle del Colegio and that, in the
rear of the Pérez establishment, a part of the ancient wall could still
be found.[17]

In April 1970, more than 22 years after Father Dunne had
visited Parral, I set out to find the fragment of wall. The *Ferretería*

Pérez was still on Calle del Colegio, but Señor Pérez told me that the wall of the college was not behind his present store, but was the rear wall of the building from which he had moved several years before.

About two blocks west of his new store he showed me an empty two-story warehouse-type building with the words "Pérez Hermanos" across the front. Since Jorge had sold the building, he had no key, but we walked around to the back, where the rear wall of what was really a three-story building was literally built up from the masonry dike which formed the riverbank. There was an entrance to the basement at below the obvious high water mark, and at about what would be the first floor was a single tall door surmounted by two bas-relief triangles, one on either side of a large bas-relief masonry cross.

Jorge told me that the entire rear wall was in its original condition, but that the roof, the front, two sides and the interior partitions were all relatively new. He also told me that from the basement of the college there had once been a tunnel big enough for a man to walk, crouched, to the northeast under his new hardware store and for another quarter of a mile to an opening through an arroyo at right angles to the river.

For what purpose the tunnel? For escape in case of attack? But the only attack was in 1767, when the last Jesuits were peacefully arrested and the Society of Jesus was banished from New Spain.

San Miguel de las Bocas

Finding San Miguel de las Bocas was more trouble than it should have been because I was slow in discovering that the name has been changed to Villa Ocampo. On the other hand, finding Villa Ocampo was easy. It's about 40 miles southeast of Parral, just west of the paved highway to Durango, and the turn is plainly marked. The town, with a reported population of about 1,000 in 1960,[18] is in two parts—the newer, and relatively more modern section, lies east of the river and is laid out with squares and blocks, in the European fashion.

West of the river, the smaller, older and less formal area is totally dominated by the very massive Iglesia de San Miguel con sus Angeles, facing the east. With due allowance for the rebuilding and repairs required in 200 years, the church of San Miguel appeared to us to be essentially the same as on the occasion of its dedication on May 6, 1668.[19] Years ago the bell tower fell, and the bells were hung in a three-aperture *campanario,* or rack, above the façade. When we were there in April 1970, a new bell tower was under construction, the plaster had been replaced many times, and the roof was new. But the entrance, although marred by an electric switchbox and very visible wires, was certainly little changed. The coat of arms of the Archangel Michael was emblazoned in bas-relief in the keystone over the doorway arch and also over a side door leading into the nave from the north. The heavy buttresses at the sides were probably part of the original construction.

Inside, the hand-hewn beams and corbels were old, as was the arch at the front of the sanctuary. The elaborate blue-veined simulated marble pilasters at the rear of the freestanding altar detracted very little from the large central figure of the Archangel, complete with sword.

In 1623 the Valle del Espíritu Santo near Río Florido was chosen as the site for a new pueblo of Tepehuanes and Tarahumaras,[20] and preliminary work was done by Father Martín Larios in that year.[21] But San Miguel de las Bocas was not officially founded until 1630, when Captain Juan Barraza and Father Juan Heredía brought about 400 Tarahumaras from Valle de San Pablo and from as far north as Nonoava to establish a town.[22] Father Heredía stayed only a few months, but his replacement, Gabriel Díaz, built the first church and remained in charge of the Jesuit experiment until his death in 1648.[23] Díaz was not without help. Nicolás Estrada was assigned to assist in 1630 and may have remained as long as two years; in 1639 José Pascual came to learn Rarámuri;[24] in 1644 and early in 1645, Nicolás Zepeda was in Las Bocas from his visita at Tizonazo.[25]

In 1645 the bishop of Durango, Diego Evía, ordered the removal of the Jesuits from Tizonazo and San Miguel and their replacement with secular priests.[26] Zepeda didn't immediately comply with the order, which was only temporarily and partially effective. Díaz remained until his death in 1648, but the partido was apparently without Jesuits from then until the arrival of Rodrigo Castillo, probably in 1651 or a little later.[27]

In April 1970 a new bell tower was under construction at San Miguel con sus Angeles.

By 1662 a series of plagues, one of which had taken the life of Father Felipe Duque (about whom nothing else is known) had reduced the population of Las Bocas to 150, but the church was said to have been well adorned, with three altars, one to the Archangel Michael, one to Our Lady of Pópulo, and another to Christ our Lord Crucified.[28] Five years later, in 1667, Father Castillo was at work on a new church, or at least on a total rebuilding of the old,[29] which was dedicated with a great fiesta on May 6, 1668.[30] The preceding June rebel Tobosos had captured Castillo and released him after serious mistreatment from which he didn't recover. He died four months after the church dedication.[31]

Before Father Castillo died, José Pascual came from the north to assist him,[32] and served until 1673, when his place was taken by Pedro Escalante. Escalante was still there in 1678, when the visitador Ortiz described the church as beautiful and well adorned,[33] and he may have been there until Francisco Medrano came, sometime before 1685.[34] How long Medrano was at San Miguel is uncertain, but by 1723 the church was in the charge of Francisco

Bañuelos. Bañuelos died soon thereafter and was succeeded by Bernardo Treviño, who was still there in 1731. By 1744 José Calderón, a native of Nicaragua, had come to Las Bocas, to serve for four years before going on to the college in Durango. The last Jesuit was Juan Hauga, who had the sad task of delivering a secularized San Miguel to the representatives of the bishop of Durango on September 14, 1753.[35]

San Gabriel

San Gabriel, a visita of Las Bocas, was founded by Father Díaz in 1630[36] as a second Tarahumara town. It never had a priest of its own, and was so small that two modern authorities are solemnly of the opinion that it simply passed out of human ken immediately after it was established.[37] Actually San Gabriel has functioned all along, and as late as 1753, when it was secularized with its cabecera, it had 30 families of Tarahumaras and a small chapel for the celebration of Mass.[38]

The town is about an hour west and a little south of Villa Ocampo and lies just upstream from some mountain outcroppings through which the river passes. The countryside is lush, with good grazing lands on both sides of the river. The 1753 chapel has been replaced by a modern rectangular church, which is thoroughly conventional. The new church may have been built on the location of the 1753 chapel, but there is simply no evidence to prove it one way or another, and there is no local tradition of an earlier church.

San José de Tizonazo

The church at Tizonazo is a large and graceful structure whose last reconstruction was finished in 1946. The east-facing masonry building totally dominates a very small town a long way south and west of Villa Ocampo.

While we found a twentieth century date above the doorway, a lintel stone over a side door in the north wall was inscribed "Ano de 1641." In part because a dated stone, when found at all, is not common at such a location, it was easy, and probably accurate, to conclude that the 1641 wall had been destroyed, perhaps in the Toboso revolt four years after its erection, and that a later builder saved and reused the old stone. While probably not as old as 1641, both the side walls, as well as the rear wall of the sanctuary, were quite old and certainly long antedate the twentieth century façade.

The interior of San José was worth the long and dusty trip from Villa Ocampo. The vigas and corbels, both at the ceiling and the choir loft, were well and attractively made, but were not old. The most unusual feature was a fixed, but freestanding, masonry altar at the modern location, well in front of an older conventional altar and retablo, also of stone. Both were tastefully decorated, and the effect was quite pleasing.

Tizonazo was established by Nicolás Zepeda in 1639 as a third gathering place for Tarahumaras from the north,[39] but it didn't remain Tarahumara for very long. Certainly there were no Tarahumaras so far south after 1687,[40] and perhaps there were none after the Toboso revolt of 1645, when the place was depopulated.[41] Before the revolt, Diego Osorio had come to help Zepeda and probably also to help finish the 1641 church, but he stayed only until April 1645, when he left for Indé ahead of the Toboso attack.[42]

The abandonment of 1645 didn't last long, since by the next year a priest, either Osorio or Zepeda,[43] was back in residence and there were enough people for a miracle to have been reported.[44] In 1659, Bernabé Soto took charge, and he was there at least until 1667.[45] By 1678 the priest at Tizonazo was Francisco Vera, but the length of his stay doesn't appear in any available source. For that matter, a record can be found of only two of his successors, Sebastián Pardo, who was there in 1692 or 1693, and Manuel Vivanco, who came by 1745 and stayed until he delivered the church to the bishop's representatives on September 7, 1753.[46]

San Gerónimo de Huejotitlán

La Iglesia de San Gerónimo de Huejotitlán

Huejotitlán, which dates from the end of 1639, was founded by
Gerónimo Figueroa immediately after he established San Felipe de
Jesús in the summer of that year.[1] This was then the edge of the
Tarahumara country, and the population tended to be mixed
Tarahumara and Tepehuán, with the Tepehuanes predominating in
the immediate area of Huejotitlán and the Tarahumaras more
numerous to the west and north.[2]

Early in 1640, Figueroa reestablished San Pablo Balleza, and
he apparently took care of both locations until Gabriel Villar came
to help him, first at Balleza and then, from 1648, at Huejotitlán,
leaving Figueroa free from the latter date to devote his full time
to Balleza. Villar served Huejotitlán for 41 years, and it was undoubtedly he who built the massive rectangular church named
San Gerónimo.

In 1678 the Villar church was described as very large, well
decorated, with rich ornaments and much silver.[3] It was still large
and richly ornamented and decorated when I visited it in the 1960s
and 1970s. The façade was plain, and if there were ever a bell tower,
it must have been on the side and must have fallen long ago.
Columns framed the simple doorway below a square choir loft win-

dow adorned with handsomely carved spindles. Centered at the top was a rude seated stone figure of St. Jerome. Whenever Paul and I inspected the church, we drew a crowd, many of whom were inordinately amused at the figure of the saint, whom they associated not with the Vulgate but with the war chief of the Chiricahua Apaches.

The church was not cruciform, but there was a partial transept or deep bay at the gospel side of the nave with a small altar before the usual picture of the Virgin of Guadalupe. The main altar was freestanding in front of a glassed-in ark with a statue of St. Jerome. On either side were columns surmounted by angels and at the very top, almost to the ceiling, was a large crucifix.

By all odds the most striking decoration was at a slightly recessed shrine on the epistle side of the nave. Here was a small stone altar surrounded by four carved and painted wood pillars which framed a life-sized crucifix suspended below not the familiar INRI but instead the full text *Jesus Nazarenus Rex Judaeorum*, not just in Latin but, as at the crucifixion itself, also in Greek and Hebrew.[4] The crucifix was above and behind a life-sized madonna, and both were in front of a masonry wall on which successive generations of the faithful had painted, in giant scale, subdued pastel flowers.

By 1678, Father Villar had an assistant in the person of Manuel Gutiérrez, and the two priests took care not only of Huejotitlán but of its two visitas, San Ignacio and San Javier, whose population, unlike that of the cabecera, was more Tarahumara than Tepehuán. The following year José Sánchez came to help, since Villar was by now old and feeble and the area was thriving. In fact it was at about this time that Huejotitlán was described as the wealthiest of all of the Jesuit missions, with Indians who were expert smiths and carpenters.[5]

Villar died in 1689 and the following year saw the arrival of Luis Fernández and, more significantly, Tomás Guadalajara, who made Huejotitlán his headquarters until his death in 1720. As was usual, Guadalajara was buried in front of the church where his tombstone could still be identified in the late 1940s.[6] Since then the graveyard has given way to a civic compulsion to tidy things up, and many of the gravestones have been dug up and moved around. Paul and I have never been able to find any symbols or writing on the stones, and we have been at a loss to locate the Guadalajara grave. None of the local people had any knowledge of it nor were they aware of a priest of that name.

In 1692, Cristóbal Condarco came to assist at Huejotitlán, and from then until secularization in 1753 there were undoubtedly others, although I find records only of Cristóbal Laris, who was there in 1723, and Benito Rinaldini, who was there at least from 1748 until September 1753, when he delivered the partido to the bishop's representatives.[7]

San José de los Olivos

Typhus is said to have wrought more havoc among Napoleon's retreating troops than the snows of Russia or the Czar's armies. A seriously debilitating disease, marked by a high fever, typhus is spread by fleas which infest rats. Once diagnosed, its course can be quickly checked by one of the modern wonder drugs, but in the twentieth century the condition is so rare that every other possibility is tested first, and the patient has become very, very sick before a diagnosis is confirmed by the laboratory. No one knows how many cases go undetected or unreported or both, but when Paul brought typhus back from Valle de Olivos in October 1972, the pathological laboratory which finally gave his doctor the diagnosis was told by the Health Department that there hadn't been a case of typhus reported in Arizona in 25 years. By that time Paul was pretty sick, and since then he has refused to spend the night in grain storage rooms, tack rooms, or in any building where he is likely to be lulled to sleep by the patter of little feet.

We were entertained in Valle de Olivos by what may well have been the only family with a spare room. The room was not attached to the main house, but instead was across the patio, and one end of it was half full of grain sacks, saddles and miscellaneous equipment. Paul and I both spread our bedrolls on the dirt floor, but by pure chance he was closer to the grain sacks and thus exposed to the fleas.

Olivos is on the east bank of Río Balleza, a little downstream or north of San Javier, and although it's possible to get there from San Javier if the river is low enough to be crossed, the simpler route is from Huejotitlán. We were told there that the road turns off to the north from the Huejotitlán-Balleza highway about seven or eight kilometers west of Huejotitlán, and we were also told that the pueblo was only one hour away. After a false start or two, we found the turnoff, which is on the mesa precisely 11 kilometers west of Huejotitlán. After traveling 2½ hours through pleasantly rolling country, we reached the town.

Valle de Olivos is said to have been established in 1680,[8] but I doubt it very much and believe the report represents a confusion with the San Felipe visita on the north bank of Río Conchos, which was also known as San José. Olivos was undoubtedly established in Jesuit times and was flourishing in 1753, when it was secularized with Huejotitlán, its cabecera.[9] But I find nothing to indicate any greater antiquity.

After secularization Olivos was important enough to displace Huejotitlán as the cabecera and to be given a priest of its own, Joaquín Loya, who was also put in charge of San Pablo and Santa Cruz.[10] Eight years later, when Bishop Tamarón made his report, the roles had been again reversed, and Olivos, then called Ciénaga de los Olivos, was a visita of Huejotitlán,[11] with a population of only 740.

In 1788 the town was supposed to have had 10,094 inhabitants and to have been the third largest place in the state, exceeded only by Chihuahua and Cusihuiriáchic.[12] Nothing about the countryside indicates why so many people lived there or how they were supported, and certainly nothing about the town itself suggests that it has ever had as many as even 1,000 people. When I visited there in the early 1970s, the buildings extended from the plaza in front of the church scarcely more than a city block in any direction.

Bishop Tamarón reported the existence of a church,[13] and indeed there must have been a church well before secularization. And it may be that today's building is the same as the one Father Loya took over in 1753, but if so, it has been obviously remodeled and kept in repair. In the 1970s the church was a large adobe and masonry building facing east with a well-made arched stone doorway, four good-sized engaged columns of stone at the entrance and a relatively recent masonry repair job across the top half of the façade. In fact the masonry repair job made the whole structure, except for the stonework at the door, look like a very large grain warehouse.

The inside was surprising. There was a wood floor, wooden pews, plastered pillars and a well-painted plastered retablo behind a conventional freestanding altar, tastefully but unimaginatively decorated. The building was cruciform but was without side altars at the arms of the transept. Quite obviously there was once a dome on squinches over the crossing of the transept and nave, but it has long since fallen and been replaced by a new and perfectly plain ceiling and roof, with peeled poles as vigas. There was no dome over the sanctuary, but the squinches formed an archway at the communion rail. A pitched sheet-metal roof completed the modernization.

La Virgen de Guadalupe

Huejotitlán's other visitas never had any independent importance. Guadalupe is, and probably always was, the least of them. Closer to Balleza than to Huejotitlán, it lies near the east bank of Río Balleza, a short distance downstream or north of the Huejotitlán-Balleza highway, on the last turnoff before the road reaches the river. The all-mestizo town is very small, and all that I could find of the church, which faced the south, were partial adobe walls with an arch over a doorway.

Guadalupe apparently was not in existence until the eighteenth century, since the first mention of the visita was in 1753, when an inventory of the secularized churches showed that it had 20 families of Tarahumaras, with 40 children and two widowers, or a total population of 82. The church must then have been standing, because the inventory showed a chapel with an altar surmounted by a painting of the Virgin of Guadalupe.[14] Eight years later, there was even less population. Bishop Tamarón recorded only six Indian families for a total of 30 persons.[15]

San Ignacio

San Ignacio, the next town north of Guadalupe, on the same road, is older and larger. The first church here was built and dedicated by Father Figueroa sometime between 1664 and 1668,[16] and was said to have been both elaborate and beautiful.[17] Its condition at secularization was not stated, although the inventory showed that in a community of 115 Tarahumaras, the church had one good bell and another which was unusable.[18]

When I visited San Ignacio there was still one bell, but it was in what was obviously a new and very plain church facing south on the town square. There were old burials in front of the church, and from this and local tradition, it seemed clear that the new church was built on the foundations of the old.

San Javier

San Javier may have been established in the 1640s, because there is a report that it was destroyed in the Tarahumara revolt of 1652.[19] In 1678 the church was described as big and beautiful.[20]

San Javier is the most northerly of the three Huejotitlán visitas on the east bank of Río Balleza, and while it must once have been a thriving place, it has become almost as small as Guadalupe. In 1971 the church was square, faced south, was entirely plain, both inside and out, and resembled its predecessor only in that it was big.

In 1753, San Javier was a community of 316 Tarahumaras,[21] and when the bishop inspected the secularized churches eight years later, he reported that both the church and the house for the missionary were in good condition. He recommended that San Javier be established as the cabecera, with jurisdiction even over Huejotitlán.[22] There is no evidence that the transfer ever happened.

San Antonio de Guasárachic

I can't explain why San Antonio de Guasárachic was ever a visita of Huejotitlán, since it is miles to the west of Río Balleza and thus much closer to San Pablo. On the other hand, when Huejotitlán was secularized in 1753, its visitas were included, and Guasárachic was listed as a Tarahumara community of 172 people with a church, an altar and a statue of San Antonio.[23]

The road to Guasárachic turns north and quickly west from the Balleza-Guachóchic highway, about halfway between those towns, near a mesa with natural summer pasturage. Guasárachic is spread out like all Tarahumara settlements, but near the old graveyard in 1971 there was indeed a very old church, rectangular in shape, facing east, with crumbling adobe walls. There was no roof, but the ceiling beams filtered the sun and made intricate geometric patterns on the bare walls and neatly swept dirt floor.

It seems possible that Guasárachic is identical to Santa Inés Sacárachic, to which there is a 1683 reference[24] as a visita of Huejotitlán. Writing five years earlier, the visitador Ortiz mentioned neither Sacárachic nor Guasárachic, which is not surprising. I can find no later reference to Sacárachic, and thus there is at least negative evidence that the two places could be the same.

6

San Pablo de los Tepehuanes

San Pablo Balleza

Balleza is the oldest Christianized Tarahumara town and the oldest missionary settlement in what is now Chihuahua. But for the first 200 years of its life, it was never called anything but San Pablo or San Pablo de los Tepehuanes.[1] The valley and the river were apparently named San Pablo by Father Juan Font when he first visited them in 1607, but at that time there was no native population to supply an Indian place name, and the Tarahumaras whom he later brought out of their caves to establish the town lived largely to the northwest and as far as 18 leagues away.[2] By 1678 there were both Tepehuanes and Tarahumaras,[3] but originally San Pablo was a Tarahumara town and the "de los Tepehuanes" in its name arose not from the population but from its location at the northern edge of the Tepehuán homeland.

There is no information about the church which Juan Font must have built in the five years before he and Gerónimo Moranta were killed in the Tepehuán revolt, but regardless of its size, it certainly didn't survive the 24 years of abandonment which followed the revolt. Between 1616 and 1640 there were continued efforts at the Christianization of San Pablo, but there is no suggestion of church building. The brief visit of José Lomas after 1618 was

too short for construction work,[4] and while Nicolás Estrada and
Juan Sanguesa stayed in Valle de San Pablo for several months in
1620, there is no report that they started to build a church. Indeed,
the fact that they left because the Indians were restless suggests
quite the contrary.[5] No building is required for the sacrament of
confirmation, and thus when Gonzalo Hermosillo, the first bishop
of Durango, visited San Pablo in 1624 and confirmed the first
Tarahumaras in the Christian faith,[6] he probably used an open field
or perhaps a temporary jacal or ramada. It is true that Sanguesa
came back to San Pablo in 1626 and 1630,[7] but his trips may have
lasted no longer than that of the bishop.

Notwithstanding the visits of the priests and the bishop, San
Pablo is not considered to have been reestablished until Gerónimo
Figueroa, after founding San Felipe de Jesús in 1639, moved south
to establish first San Gerónimo de Huejotitlán and then, undoubtedly not before 1640, San Pablo.[8] Figueroa may well have begun to
build churches in both Huejotitlán and San Pablo during the early
40s, since he took care of both places without help until Gabriel
Villar became the first full-time missionary at San Pablo in 1647.[9]
In the following year Villar and Figueroa traded places, and it seems
certain that the founder spent the ensuing years in completing the
church which, in 1668, he modestly described as the best and most
abundantly decorated of all the churches of Tarahumara.[10]

In 1673 Father Figueroa was succeeded at San Pablo by Martín
Prado, but apparently the older priest stayed on at least until the
following year and possibly until 1678 or 1679.[11] Prado was still
there in 1678,[12] but between 1690 and 1699[13] the partido was in
the charge of Francisco Velasco.

After Velasco the record is cloudy. Agustín Roa was certainly
at San Pablo in 1723 and may have come as early as 1708;[14] in 1745
the priest in charge was Francisco Ramos, but by 1748 he had given
way to Juan Hauga.[15] Hauga didn't stay long, since his place was
taken before 1751 by Lázaro Franco,[16] who delivered the Figueroa
church, now burned and with only half its walls standing, to secular
authorities in 1753.[17]

To get to Balleza from Parral, you must go first to Huejotitlán.
The road from Parral to Huejotitlán starts out as a westward continuation of the Calle del Colegio, and for the first hour it is

A painted pattern of black and white squares decorates the
memorable façade at San Pablo Balleza. April 1969.

magnificently paved, as part of Plan Gran Visión. In about an hour
you will pass kilometer 23 of the Plan's aerial markers and come to a
small settlement with a school beside an east-flowing stream.

From the school, new pavement goes left, but in 1974 unfortunately did not reach Guadalupe y Calvo. The right fork, a
dirt road, goes on to Huejotitlán, about two hours away. From
Huejotitlán it is a short half-day trip west to Río Balleza with its
unfinished bridge. After fording the river, the road turns south,
starting upstream and reaching first San Mateo and then the larger
and more important Terrero, where the highway goes due west to

Guachóchic. South of Terrero, in the lush Valle de San Pablo, lies Balleza, a pleasant, well-kept village of about 1500 people.[18]

In Balleza we have several times had altogether satisfactory visits among pleasant and hospitable people. But the church has always been somewhat disappointing. Father Figueroa's church in 1668 may well have been the finest in Tarahumara, and the church we saw, with a massive bell tower at the southeast corner, had good lines and was structurally attractive. But for us the whole thing was always ruined by the façade, painted in large black and white squares.

The first time Paul and I were at Balleza we got past the exterior and were pleased with the graceful and tastefully decorated nave. Above and behind the crucifix over the altar was an excellent oil painting of St. Paul on the Damascus road, and the candlesticks and altar decorations were in good taste. The best thing about the church, however, was a splendid life-sized statue of St. Paul with the Sword of the Spirit in a niche on the epistle side of the nave.

The next time we were there, in April 1971, no one had repainted the exterior, but the interior was changed. All of the pictures and altar decorations except the crucifix were gone and, unaccountably, the niche which had held the statue of San Pablo was empty. No one was there to guide us, but Paul and I made our way through several adjoining storerooms until, in a dusty corner, our flashlight revealed the statue, face to the wall. Not without some difficulty, we cleared an area and turned the statue around. I set up a tripod and, with the aid of two electronic flashguns, took what turned out to be a wholly satisfactory picture of the part of the Balleza church I thought to be most worth remembering.

But no memory of Balleza—not the checkerboard church, not the statue of San Pablo, not the pleasant people—is nearly as vivid as our memory of Río Balleza in flood.

In October 1971 we had come back to Balleza from Guachóchic, wet and miserable, rained out in the sierra. After staying the night we went north, crossing, with exquisite caution, the two tributaries of Río Balleza that come in from the west between the town and the useless bridge north of San Mateo. When we reached the main stream, we found it gorged with silt, swiftly flowing bank to bank. Three trucks were ahead of us, gathering their courage at the shore. One by one, gingerly, the trucks crossed, each following the same route through water which, though ominous, was not very deep. After the third truck, we started across on what we thought was the approved route, going first northeast downstream with the current and then, about two-thirds of the way across, turning to the southwest. Just as we turned, the water, coming in from under the doors, rose up to our knees and simultaneously swamped the distributor and spark plugs.

As I started to take off my soaking boots, Paul, who was on the upstream, or passenger side, opened his door to get out, and the result was disaster. Where before the river was only up to my knees, the flood now covered the seat and was climbing. I could feel the car sinking deeper in its hole in a succession of steady lurches, as the swift current ate the sand from under the wheels. The three trucks were still on the far bank, but too far away for a cable or rope to do any possible good.

Suddenly, without being asked, the men and boys from the trucks, 15 in all, stripped to their shorts and waded out to us in the middle of the river. While the cold rain beat down furiously, the rescuers, joined by Paul, began to push. Simultaneously I was able to make the starter motor turn the wheels and—miraculously—we moved. Slowly, at first, and then a little faster and finally, just before a three-foot wall of water came crashing down from the south, we moved out of the channel and drove up onto the edge of the opposite bank.

San Mateo

In the early 1970's the church at San Mateo was an interesting ruin facing the river on the west bank. The building was once imposing—high, with a splendid doorway faced in stone and displaying at the top the figures "1806," presumably the date of final rebuilding. But the ruin had no roof, and neither the church nor the adjoining priest's house to the north had a complete wall.

The original church was built by Father Figueroa sometime between 1664 and 1668.[19] Ten years later the visitador Ortiz said it was "sufficiently large,"[20] and by the time San Mateo was secularized with its cabecera, it was reported as a "decent church" with a picture of St. Matthew behind the altar.[21]

When I last visited San Mateo, it had only a handful of people and was little more than a ranch, but in 1745 there were 96 Tarahumara families.[22] By Bishop Tamarón's time, the population had been reduced to 31 families, with 264 persons in all,[23] and it declined steadily thereafter.

San Juan Atotonilco

Just when San Juan Atotonilco was established is uncertain, but it was in existence with a church and a priest's house by 1662.[24] The church, presumably built by Figueroa, was reported as being satisfactory in 1678, but at that time a new one was under construction which was expected to be neither less beautiful nor smaller than that at Balleza.[25] The new building probably never quite made it, because it was referred to in 1753 as merely "decent," with a picture of San Juan.[26]

Since then the place of the old church has been taken by a very plain rectangular adobe building which I found to be quite unrecognizable as a church except for a bell at the side. The building faced west, but originally there was a door, now closed with adobe, at the east. I thought the interior was utterly undistinguished.

San Juan was a Tepehuán visita of Balleza,[27] six or seven miles south on the east side of Río Balleza, there known as Río San Juan. No one I asked had ever heard the name Atotonilco, and the town was wholly mestizo. Atotonilco, on the other hand, apparently had been a popular Tepehuán place name,[28] since there are records of San Martín Atotonilco, part of the partido of Tópia,[29] and San Andrés Atotonilco, a visita of Papasquiaro.[30]

Nuestra Señora de la Concepción de Tecoríchic

Tecoríchic[31] was first mentioned as a visita of Balleza in 1745,[32] although there is an earlier reference to the existence of the place as an area whose Tarahumaras resisted baptism.[33] At secularization, the presence of a chapel was reported,[34] and I suspect that the 1753 building was the one which Paul and I found when we spent a night there in October 1971.

Tecoríchic is west of Balleza and south of the Balleza-Guachóchic highway. The turnoff is about halfway to Guachóchic, at a pasture to the west of some orchards. We had left Balleza early in the morning, but within an hour it had begun to rain. The road from Balleza to Guachóchic is not the best in the world, but the road south to Tecoríchic is one of the worst. It crosses two mountain ranges and would be difficult in dry weather. In the rain it got worse every kilometer—and before long was just short of impossible.

Ultimately, and just before dark, we drove into a very narrow valley, with perhaps a dozen houses spread out in the usual Tarahumara formless settlement. At the first dwelling I was told to go to the school, identified by a sheet metal roof. The Toyota never got there but instead totally bogged down in a streambed about a quarter of a mile shy of our goal.

We left the car and slogged through the rain to the schoolhouse, which we found to be a two-room affair, one room for the school proper and the other living quarters for the teacher, a mestizo married to a Tarahumara woman. We were told we could sleep in the schoolroom, but we still had to walk another half mile in the rain to get and bring back our sodden bedrolls. The teacher, truly a Samaritan, had a small fire by which we eagerly warmed ourselves.

By morning, the heavy rain had stopped, and in a light drizzle I took a picture of the chapel, a small rectangular building facing east with a pitched snow roof above the bare vigas. The perfectly plain doorway led into an utterly unadorned interior, empty even of an altar.

La Virgen de Guadalupe de Baquiriáchic

Baquiriáchic[35] is just to the south of the Balleza-Guachóchic highway about midway between the turnoff for Tecoríchic and the little settlement of Agua Azul. Although only a chapel was reported in 1753,[36] a fairly substantial church was evidently erected here at a later date, since in 1970 there was a good-sized ruin with an attractive arched doorway at the west side of a very large graveyard.

An attractive arched doorway watches over the large grave-yard at La Virgen de Guadalupe de Baquiriáchic. April 1970.

The arch of the doorway had a decorated keystone and there was evidence that there were once window openings at choir loft level above the door.

The small but compact town was largely or entirely mestizo. Like Tecoríchic, Baquiriáchic had been originally a Tarahumara settlement whose inhabitants resisted baptism to the bitter end.[37] Organized as a Christian pueblo not long before 1745,[38] it had 36 families in that year and by 1761 a population of 130.[39] Two centuries later the village probably had no more than half that number.

San Juan Bautista
de Tónachic

The partido of San Juan Bautista de Tónachic was created by a January 16, 1752, order of Agustín Carta, the visitador general. The order[1] divided the Misión de Norogáchic and created the new Misión de Tónachic, which the visitor hoped would include the *rancherías* of Mova, Tecabórachic, Guachóchic, Sípochic, Paguíchic, Temósachic and a seventh which is unfortunately illegible but may have been Panálachic. Yoquivo was in existence in 1752; why it wasn't included is anybody's guess. Not all the rancherías developed into pueblos, and Tamerón's report, about ten years later, lists only Tecabórachic as a visita.[2] Thus at the expulsion there were only three pueblos, Tónachic, the cabecera, and two visitas, Yoquivo and Tecabórachic.

In modern times the three older towns have lost their importance, and this portion of old Tarahumara Baja is dominated by Guachóchic, which in some ways has come to be almost a Tarahumara capital. For reasons of modern geography, I here include, in a discussion of the Tónachic partido, not only the three Jesuit towns of Tónachic, Yoquivo and Tecabórachic, but also Guachóchic, only a ranchería in Jesuit times, and two post-expulsion settlements, Cabórachic and Santa Anita.

La Virgen de Guadalupe de Cabórachic

Cabórachic is an entirely typical Tarahumara settlement in a broad valley south of the Balleza-Guachóchic carretera, a little more than half an hour south of the turnoff at the Agua Azul lumber mill.

In 1970 Cabórachic's rectangular adobe church, the headquarters of the local *ejido*, and a series of secular buildings, all connected as in city row-housing, looked east from an eminence located at the westerly end of the valley. The higher church portion had the usual false pitched roof to deflect snow and had no exterior adornment, not even a cross. The interior, on the other hand, was as fascinating an example of primitive art and of the mix of Christianity and animism as is to be found anywhere in the sierra. Against the flat sanctuary wall to the west there was a plain masonry altar, plastered, surmounted by a rectangular board covered with red cloth which served as a backdrop for a small madonna. Above the backdrop was a small and rather lonely crucifix.

Except for a second cross randomly placed, all other decoration was completely native, consisting of irregular designs covering most of the sanctuary wall and extending around the nave in a frieze just below the ceiling line. The drawings were by no means Christian—some were clearly flowers, some were scrolls, and others were quite nonrepresentational. The altar was framed by vertical lines marked on the walls that were suggestive of a doorway leading—who knows where? Most startling of all, however, was a well-executed drawing of the head of a Tarahumara man a little above the altar at the epistle side of the sanctuary wall. On the gospel side, and extending behind the cloth-covered board, there were random flower decorations which were repeated on a portion of the front of the plastered altar.

When Paul and I were in Cabórachic in April of 1970, we tried to find out whether the church was ever put to any Christian use and would have been happy to have any information about the unusual decorations. Unfortunately, we could find no one, man or boy, who could or would speak Spanish. The old records are just as uncommunicative, since the place is not mentioned in any report I have seen, either Jesuit or Franciscan. The building itself is unlikely to be older than the turn of the century.

Christianity, animism and primitive art combine to decorate the altar and sanctuary at La Virgen de Guadalupe de Cabórachic. April 1970.

La Corazón de Jesús de Guachóchic

The earliest Jesuit reference to Guachóchic is the 1752 order creating the Misión de Tónachic which refers to Guachóchic not as a pueblo, but as a ranchería.[3] The place is not mentioned in any subsequent Jesuit report,[4] and the next reference I can find is a Franciscan account[5] of about 1780, which calls it a visita of Tónachic.

Since then Guachóchic[6] has become the metropolis of southern Tarahumara, with a population much greater than the 2,612 reported in 1960.[7] When we visited the town in the 1960s and 70s it boasted two hotels, a casa de huéspedes, a pool hall (which closed early against the chill night air at almost 8,000 feet), a lumber mill, an airport, a liquor store, two establishments that sold gasoline (one with a pump), a restaurant, and the coordinating center for the National Indian Institute, which included among other things, the Escuela Normal Indígena for the training of Tarahumara teachers.

In the 1960s and early 70s there were two church structures at Guachóchic. The old church, La Corazón de Jesús, was on the hill to the north of the city beside the principal road into town. It was rectangular, plain, with a shake shingle roof and a bell rack at the side, undoubtedly replacing a tower that had fallen without a trace. The church was no longer used for any sacramental purpose, but in 1971, Father Carlos Díaz Infante, the Jesuit who for years had made his headquarters in Guachóchic and taken care of the Indians all the way to and in the Barranca del Cobre, was turning the building into a museum. His plan was to preserve the story of Tarahumara culture and something of the relationship between the Indians and Christianity.

On a more day-to-day basis, Father Díaz was in charge of the new and modern church across the street and west of the two-story hotel where Paul and I stayed several times. Very large and very fine, the church was surmounted by a strangely fashioned three-dimensional cross with two arms, at right angles to one another.

The people of Guachóchic have always been friendly, and we particularly have numbered three among our *amigos verdaderos*. The man who ran the hotel across from Father Díaz's church was always cordial and anxious to be helpful with road directions and advice. A closer friend was Adulfo Palma, who worked for the Jesuit mission to the Tarahumara and, under Father Díaz's general direction, supervised reconstruction of churches throughout the area. Adulfo guided us to distant places, in the jeep, on foot and on horseback; he entertained us in a well-furnished apartment in his home and, with his wife and family, at his table. He was charming, intelligent and a boon companion.

But the most important assistance of all came from Father Díaz. Without his ever-cheerful help it would never have been even remotely possible to find many of the more out-of-the-way places in the area. Completely tireless in his ministrations to the physical and spiritual needs of the Indians, uniformly happy, totally selfless, Father Díaz was without the slightest doubt the finest missionary priest I have ever met.

La Virgen de Guadalupe de Tónachic

San Juan Bautista de Tónachic was first a visita of Norogáchic,[8] and is said to have been founded in 1731 by Father Lorenzo Gera. However, since new visitas didn't usually get priests of their own, logic suggests that Tónachic was probably set up as a Norogáchic visita some years before, without a resident priest. Presumably Gera was at Tónachic by 1731, but how long he stayed is uncertain. Tónachic became a partido after 1752, and well before 1761 it was served by Joaquín Trujillo.

Neither Gera nor Trujillo was among the ablest of the Jesuit missionaries, and undoubtedly in part because of their personal problems, Tónachic didn't prosper. Gera was described as inconstant, ponderous, complaining, a barterer, avaricious, quick to weep, demanding, wholly unfit for a mission requiring hard work, without ability to deal with the Indians, and stubborn.[9] Trujillo does not appear to have been much better—he had an ungovernable temper, and because of that and his petty economies, most of the Indians at Tónachic left the area for Baburigame and elsewhere.[10]

In 1761, when Trujillo had been there for some years, the church was falling down.[11] By 1765, his successor, Jaime Mateu, had taken over and was inducing the Tarahumaras to return. But Mateu apparently was able to do little or nothing about repairing or rebuilding the church before the expulsion, since the Franciscans, being without a usable building, later had to build a fine new structure at a cost of more than 1,000 pesos.[12]

In April 1970, the Franciscan church, with a fair amount of intermediate rebuilding, and renamed for the Virgin of Guadalupe, was still standing.[13] Visible for many miles on an eminence at the west or lower end of the long valley beside whose single road Tónachic is strung out, the church was indeed imposing and very massive. A great buttress of rubble masonry helped support a very large masonry bell tower which in turn dominated an only slightly

The heavily buttressed church of La Virgen de Guadalupe
de Tónachic stands isolated at the lower end of a long valley.
April 1970.

smaller nave. Both the tower and the nave had pitched shingle
roofs, and the entire effect seemed wholly alien, reminding Paul
and me of Scandinavia or Switzerland. In contrast to so imposing
an exterior, the nave and altar were chaste and starkly unadorned.

Tónachic is northwest of Guachóchic, in the upper end of the
palisaded[14] canyon which forms the barranca of Río Batopilas. From
Guachóchic to Tónachic and back is a long day's trip over what is at
times a very steep and very difficult road. It is said that you can go
from Guachóchic to Tónachic on a horse in about five hours.[15] I
haven't tried it, but since you can get between the two places by
jeep in about five hours, I think the estimate is pretty close.

The population was mixed, with the mestizos owning well-cultivated fields and good orchards in the central part of the fertile valley, and the Tarahumaras living in isolated and less productive areas at both ends. There have never been many people. Tamarón reported 160 families,[16] there were said to have been 604 in 1900,[17] and there were probably about 400 living there at the time of our visit.[18]

Santa Anita

Santa Anita is not mentioned in any of the Jesuit records, but shows up as a visita of Tónachic in the earliest of the Franciscan accounts.[19] Without our friend Adulfo Palma, Paul and I never could have gotten there. But without horses, we never could have gotten back. About two hours east of Yoquivo, a barely visible road turns south off the carretera between Yoquivo and Guachóchic toward a moderately steep barranca. After about half an hour of driving, only about a third of the way down the canyon, the road stopped. Paul, Adulfo and I walked on down, taking perhaps an hour over rough country, almost all downhill.

Santa Anita was located in a typical Tarahumara valley, with perhaps half a dozen houses over the entire area, no two closer together than a quarter of a mile. In the center of the plain with only one house visible to the east and none in any other direction, stood the church, a simple rectangle with a pitched shake shingle roof and a combination sacristy and priest's lodging attached to the north. In front, to the east, was a cross and a little farther on, a single bell on a rack. Inside was a dirt floor with a very plain plaster altar affixed to the wall, framed with fresh pine branches from the trees nearby.

Paul and I were exhausted from walking down, and we were certain that unless we found horses, we would have to live in Santa Anita the rest of our lives. We sent Adulfo to try to locate some *bestias* for us to ride, took a few pictures and rested in front of the church. As we sat there, several Tarahumara men arrived and sat against the front wall of the church, on the other side of the door-way. They were soon followed by two more who carried a pole about

The bundle reverently laid between the dancing cross and the door of the church of Santa Anita contains the body of a Tarahumara child, destined for burial. April 1972.

eight feet long, each with an end over his shoulder. Midway on the pole, securely wrapped in cloth, was suspended a bundle. The men approached the cross, marched slowly around it four times, stopping at each of the four cardinal points of the compass on each circuit, then lay their burden in front of the cross and went over to join their fellows in the shade. No one said anything at all, not even the almost universal *Kwire vá*.[20] After about 15 minutes the two men picked up the bundle and marched over the hill to the west, with all of the others following some distance behind.

When we got back to Guachóchic we described the ceremony to Father Díaz and asked if we were correct in guessing that we had witnessed a Tarahumara funeral and a child had been buried out of our view over the crest of the hill. He told us our guess was without any possible doubt correct.[21]

An hour later Adulfo returned with news that he had located a horse and a mule at a ranch about half a mile away. We followed him gladly, and were pleasantly and hospitably entertained by the only mestizos in the community. While the bestias were being made ready, the lady of the house brought us coffee and gave us rather careful instructions on the making of tesguino, which she was boiling on a wood stove. When we gave her Polaroid pictures of her youngest child, her husband would accept no pay for the use of the animals, although he told me we could give a peso or two to the small boy who ran ahead of us up the mountain so he could bring them back.

By horse, the return trip took about 15 minutes less than the time it had taken us to walk downhill, but we consumed another half hour turning the jeep around and negotiating the steep and twisting trail to the rim.

Nuestra Señora de Loreto de Yoquivo

Yoquivo was once important enough to have a priest of its own, but little else is known of its history. The Christian settlement dates from sometime before 1751, when Bartolomé Braun was in residence[22] and Yoquivo was a visita, presumably of Norogáchic. We can fairly assume that the settlement was started as a Christian visita without an independent priest sometime during the preceding 20 years, but nothing I have seen suggests a date. Well before 1765, and presumably shortly after 1752, when the Tónachic partido was separated from Norogáchic, Yoquivo became a Tónachic dependency. Braun was still there in 1755,[23] but between that year and 1761 he was sent to Temósachic,[24] a transfer which may have coincided with the rearrangement of the frontier which took Yoquivo away from the jurisdiction of Tónachic and assigned it to Chínipas.[25] There is no record that Braun was replaced at Yoquivo, and no Jesuit was at this lonely post when the expulsion order was carried out.

In April 1972, Paul, Adulfo and I spent the night in Yoquivo,[26] after almost a full day of driving from Guachóchic. We had gotten there late in the afternoon, but in time to take pictures of the very massive church which lies at the west end of the broad Tarahumara valley and looks back toward Guachóchic.

The partially completed new bell tower of Nuestra Señora de
Loreto de Yoquivo can be glimpsed through the branches of
the tree. April 1972.

The adobe building was high, with a pitched snow roof. An
adobe bell tower was under construction on the south, and there
were roofless remnants of extensive cloisters attached to the church
behind and to the south of the bell tower. By local tradition the
cloisters were once a school, but their construction was obviously
newer than the nave, suggesting that the principal building was the
Jesuit church and that the addition was Franciscan. A great cross
stood in front of the church, and burials were all around.

Inside, there were only primitive decorations, with tree
boughs against the reredos behind a fairly modern and well-turned
wooden altar rail. A plastered adobe altar was surmounted by one
crooked cross. Old vigas, some looking as though they were about
to fall, supported a flat ceiling.

We stayed the night with Adulfo's cousin Geraldo. Paul and I
slept in a storeroom, our sleep somewhat disturbed by the flickering

of a small fire in the patio. But the flames served to warm a Tarahumara who, dressed only in loincloth, shirt and headband, stood the night in one position, apparently without moving a muscle.

Before we returned to Guachóchic the next morning, Geraldo asked that we take him to the sawmill at the top of the mountain lying southwest of the town so that he could use the radio telephone to order supplies from Parral. Full inspection of the sawmill was indeed worthwhile, and we would have been sorry to miss it. The mill was owned by a Tarahumara ejido, but all of the skilled work was done by mestizos in the employ of the ejido, with only the most menial tasks left to the Tarahumaras. Most of the jobs required great skill, since machinery operating at high speed and with maximum precision was used to reduce tremendous pine logs into 2″ × 12″ planks 15 and 20 feet long. Sawdust was spewed in mountainous quantities and carted away in wheelbarrows by the Tarahumara owners.

San Luis Gonzaga de Tecabórachic

There is a good deal of confusion between San Luis Gonzaga de Tecabórachic, which was a visita of Tónachic in 1761,[27] and La Virgen de Guadalupe de Aboréachic, a Franciscan visita of Tónachic 20 years later.[28] Father Díaz assured me that they were the same place and indeed, after taking substantially every southerly turnoff west of Rochéachic on the Rochéachic-Sámachic highway, I became reasonably convinced that he was right. I believe that there is a likelihood that the Aboréachic I finally found about 13 kilometers south from that highway (turning near a small lake about 45 minutes west of Rochéachic) is in fact a synthesis of the two places.

Aboréachic[29] proved to be a typical Tarahumara settlement, spread out at great distances around a small adobe church with a false snow roof behind a rude stone fence. Inside the church there was a plaster altar with two pictures of the Virgin of Guadalupe, some paper flowers and dried palm frond decorations. The vigas were relatively new, but there was no evidence that the building had been used for any purpose for many years.

Nuestra Señora del Pilar de Norogáchic

Nuestro Padre San Ignacio de Papajíchic

Getting to Papajíchic[1] is no mean task. In April 1970, Paul and I had spent the night in Rochéachic,[2] from which the road to Norogáchic goes more or less due north. After about an hour and a half, on a high cultivated mesa, we reached Papajíchic Nuevo, where we left the main road and went east down an extremely bad trail through a canyon so steep we were sure we wouldn't be able to return. At the bottom in a narrow valley we found the small and largely mestizo settlement of Papajíchic Viejo.

The church, now called La Virgen de Guadalupe de Papajíchic, faced east on the far side of a little stream beyond a rocky field. We drove through the field and to the edge of the arroyo, undoubtedly putting us closer to the church than any other wheeled vehicle in history. The building was adobe, rectangular and quite large, with the usual pitched snow roof and a rack at the front for the bells, which were probably once in a tower, long since crumbled. The doorway was gracefully framed in stone, surmounted by a Baroque variation of a rose window, also framed in stone.

The interior was unusual and quite pleasing. A small wooden altar adorned with paper flowers stood in front of three very fine oil paintings, two of the Virgin of Guadalupe and the third, a less

The decorations around the small altar at Nuestro Padre San Ignacio de Papajíchic feature a calico-draped Virgin of Guadalupe. April 1970.

conventional painting of the Virgin which was better art. The large central picture was draped with blue calico curtains, distinctly Indian drawings adorned the reredos wall below the two smaller oils, and the altar itself was framed with pine boughs.

Altogether it was a thoroughly satisfactory church,[3] and its discovery was adequate consolation for all the discomforts of the rough and tortuous road down the canyon. We found to our sorrow that the trail was a dead-end street and that we would have to return up the same canyon to Papajíchic Nuevo. But the church was worth the return trip too.

In 1725 Papajíchic had 130 families (which is about 125 more than it had at the time of our visit), and Pedro Martini, the priest at Norogáchic, was building the first church.[4] Whether Martini was then in the process of establishing the visita is uncertain, since it seems possible that Christianization of the area began a few years earlier.[5] In any event it seems highly likely that the Martini church, with a new roof and without a bell tower, is the one we visited in 1970. Neither Lizasoaín,[6] Tamarón,[7] the Franciscan survey,[8] nor any other report suggests that the 1725 church fell down or that a new one was ever built. But even though the church has remained, the people have drifted away, since Tamarón reported a population of 1,084 just before the expulsion.[9]

San Javier de Indios de Tetaguíchic

Tetaguíchic is a very small, typically Tarahumara settlement spread over a narrow valley at about 7,000 feet. When we were there in April 1971, the people were unusually friendly and a higher percentage than usual spoke to us in Spanish.

We got there totally by accident, and it was quite apparent that we were the first outsiders in many years. Several people said to us quite simply, and perhaps literally, that "people never come here." We had been traveling east from Sámachic to Rochéachic and stopped to ask directions at a ranch called Pasigóchic, about half a day from Sámachic. More to make conversation than for any other purpose, I asked about a primitive road that took out to the northeast from the main route and was told that it was the road to Tetaguíchic. Since I knew about Tetaguíchic but had despaired of ever finding it, we started out.

The road made a large arc to the northeast and then back to the southeast. After we had traversed 180° we came to a sawmill, where I was told that we had passed the turnoff to Tetaguíchic and that we should have gone north from about the center of the arc. We went back and did indeed find an even more primitive road going north and then east to the valley of Tetaguíchic. The road was a mere trail, only occasionally visible, with no sign of having known a wheel.

People around the isolated church of La Virgen de Guadalupe de Tetaguíchic said that visitors almost never came there. April 1971.

But it was not always so. Once a reasonably thriving community, Tetaguíchic was a visita of Norogáchic perhaps as early as 1720[10] and certainly well before 1744.[11] In Tamarón's time there were 207 families with 910 Indians in all,[12] which is at least 860 more people than were living there the day the entire population turned out to see us.

In April 1971 this massive oil painting occupied the entire west wall of the sanctuary of La Virgen de Guadalupe de Tetaguíchic.

The church at Tetaguíchic, originally San Javier de Indios but now La Virgen de Guadalupe, proved to be as fine as any in all Tarahumara. It was a fairly large adobe building facing east, rectangular in form, with a false snow roof and a carved stone entrance framing a splendidly carved and very old door. There may once have been a bell tower, although no visible sign remained other than the usual bells hanging outside on a rack.

The utterly magnificent interior was totally dominated by an oil painting which occupied the entire west wall of the sanctuary and dwarfed a small painting of the Virgin of Guadalupe on the rather simple altar. The oil was of an heroic figure proudly holding a crucifix, with a multitude including some Indians, behind the little hill on which he stood. Painted at each side of the canvas were two massive columns, all four with Corinthian capitals, and the two which framed the figure surmounted by cherubs who held back red brocade drapes. The drapes themselves were gathered at the center of the entablature, which was emblazoned as with the rays of the sun. Altogether it was a truly great work of art of which a Velásquez would have been proud.

As startling as the sanctuary were the artistically decorated carved vigas and corbels which spanned the width of the nave for the full length of the church and which, though of a different culture and era, blended perfectly with the painting at the reredos.

Nuestra Señora del Pilar de Norogáchic

In Norogáchic[13] I met one of the most beautiful young women I have ever seen. Sister Gabriela Mayerhof, an Austrian nun, was a member of Las Hermanas de Misericordia de San Carlos Boromeo, a European nursing order with a novitiate in Parral which operated the Clínica San Carlos in Norogáchic.

The *clínica* was a well-equipped modern hospital with x-ray equipment, operating room and fully stocked pharmacy, about 20 beds and four sisters, two of them (including Sister Gabriela) registered nurses. But the clínica had no doctors. Sister Gabriela and her companions took care of the health of all of the Tarahumaras within a 50- to 75-mile radius of Norogáchic, acting as diagnosticians, physicians and dispensing pharmacists not only from the clinic itself but from the jeep with which they traveled all the back roads.

Sister Gabriela was a remarkable person. When we met her in April 1971, she had been in Chihuahua five years from her native Austria, yet her Spanish was perfect and she had a good working knowledge of Rarámuri. But most important, she was at all times gracious, patient and loving toward the Tarahumaras, and whether dealing with the Indians, with her sisters in the order or with visiting Americans, she was at all times smilingly beautiful with an inner radiance which Paul appropriately described as "holy joy."

There were two orders of nuns at Norogáchic. The nursing order operated the clínica; in addition a teaching order operated a boarding school. Both the hospital and the school were across from the great church which stood on a hill above Río Norogáchic, a tributary of Río Urique. The rivers joined a short distance south of the town, at the foot of palisaded hills a long day north of Rochéachic.

Norogáchic was founded in 1690[14] by Ignacio Loyola (Ignace Vah), who lived in a cave until he could build a church and house. Loyola was still there in 1696,[15] but by the following year[16] he had been replaced by Guillermo Illing. Sometime after April 1698, Illing fled the area ahead of the rebelling Tarahumaras, taking with him all of the fixtures of his church.[17] When peace was restored, Illing didn't return but stayed in the Chínipas area,[18] and his place in Norogáchic was taken by Florencio Alderete, who was there until his death in December 1719.[19]

Antonio Ydiáquez served Norogáchic until the following February, when the visitador José Neumann, who had been at Norogáchic at Alderete's death, directed that the partido be delivered to Antonio Martini.[20] Two years later the new priest began to build a little church and spent the next three years vainly asking the procurador for two bells.[21] Martini went to Chínipas and Santa Ana in 1727, and was temporarily succeeded by the ubiquitous Ydiáquez, who by then was permanently established at Nonoava. José Basaldúa, who had been at Guazápares, took over for a time, but in June 1728, Ydiáquez came back,[22] undoubtedly only temporarily.

Who was there after that is by no means clear, but at least between 1747 and 1751[23] the cabecera was in the charge of the former visitador, Lorenzo Gera. Sometime before 1752,[24] Gera was succeeded by José Yáñez, who turned the mission over to Ildefonso Corro before 1762. Corro in turn was transferred to Sisoguíchic in early 1765,[25] and the vacancy may have been filled by the assignment from Guaguáchic of Antonio Aretzamovsky. More likely the reference to Aretzamovsky was in error[26] and it was Antonio Strzanowski who came in 1765. Certainly it was Strzanowski who delivered the church to the king's representatives at the expulsion two years later.

That the Jesuit visitadores took their work seriously has never been doubted, but the fact is probably no better illustrated than at Norogáchic,where a rather full record happens, by pure chance, to be available. It isn't easy to get to Norogáchic from Durango, Parral, Chihuahua, or any other metropolitan center, but the *Libro de la Parroquia de Norogáchic,*[27] which is by no means complete and has long gaps, records the following official visitations in a little more than 50 years: August 30, 1696, José Neumann; November 29, 1696, Bernardo Rolandegui, later to be procurador and provincial; January 5, 1697, Neumann; November 6, 1705, Neumann; 1710 (date illegible), Antonio Herrera, after whom a town was named; May 23, 1720, and again on January 28, 1722, Martín Benavides; April 5–8, 1723, Neumann; September 15, 1725, Juan Guenduláin, the visitador general; October 19, 1726, and ten years later, September 16, 1736, Juan Manuel del Hierro; November 27, 1736, another visitador general who was later to be provincial, Andrés Xavier García; March 19, 1743, Lucas Luis Alvarez, also a visitador general; five months later, on August 26, 1743, Juan Antonio Balthasar, like García, the visitador general and destined to succeed him as provincial; April 30, 1749, the local visitador again, Juan del Hierro; and finally on August 26, 1753, the visitador general, Agustín Carta, who was to begin his service as provincial two years later.

The list of visitations is long, but undoubtedly Norogáchic was remarkable only in that the record still exists.

Whether the building Father Martini began in 1722 survived the Jesuit period doesn't appear, but when the Franciscans took over, the church was in ruins and required total repair at a cost of 4,000 pesos.[28] The new church was both handsome and imposing. A very tall stone building with a splendid domed bell tower at the

In April 1970 the church of Nuestra Señora del Pilar de Norogáchic was without a bell tower or columns, but had a sheet metal roof.

northeast corner and a rose window above the graceful entrance, it was tastefully ornamented by columns extending the full length of the façade. But unfortunately the building burned and was otherwise rather thoroughly destroyed sometime before 1941.[29]

Since then the Jesuits have totally redone the church, repointing and replacing the stone façade, removing the bell tower in its entirety, adding a sheet metal roof, and making merely utilitarian what must have been a lovely building. I found the interior to be overly plain, with the simplest of altars and a single crucifix at the rear wall of the sanctuary.

Nuestra Señora del Camino de Echoguita

Sister Gabriela told us we could easily get from Norogáchic to Echoguita (which lies almost due northwest) in three hours, since it was only about 45 kilometers. Undoubtedly Sister Gabriela regularly made the round trip in a long half day, including time out to treat Tarahumaras when she got there. But since we got lost twice on the way to Echoguita and once on the way back, it took us from very early in the morning until after nine that night to get to Echoguita and back to the clínica.

Echoguita is a typical Tarahumara settlement spread out in all directions over a wide valley, with a large and imposing stone church on a saddle at the east. The upper part of the stone work looked relatively new, as if the walls had been rather completely repaired within the last 30 or 40 years. The church was totally bare of Christian decoration on the outside, and inside there was nothing but the simplest of freestanding altars and, behind the altar, a small wooden *baldaquino*, empty.

Echoguita[30] never had a priest of its own and apparently didn't come into existence until just before 1761, when it was reported as a visita of Bacaburiáchic.[31] When jurisdiction was transferred to Norogáchic doesn't appear.

San José de los Indios de Paguíchic

Paguíchic[32] is much older than Echoguita, since it is referred to as a visita of Norogáchic in a report which may date back to 1720.[33] It remained attached to Norogáchic through the Jesuit period[34] but under the Franciscans became a visita of Baquéachic.[35]

Paul and I visited Paguíchic in April 1971. We had been told that we couldn't get there from the north, that is to say, from Baquéachic, and after being on the road for a day and a half, we decided we couldn't get there from the south either. Sister Gabriela had said that she regularly visited the place in her jeep and that it was about three to four hours northeast of Norogáchic. Her directions and her time estimate were both undoubtedly right, but she didn't count on the fact that we would get hopelessly lost.

The third time we passed a peculiar rock outcropping with a large inhabited cave at its base, the place began to look familiar, and we knew we'd been traveling in a circle. At last, late in the morning of our second day out, we located a Tarahumara who not only spoke a little Spanish but who agreed to ride with us in the jeep to Paguíchic for a prenegotiated fee of 10 pesos. Along the way we found that our Tarahumara had been on his way (walking) to Paguíchic anyway, but I was so glad to find the place, I happily gave him 20 pesos.

The church at Paguíchic had been recently rebuilt under the direction of Father Díaz and Adulfo Palma. There was a new stone bell tower, quite modern in style, a new sheet metal roof, and the interior had been newly plastered. The building was not large and, except for the splendid handhewn corbels, relatively uninteresting. The interior, starkly plain, depressed me with its grimness. The very small town was spread out over a rather chopped-up valley north of the church.

It took us a full day and a half to get to Paguíchic, but getting back was nearly as bad, since we got lost again, and didn't reach Norogáchic until early afternoon of the third day, by now nearly out of gas. Sister Gabriela let us buy some of the clínica's gas and sent us on our way to Guachóchic.

9

Santa María del Pópulo de Guaguáchic

Nuestra Señora de los Dolores de Sámachic

Sámachic,[1] the youngest of the four settlements in the old partido of Guaguáchic, dates from the time of Antonio Strzanowski, who was in charge from 1757 to 1765. Strzanowski built churches and houses not only in his three old towns but also in the new pueblo of Sámachic, which he founded.[2]

The other three pueblos, Guaguáchic, Pámachic and Guaguevo, were officially established in 1718[3] by Jacobo Doye. But there had long been missionary activity in the area. Perhaps as early as 1700, Manuel Ordaz crossed the Barranca del Cobre from Cerocahui to spread the gospel,[4] and there is a likelihood that at about the same time Martín Benavides did some baptizing on the east side of the canyon.[5]

I have found nothing to indicate the sort of church Strzanowski built in Sámachic more than 200 years ago, but it may have been rather graceful. Writing in 1941, Filiberto Gómez reported that the outside of the small church was circular,[6] and indeed, the apse of the 1972 building, obviously much older than the modern front, consisted of a curved wall which may have dated from Strzanowski's time. The adobe front must have been added about the middle of this century and made the whole thing look like an open front porch. There was a two-stage sheet metal roof, pitched, one section over the porch and the other over the nave, with a sort of cupola at the front, made by running the sheet metal to a point in front of a cross.

I have inspected the church on more than one occasion and have always found it totally empty, although Father Díaz told me that the building contained an old statue of Nuestra Señora de los Dolores. The statue, apparently hidden away except on the most important occasions, must be of considerable antiquity to bear the original name of the church, which has been known for many years as La Virgen del Rosario de Sámachic.

Sámachic lies a little more than half a day south of Creel and about four miles southwest of the Creel-La Bufa road on a turnoff which leaves that road at a spot marked in 1971 by a small mail shack which is six or eight miles south of the turnoff to Guachóchic and Parral to the east.

Santa María del Pópulo de Guaguáchic

From Sámachic to Guaguáchic it is a short half day's trip in a generally southwesterly direction through high and magnificently timbered country. At an elevation of about 7,500 feet, Guaguáchic is spread out over a great valley in typical Tarahumara fashion.

Each time I have seen the Guaguáchic church I have found it different, but each time I have been impressed by its magnificence. Very large, it faced southeast, with a deep nave and, at the right of the door as I entered, a high adobe bell tower with a pitched roof. Attached to the bell tower was a long, low-lying residential area with one very small room with a corner fireplace and one very large room which in April 1972 was half filled with lumber and construction material. The priest's quarters had a pitched roof of rough-hewn boards, while the higher nave had a sheet metal roof.

When we were there in 1970, the nave was being rebuilt and, except for the sanctuary, the whole interior of the church was quite bare. The sanctuary area had a large conventional triptych retablo with three statues and, under construction, a freestanding stone altar. Two shallow transepts were empty.

Restoration has been an on-going project at Santa María del
Pópulo de Guaguáchic. April 1970.

On our 1972 trip to Guaguáchic we became more intimately
acquainted with the building and with its construction. This time
we went with Father Díaz and Adulfo, and the priest specially
arranged to show me the churches of the barranca while he ministered to his people and Adulfo worked on the Guaguáchic construction project. The four of us made the church our headquarters,
living in the two-room convento, where Adulfo doubled as cook,
and did very well indeed.

Father Díaz spent substantially his entire time giving his flock
candies and cookies by the hatful, marrying them and baptizing
their children by the dozens, prescribing and giving them
medicines, and going out at all hours of the day and night to
comfort the sick, to take medicines to the bedfast, to pray, to bless
and to teach—often leaving his dinner cold and uneaten.

By April 1972 the free-standing stone altar at Santa María del
Pópulo de Guaguáchic had been completed.

In 1972 the church was in only slightly better repair than it
had been two years before. The reason was obvious—Adulfo didn't
get there very often. But in the short space of our visit, progress was
made. Adulfo rounded up a large group of Tarahumaras to do the
heavy lifting and pulling, while he acted as carpenter, stonemason,
glazier, foreman, superintendent, and all-around expert. The roof
was repaired, the freestanding altar was completed, and some corbels were added to the hand-hewn vigas in the ceiling.

We also learned something about the uses to which the Tarahumara churches and their facilities are put. We had noticed before that in front of almost every Tarahumara church there is a large cross planted in the ground. At Guaguáchic there was also a smaller cross in front of the back door of the living quarters, and here in front of the cross there was a wooden box serving as a rude altar.

I asked Father Díaz about the crosses, and particularly about the box, and learned that the crosses are regularly used in a Tarahumara dance called the *yúmari.* Two dancers, each carrying a prayer gourd or rattle, and each carrying a container of food, dance slowly up to the cross. While dancing and chanting in low voices, they shake the rattles above their heads to get God's attention. This achieved, they lay their rattles on the box or altar and make their offerings to God, one man offering *carne seca* and the other tortillas. As they continue to dance and chant, the offering is elevated at each of the four cardinal points of the compass and then, the ritual completed, the containers are placed on the altar, the prayer rattles are retrieved and the men retire, still dancing and still chanting.

Officially founded by Jacobo Doye on April 28, 1718,[7] the pueblo of Guaguáchic[8] was probably actually settled sometime the year before. In December 1717, the visitador Martín Benavides came to Guaguáchic as well as to Guaguevo and Pámachic, and on February 9 of the following year was able to arrange for the official establishment of the three towns.[9]

While Doye, who was stationed at Cerocahui, apparently had general charge of Guaguáchic, the settlement was nevertheless a visita of Norogáchic,[10] and it probably so remained until it became a cabecera with a priest of its own in 1757.[11] Antonio Strzanowski, who came in that year, built a church and a house,[12] and Father Díaz is very likely correct that the church construction was finished in 1760.[13] When Strzanowski was transferred to Norogáchic in 1765, he was succeeded by José Iranzo, who was there at the expulsion.

Father Strzanowski's church didn't last long, since the Franciscans found themselves without a church and set about in 1771 to build a new large structure, selling 100 beeves to raise money.[14] Father Díaz believed that the present church building incorporated much of the 1760 structure, with subsequent rebuilding, and that the residential addition, which is certainly newer, was both later and Franciscan. That the addition is not Jesuit seems certain, since visitador Ignacio Lizasoaín reported in 1761 that there was only a church and some small houses.[15]

Father Díaz reported that the Franciscan church was burned in 1860, restored on an unknown date thereafter and again restored under his direction in 1963. With the too-intermittent help of Adulfo, the restoration has been continuing.

Señor San José de Pámachic

When Pámachic[16] was founded in 1718, it was a visita of Cerocahui,[17] but it was later technically dependent on Norogáchic,[18] and finally, after a brief period with a priest of its own,[19] became a visita of Guaguáchic.[20]

But long before 1718, probably at or near the turn of the century, the area was visited by Manuel Ordaz,[21] who was followed, or perhaps preceded, by Martín Benavides.[22] Benavides was there again as visitador in 1717, and later in the same year, undoubtedly at the visitor's suggestion, Jacobo Doye came from Cerocahui to baptize.[23] As a result of Benavides' report of February 9, 1718, San José de Pámachic was officially established on April 24, 1718, to be served by Father Doye.[24]

But even as Doye was taking the required official action, the Indians were working on a church, presumably begun as a result of the visits of the year before.[25] Juan Bautista Duquesney got to Cerocahui at least by 1726, serving as Doye's assistant until he succeeded him in 1730, and there is no' reason to suppose that during their service at Cerocahui both priests didn't continue to take care of Pámachic, even though in the 1720s the pueblo was listed as a visita of Norogáchic.[26] The Norogáchic arrangement obviously had the logic of geography, since the Barranca del Cobre separates Cerocahui and Pámachic.

Whether the Pámachic church was completed by Doye or by Duquesney doesn't show in any record I've seen, but it certainly must have been finished by the time José Miqueo became the pueblo's first and only resident priest. Miqueo was at Pámachic in

October 1744,[27] was still there in 1748,[28] but was gone by 1751.[29] Probably when he left, and certainly by 1757, Pámachic ceased to be a cabecera and reverted to a visita of Guaguáchic. I say certainly by 1757 because in that year Pámachic was under the supervision of Antonio Strzanowski, who built, or rebuilt, its church.[30]

In April 1972, with the help of the jeep, a balky horse and Adulfo Palma, Paul and I visited Pámachic, which is west and north of Guaguáchic. To get there we started north toward Sámachic, turned to the left where the Sámachic road forked to the right or northeast, bore to the right or north where the Nahuírachic road forked to the left, and followed an abandoned lumber road past Witibáchic to an abandoned sawmill.

In July 1970, Father Díaz had written me that he was then supervising the building of a road to Pámachic which would be a continuation of the existing road, which goes past the abandoned sawmill to the west above Witibáchic. He added "in a month a jeep can get to Pámachic." Twenty-one months later it wasn't too difficult for the jeep to get us to the saddle or divide from which we could see Witibáchic, a ranch which occupies a cultivated bench 1,200 feet closer to Río Urique than the saddle. From here on and for perhaps a full kilometer beyond Witibáchic, Adulfo and Paul walked ahead to clear the rapidly deteriorating road of fallen timber. But a kilometer beyond Witibáchic is still an hour and a half short of Pámachic, a settlement on the east side of the Barranca del Cobre and not more than 2,000 feet above the river.

By the strange word-of-mouth system which permits all important knowledge to be passed on quickly throughout the sierra, Father Díaz had arranged for horses to be brought up from Pámachic to meet us at Witibáchic. Indeed, not long after we got as far as the jeep would take us, one small boy did in fact arrive with one mallet-headed horse, undoubtedly the slowest animal I have ever seen. I rode the horse the 2,000 or 3,000 feet down to the bench on which Pámachic sits, but Adulfo, Paul and the small boy made immeasurably better time walking. Of course there was one advantage: the scenery was breathtaking, and I had no trouble at all stopping the horse to take pictures of the barranca from every angle and in every direction. But by the time we got to level ground, I dismounted and found that the horse and I both went faster when I led him.

The bells of Señor San José de Pámachic hang in a brick ramada. The one on the left, inscribed "S. S. Joseph 1761," is very certainly an original. April 1972.

Pámachic is almost directly across the Barranca del Cobre and Río Urique from Divisaderos, which is the spot on the west bank where the Chihuahua al Pacífico stops its passenger trains for a half hour to permit tourists to take pictures. The view from Divisaderos is magnificent, but the views from Pámachic and from anywhere along the trail between the Witibáchic saddle and Pámachic are equally magnificent—and there are more of them.

The church totally dominated the area. It was a very large adobe building with a pitched roof of random-length split boards

In April 1972 the sanctuary of Señor San José de Pámachic had
a dirt floor but a decorated wooden rood screen and several
excellent oil paintings.

and cloisters stretching a considerable distance in front and to
the west of the nave. The church proper faced north, and in front
of two magnificent carved ancient doors there was a relatively new
ramada with tapered columns of brick which held, hanging from
a crossbeam, two bells, neither very large. One was unmarked,
but the other was very certainly the original bell of the Pámachic church, since it was inscribed "S. S. Joseph 1761,"[31] which
would be just about the time that Father Strzanowski was completing construction.

Inside a totally undecorated nave with a bare dirt floor opened onto a most unusual sanctuary, unusual because it was framed by a splendidly decorated wooden rood screen between two plastered adobe pillars, the one on the gospel side bearing native designs. Against the rear wall was a very crude plastered adobe altar, quite small, but with interesting decorations. Amid the peeling plaster on the face of the altar were four Greek crosses, while on top of the altar were two small santos in movable wooden niches. Built into the reredos behind the altar was a larger plaster niche filled with dried foliage instead of a santo. Above the larger niche was a small painting and below was a simple crucifix. But on the wall on the epistle side of the altar were two excellent unframed oil paintings, one of a bishop and the other of a pope. When we were there, a larger but less well-preserved oil was leaning against the wall on the gospel side. Time had made the central figure unrecognizable, but a monstrance was clearly delineated in the painting's upper left corner.

We went to Pámachic on Sunday, and while there was no priest and no church service, most of the Indians of the settlement had as usual gathered together and were sitting in the shade beside the church, the cloisters and an unconnected building nearby.

While Paul and I were inspecting and photographing the church (and while my horse was, as usual, resting) Adulfo scared up another horse, so that Paul and I both rode back up the mountain. Adulfo, the two small boys (one to return each horse) and Paul reached the jeep a full half hour ahead of me. My horse was still the slowest in the sierra.

San Luis Rey de Francia de Guaguevo

The first European to descend into the Barranca del Cobre was Juan María Salvatierra, who went down the canyon on horseback in 1684. He reported that when he looked down, he "immediately asked . . . if it was time to dismount. . . . Without waiting for an answer I did not precisely dismount, but let myself fall off on the side opposite the precipice, sweating and trembling all over with fright. For there opened on the left a chasm whose bottom could not be seen and on the right rose perpendicular walls of living rock. In front stretched the descent, extending for at least four leagues. It did not run gently from hill to hill, but was sudden and steep and the trail was so narrow that at times we had to jump from one point to another because there was no foothold in between."[32]

I knew what I was getting into when Father Díaz and I went down the barranca from Guaguáchic to Guaguevo in April 1972. But even though the canyon was no surprise, there were a number of times when I was tempted to slip quietly off my mule and let Father Díaz and his friend Luis Mancinas go on without me.

Guaguevo lies on the east side of the barranca about four hours by horse from Nahuírachic, which can be reached by road. Nahuírachic, which is another name for Luis Mancinas' ranch, is about an hour by jeep west from Guaguáchic. The trail from Nahuírachic goes promptly to the east rim of the barranca and then in an uncounted number of switchbacks past breathtaking views in every direction goes down to the broad cultivated bench on which Guaguevo is located, about 1,500 to 2,000 feet above Río Urique almost directly across the canyon from Churo.

Father Díaz had sent word by Tarahumara "telegraph" to Mancinas, who had a house in Guaguevo as well as one at Nahuírachic, that we would meet him very early on Monday morning at his ranch and that we would like horses or, preferably, mules for the trip down the precipice. We got to the ranch ahead of Luis, who arrived from Guaguevo with one mule and one horse. Luis gave Father Díaz the horse, assigned the surer-footed mule to me, divided our bedrolls and equipment between the animals, and elected to follow us on foot. My mule was very fast. Whenever we came to a portion of the trail without rocks, we went at a trot, regardless of whether the ground was level and regardless of how steep the trail might be. Father Díaz and his horse had trouble keeping up with my mule. Luis had no trouble at all, and very certainly could have outrun either animal.

Guaguevo is not really in a valley or even on a flat bench but on a somewhat less precipitous slope. All the land which can be cultivated has been ploughed and planted, and a good bit of it is terraced, although less artfully and intensively than in Formosa or Japan. The houses are few and as usual far apart.

At the very edge of Barranca del Cobre's vertical drop-off
stands the church of San Luis Rey de Francia de Guaguevo.
April 1972.

At the very edge of the vertical dropoff to the river, facing
east and thus facing the entire expanse of the community, was
the church of San Luis Rey. Father Díaz and I stayed in the tiny sacristy, which was attached at the south and back of the rectangular
adobe building with its shake shingle roof. Neither the sacristy
nor the church was connected to an open barracks-like structure
to the south.

The church itself was perfectly bare, with a dirt floor, a communion rail and a simple altar with a very good but damaged statue
of San Luis, a couple of other santos and, on the wall behind the
altar, the usual painting of the Virgin of Guadalupe. We were there
three weeks after Easter, but the front door and the altar were still
decorated for Holy Week with what from a distance looked like
large white flowers but were really artificial floral wreaths made
from gourds.

Father Díaz asked me periodically to ring the bell while he prepared for Mass. His preparations consisted principally of dusting and cleaning the altar and altar equipment, but in addition he installed, in the middle of the nave, a little in front of the communion rail, a rather rude cross, similar in purpose and design to the usual dancing cross in front of the Tarahumara churches, but this time, like the cross at Guaguáchic, with a small box serving as an altar in front of it.

Everybody within the sound of the bell began drifting into the churchyard, the women dressed in their Sunday best and the men in Levi's. At Guaguevo I saw no Tarahumaras in loincloths, since the railroad is only one day away on foot and virtually all of the men of the community have at one time or another worked across the barranca and learned to wear Levi's. Fortunately, the railroad work week is five days, which means that a man can spend one day going from Guaguevo down the canyon to the river and up the other side to the rail line, work five days and then spend the seventh returning to Guaguevo. The arrangement seems not at all unusual to the Tarahumaras of Guaguevo, but a one-way trip between Guaguevo and Bahuichivo (the rail center west of Churo) would have taken me either a week on a horse or all my life on foot.

It took about two hours for the bell to do its work and for the congregation to gather in front of the church. No one went in until Father Díaz came out and announced that he was ready to begin. Even then, while the women and children promptly entered and sat on the floor on the gospel side, none of the men would enter the building until I urged them to do so and showed them the way by starting in first. As was customary we stood, knelt or sat on the left or epistle side. Except for the lessons, which he read first in Spanish and then translated into Rarámuri, Father Díaz offered the entire Mass in la idioma. And it was a most unusual and fascinating Mass, the full import of which I didn't understand until his later explanation.

Father Díaz reminded me that he didn't get to the outlying churches in his vast area very often, and said that neither he nor any other priest had been in Guaguevo for more than three years. Thus, because the Mass is not an everyday thing, the Indians need its significance explained again on each of his visits.

His explanations, as he detailed them to me afterward, started with the outward trappings. When he began the service he was dressed in the clothes he had worn all day, nondescript trousers and a dark blue wool sweater, but he had carefully laid his surplice, stole and other vestments on the altar. He explained the reason for the vestments, and as he described each article, put it on.

He then told the congregation that the Christian Mass is very similar to the yúmari dance, and he showed them that he had not two elements on the altar but four, a chalice with wine, a paten with hosts, and two bowls, one with carne seca and one with tortillas. He brought the four elements out from the sanctuary and laid them on the small altar in front of the dancing cross, then asked for three male volunteers from the congregation. As usual, nobody volunteered, so he selected three men on an arbitrary basis, and to each of them gave an element, retaining the paten and hosts for himself.

The priest then produced a Tarahumara prayer rattle and began a chant in which his three *compañeros* joined. After he had gotten God's attention by the rattle, the chant continued, and the men lifted the four elements up toward heaven at the cardinal points of the compass, one after another around the cross. The yúmari thus concluded, the Tarahumara men returned to their places. Father Díaz took the Christian elements back to the main altar and began the regular sacrifice of the Mass, fully explaining each prayer and each part of the service as he went.

When the Mass was concluded, the women and children stayed for baptisms. The following morning Father Díaz celebrated a second and, except that this time it was all in Rarámuri, identical Mass, with baptisms afterward. Between the two days he told me he baptized 32 children, and while he was at it, he solemnized a dozen weddings, including several between parents of children whom he had baptized.

On December 9, 1717, Jacobo Doye got to Guaguevo;[33] in the same month (probably in fact on the same visit) Martín Benavides inspected the community and as a result on February 9, 1718, asked Governor Manuel San Juan y Santa Cruz officially to establish Guaguevo and its sister towns, Pámachic and Guaguáchic.[34] The Acta de Fundación was executed on the governor's order by the *juez comisario* on May 8, 1718, and Jacobo Doye of Cerocahui was named as priest in charge.[35]

Guaguevo never had a priest of its own, but was dependent first, on Cerocahui, then on Norogáchic[36] and finally, by the time Antonio Strzanowski built the church in the 1750s, was under the control of Guaguáchic.[37] The settlement has probably always been about the size it was when I saw it. Bishop Tamarón reported 44 families in 1761,[38] and I'm sure the descendants of all 44 of them were at one or the other of the two Díaz Masses 211 years later.

10

Chihuahua and Chinarras

El Colegio de Nuestra Señora de Loreto de San Felipe el Real de Chihuahua

Compared to Santa Bárbara and Parral, Chihuahua is a new town. As was the case with the other two, Chihuahua was never a mission pueblo, but, like Parral, it was the seat of a Jesuit college and an important administrative and supply point for the Society's missionary activity. Rather than an Indian town, Chihuahua started out as a Spanish real established to be the seat of government for nearby mining developments—to the extent there were Indians in the area, they were Conchos, and the priests who ministered to them were not Jesuits but Franciscans.

The earliest of the mines was discovered in 1652 at Santa Eulalia, about 22 kilometers east of the present city of Chihuahua. The mine was soon abandoned, but was reopened in February 1707, when the real, or mining camp, was named Santa Eulalia de Chiguagua.[1] In 1697, during the period of inactivity at Santa Eulalia, two Franciscans, Gerónimo Martínez and Alonso Briones, came into the area on a mission inspection trip and, finding the natives disposed to conversion, established the mission of San Cristóbal de Nombre de Dios to serve the Conchos Indians a little north of the point at which Chihuahua was later founded.[2] Not long thereafter one of the mission vaqueros found a rich mineral outcropping and by November 1702, extensive mining activities had been begun.[3]

When the miners and settlers began to pour into the area, it became obviously desirable to establish an *alcaldía mayor* to keep the peace and to insure that the king got his share of the loot. In January 1708, Governor Juan Fernández Córdova issued an order establishing the alcaldía and naming General Juan Fernández Retana as the first alcalde mayor.[4] Fernández visited the area and determined to build a cabecera at the junction of Río Chuvíscar and Río Sacramento, now in the northern suburbs of the city. But he died before the mining camp could be established, and almost two years later, in October 1709, the new governor, Antonio Deza Ulloa, called a meeting of the miners, merchants and settlers of the entire area to determine the location. Sentiment was divided, but on October 12, Deza authorized the foundation of the Real de San Francisco de Cuéllar.[5] Nine years later, on October 1, 1718, the viceroy issued a decree which turned the Real de San Francisco de Cuéllar into the Villa de San Felipe el Real de Chihuahua, in honor of Philip V,[6] and with the native word *Chiguagua* first officially used for the city.[7]

Chihuahua grew spectacularly during its first forty years. The population rose steadily, from 16,000 in 1721[8] to 25,000 twelve years later.[9] But by midcentury, Tamarón reported only 692 families and 4,652 people.[10] The mines had begun to lose their easy productivity, and what was a good deal worse, the Apaches had turned their attention to Chihuahua and the surrounding area. A Spanish army officer who passed through Chihuahua in 1766 described it thusly: "This town is situated on arid ground on the bank of a small shallow stream. . . . Its population consists of four hundred families of Spaniards, mestizos, and mulattoes, who are perishing because of the total failure of the mines and the constant hostilities of the Indians who have stolen all the mules and horses and have killed many persons in the neighborhood. . . ."[11]

The expulsion of the Jesuits was followed by the reorganization of the Spanish colonial system and a substantial strengthening of the presidial line which served as intermittent protection for northern Sonora and Chihuahua, with the result that the city's population in 1788 was reported at 10,752, and the population in what is now the state stood at 124,151.[12] From then on the census fluctuated on the basis of the activity of the Apaches, the strength of the government, the progress of mineral exploration and the fortunes of the revolutionaries.

When Nueva Vizcaya was divided on July 19, 1823, and the province of Chihuahua was created, the city was made the capital. On July 6 of the following year, the province was turned into a state, again with the central city the seat of government.[13] Chihuahua has become truly the commercial center of Mexico's largest state. With a population which must be well above 200,000,[14] the city has a large, bustling business district because it is the supply point for a vast area in every direction.

Under the arrangement between the two Orders whereby the Jesuits were given exclusive rights in Tarahumara territory, the rest of what is now Chihuahua was reserved to the Franciscans.[15] Since the Real de San Francisco de Cuéllar was not part of Tarahumara, it was thus natural that its first church, Nuestra Señora de Regla, was established by a Franciscan, José Zamora, the only missionary in the neighborhood of Santa Eulalia in 1707 and 1708. The church, located on the site of the present cathedral,[16] was completed and dedicated before 1715,[17] but the Jesuits weren't far behind. Because the area was outside of Tarahumara, permission for Jesuit activity had to come not from the governor but from México. The governor, Manuel San Juan y Santa Cruz, was interested in having the Jesuits establish a boarding school, or "colegio," and it was he who induced the viceroy to authorize the Jesuit establishment on November 25, 1717.[18]

The location chosen for the school, "in the center of the residence quarter,"[19] has, not surprisingly, become the precise center of the business district. On January 24, 1718, Antonio Arias, then the visitador, with Ignacio Estrada and Francisco Navarrete, undertook actual erection of the school on the site now occupied by the Palacio del Gobierno at the southwest corner of Avenida Juárez and Avenida V. Carranza. On February 2, 1718, Navarrete, the first rector, laid the cornerstone of the Colegio de Nuestra Señora de Loreto de Chihuahua.[20]

Classes didn't begin until 1720,[21] and in that year Antonio Herrera, in whose honor the citizens of Santa Cruz changed the name of their pueblo, came to be the superior.[22] Herrera had returned to the valley of Río Conchos by March, 1723, when the faculty of the college numbered four—Navarrete, José Armas, professor of grammar, and two teachers, José Basaldúa and Diego Valladares—in addition to an *hermano coadjutor,* Domingo Tejería, who ran the Hacienda de Dolores, which Governor San Juan had purchased for the Society.

By that time the college had fallen on evil days and was very nearly bankrupt. Because of the "malevolence of certain persons," because of unproductivity of the hacienda, and probably as a result of general mismanagement, the institution was heavily in debt and losing money fast.[23] The new provincial undertook a rescue operation in mid-1725, sending Constancio Gallarati to take over as rector. Largely because he was a close friend of the governor and of other rich Spaniards, Father Gallarati was able to stave off creditors and make the college a going concern long before he died in 1739.

Navarrete apparently continued to serve, but not as rector, until 1737, when he was transferred south. But after that the records are sketchy. Presumably several years before 1748, Nicolás Sachi was at the college, his first assignment after ordination; at some point Lucas Merino is said to have served as rector; and in 1747 Jacobo Ramírez and José Robledo were there.

A decade and a half later Tamarón reported that the school had four or five Jesuits and a good church.[24] The bishop left no record of the names of his *"cuatro ó cinco sujetos,"* but they probably included Claudio González, the young grammar teacher who left the college in 1766 to take over Chinarras, José Ignacio Espadas, who was there only in 1761, as well as the three priests who were in residence at the expulsion—Manuel Flores, Salvador Peña and José Pereira. On June 30, 1767, Captain Lope Cuéllar closed the college forever. He took the three priests in custody, and five days later they were on their way to Zacatecas and México.[25]

Today there is no trace of the building—not even part of a wall was incorporated in the Palacio del Gobierno. But Francisco Almada has preserved and published a handsome picture of the college with three uncompleted arches and a central façade decorated with well-carved stone and a good statue. On the left of the main building is a tower which served as a prison for the father of his country, Miguel Hidalgo y Costilla.[26]

Santa Ana y San Francisco Javier de Chinarras

Like Chihuahua, Chinarras is a long way from the Tarahumara homeland, and there really should never have been a Jesuit church there. Either because he liked the Jesuits or because it would bolster the case for the establishment of a college at Chihuahua, or perhaps for both reasons, Governor San Juan gave the Society permission in 1716 to establish a mission church on the left bank of Río Chuvíscar, almost within shouting distance of the Franciscan church of San Gerónimo at the outskirts of the modern city of Aldama on the right bank of the river, about 15 miles northeast of Chihuahua.[27]

Antonio Arias took charge of Chinarras and built a house, one room of which served as a church,[28] and by 1720 he was taking care of 234 "gentiles and apostates."[29] In 1723 Chinarras was in charge of Lorenzo Mendívil, but he was gone by the end of 1725, when Juan Guenduláin reported that the church was without a missionary but was visited from time to time by priests from the college in Chihuahua.[30] Sometime before 1748, when he was at Tubares, Nicolás Sachi is said to have served Chinarras, and Dionisio Murillo got there by 1748 and remained at least through 1755. Murillo may have been replaced temporarily in the 1750s by Antonio Texeiro, and Rafael Palacios served the outpost from 1759 to 1762, when he was transferred to Santo Tomás.[31]

At the time of Tamarón's visit, Chinarras was without a missionary, but, as before, was served from the college in Chihuahua. By this time a good church, which the bishop described as expensive, with a vaulted roof, had been built and was in good condition. His grace added that since there was very little to do at the mission, a Franciscan from San Gerónimo frequently acted as a supply priest.[32]

In October 1766, Claudio González took charge of Chinarras, but he stayed only until the following June when, happening to be temporarily at the college in Chihuahua, he was taken into custody.

The church which Bishop Tamarón described has survived into modern times, probably looking very nearly as it did when he saw it. On the other hand, it was perfectly obvious to Paul and me that sometime during the course of the years a good part of the building had fallen down. The repairs, which had been only very recently done when we were there in April 1970, were quite unusual: The old church had been rebuilt with the old materials, and where the old decorative stones were broken, they had been put back in place in a broken condition. Thus, the inside stone pilasters showed distinct breaks and gaps, the stone trim on the doorways to the sacristy and baptistry was jagged, and the engaged stone columns which framed the front door looked as though they had been in a war. Of course, some new material had been used—the tile floor, patterned in sepia and white, was new, the pews were new and the walls themselves were new—the repair work was apparent only in the stone trim.

Chinarras is a little difficult to find, since there is no settlement of any sort, and no one thereabout seems to know the word "Chinarras." The church, which goes by the name "Santa Ana" is visible from the Chihuahua-Aldama highway, through the trees to the right, about two kilometers on the Chihuahua side of Aldama. It's worth trying to find, since the total effect, once you get over being somewhat startled, is very pleasing.

11

San Felipe de Jesús

La Iglesia de San Felipe de Jesús

Santa Bárbara and Parral date respectively from 1567 and 1631, but neither was founded as a mission pueblo. San Pablo Balleza, the first mission settlement in Chihuahua, had its origins in 1611, but was abandoned during the 24 years between 1616 and 1640. This makes San Felipe de Jesús, established by Gerónimo Figueroa on the south bank of Río Conchos in June 1639,[1] the oldest continuously inhabited mission town in Chihuahua. Today "de Jesús" has been dropped, and the place is known more simply but much less grandly as San Felipe. "San Felipe" has always been used, although originally there was some uncertainty about the rest of the name. The settlement has been variously called San Felipe y Navidad de Nuestra Señora,[2] San Felipe de Santiago[3] and San Felipe de Conchos.[4]

Father Figueroa stayed at San Felipe only through the summer of 1639, and there is no report that he did any church building before he left for Huejotitlán. Thus the first church was probably begun by José Pascual soon after his arrival in August 1639. It is likely that it was completed before the 1648 revolt, and it was certainly finished by 1651, when its modest builder said it was *muy curiosa* and adorned in a style personal to him.[5] A less prejudiced report called the church very graceful and well adorned, earning the admiration of all who saw it.[6]

When the 1648 revolt engulfed large parts of Tarahumara, the Indians at San Felipe didn't participate in the fighting, the pueblo was not attacked and, except for a brief excursion to Río Papigóchic with the governor and his troops in the summer of 1650,[7] Father Pascual remained at his post throughout the disturbances.[8] San Felipe was in fact a haven of safety, and Pascual was joined at the start of the revolt by Cornelio Beudín, later to be martyred at Papigóchic,[9] and by Vigilio Máez, who was forced to leave his post at Satevó to seek the safety of San Felipe.[10]

By 1665 Pedro Escalante had come to assist Pascual and, when the latter was transferred to Las Bocas two years later, to take charge of the partido.[11] By 1668 Escalante had built a new, elaborate and beautiful church,[12] which was described in 1753 as being in good condition, with a choir loft, sacristy, baptistry, baptismal font and a tower with six bells.[13]

By 1673 Francisco Díaz Valdés had come to San Felipe. Escalante and Pascual had traded places, Escalante going to Las Bocas and Pascual being again in charge of San Felipe, but only for a brief time before he went to Guadalajara.[14] Díaz Valdés continued in charge of San Felipe after Pascual went south, and is said to have served the partido, first at San Felipe and later at Santa Cruz when it became the cabecera, for an astounding total of 73 years. On February 26, 1746, by then long past 90, he died of apoplexy at Santa Cruz.[15]

I haven't found a record of the precise date that Santa Cruz became the cabecera and San Felipe the visita, but the shift had occurred by 1681[16] and was an accepted fact by 1692, when Antonio Herrera first appeared as the priest at Santa Cruz in charge of both pueblos.[17] However, even though it was the visita, San Felipe continued to be larger than Santa Cruz, and in 1728 had a population of 120 able-bodied Indian men against only 100 at the cabecera.[18]

I haven't been at San Felipe since April 1969, but the church which was there then was probably the same one which sounded so grand in 1753. It had become somewhat less grand. The building was at the west end of the small and widely dispersed town, facing east. It was perfectly plain, rectangular, of plastered adobe, with a simple wooden door and a flat roof. Inside there was a beamed ceiling with not very well carved painted corbels, a plain freestanding altar and an older fixed altar, the latter with a gilded tabernacle. The choir loft, undoubtedly the one which was there in 1753, led to the roof, where there were two very old bells suspended on a rack. The remnants of the tower, long since fallen, were at the north edge of the building.

There is a road from Satevó to San Felipe, but we have not used it. In 1969 we got to San Felipe from Valle de Zaragoza, which is on the south bank of Río Conchos, and from which a road leads south and west to Parral. The road to San Felipe was not marked by a road sign or otherwise, but it was the only turnoff to the west after leaving the valley on the road to Parral, and climbing the mesa. From the turnoff, San Felipe was about two hours by jeep.

Santa Cruz

In October 1972, Paul and I set out to locate Santa Cruz, Valle del Rosario and Padre Herrera, three small pueblos said to be on lower Río Balleza between San Javier and the junction with Río Conchos. It took a fair amount of traveling, and some rechecking, to conclude that the three were, and are, only one, now usually called Rosario.

The confusion about Santa Cruz has been very great. Santa Cruz was its only name when it was established in 1640 by José Pascual.[19] Early in the eighteenth century the name was changed to Padre Herrera, occasionally just Herrera, sometimes Santa Cruz del Padre Herrera, or sometimes even Santa Cruz del Padre, but all in honor of the Jesuit who served the community so long and faithfully. Variants of the Herrera name survived until 1826, when by action of an anticlerical legislature, the pueblo became Valle del Rosario.[20]

But at least I'm not the only one who has been confused. A leading Jesuit commentary reported in 1941 that Santa Cruz was then known as La Joya,[21] but the same work contained a map of Tarahumara Baja as it existed in 1678, on which were clearly and separately shown the pueblos of Rosario, Santa Cruz and San Nicolás Joya.[22] Another scholar, writing in 1937, identified Santa Cruz as Santa Cruz de Villegas, which is actually a small ranch a few kilometers northwest of Parral.[23]

The narthex of the impressive Nuestra Señora del Rosario probably looks much as it did when it was built around 1650, but the exterior has undergone extensive remodeling. October 1972.

By 1650 Father Pascual had built a fine church at Santa Cruz, very large, well built and well adorned. But perhaps more important for the material needs of the Tarahumaras, Pascual also built a dam on Río Conchos[24] near Santa Cruz, where the soil was reported by the good priest to be more fertile than at San Felipe.[25] In 1678 the visitador Ortiz described the Pascual church as large and very well decorated.[26] Three years later, by 1681, Santa Cruz had become the cabecera,[27] undoubtedly with Father Díaz Valdés in charge. The well-loved Father Herrera came, at least by 1692,[28] to help Díaz. Herrera was 81 when he died 40 years later,[29] but Díaz, who was probably a little younger, outlived him by 14 years.[30] Cristóbal Moreno was in charge of the partido by 1748, but very probably came earlier to help Díaz in his last days. Moreno was undoubtedly still there when Santa Cruz was delivered to secular clergy in 1753.

At secularization, the building was impressive. The inventory describes it as a most beautiful church, cruciform in design, with four galleries and a paneled and vaulted ceiling with two towers in which there were three new bells.[31]

When we finally found Valle del Rosario, the church looked not at all like the one described in 1753. It was no longer cruciform—the transepts and galleries had fallen and been replaced by adobe, and there was no dome. But the big structure was nevertheless most impressive. Most of the narthex may have been in its original condition—there was a ground-level room below the handsome Baroque-style tower at the southeast corner and, balancing at the northeast, a small chapel which may once have been below a second tower. The single remaining tower, with a circular wooden stairway, was quite lovely in a wholly unrestored condition. The façade, plastered and whitewashed, had an arched entrance, with a splendidly carved door, tastefully framed with bas-relief pilasters.

The nave was not large. The sanctuary had an old-fashioned painted retablo with Gothic cathedral spires and, below the monogram *MDR* and a signet with a lily, a central statue of Nuestra Señora del Rosario. Beside the freestanding altar were two small pictures, one of the Sacred Heart of Jesus and the other of the Virgin of Guadalupe. But I thought the finest thing about the interior was not the sanctuary but the very lovely unused choir loft, supported by carved vigas, delicately painted and decorated. Not without fear I was able to climb to the choir loft and to the new sheet metal roof, installed at a slant to let the rain run off.

The church complex was much larger than the nave, since at the back of the building and connected to it were ruins of a two-story adobe building which just possibly might have been the galleries reported in 1753. No one has done anything about restoring the galleries, if that's what they were, but the lady from whom I borrowed the key said that she was collecting funds to restore the tower.

Rosario is about an hour and a half north or downstream from Valle de Olivos and is not in fact on Río Balleza, but instead on the

The altar and retablo of Nuestra Señora del Rosario are
mainly ivory and gold, nicely set off by a pastel blue wall.
October 1972.

north side of a small tributary just upstream or east from its junction with the river. The church totally dominated the very small
town, and together they sat on a relatively high mesa visible across
the flat country at a great distance. The town surrounding the
church was no more than one block deep in any direction, and the
reported population of 594 seemed reasonably accurate.[32]

San José de Gracia

San José was established as a visita of San Felipe in time to be attacked in the great Tarahumara uprising of 1648,[33] and it is said that two years later it had about 100 people and a temporary church.[34] Ortiz reported in 1678 that there was still no church, only a jacal, but that a new building was nearly finished.[35] Sometime later that building must have fallen, because when San José was secularized with its cabecera (now Santa Cruz rather than San Felipe), the settlement was reported to have a church newly constructed from the foundations, but no equipment for saying Mass.[36]

The church which I inspected in 1974 was certainly not in its 1753 condition, but basically it may have been the same structure, plastered, with a new roof and bell tower, and with a buttress shoring up the walls at the southeast corner. The building was rectangular and boxlike, with an unplastered fired brick bell tower (with a domed roof) at the southwest corner. Except for a single bell and a cross above the tower, it could have passed for a store building.

The interior, on the other hand, was not without charm. The altar, profusely supplied with paper flowers, was draped severely in yellow, and held a small Cristo Rey with the sacred heart outlined on its breast. Atop a pedestal against the wall, and thus behind the altar, was a very large statue of St. Joseph, the left hand holding the infant Christ and the right grasping a staff. Behind the statue there was a square of green cloth and on either side were yellow drapes. Both the wall hangings and the ceiling were decorated with glass Christmas tree balls. The sanctuary was recessed, and on both sides of the wall, facing the nave, were small paintings, the Virgin on the epistle side and the Infant of Prague on the gospel.

In the seventeenth century San José was also called Salto del Agua,[37] but that name seems to have been forgotten, and the settlement now has two others: San José de Gracia and San José del Sitio.[38] Under either name, the small town is a place of some relative importance, since it is connected by road to Rosario, Nonoava and Satevó, and is a way station between Nonoava and Satevó.

For Paul and me in April 1974, San José was not merely an important way station—it represented the only indication of

Multicolored glass Christmas tree balls gaily surround this statue of St. Joseph holding the Holy Infant at San José de Gracia. April 1974.

human life in four hours of travel northwest from Rosario across Río Balleza and Río Conchos and then in a great arc north, northeast, east, southeast and finally south through San José to the place about an hour south of the pueblo, where Arroyo San José joins Río Conchos. At that point the road ended, but there was a ranch with a house or two. The guide we had brought with us from Rosario was able to find one horse, on which I started out for San Nicolás de la Joya, the guide sometimes walking and sometimes riding behind me.

San Nicolás de la Joya

The earliest mention of San Nicolás I have found is a 1728 report by Father Antonio Herrera that it was a visita of Santa Cruz with 70 able-bodied men.[39] In a later report, probably made in 1744, Father Díaz Valdés assigned to San Nicolás 147 neophytes of both sexes, 2 widowers, 12 widows and 80 children under instruction.[40] When the visita was secularized with Santa Cruz, its cabecera, in 1753, the inventory showed a church without a roof and an unconsecrated silver chalice weighing three marks and two ounces.[41]

In 1974 San Nicolás still didn't have much of a roof. The church was a tremendously large plastered adobe building whose windows, vertically barred with wooden poles, gave me something of a prison feeling. There was a two-tiered bell tower at the left or southeast corner and a ruined priest's residence and sacristy at the southwest corner, off the sanctuary. But inside there was no silver chalice. In fact there was nothing at all except a small and very plain plastered adobe altar and a relatively new choir loft which could be reached by a treacherous stairway under the bell tower off the narthex. The roof over the choir loft had been replaced in the recent past, but the central part of the nave was still open to the elements, and the vigas holding up the roof over the altar were sagging so precariously that some of them must have since fallen.

Getting to San Nicolás was somewhat of a challenge and required a prodigious amount of effort. But it was worth it.

Bishop Tamarón reported that San Nicolás was on the north bank of Río Conchos.[42] A more recent authority put it on the south bank at the junction of Río Balleza,[43] while a modern commentator wasn't able to locate it at all.[44] In October 1972, Paul and I were told in Rosario that the name had been changed to San Nicolás del Cañón and that it was west of Río Balleza. Finally, the U.S. Army showed San Nicolás on neither bank but actually in Río Conchos.[45]

In truth the army is very nearly right. San Nicolás de la Joya was most appropriately named, because geographically it is in fact a jewel. It's on a small hill forming a sort of Tiffany setting in the middle of a large circular valley totally surrounded by mountains and encircled, almost completely, by Río Conchos. The river breaks through the mountains at the northwest, flows around the outer perimeter of the valley almost 360 degrees and then breaks out

The church of San Nicolás de la Joya is almost deserted
and almost surrounded by the waters of Río Conchos.
April 1974.

again through a narrow and precipitous canyon at the northeast. My
guide told me that the shortest way to San Nicolás from the junction of Río Conchos and Arroyo San José was through that canyon,
but because of the boulders and rapids no horse could make it.
Instead, we crossed Río Conchos just downstream from the junction
with the arroyo, climbed the high mountain southeast of the gorge,
went down the other side into the valley of San Nicolás, crossed Río
Conchos again at the edge of the valley, and then went to its center.
There, on its hill, stood the massive church, deserted except for a
few dozen hearty souls who grew corn and beans on what is almost
an island nearly surrounded by the river.

San Francisco Javier
de Satevó

Santa Ana de la Joya

If you are going to Satevó, it is convenient to stop on the way at two of its visitas, Santa Ana de la Joya and San Antonio de las Cuevas. But if you start from Chihuahua, then getting to either one, or for that matter to Satevó, involves the town of General Trías,[1] the modern name applied to the seventeenth century Franciscan mission town of Santa Isabel de Tarahumares.[2] General Trías has an attractive and graceful church and, since it's about an hour and a half or two hours west of Chihuahua on the paved Chihuahua-Guerrero highway, it is a pleasant place to stop for refreshment.

The road to Satevó (and to Santa Ana de la Joya and San Antonio de las Cuevas) goes due south from a stone corral and stone cattleguard on the south side of the Chihuahua-Guerrero highway two or three miles east of General Trías. The Satevó road is not paved, but is perfectly satisfactory. After about an hour to an hour and a half, at an arroyo, another good and well-defined road comes in from the west. Take the turn and travel almost due west for about three-quarters of an hour to Santa Ana de la Joya.

The town—it is no longer called Santa Ana, but merely Joya—is quite small, and I strongly doubt the reported 450 inhabitants.[3] But I felt the church was worth driving a good distance for.

Very large, it was rectangular and buttressed by piers on either side, with a square unplastered bell tower at the southeast corner. In front of the church to the east there were a very large number of burials, with the stones flat rather than upright.

Inside there was a communion rail with decorated machine-turned uprights, but the altar, while quite plain, was decently and reverently decorated with artificial flowers and two small santos. I thought the ceiling and choir loft were particularly fine. The vigas both of the ceiling and the loft were hand hewn, and the large beam and corbels which held up the front of the loft were artistically carved. The spindles in the railing at the edge of the loft appeared to have been turned by hand, and by no means recently.

I haven't been able to find any record of when Santa Ana de la Joya was established, but it was a reasonably thriving visita in 1753 when, along with the cabecera Satevó, it was secularized. At that time 65 families were reported, in addition to a well-built church and house and one statue of the baby Jesus.[4] When I saw it the church was still well built, the house had been replaced by a small adobe sacristy to the north of the sanctuary, and while the baby Jesus was no longer there, the number of statues had increased.

San Antonio de las Cuevas

The town of San Antonio de las Cuevas[5] is only slightly larger than Santa Ana de la Joya, and I found the church a good deal less impressive. Very small, rectangular, with a single bell centered above the façade, it was totally bare on the inside.

San Antonio is much older than Santa Ana, dating back at least to 1674.[6] Four years later, both the church and the house for the padre had been finished, although apparently San Antonio was primarily a ranch rather than a pueblo.[7] At secularization it was still referred to as a ranch, and in the inventory the local livestock was carefully counted. A single bottle of wine for Mass was accounted for, but there was no mention of a church within which the Mass was said.[8]

San Antonio lies just west of the highway to Satevó. While as usual there is no road sign, the turnoff is to the southwest, about

half an hour south of the Santa Ana road. After you leave San
Antonio, you can get back to the Satevó carretera without retracing
your steps by going on another diagonal to the southeast.

San Francisco Javier de Satevó

Everyone has heard the story about the little old lady who selected a
place to live by closing her eyes and sticking a pin in a map. Paul
and I have done more than hear about her. In April 1969, we met
her in Satevó.

We got to Satevó late in the afternoon—it's perhaps a three-
hour trip south from the Chihuahua-Guerrero pavement if you don't
stop at either Santa Ana de la Joya or San Antonio de las Cuevas.
While I went to the church to take some pictures, Paul looked
around for a place to stay. When I rejoined him he was deep in
conversation—in English—with a pleasant-looking and obviously
American woman. He introduced me and they both explained that
she was a retired unmarried schoolteacher from a small town near
Portland, Oregon. She had never before been to Mexico, knew not a
word of Spanish, but had read that retirement pay stretched farther
south of the border. So she got a large map of Mexico and a pin,
closed her eyes and jabbed. The pin hit Satevó, which had a reported population of 672.[9]

Satevó was founded in 1640, undoubtedly by José Pascual of
San Felipe,[10] with Vigilio Máez as the first missionary.[11] Father
Máez had built Satevó's first church by June 1648, when the
Tarahumaras attacked the visita of San Francisco Borja,[12] and Máez
was ordered to seek the safety of San Felipe.[13] The rebels went from
Borja to Satevó, where they are reported to have killed five
Spaniards and a number of Indians.[14] Whether the Satevó church
was then damaged is not recorded. However, the town was pretty
thoroughly destroyed and both the church and the priest's house
were burned when the rebellion, after a brief peace, erupted again
in 1651.[15]

With peace precariously restored, Father Máez went back to
Satevó early the following year and undertook to rebuild,[16] only to
flee again in March 1652, when rebels led by Tepóraca, after first
destroying Villa Aguilar and San Lorenzo, attacked Satevó and

When we first visited San Francisco Javier de Satevó in April 1969, one tower was incomplete and a pyramidal top was being added.

largely leveled the pueblo.[17] A year later, on March 4, 1653, Tepóraca was captured and hung. This time the returning priest found nothing left of his church and town, but what was even worse, the Indians of Satevó had largely dispersed into the hills and caves, leaving him not only the problem of rebuilding but also of gathering up the neophytes and inducing them to return.[18]

Just how thoroughly Father Máez was able to rebuild his church in the 11 years before he left Satevó to be visitador general[19] is a little uncertain, because the building was apparently not satisfactory to Juan Sarmiento, who took over in 1665, or to the visitador Ortiz, who reported in 1678 that while there was an old and rather poor church in existence, Sarmiento was building a better and larger one.[20]

Sarmiento was joined at Satevó in 1674 by Fernando Barrionuevo, whose health had broken under the more severe climate of Papigóchic.[21] Just how long either of them stayed is unclear— Barrionuevo may have been there until 1681, when he became vice rector of the college at Durango;[22] Sarmiento left well before 1700 and probably by 1692, when Domingo Lizarralde was first recorded at Satevó.

I don't know how long Lizarralde remained at Satevó, since most commentators are vague about the period of his service.[23] But it seems probable that he was there on July 31, 1715, when Pedro Tápiz, bishop of Durango, attended a magnificent celebration of the Feast of St. Ignatius, with a fine orchestra and choir and a Pontifical Mass which was "celebrated with the solemnity and propriety which would have been possible in the cathedral."[24]

It seems probable that Lizarralde had died or been transferred by 1719, when Francisco Bosque is first recorded at Satevó. Bosque stayed no less than four years, since he and Balthasar de la Peña were there together in 1723, and Peña was there for another five years, or until his transfer to Santa María de las Cuevas shortly after November 28, 1728. Pedro Estrada, who served with Peña after 1727, stayed at least until 1737,[25] and probably for several years thereafter. Juan Antonio Núñez took Estrada's place, probably early in the 1740s, since by 1748 he had been in charge of Satevó long enough to be serving also as superior, a post he also held in 1751.[26] He was undoubtedly still there at secularization two years later.

The church which the bishop took over was described as a beautiful plastered adobe building with a beamed ceiling and a good roof.[27] The church I photographed in 1969 was not the same structure, although it was undoubtedly on the same location and probably incorporated some of the old. The rebuilt church was of masonry, principally rubble with some fired brick and cut stone. Quite large, it was cruciform in shape, with a glazed tile dome over the sanctuary and two partial towers, one at each side of the narthex. One tower was incomplete, but was having a pyramidal top added when we first visited in April, 1969.

The interior was well built, with a large nave, good-sized transepts, excellent column clusters supporting the superstructure of the dome, good pews, a freestanding altar, a few unremarkable altar pieces, and against the rear wall of the sanctuary, a lonesome and unadorned crucifix.

The carved front doors of San Francisco Javier de Satevó depict
a chalice and adoring angels. April 1969.

Three sets of splendidly carved doors impressed me as far and
away the best things about the Satevó church. Opening from the
west churchyard into the sacristy was a double door with a large
central carving of a monstrance in the form of a sunburst, half on
each door. The carving was excellent, but the wood was somewhat
unhappily overweathered from age. The similar double doors at the

front of the church, in better condition, contained a large carved chalice rather high at the center (again with half on each door) and on either side, below the base of the chalice, the kneeling figure of an adoring cherub. The third set, at the east side, contained the least carving, undoubtedly because of the subject—the lamb from the Book of Revelation.

The Satevó church was excellent without being overwhelming, and the doors were worth traveling any distance to see.

San Lorenzo

Satevó is more or less due south of the cattleguard just east of General Trías on the Chihuahua-Guerrero highway. There is a road from Satevó south and east to Valle de Zaragoza at Río Conchos, and although there is some dispute[28] there is said to be a road southwest through San José de Gracia to Nonoava. I think there is probably also a road west to Santa María de las Cuevas, but in October 1971, when Paul and I visited both towns in succession, there was too much water in Río San Pedro and its tributaries to risk an unknown route. We therefore turned back and went north to the highway, west on the pavement, and past General Trías. At a point near the small settlement of Aguaje on the mesa west of Trías a good dirt road goes south first to Gran Morelos,[29] then to La Paz, and finally, after a short half day from the pavement, to San Lorenzo, which has been unfortunately known since 1935 as Doctor Belisario Domínguez.[30]

San Lorenzo was first visited by Europeans toward the end of 1640, when José Pascual and Captain Juan Barraza went on an expedition west and north from San Felipe as far as Río San Lorenzo, on which the town is located.[31] The following May, Barraza returned, rounded up a substantial group of Tarahumaras and asked the Jesuits to establish a pueblo as a means of civilizing and keeping them in one place.[32]

In 1652 San Lorenzo was a visita of Papigóchic,[33] 90 kilometers to the northwest, but the distance didn't bother Tepóraca who, after leveling Villa Aguilar on March 3, promptly did the same thing to San Lorenzo.[34] When peace was restored, San Lorenzo

became, more logically, a visita of Satevó, and by 1678, the visitador noted the presence of a "small church" which served 89
families of Tarahumaras.[35]

The population apparently had risen to 160 families just before
an epidemic early in the next century laid low all but 8 families.[36]
When Santa María de las Cuevas was separated from Satevó and
became an independent cabecera, San Lorenzo, quite appropriately,
was attached to the nearer town, and thus it was Luis Mancuso, the
priest in charge of the Santa María partido, who built a new church
and house at San Lorenzo,[37] probably about 1720.

When San Lorenzo was secularized with its cabecera, the
inventory didn't describe the church other than to say it existed,
had the usual altar furnishings and statues, a retablo and a small
bell. There was also a good house for a priest, and the population
had grown to 166 families.[38] At the time of Bishop Tamarón's visit,
San Lorenzo had become more important than Santa María, and, on
the basis of a petition by the people of all the communities in
the partido, had been made the cabecera, with Santa María and
Santa Rosalía as visitas.[39]

San Lorenzo, or Doctor Belisario Domínguez, has remained
the most important town in the partido, with a population
approaching 1,000.[40] The church just possibly may be Father
Mancuso's, refurbished, re-roofed and kept in repair. It is large,
with a single tower at the southeast or front right corner, and in
1971 it was well plastered and well cared for. However, I found the
building to be rather uninteresting. Inside there was the simplest possible freestanding altar, with a minimum of decoration—
and no retablo.

Santa Rosalía de las Cuevas

Santa Rosalía de las Cuevas, an hour and a half to two hours south of
San Lorenzo, is deceptive. The first time we were there, in April
1969, we were on our way to San Francisco Borja and thus, after we
inspected the splendid church ruins at the north edge of town, we
turned southwest on the road to Borja. Most of Santa Rosalía lies to
the southeast along the road to Santa María de las Cuevas, but

Splendid carved columns still decorate the stone doorway of the ruin of Santa Rosalía de las Cuevas. April 1969.

because we didn't go that way, we didn't realize that it's really a
fairly large settlement, spread out over a good-sized valley.[41]

The Santa Rosalía ruins have deteriorated quite badly; at the
time of our visit all that remained of what had certainly been a large
and magnificent church were the walls of the nave, a splendid
arched stone doorway flanked by good columns and, beside the
narthex at the southeast, the remnant of what must have been a fine
bell tower with a masonry stairway. Plaster on the façade had preserved the front wall against the elements, but the interior walls
were without plaster, and I suspected that they wouldn't last many
more years.

The church and the priest's house at Santa Rosalía were built
by Luis Mancuso during his tenure at Santa María de las Cuevas,[42]
which means that the big old ruin is more than 250 years
old. When it was secularized in 1753, the church was reported as
being in good condition, with good altar furnishings, a retablo and
three bells.[43]

Santa María de las Cuevas

Santa María de las Cuevas was established as a Christian community by Juan Sarmiento, the priest at Satevó, immediately before and during 1678. In that year the visitador reported that while the inhabitants were not much interested in religion and given more to drunkenness, Sarmiento was working with them and had begun the construction of a church and priest's house.[44] He evidently completed only the church, because it was later reported that in the time of Father Lizarralde, the only building in the settlement was the church—the sacristy, dwelling and retablo were added by Mancuso sometime during the first quarter of the eighteenth century.[45]

In 1692 it was thought to establish Santa María as a separate cabecera, and Sebastián Pardo became the settlement's first priest, serving also San Lorenzo.[46] But Pardo stayed only a year before he went to Tizonazo, and Santa María reverted to visita status until the arrival of Luis Mancuso, sometime after 1696 and perhaps not until the second decade of the eighteenth century. Until his death in 1728,[47] Mancuso was in charge of the partido and was primarily responsible for completing and furnishing the churches and building the sacristies and dwelling houses in Santa María, Santa Rosalía and San Lorenzo.[48] In 1723 Mancuso was assisted by Antonio Aragón, and at his death his place was taken by Balthasar de la Peña,[49] who served until his own death in 1743.[50] Peña's place was filled by the assignment of Felipe Calderón, who was still there in 1748, but who, by 1751, had been replaced by Felipe Rico, formerly of Zape. Father Rico didn't stay long, but delivered the partido to Bernardo Treviño, who was there at secularization in 1753.[51]

The secularization inventory referred to the church only as "large enough."[52] The building, which in 1971 had weathered the years well, deserved more comment. It was very big, very high and very solid, with an imposing façade and doorway, framed by bas-relief pilasters surmounted by an armorial design in carved stone. The stone arms in turn were framed by shorter pilasters and both flanked and surmounted by tapered columns which looked for all the world like Cleopatra's Needle.

But for me it was the interior which made Santa María one of the great churches of the area. The sanctuary had a simple but

The lovely sanctuary of Santa María de las Cuevas is framed
by an arched rood screen faced with tile and herald angels.

graceful freestanding altar in front of an older retablo dominated by
an excellent softly lighted statue of the Virgin framed by simulated
marble pillars and flanked by two smaller statues of angels. Above
the marble arch behind the Virgin, painted on the reredos and
extending almost to the ceiling, was a very large, almost grotesque,
pommée cross, Latinized in shape. Friezes of decorative tile in
yellow and blue encircled the sanctuary at about the level of the
altar and again just below the ceiling. The sanctuary was defined by
pilasters supporting an arched rood screen faced with tile. Across
the arch, the tile was conventional in coloring and design, but the
area between the top of the arch and the ceiling was filled with the

painted figures of two herald angels, each with a decorative scroll. The two scrolls together spelled out the Annunciation message: *Beatam me dicent omnes generationis.*

Even more startling was the ceiling, which was entirely covered, from the rood screen extending back the full length of the nave and from wall to wall, with an intricate many-colored design formed by rows of painted wooden blocks set as tiles alternated with structural wooden members. The pattern was conceived on an overall basis, crossing the joints between the structural pieces and the wood blocks rather than, as with tile work, using the individual blocks to form the design. At the time of our visit it was unfortunate that perhaps a third of the blocks had fallen, but the design was still there, and only a little of the beauty had been lost.

The magnificence of the church contrasted strangely with the small town of Santa María, whose population seems never to have been much more than 800[53] since the days of the early eighteenth century.[54]

San Joaquín y Santa Ana

San Francisco Borja de Tagúrachic

In 1678 San Joaquín y Santa Ana was the most flourishing of the eight partidos in Tarahumara Alta, with more than 1,300 Christians in its four pueblos, San Francisco Borja de Tagúrachic, San Joaquín y Santa Ana de Teguáchic, San Xavier de Tepórachic and Nuestra Señora de Guadalupe de Saguárachic.[1] The partido had come into existence only four years before, when Juan Gamboa established San Joaquín y Santa Ana (now Santa Ana) at the site of a Tarahumara ranchería called Teguáchic on the south bank of Río San Pedro.[2]

The cabecera, San Francisco Borja de Tagúrachic[3] had been originally established in 1639 as a visita, first of San Felipe[4] and then of Satevó.[5] By 1648 San Francisco Borja had a church and a priest's house, and on the Feast of Corpus Christi that year, the visiting priest, presumably Vigilio Máez from Satevó, led a procession after Mass which included five Spaniards and 50 Tarahumaras. The following day rebels attacked the town, burning the church and house[6] and converting the pueblo to ruins.[7]

The old reports are devoid of any suggestion that Máez or anyone else did any rebuilding of Borja after the 1648 destruction, and it is reasonably certain that nothing more was done in the area until after Juan Gamboa and Fernando Barrionuevo arrived in 1673. But Gamboa and Barrionuevo, as well as their successors José Tardá and Tomás Guadalajara, used Borja and the nearby Santa Ana as headquarters for their wide-ranging missionary activities.[8] In 1677 Tardá and Guadalajara turned Borja and the partido over to Francisco Celada, who served the area until his death on January 28, 1707.[9] There is a suggestion in one report that when Celada took over in 1677 he was assisted by the famous Juan Ortiz Zapata, who could have served only until he was named visitador general late in the same year.[10] In any event, by the time Ortiz wrote his report on Borja the following year, reconstruction was complete, and there were both a commodious church and a good house.[11] Indeed, Borja flourished to the extent that Juan María Ratkay, writing in 1683, described it as the wealthiest of the missions.[12]

In 1692, Celada was named rector of the college at Querétaro, and during the four years of his service in the south, his place at Borja was taken by Luis Mancuso, later of Santa María de las Cuevas.[13] Following Celada's death, the partido was administered by Antonio Arias, who served until he became visitador in 1717. Arias was assisted, at least in 1708, when he was rector, by Ignacio Estrada, but when he became visitador, his place was filled not by Estrada, but by Francisco Navarrete, who left at the end of the same year to help Arias and Estrada establish the College of Our Lady of Loreto at Chihuahua. Perhaps not immediately, Navarrete was succeeded by Juan Landa, who may have been an assistant in the partido under Celada, Arias and Navarrete, and who had more than 40 years of missionary service in Tarahumara to his credit when he died in 1747.[14] Landa's post was taken by Luis Téllez Girón, who had followed him earlier as priest in charge of Cerocahui. In 1756 Gregorio Vargas was at the misión, and was said to have had both good churches and good houses in the cabecera as well as in the three visitas.[15] Before the expulsion, Vargas went to México and sometime after June 1765, he was replaced by Mateo Steffel, who delivered the partido to the military authorities in 1767 and was taken to Chihuahua and ultimately to Europe.

I have seen no description of the 1648 church which was destroyed the day after Corpus Christi, but the later structure served by Francisco Celada and his successors was uniformly praised. There

The doorway of the great carved stone church dedicated to San Francisco Borja is surmounted by an almost life-sized statue of the patron saint. April 1969.

is no reason to believe that the modern San Francisco Borja, refurbished and kept in good condition during the intervening 300 years, is not the same church. Very large, with twin two-tiered towers, it has certainly remained worthy of praise. We were especially impressed by the stone façade, with pseudo-Corinthian pilasters of carved stone framing a doorway surmounted by a statue of the Borja saint. Each pilaster in turn was flanked by a bas-relief filigree carving of vines which ascended from a Grecian urn to the capital. Above the saint was a large rose window, in carved stone, surmounted, almost at the top of the pediment, by a bas-relief cross, crowned.

While the nave was large and well furnished, and the sanctuary was nicely but simply adorned, the interior of the cruciform building was dominated by an unusual narthex and choir loft. At each side of the entrance, leading to rooms under the towers, one a baptistry and the other primarily a storeroom, were two splendidly carved stone doorways, each decorated with pastel tiles and each surmounted by an extremely large carved wooden eagle. Each eagle appeared to perch on a ledge which jutted out of the wall, thus permitting the eagle to appear to support, with wings and head, the front beam of the choir loft. The loft in turn was attractively fabricated of carved and decorated timbers.

Several times Paul and I have visited San Francisco Borja, which is on the north or left bank of Río San Pedro. The first time we came from Satevó through rolling hills with foot-high grama grass, and were, as was so often the case, trying to get to Nonoava. Because the weather was bad and we were told it might take as long as two days, we were easily talked out of trying. After taking pictures of the church, which we thought was really as fine as any in Tarahumara, we passed on west and north to Saguárachic and Cusihuiriáchic.

Two and a half years later, in October 1971, we were in Borja again, determined this time not only to get to Nonoava but also to Santa Ana and Tepórachic. We talked to everyone about roads. The consensus seemed to be that it would take a full day to get to Nonoava, but that in one afternoon we could get to both Santa Ana and Tepórachic and be back in Borja by dark. We got precise directions for Santa Ana and Tepórachic, but since we weren't leaving for Nonoava until the following day, we didn't then ask questions about how to get there.

Santa Ana is downstream or east on Río San Pedro, but the road doesn't follow the river. At that time, you had to backtrack on the road to Satevó for about two miles, then turn east until you got to the bluff on the north side of the river which overlooks Santa Ana.

Most of Santa Ana, including the church, is on the south bank of the river, but a few houses and a store or two are on the north. When we got there in 1971 the river was too high to cross, or at least we were so told by a truck driver whom we didn't hesitate to believe. Paul took some pictures of the church with his telephoto lens, and we retraced our steps to Borja, where we were faced with the same problem—we had to cross Río San Pedro in order to get to Tepórachic.

This time there wasn't any truck driver to tell us not to try, so Paul took off his boots and waded across, very gingerly. Since the water came only to his upper thighs, I wrapped the distributor in plastic and drove the jeep across, equally gingerly. We were back at the hotel just before dusk, only to discover that the road to Nonoava leaves not from Borja, but from Santa Ana. We left very early the next morning and at Santa Ana again I followed Paul across the river. We got to Nonoava at sunset and were back in Borja before dark on the following day.

San Joaquín y Santa Ana de Teguáchic

The church at Santa Ana was interesting without being spectacular. A reconstructed and plastered façade, surmounted by a campanario with two bells, gave an appearance of modernity which was belied by the very old unplastered adobe walls and the crumbling remains of a bell tower at the southeast, or left front, corner. Many old burials in the churchyard attested to antiquity, as did the splendid carved vigas and corbels which supported the roof. The sanctuary was framed by a plastered arch and held, in addition to a modern freestanding altar, a masonry and plaster altarpiece at the reredos, with a santo in a glass-enclosed ark, all surmounted by the usual painting of the Virgin of Guadalupe.

Under the name San Joaquín y Santa Ana, the pueblo was founded in 1674 by Juan Gamboa at a Tarahumara ranchería[16] variously called Teguáchic,[17] Yeguiáchic[18] and Yeguatzi.[19] In Ortiz's time, Santa Ana had a satisfactory church,[20] and it seems probable that the remnants of that church became the adobe walls and ruined bell tower of the building we saw.

The pueblo has apparently never been very large, not much more than a way station and river crossing between Borja and Nonoava. In 1678 there were 67 families for a total of 504 persons,[21] and in 1728 there were 146 able-bodied men.[22] In 1744 there were about 47 families,[23] while Bishop Tamarón reported 120 Indian families and 453 people.[24] In 1960 there were 501.[25]

San Xavier de Tepórachic

About two hours southwest of San Francisco Borja, over a road which the natives would describe as *regular* (that is to say, bad), through mountainous but not unusually high country, is the small but friendly community of Tepórachic, on the north bank of Río Tepórachic, which runs northeast to join Río San Pedro.

Like the rest of the pueblos in the partido, Tepórachic has had many names: Parnaguíchic,[26] Teópari,[27] and Tepónachi[28] were some of them, but Tepórachic seems to have persisted the longest.

In 1678 the church here was "satisfactory for the celebration of the Mass,"[29] but by 1725 it was reported as "lacking all the necessities."[30] When we saw the building it had deteriorated into a magnificent ruin. North of the town and a good bit of distance away from any habitation, it was not close to a road, but had to be approached through plowed fields. The church, which faced the south, was wholly surrounded by burials, some fairly recent, and all quite overgrown with weeds. At what was once the apse, there was an extremely well-built circular wall, suggesting a dome over the sanctuary. All of the entrances were gracefully arched, even the windows in the bell tower, which had not completely fallen when we were there in October 1971. The roof was totally gone, although there were still a few vigas stretching across a nave marked by an attractive archway leading into the sanctuary. Here and there a bit of plaster still adhered to the adobe walls, particularly at the arches. It seemed to us- that the adobe was crumbling fast and that we might be the last Norteamericanos ever to see the arched doorways or the tower.

Nuestra Señora de Guadalupe de Saguárachic

On December 28, 1674, José Tardá and Juan Gamboa visited the pueblo called Soyguárichi, or in English "place of thorns." Having baptized a number of neophytes, they "placed the pueblo in charge of the Most Holy Virgin, Nuestra Señora de Guadalupe, giving it this name because the thorns [of the saguaro cactus] turn themselves into flowers."[31]

Saguárachic's first (and probably only) church was apparently completed in 1677, probably under the supervision of Tardá, Guadalajara and Celada, but possibly by Juan Ortiz Zapata.[32] In the following year, Ortiz reported that it was as large and well equipped as the best in the partido.[33] But by 1725, the Saguárachic church was, like that of Tepórachic, quite without those things necessary for the Mass.[34]

In fact the Saguárachic church was probably larger than that of Tepórachic, but when we were there in April 1969, a good deal less of the structure was left than we found to be the case in Tepórachic. As at its sister church, there were burials, some relatively recent, all around the building, and there were remnants of all four walls. Unfortunately, however, there were no arches, doorways or towers, and nothing approaching a viga. The only thing of which one could be certain was that the building was big and that it faced east, in the general direction of its cabecera, about an hour and a half away.

The town itself is not close to the church, but lies to the east and somewhat to the north, on the other side of a small hill. The church and its grounds, which have become the cemetery for the surrounding area, can't be reached by road, but are within easy walking distance down a hill from the road.

Saguárachic was never large and hasn't grown. In 1744 there were 66 families,[35] and Tamarón reported 97 families and 302 people.[36] The population may have increased some since then, but not by much.

Nuestra Señora
de Monserrate de Nonoava

La Iglesia de Nuestra Señora de Monserrate de Nonoava

We got to Nonoava[1] after two and a half years of trying. I had read that after San Pablo was reestablished in 1640, Tarahumaras from Nonoava began drifting down to ask the priests for baptism,[2] and somewhere I had seen a map that showed a road from Balleza northwest to Nonoava. So the first time we were at Balleza, in April 1969, I asked about the road to Nonoava. Several people told me to go north and northwest from San Mateo rather than to cross Río Balleza toward Huejotitlán. There is indeed a road that goes off in a generally north-northwesterly direction, but before we got irretrievably lost, we met a couple of vaqueros who told us that there wasn't any road to Nonoava. We turned around and went back to San Mateo, crossed the river and went to Huejotitlán.

Later on in the same month we were at Satevó. Again, I made inquiries, and while everyone agreed that there was a road, they also advised us that we couldn't cross Río San Pedro because of the spring floods. Since it looked like it might rain some more, we gave up.

We weren't again close enough to worry about Nonoava until April 1971, when we mapped out a route from Norogáchic to Paguíchic and from thence northeast to Nonoava. But we were lost for most of a day and a half getting from Norogáchic to Paguíchic, and we couldn't find anyone who could tell us how to get from Paguíchic to Nonoava. We gave up and were lost for another day and a half getting back to Norogáchic.

That fall we made it, but barely. They told us at Borja it would take us about six hours. It took us nine to get there and seven and a half to return the following day. The road leaves not from Borja but from Santa Ana downstream or east on Río San Pedro. If it weren't for the usual turns and twists, the road would go almost due south, and between Santa Ana and Nonoava there are only two side roads or turnoffs. The first is the road that goes east to Satevó, and the turnoff is about 40 kilometers north of Río Conchos. The second is at La Libertad, a ranch about midway between the Satevó road and the river, or in other words, about an hour from each. The La Libertad road goes to Ochiláchic, from which there is a horse trail to Paguárichic.

The lack of more side roads is a blessing, since between Santa Ana and Río Conchos we saw only two ranches and not a single living soul except the dueña at La Libertad. The country is rolling, with many unusually shaped rock outcrops, several middling high mountain ranges, some of the arrow-straight, mortarless stone fences for which the country is famous, a few cattle guards, great blue mountains in the distance at all times, and almost no cattle. Altogether, it is an area of total desolation but savage beauty.

The road is bad without being terrible. Nowhere is it graded or kept up in any way, and we were at all times acutely aware that if it should start to rain (it was threatening most of the time), we would be in real danger. The entire day was spent in four-wheel drive, always in low range and usually in low gear.

Nonoava is on the east bank of Río Nonoava, sometimes called Río Humariza, but this is a fact which I had forgotten. Thus, when we got to the north bluff that overlooks Río Conchos and saw buildings on the south bluff, I told Paul we were looking at Nonoava. We drove down from the bluff about two miles to the river, passing two ranch houses along the way. At the crossing there was no one on either bank, and the river was wide, deep, swift and obviously impassable.

We drove back up the hill to the first ranch house, where we found a very old, tall, tough and wiry mestizo with a Tarahumara wife. He told us no trucks had crossed the river for several days and that there had been so much rain in the mountains upstream that it was likely to be a week or two before any could cross again. He offered to take us across in a canoe and told us that on the other side there was a telephone which we could use to arrange for a truck to come from Nonoava to pick us up.

Our guide untied his canoe from a tree upstream or west and, holding onto a rope tied to the bow, brought it down to us. He anchored the rope to a tree and laid a large hand-hewn paddle athwart the sides of the boat. Somewhat gingerly Paul and I got in and sat on the paddle. The old man then took off his shoes, pants and shorts, rolled his shirt up under his armpits, took the rope and waded into the river, walking upstream against the current. He appeared to make no progress at all but actually kept even with the bank and almost imperceptively moved, the canoe following, across the stream. At the middle of the channel the water covered his chest and was up to his armpits, soaking his shirt.

When we got to the other side, the three of us headed for the store on the bluff. Like anything else when you need it, the telephone was out of order. Since our boatman kept insisting that it was only ten minutes to town by an easy walk, we started hiking. As we walked, he most solemnly told us that in Nonoava we would find many fine hotels and restaurants, and the thought of these comforts kept me going on the rough trail.

After about half an hour we met three vaqueros, who offered us their horses. Paul chose to walk, but we gladly accepted two of the horses, one for me and one for the youngest of the cowboys, who could later return them both. Our guide went back to the river, having first arranged to meet us on the south bank at 9:00 A. M. the following morning.

Another hour brought us to Nonoava, just at dusk. When I asked the way to a hotel I learned that there were no hotels, rooms for rent, or restaurants. After a good deal of searching we located lodging in the empty second floor of a building across from the church. It was welcome shelter, since it gets cold late in October, and Nonoava is just under 5,000 feet.[3] Our luck seemed to have changed, for we also found a woman who agreed to feed us and a man who was willing to drive us back to the river the next morning.

The first European to look on the Nonoava valley was either Father Juan Font, who may have traveled this far in 1611,[4] or Captain Juan Barraza who with Father Juan Heredía came to the valley in 1630 and brought back 400 Tarahumaras to settle San Miguel de las Bocas.[5] There is no indication that there were any Spaniards in the area for another 45 years, or until José Tardá and Tomás Guadalajara visited and baptized in Nonoava in 1676.[6] As a result of their visit and the recommendation of the visitador, Bernabé Gutiérrez, who urged that new priests be stationed in Nonoava, Cárichic, Papigóchic and Tutuaca,[7] Francisco Arteaga, later to serve as provincial of all of New Spain, became Nonoava's first resident priest in 1677.[8] A year later, when the visitador Ortiz was there, Arteaga had built a satisfactory small house to live in but he had only a jacal for a church. Ortiz added, however, that the temporary church was adequate for the decent celebration of the divine office, although, being so recently established, Nonoava badly lacked bells and ornaments. Nonoava at that time had 58 families and a total population of 209, but nevertheless in a year's time Father Arteaga had baptized, in Nonoava and Paguárichic, then its only visita, a total of 352 persons.[9]

Arteaga left Nonoava in 1684, and the pueblo was without a missionary until the arrival in 1687 of Pedro Noriega. Noriega began a construction program, and by 1690 he had built a dwelling house in its entirety and had a church well under way, having in a single year made 61,000 bricks for the church.[10] Between 1690 and 1692, Noriega took Juan María Salvatierra's place in Guazápares, and Nonoava had the temporary services of Juan Verdier, who apparently helped out only until Noriega returned. During the revolt Nonoava was seriously threatened, but rather than seek safety in one of the more populous towns, Noriega sent to Parral for help and was promptly furnished a garrison of 20 soldiers who stayed until all danger was past.[11]

Who administered Nonoava after Noriega died in 1704 simply doesn't appear, since the earliest report in the eighteenth century shows that in 1723 the partido was in the charge of Antonio Ydiáquez. Probably Ydiáquez came to Nonoava in February 1720, when he left Norogáchic;[12] in theory he could have come when Noriega died in 1704. But he was still there in 1755,[13] and while a 51-year span is not unknown in the Jesuit history of Tarahumara, it is at least most unusual.[14]

I can't be sure from the reports whether or not Father Ydiáquez built a new church. Noriega's 1690 church was obviously made of

Very large and unusually high, the church of Nuestra Señora de Monserrate de Nonoava faces east with twin towers and a triangular pediment above the façade. October 1971.

brick, but 35 years later the visitador Guenduláin described the building as "fabricated of beautiful wood very curiously made and painted."[15] Since the churches of the area were never made entirely of wood, the description can hardly be taken to mean a new frame building, but can only mean a great emphasis on decorative wood trim. Except for an unhelpful 1761 statement that the church was "good,"[16] I find no subsequent description of the building.

In his *Obra de los Jesuitas*, Decorme has an undated photograph of the church,[17] which, although in very bad repair, is without any doubt the same building, prior to restoration and reconstruction, that I saw from a horse when I first approached Nonoava. The sun was then down, but there was still a little light, and the view was startling and very grand, with low-lying adobe buildings in front of the tall twin-towered church and distant high mountains black against the setting sun beyond. The Decorme church is the same immense masonry building, but, since it must have contained 10 or 20 times 61,000 bricks, it was very certainly not the one Noriega built, with or without wood trim.

Very large, and unusually high, the Nonoava church faced the east, with twin towers (rebuilt since the Decorme picture) and a new pediment above the façade with a niche containing a good likeness not of Santa María de Monserrate,[18] the *patrona*, but of the Virgin of Guadalupe, in colored tile. No longer a series of barrel vaults running the width rather than the length of the building as it was in the Decorme picture, the old roof had given way to more modern sheet metal, pitched over a flat ceiling.

The inside was simple, but very well done. The sanctuary was substantially narrower than the nave and there was probably once a dome, although the ceiling was later supported with vigas and painted corbels, hand hewn. Instead of a retablo there were heavy drapes, white and brown, extending starkly from the high ceiling to the floor, with a large crucifix behind a plain altar. The one incongruous note was an altar cloth with the English words "My Lord and My God."

Regardless of when Father Ydiáquez came to Nonoava, he was evidently less than fully effective in his latter days, for Manuel Vivanco came to help him at least by 1755.[19] Vivanco was still there in 1761,[20] but he and Ydiáquez were both gone by 1765, when Bartolomé Braun, complaining that "for more than twenty years Nonoava has had decrepit and disabled missionaries,"[21] installed Juan Hauga, who had left San Miguel de las Bocas two years earlier. Before the expulsion Hauga had gone to Cárichic, and Pedro Cuervo was serving in what was probably his first and certainly his last missionary post.

The Jesuits no longer have charge of Nonoava, although they took over the church in 1905 and established a school.[22] In 1924, the church and school were turned over to the bishop of Chihuahua,[23] and since then both have been operated by the Franciscans. When Paul and I were there in 1971, the Franciscan priest was absent, having gone to Chihuahua by plane. And that's without doubt the best way to go.

Nuestro Padre San Ignacio de Humariza

As a Tarahumara ranchería, Humariza[24] dates from about 1641,[25] but a Jesuit mission was not established there until after 1678, when the visitador Ortiz reported that the partido consisted of Nonoava, the cabecera, and a single visita, Paguárichic, but that "there are a number of gentiles who ask for baptism in a post called Humarisac, where, with the help of the Lord, it is hoped to establish a good pueblo of Christians."[26]

There seems to be no doubt that Humariza was founded very quickly after Ortiz's visit, perhaps in the same year, but who the founder was is less certain. Ydiáquez, who wrote a history of the partido 66 years later, said that Humariza was organized by Father Ignacio Loyola,[27] while Luis González Rodríguez, who wrote in 1962 but had access to records unavailable to other commentators, said the pueblo was Christianized by Francisco Arteaga, the priest at Nonoava, and Bernardo Rolandegui, who, like Arteaga, was later provincial of New Spain.[28] If either Loyola or Rolandegui was there, it was apparently only briefly and only for the purpose of helping Arteaga, since Humariza never had a full-time resident priest. Indeed, in the early part of the eighteenth century it was reportedly almost never visited by missionaries.[29]

Mines were discovered nearby in 1695,[30] which probably helped increase the population. In 1725, 100 families were reported and, in addition to the small chapel built by Arteaga, Rolandegui or Loyola, a new and good-sized church was under construction.[31] That was probably the high water mark of population, since there were 92 families in 1744[32] but only 60 when Bishop Tamarón was there.[33] In 1937 the population was reported at 322,[34] but when we were there in 1974, we were told there were only 100.

Humariza was even more difficult to get to than Nonoava. In 1975 I confirmed that there is a road from Norogáchic through Paguíchic to Nonoava, but that it doesn't go through Humariza, lying well to the west of Río Humariza, which connects the two settlements along a twisting, tortuous course through steep barrancas. In October 1972, we were told in Nonoava that the best way to get to Humariza was by air from Chihuahua, Parral or Norogáchic, that there was no passable road for a motor vehicle of any sort, and that it would take six hours on a horse along the trail which follows the river (the same trail which was reported in 1725 as crossing the river 46 times between the two pueblos)[35] In April 1974, we made it the easy way by air.

We left Parral at seven in the morning in a six-place Cessna with two other passengers, one on his way to Balleza and the other (a native of Humariza who simply couldn't understand why anyone wanted to go there) on his way to Guachóchic. After we had left the Balleza passenger at the airstrip west of town, we went northwest to the headwaters of Río Humariza and then followed the stream north, landing on an extremely short runway that sits on top of a mesa north and a little east of the town. Before he took off for Guachóchic, the pilot told us he would be back in an hour, insisting that he could not wait longer because of winds and the rising temperature.

With considerable misgivings, Paul and I started down the steep slope to the valley, carrying three cameras and a tripod. It was a very long walk, and we had only 20 minutes of our hour left when we reached the church at the far west end of the sparsely populated valley. I began to take pictures while Paul went to locate a truck which two small boys had told us was Humariza's only vehicle.

By the time the hour was up Paul found the truck, we piled in, and the owner drove us back to the mesa and the airstrip, with what seemed like all the small boys in town going along for the ride. On the way the driver confirmed that he owned the town's only motor vehicle, telling us he had brought it in the year before in about four hours over the new road from Nonoava.

When we got to the airstrip the plane wasn't there—it didn't come for another two hours.

We regretted our unnecessary rush at Humariza, for the 1725 church was still standing. It totally dominated the valley, facing the east in massive magnificence from the top of its hill. The high building was of adobe with the plaster wearing thin at the edges. Heavy attached buttresses at both front corners gave the façade an appearance of columns. It had no true tower, but an arched belfry at the front surmounted by a cross. The roof was new, but everything else outside was very old, even to the crumbling and roofless priest's dwelling adjoining the sacristy at the south.

The long nave was almost totally bare, but the sanctuary, substantially narrower than the nave, had a relatively new plain

In May 1974, the plaster on the church of Nuestro Padre San Ignacio de Humariza was wearing thin at the edges.

wooden altar, freestanding with the initials *JHS* on the front, and a plain wooden communion rail. At the reredos were four pictures, the two large ones at the top draped in rope-like bunting in the colors of the Republic. On the gospel side a draped Virgin of Guadalupe was hung above a small representation of St. George and the dragon, while on the epistle side an unidentified saint surmounted a smaller likeness of the Virgin. The four pictures surrounded a central pedestal, which held a medium-sized statue of San Ignacio. A ledge behind the altar had two small santos, Christ on the gospel side and a nun on the other. The interior was far from spectacular, but the outside made the trip seem worthwhile.

Nuestra Señora de Copacabaña de Paguárichic

We haven't been to Paguárichic, and only partly because there's no road. The first turnoff on the road north from Nonoava is at the ranch of La Libertad, about an hour away. From Libertad there is a road to Ochiláchic, and we were told that it would take only about 15 minutes to get there. However, the road stops at Ochiláchic and from there it's another 45 minutes by horse to Paguárichic. I have been assured not only that there is no church in Paguárichic, but that there are not even ruins or rubble that mark the spot where there once may have been a church. We didn't go.

I can find no suggestion anywhere in any report that there ever was a church at Paguárichic. The only reference to a place for divine services is that of the visitador Ortiz, who reported in 1678 that the place had "no more church than a small jacal."[36] There were then 33 families in residence, but by the only subsequent census, the population had dwindled to 22 families,[37] so I doubt that a church was ever built.

Halálachic

When we were at La Libertad, we were told that 15 minutes away at Ochiláchic there had once been a church, which has become no more than a small pile of rubble with no walls. I suspect that Ochiláchic is the same as Halálachic, which was reported about 1725 as a visita of Nonoava that was never visited by the missionaries.[38] We didn't visit it either.

San Francisco Rexis

At about the same time, but in the opposite direction from Nonoava there was reported to be a potential visita consisting of a ranchería of about 60 families of Tarahumaras living between Nonoava and Humariza. It seems the Indians had asked for a priest of their own and didn't wish to merge with either Nonoava or Humariza. The visitador Guenduláin reported in 1725 that he had

In April 1975 the roof of the church of San Francisco Rexis was gone, and seekers after nonexistent Jesuit gold had dug a great pit where the altar once stood. It was necessary to stand precariously astride the pit to take this picture of the choir loft and entrance.

asked the priest at Nonoava, Antonio Ydiáquez, to establish a church at the ranchería, the name of which is not given, and to dedicate it to "our venerable Juan Francisco de Rexis,"[39] the famous French Jesuit who had been beatified in 1716 and was canonized 12 years after the visitador made his recommendation.[40]

I have seen no later report which suggests that Ydiáquez followed his instructions. But Almada lists San Francisco as a rancho in the area of Nonoava,[41] and in 1975 I heard that, in a valley called San Francisco which lies south of Nonoava and almost to Humariza, there is a church ruin. I decided there was a good chance that Ydiáquez had done what he was told to do, and therefore in April of that year Paul and I determined to find out.

This time we reached Río Conchos at a dry time and had no trouble getting to Nonoava. We stayed the night and the next morning took the new road for Humariza, which for the first half hour is the old road to Norogáchic. While much less traveled than the branch which bears southwest to Norogáchic, the Humariza road is not really bad—it's well described by the usual Spanish term, regular, and, best of all, it doesn't follow the river like the 1725 trail, but instead sticks to the ridges to the west of the drainage.

After about three and a half hours, we came to what most certainly was San Francisco Rexis. A small but well-built rectangular church of adobe, partially plastered, the building, although a ruin, had retained great charm. It faced east, looking down a valley formed by a tributary of Río Humariza; it had a graceful, but ruined, three-bell campanario above a partially plastered façade with an arched stone doorway below a square window which looked into a small choir loft. The roof was gone, and seekers after nonexistent Jesuit gold had dug a great pit where the altar stood. On the rear wall there were still three recesses, the central one well plastered and arched, which once held santos. If Ydiáquez was able, he probably filled the center niche, the largest, with a representation of the French saint whose middle name is still used to mark the place. But we found San Francisco quite deserted—no one lived at the rancho, whose plowed fields came almost to the edge of the handsome but lichen-covered stone steps which fanned out from the church doorway.

We got back to Nonoava the same night, very tired but quite ready to salute both Antonio Ydiáquez and Jean François Regis.

San Bernabé
de Cusihuiriáchic

Santa Rosa de Cusihuiriáchic

For 300 years the very nearly unpronounceable Rarámuri name Cusihuiriáchic[1] has been applied to the great silver-rich mountain south and east of the modern Cuauhtémoc, as well as to the town on the north slope. For most of that time the name for both mountain and town has undoubtedly been shortened, at least by the non-Indian population, to "Cusi."

In April 1969, Paul and I spent a full afternoon and evening searching for the town. The few people we met told us that it was at the foot of the mountain,[2] but we found tremendous vagueness as to whether it was on the north side of the mountain, the west or the south. The result was that we tried every road and path which seemed to lead to the mountain, starting on the south side, working around the west and finally, at about dark, reaching the north side.[3] There, running east from the base of the peak and thence around the mountain to the southeast to join Río Satevó, we found the precipitous and narrow gorge of Río Cusihuiriáchic, lined on both banks by a thousand windowless walls. The walls are all that is left of the stately colonial buildings, many of them of two stories, which once housed a population of 10,000.[4] Cusi is still pretty grand, in a ghostly yet elegant way, but only 360 people live there.[5]

Mining made Cusi a great city, but it was a Christian settlement first. On February 13, 1674, Juan Gamboa and José Tardá,
working out of Papigóchic, united the three settlements of
Cusihuiriáchic, Coyáchic and Huizóchic into a partido under the
name San Bernabé de Cusihuiriáchic, with headquarters in Cusi,
and Gamboa stayed in the area for a time to solidify the conversion.[6]
Four years later, in 1678, Gamboa had returned to the south and
Tardá, then rector of Tarahumara Alta, was in charge of the partido,
serving Cusi's population of 327 (10 more than the 1960 figure)
from a small flat-roofed church.[7]

Three years later all hell broke loose. Two mines, San Juan and
La Concepción, were discovered, and the population influx began.
In August 1687, the great San Bernabé silver vein was uncovered in
the heart of the mountain.[8] The following year Cusi was made the
headquarters of an alcaldía mayor with General Marcos Fernández
Castañeda as the first alcalde mayor with jurisdiction over all of
Tarahumara Alta. The predictable result was described by Father
Neumann: "Extensive digging was begun, and great throngs of
people flocked to these places. Houses were built, and mills for
smelting the ore. Within a short time a town had been established,
that soon attracted a host of merchants, who fixed their residence in
it, that is to say, in the very center of Tarahumara. Now these
Spaniards needed forest-land for timber, grazing-land for their
cattle, and Indians to make the bricks of which their houses were
constructed, and to perform other services. Consequently, the
natives were summoned and forced to this labor. The result
was that from that day they began to consider how to shake off the
Spanish yoke, and to plot with other tribes which had always been
hostile to the Spaniards. They consulted with one another by
means of messengers, and the conspiracy already existed in the
year 1689."[9]

Cusihuiriáchic itself was not attacked by the rebels of 1690.
Even though the number of able-bodied men had been depleted by
the usual fickle rush to the newly discovered mines at Urique,[10] the
Spaniards at Cusi formed themselves into a citizens' militia and
took up arms to assist the king's troops against the rebels.[11] Later,
when peace came and the government troops went back to the
south, 200 Spaniards of Cusi were conscripted, formed into four

companies under their own leaders and charged with the protection of the mission should there be another revolt.[12] Thus Cusi remained secure from the later uprisings of the decade. Indeed, in the 1697 revolt, some of the Franciscan missionaries to the Conchos Indians farther north withdrew to Cusi for safety[13] and a little later, notwithstanding continued military activity in the country north and west of Papigóchic, Bishop Legazpi visited Cusi on his way back to Durango from Sonora.[14]

When the Spaniard came, the Tarahumara vanished. So it was at Cusi. By 1698 it was reported that there were only two Tarahumaras, one of them sick, still in Cusi; the rest of the natives had moved their livestock, belongings and families to Papigóchic.[15] Thus, it isn't surprising that Cusi ceased to be the Jesuit headquarters of the partido and became a visita of Coyáchic. I find no record to show when the change took place, nor have I the name of the Jesuit, if indeed there was one, who was assigned to Cusi after Father Tardá left in 1683.

Miguel Ortega was in charge of Coyáchic by February 1690, and since he was in all probability its first priest, it seems logical that he took over the partido and moved the cabecera to Coyáchic on some date between 1683 and 1690. But there continued to be Christian activity at Cusi, and a curacy was established to serve the Spanish population. Sometime before 1709 a secular priest, José García Valdez, was there as curate, and in 1718, even though it is probable that no Jesuit was in residence, a small "college" was established by the Order for the purpose of training children and helping new missionaries to learn the language.[16]

Obviously some of the Tarahumaras had come back in the meantime. The mines had been temporarily abandoned, the Spaniards were gone, and the whole place was reported to have a population of not many more than 10 families.[17] A little later the census had risen to 69 families, and Cusi had a church as good as that of Coyáchic, with a wooden ceiling.[18] In 1728 there were 42 Indian men of working age, 11 children and 11 men too old to work—nobody bothered to count Indian women in New Spain some 250 years ago.[19]

By the middle of the eighteenth century Cusi was coming to life again and was served by two priests, Marcos Andrés Sánchez de

Tagle, curate, vicar and ecclesistical judge, and the vice curate Francisco Xavier Zárate. The population had risen only to 290 by Bishop Tamarón's time,[20] which was still 30 years before the era of the town's most spectacular activity.

There were new mineral strikes in the last quarter of the century, and the miners and merchants came back. Indeed, in 1788 the population reached 10,750, and Cusi was the area's second largest city, barely exceeded by Chihuahua at 10,752.[21] It was doubtless this period which saw the construction of most of the graceful, balconied buildings whose pitiful remnants line the arroyo today.

The mountain continued to spew forth its riches,[22] but Cusi's fortunes took a nose dive in 1811. In that year, supplies having been choked off by the revolution, the proprietors of the mines, with a caravan of 70 people and a train of 600 mules, set out for Veracruz to get supplies. On reaching the coast, the party was stricken with yellow fever. The proprietors died, and only nine of the original party were able to return to Cusi two years later.[23] The calamity, combined with the continuing revolution, paralyzed the mines, and while there was some resurgence of activity, principally with North American capital, around the turn of the century, Cusi was clearly destined then to become what it is today—a town of crumbling walls, empty balconies, faded magnificence and ghostly winds rustling the leaves of the poplars down the single street which borders the left bank of Arroyo de Cusihuiriáchic.

That single street, with ruined walls on both sides, begins at the upper end of the arroyo near the tie-less roadbed of the mining company railroad which once briefly connected Cusi with the outside world. It goes past splendid stone and masonry entrances to tunnels, stopes and drifts from which the timbers have long since disappeared, past the ancient church bell now standing lonely in a narrow town square, and finally, almost at the foot of the canyon, arrives at Cusi's magnificent church.

In 1725 the Cusi church didn't amount to much, and when the final structure[24] was built, and by whom, is anybody's guess. When we first found the tall church in the moonlight at the low end of the town, the beauty of its single-domed tower, rising in three tiers, with delicate arches, made up for the long and tiring search. In

The single-domed tower of Santa Rosa de Cusihuiriáchic rises in three tiers, with delicate arches. This view from the back mercifully hides the peeling plaster and crumbling walls. April 1969.

the morning we saw that the exterior was in bad repair—the plaster was falling; the walls, although protected by a sheet metal roof, were crumbling.

Inside, beneath a splendid beamed ceiling with carved vigas and corbels, was one of the most magnificent retablos in all of Tarahumara, rivaled only by the three-fold splendor of Santo Tomás. In gold leaf, extending from the floor behind the altar up to the high ceiling, it was tri-partite, with highly decorated and chased gold columns ascending at the outer margins to form a delicate curve at the top, and with two additional and substantially identical gold columns acting as dividers to help frame ten excellent oil paintings, four in a vertical row on either side and two in the center above a splendid statue of the Virgin in a gold niche. The Virgin, whose niche stood out from the rest of the retablo, was immediately behind a five-tiered altar with a veiled tabernacle and artfully placed candles, which reflected a halo from the gold leaf above and behind her head.

The paintings were both well done and well preserved, although I was not able to identify all of them. At the top of each outer row the apertures were both small and triangular, and each was appropriately filled with a painting of an angel. The two central oils above the statue apparently depicted, immediately above the niche, the Assumption of the Holy Virgin and, appropriately at the very top, the Trinity in the figures of the Father, Son and Holy Spirit. Flanking the Assumption and, in part, the Virgin in her niche were a scourged figure and a kneeling saint, while the lower panels showed Christ taken from the cross and the Adoration.

San Ignacio Loyola de Coyáchic

Coyáchic is northeast of Cusi and, as the crow flies, it really isn't very far. To get there otherwise than by crow, we had to go northwest back up the arroyo, coming out on the mesa where the old mine railroad began the descent to the pueblo. From here we started on the road to Cuauhtémoc, but less than halfway to the city, turned sharply to the right, and went on a much poorer road to Colonia México, and from thence south and east to the pleasant valley in which Coyáchic is located.[25]

The church of San Ignacio Loyola was established by Fathers Gamboa and Tardá in 1673 and 1674 as part of their Misión de San Bernabé.[26] Tardá stayed in and around Coyáchic until 1683, and by 1678 he had built a small church and was planning a new and finer one to serve his 466 neophytes.[27] Throughout this period Cusi was the cabecera, but Father Tardá seemed to spend much time in Coyáchic—for example, Neumann and Ratkay reported to him at Coyáchic for assignment and spent the first two months of 1681 there, studying Rarámuri.[28]

Coyáchic is at an altitude of about 6,000 feet and in the spring the blooming fruit trees and numerous flowers give it a bucolic charm which contrasts sharply with Cusi. Since the Jesuits undoubtedly started the fruit trees and planted the first flowers, Coyáchic today probably differs little from the pueblo of 1684, before the calm was shattered by the discovery of silver.[29] Fortune-seekers and miners flocked to Coyáchic and nearby Cusi,[30] with the result that by 1690 Father Neumann reported that "the mission . . . is completely ruined by reason of the two mining camps nearby."[31]

By 1690 Miguel Ortega was in Coyáchic, presumably in charge of the partido, but from then on it isn't possible to develop an administrative chronology. It seems likely that after the Coyáchic mines played out the pueblo was taken care of mainly by the secular clergy serving Cusi. At the end of the first quarter of the eighteenth century, only 45 to 50 families lived in and around Coyáchic,[32] but a Jesuit, Andrés Sotomayor, was in charge of the church. The building, presumably completed on the basis of the Tardá plans of 1678, was very large, with curiously worked wood trim and a neatly finished vaulted ceiling of hand-hewn beams. The church was well painted, richly ornamented and adequately supplied, as befitted the cabecera. And Father Sotomayor was comfortable in what the visitador described as a "good house."[33]

By 1747 Francisco Osorio was at Coyáchic, but four years later his place had been taken by José Hidalgo. By 1755 Hidalgo had given way to Luis Yáñez, who was transferred back to Cárichic well before 1765, undoubtedly because of his failing health. In 1759, either to assist Yáñez or to replace him, Benito Rinaldini took over Coyáchic, but still served as visitador.[34] Doubtless early in the decade, Coyáchic welcomed its last Jesuit, Francisco Badillo.

In 1753 Satevó and the other eastern and southern churches had been secularized. Coyáchic was thus the first Jesuit cabecera west of Chihuahua in 1767, and Father Badillo was the first Tarahumara missionary to hear the royal order of expulsion. He suggested to Captain Cuéllar, who came both to arrest him and to ask his advice, that he notify Bartolomé Braun, the superior of Tarahumara Alta then stationed at Temósachic, or, because he was closer, Felipe Ruanova, the visitador then at Mátachic. Cuéllar went on from Coyáchic to Mátachic, and from there Ruanova sent orders throughout the area, bringing all of the Jesuits dutifully and docilely to Chihuahua for imprisonment and exile.[35]

Indians no longer live in Coyáchic, but the pleasant pueblo has become home to 263 mestizos.[36] The large church which Father Tardá was planning in 1678 has undergone considerable rebuilding. In 1970 the exterior was dominated by an arched doorway of fluted stone and, above the stonework, the Jesuit insignia in bas-relief, all neatly plastered. The tower and belfry fell down long ago, and three bells were suspended in a campanario extending up from the front wall.

Inside, the vaulted ceiling had been replaced by sheet metal laid on rather poorly made modern trusses to form a central pitch. I found the sanctuary both pleasing and unusual. Framed by a white brick arch forming a rood screen with a bas-relief heart at the keystone, the rear wall was covered by a gold drape, which began near the ceiling and fell gracefully to a line below the altar to form a backdrop for a statue of the founder of the Society of Jesus. The statue stood on a pillar of white brick, pointed with dark mortar, which was immediately behind a simple freestanding altar and flanked on either side by smaller, but otherwise identical, pillars, each with a smaller santo.

San Miguel de Napabéchic

Napabéchic is not very far northwest of Cuauhtémoc, a sizable town we have always used as a way station, supply depot, and auto repair center between Chihuahua and the sierra. A pleasant, energetic, bustling community, Cuauhtémoc owes its existence to the Mennonites and the railroad. Before the advent of either, the place was a rancho of no importance called San Antonio de Arenales.[37]

The Mennonites came to Chihuahua from Canada in 1921 and 1922, with assurances from President Alvaro Obregón that they would be exempt from military service, would never be required to swear to an oath, could have total freedom of religion, could establish their own schools, and could carry on their theocratic government and highly efficient farming operations without interference.[38]

The Mexican government has kept Obregón's promise, and the splendidly manicured Mennonite fields extend out from Cuauhtémoc uncounted kilometers to the south, the north and the northwest. It is here that the *queso de Chihuahua* is made—and it is a cheese justly famous throughout all of northern Mexico.

Most of the people in Cuauhtémoc had never heard of Napabéchic, and only a few of those who had tried to tell us how to get there. None of these agreed as to the route or direction, which may be the result of the fact that, while neither shows on any map I have seen, there are said to be two pueblos of this name, Napabéchic Abajo with 48 inhabitants and Napabéchic Arriba with a population of 97.[39] The Napabéchic Paul and I finally found is a small ejido beyond the Mennonite fields with a small modern church and, some little distance northeast of the town proper and beyond a sturdy fence, the remnants of the adobe walls of a much older church building.

Napabéchic was not part of the San Bernabé partido when it was first established. In February 1676, Fathers Tardá and Guadalajara reported that Tarahumaras from Napabéchic had come to San Francisco Borja to ask for baptism. One of the priests went to the distant settlement, baptized a goodly number and concluded that it would be better to try to move the Indians closer than to establish a new visita.[40] But by 1678 Tardá had changed his mind, and Napabéchic was a full-fledged visita with a little jacal serving as the church for 92 Christians.[41] It seems likely that the jacal served for nearly 50 years, since Guenduláin reported in 1725 that the church, recently built, was located on the plain.[42] We found the ruins still on the plain at the edge of the foothills in which Napabéchic is built.

Huizóchic

Huizóchic lies due south of Cusi and south of the pueblo of San Bernabé. We haven't been there because the people to whom we talked were sure that Huizóchic had neither church nor ruins.

Huizóchic was one of the three towns (Cusi and Coyáchic were the others) which were joined together in 1674 to form the Misión de San Bernabé.[43] But there is no record of a church having been built at Huizóchic or of a visita ever having been established. In 1678 Cusi's visitas were Coyáchic and Napabéchic;[44] in 1725 Coyáchic was the cabecera and the visitas were Cusi and Napabéchic;[45] in 1761 Coyáchic was still the cabecera and Napabéchic and Cusi were still visitas.[46] Nowhere in the records is there a mention of Huizóchic.

San Bernabé

At San Bernabé, on the other hand, we found a church. Although not in good repair, it is undoubtedly not older than the turn of the century. It was rectangular, with a slightly pitched sheet metal roof, and its only exterior decorations were some stonework around the door and a bas-relief cross above the choir loft window. Inside it was without adornment of any kind. The building probably never had a bell tower, but at the northeast corner, detached from the wall, a new tower had just been finished when we were there in October 1971.

Because many of the old references to Cusi, or to the partido, are references to San Bernabé, many people have fallen into the trap of believing that the pueblo of that name is ancient. The leading modern authority on Chihuahua has even reported that the pueblo was founded in 1673 by Juan Gamboa and Fernando Barrionuevo.[47] Nothing about the church or about any other building in the little pueblo suggests he is right, and nowhere in any of the reports, Jesuit or Franciscan, is there any reference to the town of San Bernabé as a visita, either of Cusi or of Coyáchic.

16

Señor San José
de Temeýchic

Cristo Rey de Temeýchic

On the right or east wall of the narthex of the church of Cristo Rey de Temeýchic[1] there is a plaque which, when translated, says:

> Misión de Sn. José
> Founded by the Martyred Fathers
> Cornelio Beudín, S.J.
> and Jacome Basile, S.J. in
> 1650
> It was rebuilt in 1675 by the
> Fathers Tomás Guadalajara, S.J.
> and José Tardá, S.J.

The plaque is nicely done and shows a reverence for the martyrs Beudín and Basilio as well as a decent respect for two of the really great Jesuits of the Tarahumara frontier, Tardá and Guadalajara. Unfortunately, what the plaque says is not strictly accurate.

Cornelio Beudín was martyred in Papigóchic on June 4, 1650,[2] and there is no evidence that either he or any other European set foot in Temeýchic prior to his death. Giacomo Basilio didn't reach Papigóchic to replace the martyred Beudín until the summer of 1651.[3] Since Basilio built a little church[4] in Temeýchic before he was killed in Papigóchic on March 3, 1652,[5] Father Dunne was probably right in fixing 1651 as the date of the establishment of Temeýchic as a visita of Papigóchic.[6]

With the death of Basilio no further attempt was made to Christianize Temeýchic or the more important Papigóchic for more than two decades. Fathers Tardá and Guadalajara did indeed reach Temeýchic on August 13, 1675, and the following February reported that they had found vestiges of the church and house which Basilio had built and that another priest, whom they didn't name but who must have been Barrionuevo or Gamboa, had entered Temeýchic a few months ahead of them.[7] Neither Guadalajara nor Tardá stayed at Temeýchic, and there is no suggestion in the records that either of them reconstructed the Basilio church. It seems much more likely that rebuilding was begun by José Sánchez Guevara, Temeýchic's first resident priest, who came in 1678 to take charge of the new partido.

At first, Sánchez stayed in Cusi under Tardá's supervision, and he apparently served not only Temeýchic but its visitas, Pachera, Tosaboréachic and Píchachic. When the visitador Ortiz reached the partido later in the year, Sánchez, although still living at Cusi, was firmly in charge, and the small church was newly roofed.[8] The following year Sánchez moved on,[9] and his place was taken by Gaspar Varillas, who stayed for six years or until the arrival in 1685 of Juan Francisco Fernández.

Father Fernández either did or didn't move the entire town of Temeýchic away from its original site to a location about seven leagues west of the Sánchez church. Father Roque Andonaegui, who was Temeýchic's most famous (or infamous) citizen, reported in 1744 that seven leagues away, on "a broad and pleasant plain," there were to be found the ruins of a chapel marking the original site of Temeýchic. Andonaegui says that because the Indians wanted him to, Father Fernández moved the entire town and established a new settlement at the 1744 location, "in a very dismal valley at the foot of a mountain range and in the shadows of the mountain," a location which was wholly unacceptable to Andonaegui.[10]

The trouble with the Andonaegui report is that Temeýchic today is neither in the shadow of a mountain nor on a broad plain, but instead is at the edge of the high plateau which runs east from Río Papigóchic and its tributaries almost as far as Cusi. Immediately west of the town is Río Temeýchic, a north-flowing tributary, and farther west is the sierra, but in between there are good orchards with abundant apples, and there certainly is no mountain either close enough or high enough to cast a shadow over the town. Assuredly Temeýchic was not moved twice, and the account of the move by Fernández rests only on the report of Father Roque Andonaegui, whose reliability one may certainly legitimately hold in question.

Father Fernández left Temeýchic during the last Tarahumara revolt at the end of the century, and after peace was restored, his place was taken by Gaspar Zanna, who didn't stay long. Zanna was thought by the Tarahumaras at Pachera to have been unduly harsh in reproving them for some of the usual vices of the period, with the result that a group from Pachera came to Temeýchic and attempted to burn down the church and the priest's house. No serious damage was done, but Zanna, who was temporarily in Cusi, got the message and, in defiance of orders from the visitador, started for México and kept going.[11] He was succeeded, undoubtedly not immediately but certainly by 1708, by Ignacio Javier Estrada.[12]

In 1725 the Sánchez church of 1678 was "small, bad and very old,"[13] and Estrada was at work on a new building. Estrada was unwell during the 1730s—his occasional entries in the baptismal register are shaky and unsure, and he received fairly frequent help from other priests, including Blas de la Palma of Santo Tomás and Luis Téllez Girón for half a year before he went to Cerocahui. Thus Estrada may not have finished the church before his death in June 1741, or if he did, it didn't long outlast its builder.

After Estrada's death, Temeýchic was intermittently served for a few months by Blas de la Palma and Francisco Osorio, who had been at Cárichic, but in September of 1741, Roque Andonaegui took over and later claimed to have built and finished in only 13 months[14] a church which was contemporaneously described as ten times more beautiful than that of Mátachic.[15]

Father Andonaegui had time for other things, too. He was said to have engaged extensively in questionable commercial transactions through which both he and the mission contracted very heavy

debts, to have spent most of his time in Cusi gambling and drinking, to have installed a paramour in a home he owned in Cusi and
to have been the father of perhaps as many as three of her children.
After he was removed in June 1747, his activities were characterized as a scandal in "all the land, in Cusihuiriáchic and even in
Chihuahua."[16]

Bernardo Treviño was sent from the college at Chihuahua to
succeed Andonaegui, but in the summer of 1748 his place was taken
by José Miqueo, who remained in charge until his death in June or
July 1764. Miqueo was briefly succeeded by Ysidro Saavedra of
Papigóchic, who helped out only until the partido's last Jesuit,
Antonio Hitl, arrived in September.[17]

You can get to Temeýchic by going south from the Guerrero-
Chihuahua highway to Miñaca, which is the first station after you
leave La Junta on the La Junta-Los Mochis segment of the railroad.
From there the old road more or less follows the tracks to Terrero,
where a turnoff to the northeast will take you first to Pachera and
then, going upstream (southeast) along Río Papigóchic through San
Miguel, to Temeýchic. In Temeýchic the road goes east to Los
Alamos and from thence it is an easy run over the plain past Laguna
de los Mexicanos on any one of the many roads which lead
to Cuauhtémoc.

Paul and I got to Temeýchic late in the afternoon one fall day
in 1969, and we found the handful of people[18] to be hospitable and
friendly. The big fired brick church at Temeýchic, called Cristo Rey
(it had a large figure of Christ the King atop the dome on the single
two tiered tower), was not old enough to be the church that Andonaegui built, but it was very likely on the same foundations and
may have incorporated portions of the old walls. The town's few
buildings were to the west and south of the church, and it thus
stood quite alone and impressively large at the edge of the broad
plain, totally dominating the area for a great distance.

The sanctuary, appreciably narrower than the nave, was pleasantly lighted by two high windows, one at either side. A conventional wooden retablo, painted, with a statue of Joseph and the
Christ, stood behind a freestanding altar covered with a fine lace
cloth. A small santo, a painting of Guadalupe, and some artificial
flowers completed the decoration.

Buttresses, both lateral and frontal, dominate Santa Rosa de
Santa María de Pachera. October 1969.

Santa Rosa de Santa María de Pachera

Pachera, a pleasant little settlement,[19] is spread over a broad valley
near the junction of Río Terrero and Río Papigóchic.[20] In 1969
there were no buildings near the church, which faced the sunrise.
Imposing and substantial, it would probably stand for many years
to come. There were heavy buttresses at both sides and also extending laterally as part of the front wall of the building, but even more
curious were the extra-thick curved buttresses against the façade, at
either side of the front door. If there had been a tower, it had fallen
and been replaced by a square opening above the doorway with two

small bells. The doorway itself was dignified, with bas-relief pilasters, a double stone pediment forming a horizontal line above the lintel and a small bas-relief cross.

The interior had an embroidered gold-colored altar cloth, a central framed portrait of the Virgin and Child, flanked by two santos, one presumably Santa Rosa and the other San Martín de Porres. The portrait and the santos rested on an old-fashioned fixed altar with a built-in tabernacle. At the sanctuary wall a figured drape extended from ceiling to floor, white in the center with a few appliquéd red roses, and at each side, pastel pink.

Pachera was visited by Tardá and Guadalajara in 1675[21] and was established as a pueblo in the following year[22] or at least before 1678. In that year Pachera was very certainly a visita of Temeýchic, but it was probably without a church and was certainly without a single Christian, *"porque el demonio ha hecho mas resistencia. . . ."*[23]

Silver was discovered in the vicinity early in 1697,[24] and two years later the Tarahumaras of Pachera tried to burn the Temeýchic church. Whether their revolt was the result of the unrest which so frequently followed the arrival of Spanish miners or was the work of el demonio doesn't appear, but the Indians fled into the sierra ahead of the Spanish troops and remained until early in the next century.[25]

What Pachera had in the way of a church when its people attempted to burn the building at Temeýchic is wholly unreported. Indeed, not only is there no mention of a church in the report of the visitador Ortiz, but nothing is said about such a building in any subsequent visitation report which I have seen. Thus, while the church I inspected was certainly old, I have no way of relating it to any particular era or structure.

San Francisco de Asís de los Alamos

In December 1675, Fathers Tardá and Guadalajara traveled between Cárichic and Papigóchic and passed through Tosaboréachic.[26] Three years later Father Ortiz reported that San Juan Toraboréachic was a Temeýchic visita seven or eight leagues to the east, near the road between Temeýchic and Cusi, that it had a satisfactory jacal for a church and a small house for the priest, that there were thirty families of Christians numbering 92 people of both sexes, and that the rest of the people were gentiles who would probably soon be brought into the sheepfold of the church.[27]

There are no subsequent references to Tosaboréachic or to San Juan Toraboréachic, and we can only guess what happened to the gentiles. No map, ancient or modern, shows Toraboréachic or Tosaboréachic, and neither word is mentioned in any modern compendium or gazetteer I have seen.

Nevertheless I am convinced that Tosaboréachic still exists and that it is identical with Nuestra Señora del Pópulo de los Alamos, which was first reported in 1725 as a visita of Temeýchic with 90 families and 115 children.[28] The 1725 report was sketchy, but in 1744 Roque Andonaegui not only reported that Alamos was a visita of Temeýchic about eight leagues away to the southeast, but that it had recorded 505 baptisms between 1679 and 1744,[29] which seems conclusive.

In Tamarón's time Los Alamos had 87 families, totaling 243 Indians,[30] but the bishop's annotator wasn't able to locate the pueblo anywhere.[31] Paul and I found it with no difficulty at all in April 1970, on the road from Temeýchic to Cusi, in an orchard-filled valley on the plain about eight leagues from Temeýchic. Both the town and the modern-looking rectangular church, called San Francisco de Asís de los Alamos, are quite small, but both are neat and well kept.

The exterior of the church, which had a single small bell tower, was of little or no significance, but not so the interior. The nave and altar were conventional, but almost the entire rear wall of the sanctuary was filled with a tremendous and very fine oil painting of St. Francis of Assisi in ecstasy and the Seraphic Doctor, St. Bonaventure.

San Marcos Píchachic

The church at Píchachic is at the west edge of the railroad right-of-way, but the passenger trains don't stop. The first time I was there, the *autovía,* a self-contained diesel electric car which travels between Los Mochis and Chihuahua in twelve daylight hours, was going so fast toward Chihuahua that the town and church were out of sight before I could unpack my camera. When we came back toward Los Mochis, I had the conductor warn me a few miles in advance, and I took a surprisingly good picture of the church from the back platform.

Five years later, in May 1973, Paul and I rented a flatcar in Chihuahua, lashed the jeep to it, and hooked onto a freight train for Témoris. The excursion took two full weeks and involved building (and tearing down) a ramp to get the jeep on and off the flatcar at Témoris and at a number of intermediate points where there are passable roads leading from the railroad to interior church towns in the old Jesuit province of Chínipas. This time the freight train stopped in Píchachic (and everywhere else between Chihuahua and Témoris), and I took more pictures of San Marcos on the way in and on the way back.

We were surprised to find the building still standing in 1973. For in October 1969, when Paul and I had been at Píchachic in the Toyota without the aid of the railroad, we both had been entirely certain that the building would soon totally collapse. It had no roof, and while there was still a little plaster on the front wall and the tower, the adobe was deteriorating. In its day the church had been spacious, graceful and quite impressive. Even in its state of decay, really not much worse in 1973 than four years before, its columned tower, arched and domed, was still graceful and well built, as was the doorway, with pilasters framing an arched opening below the bas-relief letters *IHS*.

Getting to Píchachic by road is no picnic, although as the crow flies it isn't far from its cabecera, Temeýchic. The railroad goes generally south from Terrero along Río Terrero through Vergel and Sigoyna to Píchachic, but the road (on which we had come to Terrero from Miñaca to the north in 1969) leaves the railroad at Terrero and turns west into the heavy forest to make a wide loop west, southwest, south and finally southeast to San Juanito, the most important of the railroad towns in the area. About an hour out of Terrero, there is a fork, where, at a place called Caseta (consisting solely of a combination restaurant and store), a very bad road goes southeast to join the railroad quite a few difficult miles north of Píchachic.

The first mention of Píchachic is in the year 1678, when the pueblo may have been founded by José Sánchez Guevara.[32] Ortiz described the settlement as a visita of Temeýchic with only four families of Christians and unnumbered gentiles. If it had a church, he didn't mention it.[33] In fact no subsequent visitador said anything about a church, although there must have been a jacal at least by 1679, since Andonaegui reported a total of 1,677 baptisms at Píchachic between that year and 1744.[34] Mines were discovered in the vicinity in 1860,[35] undoubtedly with the usual stimulating effect on the population. But the stimulus was temporary, since the 265 inhabitants reported in 1759[36] have shrunk by more than 100.[37]

The appearance of the Píchachic church in 1973 suggested that the roof had fallen at least 50 years earlier and that it had been a good deal longer since the building had had any attention at all. On the other hand, between November 1939 and July 1942, one of the Jesuits from the Tarahumara Mission was stationed at Píchachic.[38] Thus it would seem either that the roof fell relatively recently or that the priest, for reasons which don't appear, was unable to preserve and restore what was once a lovely church.

17

La Purísima Concepción de Papigóchic

La Iglesia de la Purísima Concepción de Papigóchic

Ciudad Guerrero[1] has had various names: first there was Papigóchic,[2] the Tarahumara ranchería; then, early in 1649, when Governor Diego Guajardo ordered a presidio and Christian town to be built,[3] it became Villa Aguilar; later, for the 33 years between 1826 and 1859, it was called Villa de la Concepción.[4] But regardless of what name it has carried, Guerrero has always been important—indeed, during most of its three and a quarter centuries, it has been the most important settlement in Tarahumara Alta.

Villa Aguilar was the child of violence, and it had a violent youth. Established during the first Tarahumara revolt, the presidio was to serve three functions: a fortress to enforce the peace,[5] a permanent Spanish settlement,[6] and a Christian mission to the Indians. To take care of the third purpose, the governor asked the Jesuits to assign a priest, not only to serve the Indians but also to minister to the soldiers and settlers. Cornelio Beudín came from San Felipe in the fall of 1649 and promptly built Papigóchic's first church, La Purísima Concepción, a little north of the presidio and thus closer to the Tarahumaras.[7]

The rest is history. On June 4, 1650, the Tarahumaras revolted, killing Father Beudín and Fernando Vásquez, his soldier guard. The church and house were burned, and the bodies of the two Europeans, shot through with arrows, were lashed to the cross in the churchyard. The soldiers at Villa Aguilar recovered the bodies and saw to their burial, not at the ruined La Purísima, but instead at the presidio chapel.[8] The soldiers were too few to follow the rebelling Tarahumaras, but troops came from Parral, and limited peace was restored.

As a condition of the peace, Governor Guajardo required the Indians to restore La Purísima,[9] and the church had been rebuilt by early 1651 when Giacomo Basilio arrived to take Beudín's place.[10] On March 3, 1652, Father Basilio was killed in the third revolt, and this time the destruction was more complete. Purísima was devastated, and so were the presidial church, the presidio itself and the Spanish settlement.[11] In the words of a later commentator, "This time, no one escaped with his life."[12] In the face of such total destruction, Papigóchic, Villa Aguilar, and for that matter all of northwestern Tarahumara Alta were abandoned by the Spanish for more than 20 years.[13]

On September 30, 1673, in Parral, Governor José García Salcedo presided over a meeting typical of the Spanish bureaucracy—a strategy session to determine what could be done to bring Tarahumara Alta under the yoke of Christianity and European civilization. The meeting, attended by representatives of the army, the bishop, the Jesuits and the Indians, resulted in a determination to reestablish Villa Aguilar and Papigóchic;[14] a month after adjournment, Fernando Barrionuevo and Juan Gamboa left Parral for the north.[15]

While Barrionuevo and Gamboa certainly visited the Papigóchic area, it fell to their successors, José Tardá and Tomás Guadalajara, actually to reestablish the settlement and to see to the building of a chapel, probably at the presidio. In December 1675,[16] Tardá and Guadalajara reported at length on the rediscovered mission field, and, based on their request and the recommendation of the visitador general, Bernabé Gutiérrez,[17] six new Jesuits[18] were assigned to Tarahumara Alta: Francisco Celada, who was sent to San Francisco Borja; Francisco Arteaga, who came to Nonoava; Diego Ruiz Contreras, who was placed in charge of Cárichic; Antonio Oreña, who took over Sisoguíchic; José Sánchez Guevara, at Temeýchic; and for Papigóchic, Nicolás Ferrer.

By 1678, Ferrer was firmly in charge of his partido, had built a small jacal to serve as a church on the ruins of the old La Purísima, had plans for a very fine large church as a permanent replacement, and, in addition to the cabecera, was serving the three visitas of San Cornelio Paguírachic, Santo Tomás de Villanueva de Tojorare and San Pablo de Basúchic.[19]

Ferrer was in poor health, and he was replaced by Juan Bautista Copart not long after the report of the visitador. Copart left for California in 1684,[20] and Papigóchic was without a priest until the arrival of Domingo Créscoli, who may have come as early as 1688 but was certainly there on April 1, 1690, when the Tarahumaras again revolted. Créscoli didn't return after the peace, but instead his place was taken by Juan Verdier.[21] Verdier in turn was transferred to Sonora in October 1695, and the partido was put in charge of Venceslao Eymer.

Eymer stayed in Papigóchic until his death in 1709,[22] and was thus serving the partido during the last of the Tarahumara insurrections. At that time Papigóchic, a haven of safety in a violent land, was home to a total of six Jesuits—Father Eymer's temporary guests were Pedro Proto of Cocomórachic, Juan Bautista Haller of Yepómera, Jorge Hostinsky of Tomóchic, Florencio Alderete of Mátachic and Balthasar de la Peña of Santo Tomás.

Papigóchic and Villa Aguilar were not attacked in the 1697 revolt, but the year before there were horrendous portents from which Father Eymer and his neophytes might well have guessed that evil was about to fall on the land. According to Father Neumann: "In the month of April, 1696, this province of Tarahumara Alta was shaken by an earthquake, notwithstanding the fact that earthquakes are unusual in this region. At the end of October, just before dawn, a dreadful comet became visible. At first it had no head, but later a head, very dark, took shape, facing the East, while the tail streamed toward the West. For about three weeks it shown in the sky, terrifying all beholders, and then vanished from sight. On the first night when the comet appeared, fires were seen on the hills near the church of Papigóchic; they darted to and fro, making a ghastly light, and a fiery ball hung in the air, which presently fell to the earth with a crash like that of a thunderbolt. During the night between Friday and Holy Saturday the bells of this same church twice sounded a mournful peal, though no man laid hand to them; the sound was like the tolling heard at a funeral. The river which flows through Papigóchic was seen to break into waves. They rose to a great cone, twelve feet in height; then, with a mighty roar, sank back into the channel, and the stream resumed its flow."[23]

That there should be supernatural portents in Tarahumara in 1696 is not surprising. Indeed, in the same decade as the 1692 Salem witch trials, a Papigóchic sorcerer, after first confessing and receiving absolution and the final consolation of the church, was burned alive.[24]

The records before 1742 are a little sketchy, but it seems probable that during most of the 17 years which followed Eymer's death in 1709, Papigóchic was in the charge of Jorge Hostinsky, who also served Santo Tomás and a number of churches in the higher and more inaccessible sierra. The year before Hostinsky's death in 1726, he was reported to have at Papigóchic a well-decorated, very large and very beautiful church, from which he served two visitas, both on the left bank of the river, San Cornelio de Paguírachic and San Javier de Mogúriachic.[25] Hostinsky's place was apparently taken by Bernardo Gaspar, but I haven't been able to determine how long he stayed. Nor, except that he probably left toward the end of 1741 or early in 1742,[26] have I discovered anything at all about the Papigóchic service of Lucas Alvarez, later visitador general.

By July 1742, when the 14th bishop of Durango, Martín Elizacoechea, visited Papigóchic, Dionisio Murillo was in charge of the partido.[27] Murillo left the following January, perhaps to take over Chinarras, and his place at Papigóchic was filled, very briefly, by Lucas Merino. In May 1743, Francisco Osorio, who had served in Cárichic, came to Papigóchic, to remain for almost three years.[28]

Osorio filed a rather full report in 1744, recording the fact that Papigóchic had a good church, that the pueblo consisted of some 200 houses, that epidemics had reduced the population to about 250 from a high of 800, that Paguírachic and Mogúriachic were the visitas and that from 1683 to 1744 there had been a total of 5,093 baptisms.[29] Before he left for Coyáchic early in 1746,[30] Osorio was assisted occasionally by Blas de la Palma of nearby Santo Tomás and, in January and February 1746, by Xavier Félix Mier, then or soon thereafter to be stationed at Sisoguíchic, by Antonio de San José Carral and by Lorenzo Gera, then the visitador.[31]

Papigóchic hadn't prospered under Osorio, but conditions got worse. A year and a half after he left, it was predicted that if his successor, Domingo Cosío, were not promptly removed, the mission would be utterly finished.[32] The visitador, Juan Manuel Hierro, didn't succeed in getting Cosío retired to a college until September 1748, when Luis Angel Yáñez came from Tutuaca to replace him.[33] Yáñez served only for a few months, since by the following April he had traded places with Sebastián Prieto, who had been at Cárichic since the preceding fall.[34] Prieto served, apparently quietly and well, for the next nine years, although, perhaps because of failing health, he was frequently assisted by neighbors and visitors, including Martín Vallarta of Cárichic and José Zamora, later to be at Santo Tomás. Prieto's last entry in the surviving parish registers is dated June 27, 1758, and it may be assumed that he died not long thereafter.

After Prieto, Blas de la Palma from Santo Tomás helped out temporarily, as did José Zamora and José Miqueo of Temeýchic, but by November 1758, the partido was again served on a permanent basis—the young Ysidro Saavedra came in that month and served through July 1764. In 1761, when Saavedra was in charge, Tomás Lizasoaín reported that the church and the house were good.[35]

Saavedra left in July 1764, and Diego Barrera, a visitor from Santa María Suamca in Sonora, as well as Rafael Palacios, then at Santo Tomás, helped out during the summer,[36] or until José Vega, also a young man, came to take over in September. In the following March, Manuel Vivanco, now old and almost blind, was transferred to Papigóchic from Nonoava,[37] and two years later, at the expulsion, Vivanco and Vega delivered the partido to the military authorities. It was promptly secularized.[38]

Ciudad Guerrero is no longer a place of violence or a peaceful island in the center of violence. Instead, it's a pleasant, hospitable small city[39] which can serve very satisfactorily as a central point from which to explore Tarahumara Alta.

No amount of inquiry and searching has ever permitted me to fix with certainty the location of the old presidio, although I believe it was in the general vicinity of the most easterly of Guerrero's three churches, La Refugia, on the south side of the highway approaching the town. If I am right as to the general location of the presidio, then La Refugia, which is without doubt the second oldest of the three churches, may well be built on the foundations of the presidial chapel, which housed the bones of Fathers Beudín and Basilio.

I found the exterior of this church to be interesting without being spectacular, with a single square bell tower at the southeast corner, bas-relief pilasters framing an arched doorway, and a church-yard full of old burials, some in low crypts above the ground. The nave was plain, but the narrow sanctuary was not without charm. A plain wood table stood in front of an extremely simple altar, decorated by a blue and white cloth and surmounted by a picture of the Madonna and Child. Both altars, with their meager decorations, were framed by an arched entrance of stone, not unattractively painted with blue conventional figures.

No one locally, including the priest, seemed to know anything about it, but I believe that the oldest of the three churches, the one locally called Guadalupe, is all that remains[40] of La Purísima Concepción, where both Beudín and Basilio were martyred. The location is about right; Guadalupe is due north of La Refugia and at the very edge of town. In 1969 the back wall and roof were gone, as were most of the two sides, but the front wall, facing south, was largely standing with a graceful arched doorway, flanked by two ornamental pilasters, each topped by a decorative element serving no structural purpose. Above the doorway was a circular opening into what was probably once the choir loft. The churchyard was, as usual, full of burials.

The final church, an imposing structure on the west side of the plaza, is called, appropriately, La Purísima Concepción. But it's in the wrong location for the old mission church, and is altogether too large to be even a reconstruction of what was very certainly a small building. La Purísima Concepción on the plaza had a three-tiered bell tower, an arched door set in a square frame with bas-relief pilasters and, above the door, a small round window surmounted by a niche for a santo.

The interior was very splendid. A conventional sanctuary, narrower than the nave, was framed by simple pilasters at the ornate marble communion rail. Inside the sanctuary there was not an altar, but instead a lectern and then, at the back wall, a second and narrower sanctuary or niche defined by an arched opening. At each side of the opening, on the wall beneath a Gothic gold canopy, was an excellent statue, the Virgin at the epistle side and Christ at the gospel. Within the inner sanctuary, which was almost square, with a decorative tile ceiling, there was a fluted marble baldaquino, surmounted by a cross and holding a large statue of the Virgin, with gold halo. Before the statue stood two altars, both of marble, the higher one fixed at the rear and the lower one freestanding, almost on a line with the wall which held the canopied santos.

San Cornelio de Paguírachic

In 1678, San Cornelio de Paguírachic was an established visita of Papigóchic with nine Christian families,[41] but the visitador didn't say anything about a church. By 1725 there was a house for the priest and a wholly undecorated church called Nuestro Padre San Ignacio,[42] the name which has persisted into modern times.

But the church hasn't persisted.

I knew from the old accounts that Paguírachic was south and east of Papigóchic on the river; and in October 1969, Paul and I were told in Guerrero that we could get there by going south and west from Miñaca. About an hour out from Miñaca, lying south and east of a wooded hill, we found Paguírachic Nuevo, a small community[43] spread out over a fairly wide area with a new church (still called San Ignacio) under construction. We were told that the old church was in Paguírachic Viejo on the other side of the hill to the northwest. We followed a very bad road around the hill, overtaking one or two parties of Indian women with children. In each case, we were told that Paguírachic Viejo was farther up the road. On the other side of the hill we found not the river we expected but instead, a large lake backed up from a dam some distance downstream. We went to the margin of the lake without finding any sign of habitation or ruins, left the very primitive road and went overland back up to the top of the hill, exploring in all directions, but locating only a single small ranch house, guarded by a friendly dog, but with no people. We turned back and met some of the same Indians gathering pine nuts. Here we learned the answer: the elusive Paguírachic Viejo and the old church were covered by the lake!

San Pablo de Basúchic

In 1678, Basúchic was a well established visita, with 36 Christian families worshipping at San Pablo, the very small jacal which was used for a church.[44] Modern Basúchil is a small and not very important stop on the railroad, a few miles east of Guerrero. The town lies entirely south of the tracks and includes the new, small and conventional church of La Virgen de Guadalupe. While it is possible that the new church is on the foundations of the old, it seems a good deal more likely that the jacal was at the graveyard in the middle of the plain north of the railroad. But I haven't been able to find any foundations or ruins. Nor do I know why the place name is now spelled Basúchil instead of Basúchic.

San Francisco Xavier de Mogúriachic

Today it's pronounced as though it were spelled Mogúriachic, but that hasn't always been so.

In 1725 it was reported that Guadalupe Moleachi, a Papigóchic visita on the other bank of the river, had a house for the priest and an undecorated church.[45] The 1744 report refers to San Francisco Xavier de Noguriachi, a visita of Papigóchic, to the west of the cabecera and away from the river, with no arable lands in the immediate vicinity of the town.[46] According to Bishop Tamarón, the pueblo of San Javier de Muguriachi was a visita of Papigóchic three leagues to the west and was served by the curate from Cusi.[47] Lizasoaín called it San Xavier de Mogurichic,[48] and Decorme quoted Tamarón but changed the spelling to Moguiarachi.[49] Bancroft also relied on the bishop, but called it both Muguriachic and Moleachic.[50] And finally, Almada, who said the mission was destroyed by Apaches in 1770, preferred the spelling Magurúachi.[51]

In April 1971, the storekeeper at Miñaca said we would be likely to miss the turn for Mogúriachic, but that he would send a friend to show us the way. The road from Miñaca turned out to be familiar, since we went first to Paguírachic and then toward Tomóchic. But nevertheless, without our guide, we couldn't possibly have found our way—the turnoff, about an hour west of Miñaca, is unmarked and nearly invisible. Mogúriachic is only a few kilometers north of the Miñaca-Tomóchic highway, in an entirely typical Tarahumara valley with only two visible houses. People at both houses (as well as our guide) assured us that the large mound in a plowed field at about the middle of the valley was the church. There were no walls, but at the edges of the mound there were adobes and, as nearly as I could make out, the size of the building was entirely consistent with a church destroyed by the Apaches 200 years before.

San Miguel

San Miguel was never a visita of Papigóchic, and I include it here only because its cabecera, Santo Tomás, which started out as a visita of Papigóchic, is also included.

The first reference to San Miguel was in 1725, when it was reportedly less than a league from Santo Tomás with its own church and a small house.[52] Bishop Tamarón said only that the visita had 44 families with a total of 228 Indians.[53]

Modern San Miguel is little more than a ranch about two kilometers west of Santo Tomás on the east side of Río Papigóchic. I haven't been able to locate any walls or foundations of the 1725 church, nor does there seem to be any local tradition that an old church ever existed.

Santo Tomás de Villanueva de Tojorare

Santo Tomás is the only Papigóchic visita entitled to be called magnificent. It was in April 1969 that we first looked up from the pleasant, tree-shaded town at the great white twin-towered building presiding serenely over its churchyard.

Inside, there was as fine a display of churrigueresque gold leaf and statuary as is to be found anywhere in Chihuahua outside the cathedral. The nave was rectangular without transepts, but three complete, highly ornate and profusely decorated retablos, each worthy of a cathedral, gave the effect of a three-altared church. The

The great white twin-towered church of Santo Tomás de Villanueva de Tojorare looks out to the south over a pleasant tree-shaded town through a churchyard crammed with burials. October 1969.

central gold retablo, only slightly recessed behind an opening framed by an arch of pink stone, was, appropriately, the finest, but it was not necessarily the largest. Almost life-sized statues of St. Thomas and of Mary, Queen of Heaven, were in the two central niches, the Virgin at the top and St. Thomas, with spear and book, in the central position. Both were flanked by gold-filigreed columns and together they were surrounded by four large and very fine oil paintings, framed in gold. Six smaller paintings, each in its golden niche, formed a bottom border at the level of the freestanding altar. On either side of the stone archway into which the central retablo was recessed were good statues on fixed pedestals: on the epistle

Of all Tarahumara's Jesuit churches, only Santo Tomás de
Villanueva de Tojorare has three retablos. April 1969.

side the Virgin standing as Diana on a half-moon, with cherubs
below, and at the gospel side Jesus of the Sacred Heart standing
on the globe.

The two other retablos were lesser only by comparison. On the
epistle side of the nave, beside the first half-dozen pews, was a gold
and blue retablo of four sculptured columns framing, at the center,
three good statues, the two on either side almost identical scarlet-

draped figures of Christ of the Passion and the third, in the middle, Joseph walking with the boy Christ. Highly ornamented blue and gold columns separated the panels, and each column appeared to be supported by a cherub, carved and gilded. At the very top, surmounting the central statue and flanked by ornate gold, was the familiar picture of the Virgin of Guadalupe.

Directly across on the gospel side was a retablo of extremely similar but not identical design. Here there was more gold leaf and less blue, but, as on the epistle side, there were three statues, Mary at the Cross in the center, an unidentified saint, perhaps Martha, on the left and another, perhaps Mary Magdalene, on the right. At the top, facing the picture of the Virgin of Guadalupe across the nave, was an exceptionally well carved crucifix, with the body of the Savior modestly draped from the waist down. On the small altar, immediately below the Virgin, was a small statue of the Infant of Prague. All of the statues were tastefully and colorfully dressed, and the result was a breathtakingly rich assembly of gold, brilliant blues, deep reds, and pastel shades of blue and pink.

The Santo Tomás church has not always been so impressive. In 1678 Ortiz reported that three or four leagues north of Papigóchic was the pueblo called Santo Tomás de Villanueva, formerly known as Tojorare, with a small jacal for a church.[54]

Santo Tomás was not a visita very long, but had a priest of its own in the person of José Guerrero Villaseca at least by April 1, 1690, when the frontier broke open in revolt.[55] Guerrero didn't return after peace was restored, but his place was taken by Jorge Hostinsky, who in turn yielded to Balthasar de la Peña in 1695.[56]

In the 1697 revolt, the church at Santo Tomás was completely destroyed,[57] and Peña, who had gone to Villa Aguilar for safety, didn't return. His place was taken by Pedro Proto, who had been in Cocomórachic[58] and who was transferred to Yécora in 1701.[59] Then or soon thereafter Hostinsky returned and lived in Santo Tomás but served a much wider area of the sierra until his death in Papigóchic in 1723.[60] After Hostinsky's death, Santo Tomás may have slipped back into visita status for a few years, but by January 1, 1727, Antonio Arias had returned to Tarahumara and was in charge. In April of that year, Arias was succeeded by Blas de la Palma, who stayed for 35 years, or until the summer of 1762, when he probably died. In that year, Palma's house and church were described by the visitador as the best in all the missions,[61] and indeed they must have been, for they attracted more than their share of visiting priests, whose signatures are preserved in the registers of baptisms and marriages for the 40 years before the expulsion.[62]

José Calderón was at Santo Tomás in February 1730; Bernardo Garfias, who had been visitador of the Chínipas missions, was there for part of the summer of 1732; and a year or so later Antonio García performed a baptism. In August 1748, Sebastián Prieto, then at Cocomórachic and later to move to Cárichic, was a visitor. In 1761 and 1762 there were more visitors, probably because Blas de la Palma's health was failing and he needed help more frequently. José Miqueo came often from Temeýchic, and José Montaño was there for several months, as was Francisco de los Ríos. Palma's last entry in the register is dated August, 1762, but before Rafael Palacios, his permanent successor, came from Chinarras in December, Santo Tomás saw the temporary services of Joaquín Trujillo and of José Espadas, later a teacher at the seminary in Durango.

Palacios stayed at Santo Tomás until the expulsion,[63] but, perhaps because the beauty of the church continued to attract visiting priests, he had frequent help: José Zamora, who had served briefly in September 1762, was there again in the spring of 1766; José Vega, who had visited Santo Tomás when he was at the Chihuahua college in 1764, came more frequently after June 1765, when he became the assistant at Papigóchic; Antonio Hitl of Temeýchic was there in 1765; and Bartolomé Braun of Temósachic came in 1766. Indeed the church was then a fine one—and it has remained so.

18

San Rafael de Mátachic

Nuestra Señora de Loreto de Tejolocáchic

Tejolocáchic[1] is on the railroad, the Guerrero-Madera highway and Río Papigóchic, about midway between Santo Tomás and Mátachic. It's a very small town[2] with a very plain, severely whitewashed conventional church with twin two-tiered towers, each with a wooden pyramidal dome surmounted by a cross. When we were there, the two large Coca-Cola signs beside the church seemed to us not at all incongruous.

Tejolocáchic has never been very large. In 1677 Tomás Guadalajara, who was in charge of the partido, then called La Misión del Triunfo de los Angeles, referred to Tejolocáchic as a visita.[3] But a year later, Juan Ortiz, the visitador, reported on the misión in some detail without mentioning the place.[4] In October 1700, the new governor, Juan Larrea, visited the settlement on a pacification trip,[5] but the first suggestion that there was much Christian activity in Tejolocáchic dates from 1725. In that year the visitador Guenduláin said that Nuestra Señora de Loreto had 50 families, a church and a small house, but none of the necessities for a visita. And, he added, quite incredibly, that at an earlier time it had been a cabecera with Cocomórachic as its visita.[6]

[169]

By Bishop Tamarón's era, the church name had changed to San Gabriel, and the town was still a visita of Mátachic with a population of 143.[7] While Tamarón didn't say, his contemporary, Lizasoaín, said that the church and house were good.[8] Since then, the name has been again changed, this time to San Miguel.

San Rafael de Mátachic

The great missionary pioneers, José Tardá and Tomás Guadalajara, went downstream along Río Papigóchic in 1675 and, reaching Mátachic,[9] named it San Rafael,[10] the name it bears to this day. The following year Guadalajara returned to make Mátachic the cabecera of the Misión del Triunfo de los Angeles and his own headquarters until 1684, when, tired and ill, he went permanently to the south. Two years after he began his work, Guadalajara had built a very fine church and had firmly established Christianity in Mátachic and its three visitas, Temósachic, Yepómera and Cocomórachic.[11]

Guadalajara was succeeded by Francisco Velasco, who stayed until the 1690 revolt, when the church was burned, the sacred vessels were destroyed and the town was devastated.[12] Rebuilding fell to Florencio Alderete, who had been at Cocomórachic before the war and who was now serving as the superior. Alderete stayed for a short time in Mátachic and then went back to Cocomórachic to make a place for a newcomer, Nicolás Grisoni. Grisoni was here only until 1693, when Alderete returned, to stay until the area was engulfed by a new tide of revolt in 1697. In 1690 Alderete had fled from Cocomórachic, and this time, when word reached Mátachic that the Tarahumaras had risen and that Cocomórachic had been plundered, Pedro Proto, then the priest at Cocomórachic, was visiting at Mátachic.[13] Both priests went posthaste to Papigóchic with Mátachic's sacred vessels.

When peace came, Alderete didn't return, but Diego Lilín, who came from México, took charge of Mátachic and for the next two years also ministered to Cocomórachic.[14] Lilín served Mátachic until 1705,[15] and he must have done something about building a church, but I've found no record of it. The first of Lilín's successors of whom I can find any account was Juan Morales, who may well have come when Lilín left. He was certainly in the area in 1708, and in Mátachic in 1723. It is recorded that Morales began a church,[16] and a 1725 report shows that at Mátachic there was a church, both small and new, as well as a larger one under construction.[17]

In 1755 Mátachic was in the charge of Francisco Santa Cruz, and six years later the visitador reported that the church and house were both good.[18] By that time Mátachic was the home of its last Jesuit, Felipe Ruanova, visitador of Tarahumara Alta, to whom fell the sad task of helping Captain Cuéllar gather up the Jesuits for expulsion.[19]

Father Dunne published[20] a picture of the façade of a church which was once tall but had crumbled to nothing more than a wall, with its peeling plaster defaced by the remnants of a political sign. The arched doorway was flanked with pilasters which rose to frame a window surmounted by a pediment containing, in bas-relief, a seal with the letters *JHS*. The façade was not beautiful, but it was certainly interesting, and I was looking forward to seeing it. In a paragraph which begins, "The walls of these ancient churches are for the most part still standing," Father Dunne said that "the traveler today can admire the mission churches of Mátachic. . . . "[21]

Unfortunately, this is no longer so. In 1969, a church at Mátachic was certainly standing, but it was both large and recent. Black with white trim, it had a tripartite façade with a single tower surmounted by a cross. The interior was plain and unprepossessing, with an unadorned freestanding altar and a middle-sized crucifix suspended against and partially above a knotty pine wall which didn't reach to the ceiling. Diligent inquiry around the community yielded the consensus that the present church was built about 1945 after the old church in the Dunne photo, on the same site, had been torn down completely.

Mátachic is by all odds the most important place between Guerrero and Madera. It's somewhat of a supply center for mining and lumbering activities in the sierra, with a passable road leading across the river to Cocomórachic, Tutuaca and Yepáchic.

San Pablo de Cocomórachic

To get to Cocomórachic,[22] you must cross the river at Mátachic and travel into the sierra southwest for about two hours. A very small town,[23] it had a crumbling old church, called La Virgen de Guadalupe, when we were there in October 1969. At that time plaster was going fast on the facade and had already gone on the walls. A campanario above the roofline held two bells, but the building was otherwise totally undistinguished, both inside and out. A new school and church, the pride of the pueblo, were under construction. Since the time of our trip, the old church may well have completely fallen.

In 1678 Cocomórachic was a recently established visita of Mátachic with 41 Christian families but no church;[24] five years later, it was an independent cabecera with a priest of its own in the person of Florencio Alderete.[25] By 1690, Alderete had certainly completed a church because the rebelling Tarahumaras burned it to the ground, set fire to his house, destroyed the sacred vessels and devastated the area.[26] When the Jesuits returned to their posts in 1692, Alderete went first to Mátachic, but a short time later took over Cocomórachic, staying only until 1693, when he could trade places with the newly arrived Pedro Proto.[27]

It was Proto who reported seeing a strange giant in 1696, an appearance which was believed to be one of several portents from which the Europeans should have been able to predict the revolt of the following year: "At the mission of Cocomórachic, in the month of May, 1696, on a clear day and at about three o'clock in the afternoon, the missionary chanced to be at the door of his house. Suddenly, on a hill close by, he saw a giant standing. He was of enormous size, so that the tallest of the trees around him reached only to his breast. His face was averted. He bent down as if to gather stones. For nearly a quarter of an hour, the father watched him, and then he vanished."[28]

The giant didn't keep Proto from rebuilding the Cocomórachic church in time for it to be destroyed a second time in 1697.[29] It was to Cocomórachic in March 1697, that General Fernández Retana brought some 60 captives from Sírupa. All were sentenced to death and on March 25, about 30 were shot, and, "as as a salutary example to the rest, their heads were cut off, set upon spears, and displayed to the public view, some of them in Cocomórachic, others along the road to Yepómera; and thus they were left to become the food of crows."[30]

When peace came, a missionary was not immediately sent to Cocomórachic, and it reverted to its old status as a Mátachic visita. The contemporary reasons were probably accurate: settlements like Cocomórachic were believed to be "too unstable and too insecure;

moreover, the results seemed incommensurate with the labor, except in the case of children who died before they had lost their baptismal innocence."[31] But even if Cocomórachic had no full-time missionary, somebody rebuilt the church, which was described in 1725 as adequate although destitute of those things necessary for the divine office.[32]

Cocomórachic was again established as a cabecera sometime before 1748, when Sesbastián Prieto was in charge.[33] But the status didn't last long, because Prieto had gone to Papigóchic by 1751,[34] and in Tamarón's time, the pueblo was a visita not of Mátachic but of Santo Tomás.[35]

San Miguel de Temósachic

Temósachic[36] was established by Tomás Guadalajara in 1676 as part of the Misión del Triunfo de los Angeles.[37] The visitador Ortiz recorded in 1678 that San Miguel was two leagues north of Mátachic, and that while the visita had only a jacal for a church, a large permanent one was planned.[38] By 1690, Temósachic was a visita not of Mátachic, but of Yepómera,[39] and its church, planned by Guadalajara in 1678, had been finished. Finished, that is, in time to be destroyed.[40] It was rebuilt after 1692, and undoubtedly was rebuilt again after the 1697 revolt.

The church was apparently quite magnificent in 1725. By then Temósachic was the cabecera—Juan Manuel Hierro, the priest in charge of the partido, had moved his headquarters from Yepómera the year before. The visitador described the Hierro building, dedicated to San Francisco Javier,[41] as "fine, large and beautiful with its roof supported with beams curiously wrought, sculptured, and painted. The retablo of the main altar was formed by a large and good painting which covered the whole space, and each of the side altars was adorned with paintings in its turn."[42]

Father Hierro remained at Temósachic until his retirement in 1758, thus serving the partido, God and his fellow men for a total of 50 years. From Yoquivo Bartolomé Braun came to take his place, to work for the nine brief years which remained before the expulsion, and then to die at sea.

Father Hierro's church was reported to have collapsed in January 1907,[43] and I doubt that any part of it, except possibly some of the rubble and sand for the mortar, has been incorporated in the very unusual church complex which was under construction when Paul and I first visited Temósachic in April 1969. At that time we examined three buildings or parts of buildings, all facing east in the central plaza. In the middle was a completed boxlike structure in black plaster with three wide horizontal lines above a curved doorway. From the interior, then used as the church, it was possible to climb through the old bell tower at the northeast corner onto the roof of the adjoining building to the north. At street level the north building was unfinished and empty, but above the roofline was a graceful three-arched campanario of rubble masonry. There were three bells, the two smaller ones unmarked but the one in the center bearing the legend "San José 1899." South of the church proper a new building, as yet generally formless, was under construction.

In May 1976, the three parts had not only been joined, but portions of them had been largely rebuilt. The building at the north had been incorporated into the whole, but without its campanario; the façade of the middle building had been redone to include the fronts of all three, with the result that the curved doorway was the only entrance, the old horizontal lines were gone, and there was a new roof pitched from a central ridge pole. The building at the south turned out to be a new and attractive bell tower, square, with two arched apertures on each of the four sides, surmounted by a dome. The effect was altogether pleasing.

San Gabriel
de Yepómera

La Iglesia de San Gabriel de Yepómera

I'm convinced that Yepómera[1] is not, and never has been, the same as Temósachic; but not everybody is, or has been.

The first to be confused by the two was Benito Rinaldini. His list of Jesuit partidos in Tarahumara contains this entry: *"Temósachic, alias Yepómera: Padre Rector de este Rectorado: Juan Ma. del Hierro."*[2] Rinaldini didn't explain what he meant by the "alias" and, unless the two pueblos were one, I can only suggest that his reference is to the fact that when Hierro was first in charge of the partido, the cabecera was in Yepómera but was moved to Temósachic about the time Rinaldini came to the mission field.

But Campbell Pennington, who is a distinguished geographer, said, "The modern Yepómera is located to the north of the site of the seventeenth-century Yepómera (Temósachic)."[3] Even with Pennington's help, I can find no convincing evidence to support the assertion. Indeed, such evidence as there is suggests that at least since 1677, when Tomás Guadalajara, the founder of both pueblos, referred to both, separately, in the same letter,[4] Temósachic and Yepómera have been quite distinct. Pennington has been misled by the fact that the modern Yepómera is not on Río Papigóchic, and he somehow thinks that the ancient town ought to have been.[5] More particularly, he seems to be confused by Father Guadalajara's description of what was essentially a "string town" along an arroyo which joined Río Papigóchic and which had at its upper end Yepómera la Alta, then called Xicuríchic and, at the lower end, nearer to the river, Yepómera la Baja, then called Tlaxómoho. In Guadalajara's time, in each of the two barrios or neighborhoods of Yepómera, there was a church, one at the lower and one at the upper end of the arroyo.[6] Indeed, both churches were there until relatively recently, and traces of both have remained.

Yepómera isn't on the road between Temósachic and Madera, and it is easy to miss—the first time we were in the area we got all the way to Madera without having found it and had to turn back. The Yepómera road, which eventually becomes its main street, leaves the highway about a half to three-quarters of an hour south from Madera and goes parallel to the left bank of Arroyo de las Burras, cutting off at almost a right angle from the highway and following the arroyo in a wide curve to the left, with ranch houses and ruined buildings dotting the way. If you go this way, you will first reach Yepómera la Alta, which no one any longer knows as Xicuríchic.

Here, to the left of the road and near to the crest of a hill, is an old graveyard, which marks the location of the upper church. While the stone markers are readily visible, I haven't been able to find anything which I can say positively is a foundation or was once part of a wall of a church. On the other hand, old residents have told me that they remember the church ruins, and it is accepted folklore that the bell[7] which was hung on a rack at the front wall of the church compound in Yepómera la Baja, or Tlaxómoho, was brought from the old church at the upper location.

It's a fair distance from the upper town to the lower. The lower has obviously long been the principal location and is close to the junction of Arroyo de las Burras and Arroyo de los Poños, which comes in from the east and augments the larger stream as it flows south to Río Papigóchic.

When we last did a detailed exploration at Yepómera, a new church, facing south beside the main street, was nearing completion. It was obvious to us that it was in the general location of the old church because of the numerous burials in the churchyard which surrounded and crowded in upon the rack with its old bell. After a good deal of inquiry, we found an old gentleman who was interested in local history and who showed us the clearly discernible foundation and a remnant of what was undoubtedly the west wall of the old church. The old wall was parallel to the west wall of the new structure but lay about five feet farther west or toward the arroyo. The old east wall was, of course, covered by the new building, but the only picture of the Yepómera church which I've seen[8] shows a relatively narrow façade, about the width of the present building, suggesting that the new church simply moved over closer to the street.

In 1675 Tomás Guadalajara and José Tardá established San Gabriel de Yepómera as a visita of Mátachic and thus as part of the Misión del Triunfo de los Angeles.[9] But it wasn't easy. The Franciscans, and in particular Fray Alonso Mesa, objected to the institution of Jesuit work at Yepómera and indeed, at any point on or beyond the northeast bank of Río Papigóchic, which was said to be the dividing line between the country of the Conchos, to whom the Franciscans were authorized to minister, and that of the Tarahumaras, the exclusive domain of the Jesuits.

On the basis of a claim that Río Papigóchic had been recognized as the boundary in an agreement between the two Orders signed on some date between 1649 and 1653, Mesa apparently undertook missionary work at least in the upper end of Yepómera. Guadalajara, who was not entirely charitable toward the Franciscans,[10] professed ignorance of the agreement and asserted that the division should be based on tribal location, thus conceding to the Franciscans jurisdiction over the Conchos but nevertheless claiming both that there were no Conchos in Yepómera and that the Franciscans hadn't baptized anyone there.[11] And well might Guadalajara be concerned—not only was Yepómera beyond Río Papigóchic, all the pueblos of the Misión del Triunfo de los Angeles were on either the north or east bank, as were Papigóchic and Santo Tomás. Needless to say, Guadalajara won—the dispute was "compromised" in his favor: the Jesuits could continue to minister to the Tarahumaras without worrying about river boundaries, and the Franciscans could continue to take care of the spiritual needs of the Conchos of the plains.[12]

The visitador Ortiz doesn't say anything about two churches at Yepómera, reporting only that the 44 Christian families used a jacal for a church and were planning a new one.[13] Three years later, in February 1681, Yepómera for the first time had a priest of its own; but Juan María Ratkay couldn't stand the winter and moved on after a few months.[14] By 1690, when Ratkay's successor, Juan Ortiz Foronda, became the first martyr of the April revolt, Yepómera was firmly established as the cabecera of a new partido which included, as visitas, Temósachic, Nahuárachic and Sírupa.[15] And we know that Ortiz had both a church and a house, for both were burned to the ground.[16] I find nothing directly to indicate who built the church, but since there was only a jacal in 1678 and Ratkay stayed only a few months, I must conclude Ortiz came to Yepómera from Parral well before his death, probably as early as 1688, and took care of the necessary construction.

After the destruction at Yepómera, the Tarahumara fury moved on, but it was not until June 16, 1690, that Governor Pardiñas reached Yepómera, found the village burned and the church reduced to its foundations. The bodies of the priest and the two Spaniards who had died with him were buried together by the visitador, Francisco María Pícolo, and by Tomás Guadalajara, then rector of the college at Parral.[17]

When the Jesuits came back after the uneasy peace of 1692, Juan Calvo was very briefly at Yepómera, being succeeded almost immediately by Juan Bautista Haller. Haller set to work to rebuild Yepómera, and a year later had "built a fine house and church."[18] Like that of Ortiz, Haller's church was doomed. In the 1697 revolt, he escaped with his life, but the new church was burned and the town again leveled.[19] After the peace, he went back to rebuild for the second time a church which had been "completely destroyed."[20]

It is recorded that on the road which Haller traveled from Papigóchic to Yepómera, General Fernández Retana had lined the way with spears, each spear carrying the severed head of a rebel Tarahumara as "a promise of death and Spanish vengeance."[21] What is not recorded is whether the heads were still there when Haller rode downstream to Yepómera, and there is no record of his feelings as he began to build a third church. He died in 1708, but that gave him nine years to build the church which Juan Hierro served at least until 1723.[22]

The visitador Guenduláin gave no description of the Yepómera church in 1725, merely reporting that there was a church which served 129 families.[23] Since his casual reference to the church and house appears on the same page as his somewhat ecstatic description of the church at Temósachic, we can assume that it wasn't much— or that, since Yepómera was now a visita, he found it politic to give more space to the cabecera. There is no subsequent mention of the church, although there is at least a suspicion that the church was badly treated if not totally ruined on June 18, 1842, when the pueblo was attacked by Apaches and 42 people were killed.[24]

San Andrés de Sírupa

The start of the 1697 revolt was thus recorded: "...the Indians were assembled in the valley of Sírupa, at a very steep place which resembled a fortress and which was inaccessible to cavalry;... Retana...had brought with him a band of Indians, belonging to other, and friendly, nations. He now sent these Indians ahead, with orders to encircle the height where the fugitives were gathered, and to hold them in a state of siege until the following day, when he himself would come with the cavalry. But the besieged sent a shower of arrows against Retana's allies, killed a few of them, wounded others, and forced the rest to fall back.

"Yet the rebels feared the sudden arrival of the Basque captain. And so, with the utmost silence, they stole away from that fortress which Nature had reared; but they left their sheep behind, in order that the bleating of the flocks might remove any suspicion that the owners had fled. On the next day Retana and his soldiers arrived; ...he bade his men ascend the cliff, steep and rough though it was. But they found no living thing except the sheep...."[25]

The cliff from which the rebels showered death and destruction on their pursuers is still there, west of what is left of the settlement of Sírupa and surrounded on three sides by the river, which travels first northwest between Sírupa and the escarpment, makes a 360° loop and then comes back to the southeast on the other side.

Sírupa, which has shrunk to no more than a ranch, is about two hours southwest of Madera, across magnificent distances and an 8,000-foot mountain, and lies in a broad and rugged valley, itself at

5,000 feet. In 1969 the ranch had a goodly number of buildings and houses, many of them connected together as in a small pueblo. Uphill or east from the ranch was an extensive graveyard with the clearly distinguishable foundations and partial wall of the hewn stone church of San Andrés de Sírupa, a portion of it covered from the elements by a rude ramada. The people of the ranch seemed to know nothing of the history of the steep cliff across the river, but they were proud of their church ruin, which they recognized as being very ancient.

In 1678, accompanied by Tomás Guadalajara, the visitador Ortiz inspected San Andrés de Xiripa, which had 17 Christian families but was not yet an organized visita.[26] But by 1690, the valley had become a visita of Yepómera and was one of the places where rebel Tarahumaras gathered in preparation for the assault against the Spaniards.[27] There is no indication of the existence of a church in any of the early reports, and it seems unlikely that the ruin under the ramada is older than the very end of the Jesuit period.

La Consolación de Nahuárachic

Father Dunne said that in 1687 Guadalajara and Ortiz visited Nahuárachic after they left Sírupa,[28] but Ortiz then called it Negarachi.[29] In the first identification of Nahuárachic as a 1690 visita of Yepómera, Father Neumann spelled it Nagrurachi.[30] The small pueblo's only claim to fame is that the martyred Ortiz Foronda was at his visita, Nahuárachic, when Yepómera was attacked and that he went back to the cabecera to meet his death.[31]

Getting to Nahuárachic is not difficult. On the highway from Madera to Mátachic, just beyond a church and school on the outskirts of Madera, a road turns to the west and leads in 15 or 20 minutes to Nahuárachic. The town is in a valley and is relatively compact, with a graveyard on high ground at a little distance. We could find no evidence of a church at the graveyard, although that was altogether the most likely place. Local opinion seemed about equally divided between those who said there neither was nor ever had been a church in Nahuárachic and those who contended, quite unaccountably, that an uncompleted new adobe building on old foundations was the church. It is true that the old foundations may have underpinned a church, but the new building looked singularly unlike a religious structure and resembled nothing so much as a partially roofed corral. I have no evidence, ancient or contemporary, that there ever has been a church building.

Jesús del Monte
de Tutuaca

San Juan Evangelista de Tosánachic

In 1678 Tosánachic[1] was a visita seven or eight leagues east of
Tutuaca, its cabecera, with a jacal that served as a church for six
Christian families.[2] If there's any subsequent mention of Tosánachic
in the church reports, I've missed it.

Modern Tosánachic is a very wide valley, quite sparsely settled,[3] approximately midway between Cocomórachic and Tutuaca,
at the junction of the road which goes south to Huajumar and
Cajuríchic. The valley, fertile and pleasant at about 7,000 feet,
is completely surrounded by high mountains and buttressed at
the west by white chalk cliffs, a thousand feet high. As in Ortiz'
time, there is no church, and the ancient jacal has long since
disintegrated.

In almost the geographic center of the valley, close to the
pueblo's only store is a *campo santo* where once a church, or at least a
jacal, may well have stood. But when Paul and I were there in
October 1969, we could find nothing to suggest the foundations of
a church within the stone wall which surrounded the graveyard.
Outside, if there was ever a church building, it was long ago mixed
with the soil, churned by at least 300 years of plowing.

In Tosánachic we talked to everyone we could find about a possible church location and church ruins, but no one had any information, nor even a suggestion of a tradition.

Ciudad de Jesús del Monte de Tutuaca

Tutuaca has had a more illustrious history, and it has a church, although probably not a century old.

In the fall of 1675, when José Tardá and Tomás Guadalajara were making their headquarters at San Francisco Borja, a delegation of Tarahumaras from Tutuaca traveled the 40 leagues to ask for baptism and to offer to build a home and a church for a padre. In December, the two missionaries went to Tutuaca, "a very distant town."[4] The Indians[5] treated the missionaries with the utmost kindness and the greatest courtesy. In fact the natives were so overjoyed with their visit that they held a very drunken fiesta with much tesguino. Alarmed and in actual fear for their lives, the two priests took their equipment and retired to high ground overnight. By the evening of the second day, they talked the Indians into sobering up, poured out the rest of the tesguino, catechized, baptized some 30 adults, and, on the Feast of the Circumcision, January 1, 1676, named the pueblo Ciudad de Jesús.[6]

In the spring, after Tardá and Guadalajara had reported their success, the visitador Gutiérrez recommended that six new Jesuits be sent to Tarahumara Alta and that one of them be permanently stationed at Tutuaca.[7] But it wasn't quite that easy. Two years later Jesús del Monte de Tutuaca was indeed a cabecera with 126 Christians and three visitas: Tosánachic, Yepáchic and Maguina. But there was only a jacal for a church, and there was no priest— Guadalajara took care of the cabecera from Mátachic.[8]

Juan María Ratkay was Tutuaca's first full-time priest, but he was there only a few weeks in the spring or early summer of 1681 before going to his final assignment at Cárichic.[9] Tutuaca was next served by Francisco Velasco, who probably came in 1682. But by 1687 he had been transferred to Mátachic in a reassignment which saw Manuel Sánchez come from Yécora to Jesús del Monte.[10]

Sometime between the jacal of 1678 and the death of Father Sánchez in the April 1690 revolt, a church was built in Tutuaca.

But nothing tells us whether it was Velasco or Sánchez who was the builder, nor is there any description of the temple, which was burned and utterly destroyed in the devastation of that year.[11] After the peace, Tutuaca was ruled unsafe, undoubtedly in part because its Indian governor was a notorious polygamist and unrepentant murderer.[12]

Without a priest, the partido was virtually closed for 22 years.[13] It's true that after the second peace of the decade, Venceslao Eymer occasionally visited Tutuaca from Papigóchic;[14] that in October 1700 a new Indian governor was named,[15] thus making the post less unattractive; and that in 1708 Francisco Bosque was assigned to Tutuaca and may have served very briefly. But it seems certain that the partido had nothing approaching regular clerical attention until 1713, when Jorge Hostinsky, a veteran of the area, began to take care of Tutuaca from Santo Tomás.[16]

In 1717 or 1718, Jorge Villanueva came to the sierra, and Tutuaca again had a full-time priest. But not for long. Like Ratkay, Villanueva suffered from the cold, and left after one winter.

A few years later when Francisco Glandorff took over Tomóchic, he began also to serve Tutuaca,[17] an arrangement which continued until Luis Yáñez was permanently assigned to Tutuaca a year or so before 1748.[18] Yáñez went to Cárichic in 1749,[19] and in the following year Bartholomé Braun came to Tutuaca,[20] spending a year before he moved to Yoquivo.[21] Cristóbal Moreno, whose health was not the best, was in charge of the partido by 1755,[22] and probably had come in 1753, when Santa Cruz, his former post, was secularized, which means that Tutuaca was without a priest for the two years after 1751.

When Lizasoaín reached Tutuaca in 1761, the church, now called San Miguel, was described as not very good, and because of the bad health and advanced age of the missionary, the partido had fallen on sorry times. The visitador recommended that the pueblos of Yepáchic and Tutuaca either be given another and more robust priest or that they be joined to Moris and Maicoba for easier administration.[23] The administration didn't get any simpler, but by the time of the expulsion, Tutuaca was in the care of the young Juan Nortier, and Cristóbal Moreno had almost certainly died.

Tutuaca bears less resemblance to a town than most of the populated ciénagas of Tarahumara. The valley is bigger than the

In October 1969 the altar at San Miguel de Tutuaca held an interesting display of santos, including St. Peter and the Infant of Prague.

average, and it's cut more deeply than is usual by Río Tutuaca, a good-sized river. Instead of half a dozen houses spread out at great intervals, there are half a dozen ranches[24] separated at even greater intervals. At about the center of the valley, with no building closer than half a mile, is the church of San Miguel de Tutuaca.[25] Facing the east, it sits in the middle of a neglected field, surrounded by the low crumbling walls of older buildings and 300 years of burials. A rectangular plastered adobe with a steeply pitched shingle roof, a window at each side and a rectangular doorway, it could pass for a school or warehouse were it not for the two bells which look out from perfectly square apertures above the doorway. No one in the area could help us estimate the age of the building, but it was not old.

The interior was most unusual. The nave was without adornment, but behind the severely simple altar covered by a white tablecloth and against a blue-green plastered wall were three large santos. Standing on the altar and thus in front of the other two was St. Peter, a very large key in his right hand, an open book in his left, and the Infant of Prague at his feet. Behind him, slightly out from the wall and supported by a cloth-covered box which permitted him to stand high enough so that his chest, shoulders and head were visible over the statue of Peter, was a figure which may have been St. Michael, but without sword. His right hand was raised, and thus nearly touched the outstretched right hand of a most extraordinary statue affixed to the wall and standing on a block: he had obviously been crucified—there were holes in his hands and shins; his head held a crown of thorns; his arms, torso and legs were bloodied; and his head was inclined at an angle typical of a crucifixion. But otherwise he was most unlike Christ in appearance— among other things, his arms were outstretched as in a semaphore, with each arm at 45° from the horizontal. To the right, and a little below the middle santo, was a small and simple crucifix.

Señor Santiago de Yepáchic

By the spring of 1976 Plan Gran Visión had paved the road from La Junta west to Tomóchic, then southwest to Basaséachic, the 1,000-foot waterfall,[26] and work was progressing on the extension to Yepáchic.[27] I suspect that even without completion of the pavement the Tomóchic route is a better way than the road from Mátachic south and west through Cocomórachic, Tosánachic and Tutuaca. It was the latter road which the visitador called *camino fragoso* in 1678.[28] It was still rough when Paul and I spent a whole day on it 291 years later.

Ortiz considered Yepáchic to be at the western limit of the Tarahumara mission,[29] but in fact it has always been more Pima than Tarahumara—indeed Neumann referred to it as "the first village across the border in Pimería."[30] Nevertheless, even though Pimas predominated, Yepáchic was administered as part of Tarahumara, and almost uniformly as a visita of Tutuaca. I say "almost" because for a brief period, probably from 1751 to 1761,[31] Joaquín Trujillo was at Yepáchic, and the village had a priest of its own. The result was nearly disastrous. Because of his bad temper and ill-advised economies, Trujillo left Yepáchic in a sad state, both spiritually and materially, so sad in fact that while he was there many of its neophytes deserted the settlement and in 1765 were only beginning to drift back to their old homes.[32]

The border of the state of Sonora lies behind the massive
stone church of Señor Santiago de Yepáchic. October 1969.

None of the seventeenth century reports says anything at all
about a church at Yepáchic, the first reference being that of
Lizasoaín, who reported after his visit in May 1761, that the
churches, both at Yepáchic and its cabecera, were *"no muy buenas."*[33]
That is no longer true of Yepáchic.

In October 1969, most of the town was concentrated on high
ground at the west side of the broad valley, and it is there that the
massive church stood, its back to the mountains which mark the
Sonora boundary and its façade resolutely facing the ciénaga and
fields in the middle and the forest on the east edge of the valley. It
was a stone building, with a large courtyard enclosed by a stone
fence. A high but graceful bell tower with two arches was at the
left, undoubtedly representing newer stonework which replaced the
original tower when the pitched roof was added. A heavy door was
framed in a modern jamb below a semicircular doorlight.

The door was locked, and while there were houses immediately
in front of the chuch, at its side and all around, the key was with an
old Pima who lived a good three miles across the river at the other
side of the valley.

The decorated retablo at Señor Santiago de Yepáchic is
of the same general type as those at Cusihuiriáchic and
Santo Tomás, and of almost equal quality. October 1969.

But the church was worth the trouble. The nave was of no
particular interest, but behind the simple altar was as fine a retablo
as any I have seen. There were seven really excellent oil paintings,
six of them framed as part of the painted and decorated altarpiece.
The seventh, a Madonna and Child, was separately framed in blue
and, surrounded by artificial flowers, stood immediately behind the
altar. At the very top was a splendid painting of the Trinity, the
Father in the middle and the Son on the Father's right facing
the Holy Spirit in a scarlet robe commemorating the Pentecost.[34]
Framing the Trinity were two highly decorative angels, while
below, and thus in a central position between the Trinity and
the blue Madonna, was St. Francis of Padua, flanked by the Virgin
of Guadalupe on the left and St. Francis of Assisi on the right.

San Juan Bautista de Maguina

In 1678 the visitador reported that San Juan Bautista de Maguina was three or four leagues from Tutuaca, that it had six Christian families totaling 25 to 30 people as well as a fairly substantial quantity of gentiles.[35] He said nothing at all about a church, and no subsequent commentator says anything at all about Maguina.

I found the people in Tutuaca and Yepáchic to be equally uncommunicative. I've simply never been able to find anyone who ever heard of Maguina or of a place in the area with a name sufficiently similar to run a reasonable chance of being the same. I find the settlement on no map and, quite reluctantly, I've given up looking.

La Purísima Concepción
de Tomóchic

La Iglesia de la Purísima Concepción de Tomóchic

Reports with respect to the partido of Tomóchic are remarkably confused and confusing. Father Dunne tells us that "Shortly. . . after [1675] the partido of Tomóchic was created,"[1] but it couldn't have been very shortly, since the visitador Ortiz makes no mention of the partido nor of any of its pueblos. It seems probable that Tomóchic itself was founded by Hostinsky in 1688;[2] that Illing, who came to Tarahumara with Hostinsky, organized Cajuríchic the same year;[3] and that Eymer was the first Jesuit at Arisiáchic in 1692.[4] But there is no mention of Peguáchic before 1725,[5] nor of Teséachic before 1697, when Hostinsky was in charge.[6]

The confusion is compounded as much as anything else by a total inconsistency with respect to the names of the several pueblos. The priest for whom Tomóchic will be always remembered, Francisco Glandorff, got there from Cárichic in February of 1722,[7] and three years later the visitador Guenduláin reported with respect to the partido that the cabecera, Concepción de Nuestra Señora de Temotzi, had as visitas three rancherías which would ultimately become pueblos: San José de Aleasachi (which must be Arisiáchic), El Venerable Estanislao de Culiachi (which by its location can only be Cajuríchic) and El Beato Luis Gonzaga (which must be

Peguáchic). He told us that in the four locations churches had been commenced, but he said nothing of Teséachic.[8]

In another three years, Glandorff furnished the information for the 1728 Administrative Census and listed his towns as Hororachi (which, if it's anything, is Arisiáchic), Temochi, Tepete (which may have been Teséachic), Tutuaca (of which Glandorff had occasional oversight), Cuiquíachic (Cajuríchic) and a ranchería called Paguáchic.[9]

In two more years, Glandorff reported that since his arrival he had built four churches, one of them dedicated to La Immaculada (obviously Tomóchic), another to San José (certainly Arisiáchic) and the other two unnamed.[10] Evidently after the 1730 letter, he built another church, because when he described his work 22 years later, Glandorff claimed the construction of five *templos*, one (Tomóchic) dedicated to the Virgin of the Immaculate Conception, one (evidently Teséachic) to St. Michael the Archangel, one (Arisiáchic) to St. Joseph the Worker, a fourth (Peguáchic) to St. Aloysius Gonzaga, and finally, at Cajuríchic, one to the Mother of God, St. Mary of Aranzazú.[11]

In 1693 Tomóchic[12] was said to be "the seat of Satan, and has always been the fountainhead of rebellion in Tarahumara."[13] Indeed, 40 years before Hostinsky arrived as its first resident priest, Tomóchic was the rallying place and the center of the 1648 revolt and "the pueblo which forever, from that date forward, became the axis of war and of rebellion in Chihuahua."[14]

It was at Tomóchic that because of their hunger the rebels of 1648 asked for peace. But Governor Guajardo's price for peace was hard: the heads of the four rebel chiefs. Ochavarri and Supichiochi had disappeared into the sierra never again to be seen, but Bartolomé and Tepox, the other two leaders, were still in the area, and their heads, severed by their own followers, were placed at the feet of the governor. "In April 1649, Guajardo returned triumphantly to Parral. He had made peace, and 2,000 Indians, exhausted by the fatigue of a useless war and debilitated by the treason which had delivered the heads of their leaders, had been conquered. The bodies of 150 dead Indians were left abandoned in the neighborhood of Tomóchic, bodies which would improve the land and render it more fertile in valor and in pride."[15]

And revenge also concluded the revolt of 1652, which ended with the capture of Tepóraca and his Christian hanging at Tomóchic on March 4, 1653. His body, riddled with arrows, was left hanging from a pine tree, as a symbol and a warning.[16] By 1690 revolt was a familiar thing, and Jorge Hostinsky, who had built a church and a house in the two years he had been there, barely escaped with his life. The church was burned, his dwelling was laid waste, and the pueblo was devastated.[17]

When the Jesuits went back after the uncertain peace of 1692, Hostinsky's place was taken by Venceslao Eymer,[18] but on October 9, 1695, Eymer went to Papigóchic, and Hostinsky was back in charge of the partido.[19] Less than two years later, in March 1697, it was the same old story. While Hostinsky was away at Arisiáchic, rebels struck Tomóchic, burned the rebuilt church and the priest's house, laid waste the town, killed all the mission cattle, and divided the corn and other supplies among themselves. Again, Tomóchic was the headquarters, and the rebels installed themselves on a peñol beside Río Tomóchic which they called Sopezi. "On one side the river flowed past the rock...on the other the cliff was too precipitous to be scaled...it could not be surrounded, since at the rear it merged into the mountain."[20]

After the peace, the continued danger was thought to be so great that no Jesuit was reassigned to Tomóchic or the other pueblos of the partido.[21] "Indeed, it seemed advisable completely to abandon... [Tomóchic and Cajuríchic], since many of their inhabitants had been taken elsewhere."[22] Until 1722 no resident missionary served any part of the partido, but in that year not only did Glandorff come from Cárichic, but 800 families congregated in Tomóchic, Arisiáchic, and Cajuríchic and, despite an epidemic which cost the lives of 1,817 adults and more than 3,000 children, the area began an era of progress and peaceful prosperity.[23] By 1725 Father Glandorff had commenced a church, and meanwhile Tomóchic's 300 families used one room of his house for services.[24] Thirty-eight years later, long since a living legend, Glandorff died,[25] and at the time of his death both the church and the house were said to be good, although the population had dwindled to 101 families.[26]

Glandorff was succeeded by Mateo Steffel,[27] who moved to San Francisco Borja before the expulsion,[28] thus making way for Tomóchic's last Jesuit, Juan Manuel González.

Tomóchic is spread out over a wide valley formed by the curving Río Tomóchic. In October 1969, the church, La Virgen de la Refugia, faced east from about the center of the valley, completely surrounded by the ruins of prior church buildings. It was quite plain with a two-bell campanario at the façade and a door with a red panel and two crosses. The interior was equally plain, with a simple altar in a small recessed sanctuary, with loops of pine branches framing a rather conventional picture of the Madomna and Child.

The last Tarahumara revolt came to a close in 1698, but some say that rebellion never ends in Tomóchic. Almost 200 years later, in 1892, influenced by heretical followers of Teresa Urrea, a mystic known as the Santa de Cabora, a group of citizens defied the local authorities and proclaimed that they bore allegiance solely to God. Reports reached Guerrero that Tomóchic was in open revolt, and 1,200 federal soldiers with one cannon attacked the town, burning the church to which the defenders retired and ultimately achieving total victory at the expense of more than 200 dead and 100 wounded.[29]

San José Laborando de Arisiáchic

Father Glandorff was famous for running between the three principal towns of his partido and throughout the sierra, but before Plan Gran Visión there were no modern roads connecting Arisiáchic, Tomóchic and Cajuríchic, and we have had to make entirely separate excursions to each. When Paul and I went to Arisiáchic in April 1970, it was totally Tarahumara except for two mestizo schoolteachers, who were so glad to see a couple of non-Indians that they dismissed their classes so that they could talk with us. The church, a very old and crudely built adobe, faced east in the center of a typical Tarahumara valley. Called La Virgen de Guadalupe, the exterior was undistinguished except for two old bells in a square opening at the top.

The nave was substantially undecorated, but the sanctuary was graced by eight really excellent oil paintings in a poorly framed retablo behind a fixed altar. When we were there three rows of yellow flowers, each shaped from a gourd and resembling a large sunflower, framed the altar in a way seriously to obscure the paintings. While the centuries have not wholly spared them, the oils have, as usual, been reverently preserved, and they are truly lovely. Above the altar was a central portrait of the infant Christ, with Joseph and another, while at the very top were the familiar figures of the Trinity, similar in arrangement to those at Santo Tomás and Yepáchic but superior to either. The Trinity was flanked by two paintings of battle scenes, while the painting of Jesus and Joseph had at its right St. Francis of Assisi and at its left a Madonna and Child.

The Christian history of Arisiáchic begins with Venceslao Eymer, who started his missionary activity here in 1692.[30] Eymer soon moved on to Tomóchic and was transferred to Papigóchic in October 1695, leaving the partido once more in the hands of Jorge Hostinsky.[31] Before the 1697 revolt, a church had been built at Arisiáchic, probably partly by Eymer and partly by Hostinsky, but the extent to which Christian influence had penetrated may well be questionable. One event which was a principal cause of the revolt was Indian resentment at the Spanish execution of Nicolás el Tuerto,[32] the chief at Arisiáchic who was said to have been a sorcerer, to have encouraged polygamy and to have been guilty of a dozen homicides.[33]

The trouble brewing in Arisiáchic was apparent for some time before the actual revolt, since Neumann reports that on three occasions the faithful of the pueblo sent messengers to Villa Aguilar asking for soldiers to defend against a threatened attack. Suspecting a trick, Fernández Retana sent no soldiers, but instead dispatched 150 Indians from Papigóchic. By the time they got there, the revolt had begun, so the Indians from Papigóchic joined in, burning the Arisiáchic church, destroying the house from which Father Hostinsky had fled, and laying waste to the town.[34]

Like its cabecera, Arisiáchic was not reoccupied by the Jesuits until Glandorff took over the partido and rebuilt the church. But the building Paul and I visited in 1970 had very certainly been rebuilt since Glandorff's time. The interior plaster was very old, and so was the adobe, but the roof had seen only a handful of decades, and it seemed highly probable that rebuilding and repair had been more or less continuous for more than 250 years, with particular attention at all times to preserving the oil paintings, which were at least 200 years old.

Nuestra Señora de Aranzazú de Cajuríchic

Cajuríchic, the third principal town of the Tomóchic partido, was established by Guillermo Illing in 1688.[35] In the next two years he built a church and a house, but in the 1690 revolt both were burned, the town was devastated, and he barely escaped with his life.[36] There is a suggestion that after the peace, Juan Bautista Barli may have served very briefly at Cajuríchic, but if so, then certainly it was a passing thing, for it was determined that Cajuríchic didn't offer enough security to justify the permanent assignment of a priest.[37] If there had been any doubt at all respecting that conclusion, it vanished in the fires of the last revolt of the century, when Governor Larrea told the residents of Cajuríchic to move to Papigóchic and declared the town officially abandoned.[38]

But as in the case of Tomóchic, the abandonment was not permanent, and by 1730, the ubiquitous Father Glandorff had built a church which he dedicated to the Virgin of Aranzazú.[39]

The church Glandorff built is certainly not now standing, or at least not in its original condition. But he would have been equally proud of La Virgen de Guadalupe, a splendid twin-towered building which shows definite Gothic influences in the pointed arch at the main entrance and on either side of the altar. In 1969 the altar was simply and tastefully decorated with a cloth whose edge repeated the triangular design of the unusual communion rail covering. Behind the altar was the only conventional work of art in the church—the usual representation of the Virgin of Guadalupe.

The other paintings at Cajuríchic were far from conventional, and comprised a truly remarkable collection of church art—remarkable not merely for the total isolation of the pueblo, but also for the catholicity of subject matter and the excellence of the paintings. Within the sanctuary, on the epistle side, behind two very well done busts, one of a woman and the other a man, was an almost life-sized portrait of what may just possibly have been the Virgin of Aranzazú, with melancholy eyes, a crown and flowing robe and, supported by a pillow on her left knee, a blond Jesus, fully dressed but without shoes. In the nave, on the epistle side, were three very large oils: the first a kneeling saint who may have been San Isidro, flanked by cherubs, with an apparition of the Virgin above him; the

In October 1969, repairs were underway on the Gothic-influenced church of La Virgen de Guadalupe de Cajuríchic.

second a most lifelike and extremely well drawn Christ crucified; and the third, behind and above some excellent small santos, a painting reminiscent of Gainsborough's *Blue Boy*. It was of a man, dressed in blue and holding a pail which probably contained "five barley loaves, and two small fishes."[40] On the gospel side of the nave, there were only three paintings: the first, closest to the pulpit, St. Simon carrying the cross to Calvary; the second a foolish virgin whose lamp has gone out; and the third a seated Christ, scourged and naked except for the royal robe put on in mockery, strapped at the wrists, with crown of thorns in place.

Cajuríchic is about as remote as any church in the sierra, but both times we have visited we have found it worth every bit of the trouble getting there. We first tried it from Tosánachic, from which the old road goes south toward Huajumar. We had spent the night before in Yepáchic, and in mid-afternoon reached Tosánachic and turned south. When night fell—quickly and without warning, as always in the sierra—we were at about 8,500 feet and in a dense forest. We spent the night at a ranch, where we learned it was much farther to Cajuríchic than we had expected. Concerned, perhaps unduly, about our gas supply, we regretfully turned back to Tosánachic.

Later on the same trip, we got to Cajuríchic, this time by going almost due west from San Juanito, deep into the sierra and through heavy forests, over a relatively good road hacked out to serve the lumbering and mining men of the area. The drive from San Juanito to Cajuríchic took from six to eight hours, depending somewhat on how many lumber trucks you met, and whether you met them at the top of a grade or the bottom. Because wherever a car meets a lumber truck in the sierra, the truck has the right of way, and the smaller vehicle must go, in reverse, either up or down to a point wide enough for the truck to pass.

The timber between San Juanito and Cajuríchic is magnificent: between the two towns, we must have seen trees enough to provide masts for all the ships that sailed the seas for a thousand years. When we were there again, in 1976, we found just as many trees, but the eastern half of the old road, splendidly rebuilt, reduced the time between the two towns by half.

Cajuríchic itself is in the middle of the usual valley, not much different from a dozen others nestled in the pine-clad sierra. The settlement has only a few buildings beside the magnificent church. The few people were friendly and helpful and as interested as we in their church and its splendid decorations.

At La Virgen de Guadalupe de Cajuríchic, the artwork is magnificent. This painting is particularly interesting, for it may depict the original patrona, Nuestra Señora de Aranzazú. October 1969.

El Beato Luis Gonzaga de Peguáchic

In 1725 the visitador Guenduláin reported that between Tomóchic and Cajuríchic there was a ranchería dedicated to El Beato Luis Gonzaga where a church and a house had been commenced and where 23 Christian families were served by a temporary chapel.[41] Aloysius Gonzaga had been canonized by Tamarón's time, and therefore the bishop reported that the pueblo of San Luis Gonzaga de Peguáchic, located nine leagues west of Tomóchic, had 36 families with a total population of 164 Indians.[42] The bishop's editor couldn't locate the pueblo at all,[43] and not only have Paul and I been unable to find the place, but we haven't found anyone who has ever heard of it.

San Ignacio de Teséachic

I haven't been able to do any better on Teséachic. Hostinsky was supposed to have been here as early as May 1697,[44] but the location isn't mentioned again until Tamarón's time, when he reported that it was a visita of Tomóchic, nine leagues to the north with 103 families, totalling 204 Indians.[45]

No one we have talked to in Tomóchic has had any suggestion at all as to the direction or location of Teséachic. This doesn't mean, however, that I've given up. Paul and I plan to go back, and someday, somewhere, we shall find someone who can tell us how to get not only to Teséachic, but also to Peguáchic—I hope.

El Nombre de Jesús
de Cárichic

La Iglesia del Nombre de Jesús de Cárichic

Cárichic[1] was founded by Tomás Guadalajara[2] on November 9, 1675, the Feast of the Basilica of Our Savior. The natives of Cárichic were not initially friendly. Before Guadalajara and Tardá made their summer excursion down Río Papigóchic as far as Yepómera, the Indians of Guerucárichic—for so it was then called—sent word that no priests would be permitted to enter the village. But later in the fall, gentiles from Cárichic made three trips to Borja to ask for missionaries, and the third time Guadalajara, who was temporarily alone, broke their mutual promise never to travel without the other into new country.

When Guadalajara got to Cárichic, he was greeted with wild enthusiasm—in their letter the priests compared it to a riot of European university students. After he had baptized about a hundred, the Jesuit named the place El Nombre de Jesús de Cárichic, which soon became, in approximation of the original name, Jesús Cárichic, or, as a single word, Jesuscárichic. The new Christians begged Guadalajara to stay among them, promising to build a church for his use. In fact, they were able, in the space of the next 15 days, to construct a serviceable jacal with a thatched roof.[3] Based on the enthusiastic report of Guadalajara and Tardá, the visitador Bernabé Gutiérrez recommended in April 1676, that four new priests be sent to Tarahumara Alta, and that one be assigned to Jesús Cárichic.[4]

Thus it was that when Juan Ortiz came to Cárichic in 1678, he found the newly installed Diego Ruiz Contreras in charge of a cabecera with a small house, the inadequate church which Guadala-jara's faithful had built in 1675, and the people at work on a new church, large and well proportioned.[5] Ruiz probably didn't stay long enough to finish the building project, because he was replaced the following year[6] by Bernardo Rolandegui, the Basque who suc-ceeded Juan María Salvatierra as provincial in 1706.[7] Rolandegui probably finished the church, but sometime between March and August 1681, he left for México[8] and was replaced by Juan María Ratkay.

There's nothing to suggest that Ratkay, whose training didn't include the construction arts, did any church building before he died on December 26, 1683,[9] but not so with his successor, Fran-cisco María Pícolo.[10]

It seems very certain that Pícolo started from scratch, abandon-ing the 1675 straw-thatched church, if it still existed, as well as the one on which Ruiz Contreras was working in 1678. For in February 1690, Neumann reported: "a very pretty church with three aisles is being built there; much stone-cutting is going on, which the master-builder is doing with the help of the Indians."[11] Later, when Pícolo had gone to California and Neumann was describing his own headquarters, he called the church "... a large one, and very beautifully built with a double row of columns; there was none like it to be seen elsewhere at the missions, in all this vast province of Mexico. With the assistance of many friends, Father Francisco María Pícolo built it, and upon its construction he lavished great care."[12]

Indeed, while it may not be quite true that "the saintly Pícolo... built the finest church in all the land,"[13] it is certainly true that it was, and has remained, a magnificent structure. The nearly 300 years since Pícolo left Cárichic have been kind to his Romanesque church. There has been no change in its most unusual feature, the 12 structural columns which he used to define the central nave, each column hand hewn from a single tree, and each

This view of the nave and sanctuary at El Nombre de Jesús de Cárichic shows six of Father Pícolo's beautiful columns, which were hand-hewn in the 1690s.

tree brought at a great expenditure of muscle power and sweat from the high-pine country a good 20 miles to the west. In modern times the columns have flanked the center aisle and supported both the lowered roof over the side aisles and the higher central walls with clerestory lighting. The columns, with pseudo-Corinthian capitals, were topped by bolsters which in turn carried the beams supporting the clerestory walls. I was sure the columns differed little from their appearance in 1725, when they were called large and fine and when it was said that they were sculptured and painted so that at first sight they seemed to be made of stone.[14] Modern pews, a modern ceiling and roof, and a modern altar and altarpiece dedicated to the

Holy Family did not seem at all incongruous, and didn't really spoil the Pícolo church, behind whose altar repose the bones of both Ratkay and Neumann.[15]

The outside of the church at Cárichic, while substantial and tasteful, could hardly measure up to the striking nave. And there is evidence of a good deal more change since Pícolo's time than has been true in the case of the interior.[16] In 1904[17] the façade had the same general outlines it had on my visits, but at the southeast corner there was then a crumbling brick bell tower which fell sometime before the middle 1940s.[18] By April 1969, when I first visited Cárichic, the old tower had been completely replaced by a modern, boxy structure capped with a pyramidal roof. The doorway, tastefully done in stone, with *IHS* and a cross in bas-relief at the top, was largely as it was in 1904, and probably also largely as it was in 1697. At the extreme height of the façade, the church then and since has had a low-relief cross, a graceful addition which seems not to have been present either in 1904 or the middle 1940s.

When Father Pícolo was building his church in the 1690s, he had some temporary help in the person of Juan Verdier of Papigóchic,[19] and in 1697, when the construction must have been finished or almost finished, he had more company. In June of that year, driven from his post at Sisoguíchic by the last Tarahumara rebellion, José Neumann came to Cárichic,[20] there to remain for almost 35 years. By the first days of September, Pedro Proto, another fugitive from the wars, was helping out,[21] but by mid-October Pícolo, the master builder, had left for California.[22] In the fall of 1697, when Bishop Legazpi visited Cárichic, he was received not only by Neumann, who was then in charge both as visitor and as Pícolo's replacement, but by seven other Jesuits, undoubtedly including Proto and others who were accompanying the bishop on his tour. He remained four days in Cárichic and confirmed more than 2,000.[23]

Two years after the bishop's visit, when peace seemed secure, Neumann's term as visitador expired, and he devoted himself wholeheartedly to Cárichic and its three visitas, Tagírachic, Pasigóchic and Bacaburiáchic. In each he proceeded to build dwelling houses and churches, and he caused each to be beautifully decorated and abundantly provided with sacred vessels.[24]

By April 1969 the crumbling brick bell tower of El
Nombre de Jesús de Cárichic had been replaced by this
modern structure.

Until 1732 Neumann administered Cárichic, apparently with
only occasional assistance. In 1712 Miguel Ortega, who may still
have been serving as visitador, died in Cárichic,[25] and in the summer of 1715 Juan Morales showed up briefly in the parish registers.[26] In September 1715, another bishop, this time Pedro Tápiz,
visited Cárichic,[27] and in March 1721, the legendary Francisco
Glandorff arrived, to spend a year helping Neumann and learning
Rarámuri.[28] From June to October 1722,[29] Balthasar Rauch took
Glandorff's place at Cárichic, probably also to learn the language.
Although now in advanced years, Neumann got no more help until
April 1731, when Antonio Martini came from Chínipas. But Mar-

tini went back after a brief time,[30] his place taken, at least by November,[31] by Gaspar Stiger. It was Stiger who gave extreme unction to the dying Neumann on May 1, 1732, and saw to his burial under the floor of the church he loved so well, on the gospel side of the altar.[32]

Gaspar Stiger left Cárichic for Pimería Alta in 1733,[33] and the vacancy was undoubtedly filled more or less immediately. But by whom? Francisco Osorio was in charge between August 1738 and May 1739,[34] and since there is no record of his being anywhere else after 1727, it's entirely possible that he was Stiger's immediate successor. But it's equally possible that Stiger was succeeded by Manuel Romero, who was there between May and December 1738,[35] and who may just as easily have come five years before. Osorio may have remained until 1744, when he was at Papigóchic,[36] but it's more likely that he left at the end of 1741 or in January 1742, when the signature of Julián Fernández Abeé first appears in the parish books.[37] Fernández was there in July 1742, when Bishop Elizacoechea came to confirm.[38] Indeed, he was still there in 1748,[39] but he was succeeded that fall by Sebastián Prieto,[40] whose place was taken in turn by Luis Yáñez the following April.[41] But by 1755 Yáñez was at Coyáchic, and Lázaro Franco had come to Cárichic from San Pablo.[42] Franco probably stayed until 1761, when Yáñez returned.[43] Four years later Yáñez was in failing health,[44] and by the time of the expulsion he was being assisted by the younger Juan Hauga.[45] Together, they delivered the Pícolo church to the representatives of the crown and trudged off to Veracruz, both to die in distant Bologna.[46]

El Beato Luis Gonzaga de Tagírachic

Cárichic is about two hours south and a little west of Cuauhtémoc, in rolling scrub oak country below the timber line.[47] Its visitas are northwest, west and south, but I thought only one to be worth visiting. Tagírachic isn't the one.

After two false starts in previous years, we finally located Tagírachic in 1975. Just south of the divide below Laguna de los Mexicanos and north of Cárichic, there was a new road which led to, but not beyond, Tagírachic, a small but not unpleasing town at the edge of the timber line. In the very center of town, on a mound of crumbled adobe formed over the course of almost 300 years, stood a corner of a wall, perhaps eight feet high, which was all that was left of the Tagírachic church.

Tagírachic[48] may have been visited in December 1675 by Tardá and Guadalajara,[49] and it's certain that three years later, when Diego Ruiz Contreras[50] was in charge of the partido, Tagírachic was flourishing as a Christian village with a jacal for a church.[51] Apparently by 1684, when Ratkay was beginning his work at the cabecera, Tagírachic had become important enough to have a priest of its own. For in that year Juan Ortiz Foronda, later a victim of the 1690 rebellion, came to the visita and spent three years before being transferred to Parral.[52] And indeed the place must have been important, since by December 1690, it contained 300 baptized Christians.[53]

Pícolo was too busy at Cárichic to build churches in his visitas, but when Neumann was free of his duties as visitador in 1699, he undertook the task and in three years had completed churches in Tagírachic, Pasigóchic and Bacaburiáchic, all with dwelling houses and all beautifully decorated and adequately supplied.[54] In 1725 Neumann's Tagírachic church and house were in good condition and quite adequate,[55] but there's no later report of either, and by Tamarón's time the place had only 40 families.[56] There are probably a few more today, but there isn't much by which to remember Neumann's church.

El Santo Angel de la Guarda de Pasigóchic

Except that it never had a priest of its own, the story of Pasigóchic parallels that of Tagírachic. In 1678, Pasigóchic had a jacal for a church,[57] and at the turn of the century, Neumann built here a church of which he was proud.[58] In 1744, both the church and the house were still in good condition and well equipped.[59]

I wish it were still true. In 1971 the church stood quite alone in the center of the usual Tarahumara "settlement," with the closest building half a mile away. It was of rubble stone, with a partial roof and an exposed beam ceiling. The interior was utterly bare, although it had been kept neat and there was no accumulation of trash. While there was evidence of burials outside, it seemed certain that the building had been without sacramental use for many decades.

Nuestra Señora del Pilar de Zaragoza de Bacaburiáchic

Bacaburiáchic may have been founded as early as 1676,[60] and it was certainly well established in 1678, with a church of sorts.[61] Five years later Juan Ratkay called it San Casimiro Bacaqueriáchic[62] and it seems certain that this is the third visita in which Neumann built an ample, beautifully decorated and abundantly provided church at the turn of the century.[63] Neumann's church and house were still quite adequate and had all the necessary equipment in 1725, when the settlement had 211 families and was recorded as Nuestra Señora del Pilar de Bucaguarachi.[64]

Bacaburiáchic is a very long two hours south and a little west of Cárichic, and, because of the way the country is cut up with barrancas and by erosion, it would take as long on a horse or on foot as in a four-wheel-drive vehicle. Perhaps it was the distance from Cárichic which accounted for the fact that six years before the Jesuit expulsion a new partido was in the process of being formed, with Bacaburiáchic as the cabecera and three visitas:[65] Teguérichic, to be taken from under the jurisdiction of Cárichic; Narárachic, just then being established as a Christian community; and Choguita, a visita of Norogáchic which Paul and I found to be a long distance from everything. But the expulsion kept the new partido from actually getting established, and the Franciscans did nothing about it at all. Under their guidance, neither Bacaburiáchic nor Choguita was reestablished, and both Narárachic and Teguérichic became visitas of Baquéachic.[66]

In October 1971, Paul and I went to Bacaburiáchic, taking with us as a guide an ancient Indian cowboy named Mariano. Our guide took us south and a little east of Cárichic over a very bad road which got progressively worse as it crossed deep barrancas and wound through an area thick with inhabited caves to a deeper barranca through which a medium-sized fast-flowing river moves east to join Río Conchos.

La Virgen de Guadalupe de Bacaburiáchic, as it's now called, is quite definitely not Neumann's church. The masonry building, with a pitched shingle roof and a square bell tower whose flat roof was angled, couldn't have been much more than 25 years old. The interior was quite plain, with a wooden altar against the wall and a cement floor without pews. Two santos as well as candles and paper flowers graced the altar, which was surmounted by the usual picture of the Virgin of Guadalupe, this time trimmed with a wreath of paper flowers.

San José de Baquéachic

In 1744 Fernández Abeé, the priest at Cárichic, reported that Baquéachic was one of seven pueblos which together went to make up Nuestra Señora del Pilar de Zaragoza de Bacaburiáchic.[67] I have found no other Jesuit reference to Baquéachic,[68] and when the Franciscans took over in 1768, the place was without either church or house.[69] The friars remedied the lack and set Baquéachic up as a cabecera with three visitas:[70] Narárachic, an independent cabecera in 1767, Paguíchic, a visita of Norogáchic under the Jesuits, and Teguérichic, formerly a Cárichic visita.

Until 1975 I simply didn't know what was left of the Baquéachic church. Our friends at Cárichic had always told us that the pueblo was only five hours away, on a road to the southeast which turned off from the road to Bacaburiáchic. We made plans to get there on four occasions: twice we were prevented from starting because it was fall and the rains and rising rivers had made the road impassable—the third time we were stopped by a serious gas leak. In 1975 we tried it again, this time with Francisco, a small and frightened, but competent, guide. At the end of five very long and indescribably difficult hours, over what is by all odds the worst road I've ever seen, we reached Baquéachic. We found its church by far the finest of any of the Cárichic visitas.

The superb stone building, with a pitched sheet metal roof[71] and a two-tiered bell tower surmounted by a domed cupola, totally dominated the usual spread-out valley settlement, part Tarahumara

The superb stone church of San José de Baquéachic dominates
its rural valley settlement. April 1975.

and part mestizo. The interior was dignified, with white plastered
walls rising to good carved vigas and corbels. A light blue altarpiece
framed a crucifix, with the figure modestly draped from the waist,
which was in turn surmounted by a quite excellent unframed oil
painting of San José and the Infant Jesus. A black-draped santo was
on a pedestal at the epistle side.

From Baquéachic, a somewhat bustling small community of
relatively well built houses and splendidly constructed stone corrals,
a road crossed the river at the south edge of the valley and rose

spectacularly up the barranca and to the top of the mesa. We were told it went to Norogáchic, and undoubtedly it did. I only hope it's better than the one we had traveled from Cárichic to Baquéachic or the earlier road from Cárichic to Bacaburiáchic. We returned to Cárichic through Bacaburiáchic and thus discovered a new and better road from Bacaburiáchic to Cárichic—it went north and west in a great loop to connect with the Sisoguíchic-Cárichic highway and thus avoided perhaps a third of the direct spine-crunching route between Cárichic and Baquéachic. We didn't take it on the way out because Francisco was evidently too unfamiliar with the country to tell us that the best way to get from Cárichic to Baquéachic is to start west on the road to Sisoguíchic.

Santa Ana de Teguérichic

Tamarón listed Santa Ana de Teguérichic as a visita of Cárichic with 66 families and 276 Indians,[72] and Lizasoaín, writing at about the same time, said that the place was about to be organized as a visita of the new cabecera Bacaburiáchic.[73] Probably nothing much happened in the Jesuit twilight, but under the Franciscans Teguérichic became a visita of Baquéachic. It was then said to be six leagues north of its cabecera and to be five leagues south of Cárichic by wind and eight by road, to be on the same side of the river as Baquéachic, and to have 48 people.[74]

We have been told conflicting stories about how to get to Teguérichic, and thus far we haven't been greatly motivated to try. In April 1972, Father Benjamín Tapia, then the Jesuit superior, as well as the other priests and brothers at Sisoguíchic, insisted that the old church at Teguérichic had been totally torn down and that even the foundations had been completely covered by a school. The town was served, they told us, by a new church which occupied a wholly different location.

El Dulce Nombre
de María
de Sisoguíchic

La Iglesia del Dulce Nombre de María de Sisoguíchic

On October 12, 1900, four modern Jesuits—three priests and a brother—reestablished at Sisoguíchic[1] the Misión de la Tarahumara.[2] Ever since, Sisoguíchic has been the most important center of Christian activity in Tarahumara and, after Chihuahua and Ciudad Juárez, the most important in the state.

The misión was made a vicariate apostolic by Pius XII on June 23, 1958. Salvador Martínez Aguirre, a Jesuit missionary whose endurance and ardor match those of the indefatigable Glandorff, was appointed vicar apostolic and, on September 9, 1958, in the most solemn ceremony Sisoguíchic had ever seen, was consecrated bishop of Arca, a nonfunctioning diocese in Armenia.[3] One of the finest pastors I have known, Bishop Martínez, who was as much at home on a horse in the sierra as at the altar, served Sisoguíchic and the misión with distinction until June 16, 1973, when his resignation as vicar apostolic was accepted and he retired to Chínipas. Simultaneously with his retirement, José A. Llaguno, an airplane pilot as well as a dedicated Jesuit missionary and a distinguished scholar, was appointed in his place. On May 13, 1975, the new vicar apostolic was in his own right consecrated bishop in a ceremony which, because the jeep broke down this side of Sisoguíchic, Paul and I were regretfully obliged to miss.[4]

No one would have predicted so grand an ecclesiastical future when Antonio Oreña established Sisoguíchic as a Christian pueblo in 1676.[5] Oreña apparently built two churches and two houses: the first set were no more than small jacales,[6] but the second church and house were much more substantial and were almost finished in 1678 when the visitador described a splendid flat-roofed church and said it lacked only doors for its dedication.[7]

Oreña probably left for Bácum not long after the 1678 visit,[8] when the church still didn't have any doors. There is a report that Sisoguíchic was served by José Sánchez Guevara from 1679 until 1681,[9] but the account seems doubtful, since during the period nothing was done to finish the big church and the larger house.[10]

It seems altogether more likely that the partido was without a priest until March 7, 1681, when Bernardo Rolandegui, of Cárichic, took José Neumann to his new post at Sisoguíchic. Neumann, the sophisticated European, was aghast at both the house and church. He reported that the pueblo had a "little old straw thatched church, which seemed rather a hovel than a church," and that the dwelling house he was expected to occupy "was another hut, or hovel, built beside the church."[11]

Rolandegui told the Indians that their new priest couldn't stay with them unless they immediately finished the larger church and built him a proper house. The Tarahumaras finished the church within three weeks, so that Neumann was able to celebrate there for the first time at Easter. Within another three weeks he was comfortably situated in the completed house.[12]

But Neumann had even grander ideas, and in July 1686 he was at work on a new church.[13] By February 1690 Sisoguíchic's third church, as well as a new house, was finished.[14] The construction expense had been largely borne by "one of the Spaniards at the silver mine . . . [who] had also provided the sacred vessels . . . and all the necessary furnishing," not only for the church at Sisoguíchic but also for that at Echoguita.[15] And the Sisoguíchic furnishings were rather special: "Scarcely any other mission is as well provided with sacred furnishings and equipment as is this one; it has fifteen chasubles, altar-frontals of many colors and all of silk, both damask and flowered, and three paraments worked with gold and silver. Upon these things I have spent more than 2,000 imperials."[16]

And all Neumann's work went up in smoke.

After the 1697 rebels burned the church and the priest's house at Echoguita, Neumann was warned that they were on their way to Sisoguíchic. He packed up the sacred vessels, gave them to trusted Indians to hide in the caves, and late at night, on June 21, left Sisoguíchic for Cárichic. From a height he "... looked back at the village, and saw many fires moving to and fro; they were the flames of pine torches, and by their light the loyal Indians were carrying away the furnishings of the church and the dwelling-house."[17] From Cárichic he dispatched Indians to help the defenders of Sisoguíchic, but before they arrived, the rebels had burned the church, all of the houses, and even the crops.

Sisoguíchic was still in the control of the revolutionaries when Captain Fernández Retana arrived with Spanish troops and Indian auxiliaries. In the ensuing fighting 61 rebels were killed, the others fled, and on June 25, the heads of 33 of the slain apostates were severed and put on spears planted on a hill near the ruins of the Sisoguíchic church.[18]

What happened to Sisoguíchic after the war is by no means clear. There is no record of any priest being assigned before Balthasar Rauch, and there is no evidence that he was there before 1720.[19] In 1725 it was reported that Rauch, who by then had been replaced by Juan Francisco Rexis, had built at Sisoguíchic a handsome new church that was large but inadequately adorned, as well as a good new house.[20] How long Rexis stayed after 1725 no one seems to know, and there is a good chance that the post was vacant for at least some of the time before 1744, when José Escalona came over from the Chínipas area to serve the partido. Certainly by 1747 and perhaps as early as 1746 Escalona had gone back to Santa Ana and Félix Mier had taken his place, only to give way before July 1751, to Martín Vallarta. Two years later Felipe Ruanova was transferred from the Tepehuán country,[21] but by 1761 Ruanova had gone to Mátachic, leaving Sisoguíchic in the charge of Antonio Hitl.[22] Hitl was reported to have a good church but an inferior house.[23] He vacated the house before June 1765, when Ildefonso Corro took over in time for the expulsion.[24]

The big church which Hitl served in 1761 was probably the same handsome building which Balthasar Rauch built after 1720.

The great stone cruciform church of El Dulce Nombre de María de Sisoguíchic was erected in the 1720s, but over the years the original structure has undergone extensive remodeling.

Remodeled extensively in 1875,[25] it's undoubtedly the one which we first saw in 1968, with the Jesuit priests' residence on its left and the school on its right. Structurally the great stone cruciform building was essentially identical to that shown in a picture made shortly after the turn of the century,[26] when repairs, including the installation of a new roof, were underway. In addition to the new roof, which required the addition of a pediment to the façade, a cone-shaped and cross-surmounted cap was added to the bell tower.

When we were at Sisoguíchic in May 1976, the church was undergoing extensive remodeling, but on our prior visits we had found the nave to be large and well appointed in the modern style, as befitted the premier church of the Misión de la Tarahumara. The main altar featured a very high, three-tiered altarpiece with three good statues, the central one under a splendid canopy. Sometime after our first visit in 1968 the reredos was tastefully draped, from ceiling to floor, with red behind the retablo and white at each side. By the early 1970s the transept altars and their decorations had become considerably more modest than they had been in 1968, when the gospel side altar had displayed a good statue of San Ignacio Loyola under a canopy and the epistle side had the usual representation of the Virgin of Guadalupe below a bas-relief arch supported by simulated marble pilasters.

In this century Sisoguíchic has been above all a church town. In addition to the Jesuit headquarters and a hospital run by nuns who belong to a nursing order, for years there have been two schools—one run by the Jesuits and another by an order of nuns— and more recently established in splendid isolation on a hill up from the church (probably the hill on which the 33 Tarahumara heads were displayed), a convent of contemplative sisters. The three orders could be readily distinguished by their habits—the Jesuits call them the blacks, the reds and the whites. But only two, the blacks and whites, came to daily morning Mass, and the Jesuits were obliged always to have two priests available at Sisoguíchic, since the contemplative nuns with their red habits could leave the convent only on a very limited basis and the sacrament had to be taken to them.

Paul and I have only the fondest memories of Sisoguíchic. The priests and brothers were always helpful with directions and counsel about the roads; they saw to the automotive repairs; they furnished us with food and lodging on many occasions; they were most generous in sending us to inaccessible places in one of the two airplanes from which they served their vast territory. In short, we found them boon companions, and they have become honored friends.

San José de Panálachic

Sisoguíchic is on the eastern slope of the continent, near the headwaters of Río Conchos, about half a day west and a bit south of Cárichic. Neumann called it "the farthest corner of this region"[27] and said, "This valley of Sisoguíchic is the highest of all the valleys in Tarahumara. This is evident from the fact that the river which flows through it which has its source a few leagues hence, among very lofty mountains . . . is the last river of all to flow eastward. . . . In consequence the cold is more intense here than elsewhere, partly because of the altitude and the bleakness of the mountains, where only pine-trees grow, and partly because of the violence of the winds, which rush hither from every direction, and, as it were, do battle with one another."[28]

Neumann's description is accurate—Sisoguíchic is near the top of the world, and its visitas are spread about, in a descending circle, most of them at lower levels, and in warmer areas. Typical of the pattern, Panálachic is about an hour and a half southeast, or downstream, on a passable road. Paul and I were there in April 1972, and we probably could have made it alone without help. But the ever gracious and helpful Father Tapia insisted that we have a guide, and sent with us a pleasant and intelligent 13-year-old, fittingly named Pablo.

The town is fairly good sized and, while spread out in the usual Tarahumara fashion, has more of a mestizo appearance than is usual in these valleys. The community is totally dominated by two churches near its eastern edge. The older, of adobe and stone, with a single bell in the tower, is not unlike the churches at Cuzárare and Pámachic. But when we were there it was in the process of being abandoned in favor of a totally modern building under construction across the road, with a plywood roof and circular walls of ornamental masonry.

The old church was being used to store construction materials for the new. The careless builders had left, totally unprotected amid stacks of lumber and bags of cement, two large oil paintings, one leaning against the altar at floor level and the other at the side of the nave. Both pictures were originally very fine, and even in 1972 preserved remnants of greatness. In one a Madonna with Child was surrounded by angels and admiring mortals and in the other Joseph was holding the Christ child. Unless they received better protection, both were probably completely ruined during the period of construction.

In 1682 Neumann considered Panálachic as only a potential visita, full of unconverted Tarahumaras but within the logical range

of his prospective missionary activity.[29] But there's no evidence that
a church was established there much before 1744, when San José de
Panálachic was called a new visita of Sisoguíchic.[30] I can find nothing to indicate when the fine old church we saw in 1972 was built,
but it may well be as old as the 1744 report. Since our visit it
probably has been razed—a victim of progress.

Nuestra Señora de la Luz de Narárachic

In 1972 Narárachic was a visita of Sisoguíchic, but it was never so
in Spanish times. The settlement was first reported in 1761, but it
was listed as a visita of Bacaburiáchic.[31] Four years later it was
reported to be a visita of Nonoava,[32] but by the time of the expulsion Narárachic was a full-fledged cabecera with a priest of its own.
When the expulsion order came, the young Cosme Díaz was hard at
work building Nuestra Señora de la Luz—but the Franciscans, with
less grandiose ideas, reverted Narárachic to visita status, this time
under Baquéachic.[33]

There are said to be roads to Narárachic, but I haven't found
anyone who has used one or knows anyone who has. In April 1972,
when Paul and I were guests of the Jesuits at Sisoguíchic, Father
Tapia told us not to try to drive, and instead arranged for us to fly in
one of the Jesuits' two single-engined planes.

Narárachic is on the west bank of a south-flowing bend of Río
Conchos, but its airstrip is on much higher ground and a good
many miles away, on the south edge of a 1,000-foot barranca made
by the river before it turns south to pass by the town. The runway is
very short, and the skillful pilot had to touch the wheels gently on
the very edge of the barranca, so as to use every possible foot of
length in decelerating, stopping neatly just short of a deep arroyo.
Later, when we took off to return to Sisoguíchic, I was numb when
we left the edge of the barranca, not yet airborne, and dropped 500
feet before beginning slowly to lift out of the canyon.

On our walk from the airstrip to the church, we were met by a
yellow-haired young man of about 25 who was Narárachic's only
non-Indian. He was a missionary volunteer from the city of
Chihuahua who had spent the past ten months teaching Tarahumara
children and helping to feed the adults who live in the caves[34] on

By April 1972 the crude masonry façade of the church of Nuestra Señora de la Luz de Narárachic needed the support of a pine tree.

the other side of Río Conchos and in the handful of huts on the Narárachic side of the river. His one-room school (in which he also lived) was on the very edge of the barranca, affording him a magnificent view but little else. He was supplied periodically from Sisoguíchic, and the infrequent visits of the Jesuit airplane provided his only opportunity to talk with anyone from the outside world. Utterly devoted and utterly committed, he made his most impressive statement to me upon parting, when I thanked him for his hospitality. "No," he said, "thanks are only for God."

The Narárachic church was of stone, very crudely done by primitive or unskilled masons. Its precarious condition was substantially identical to that evident in a picture taken in the middle 1940s,[35] except that in 1972 a long pine tree was holding up the front wall at about a 45° angle.

The interior was an interesting mixture of primitive and modern. The fixed plaster altar and the sanctuary wall were totally covered with primitive Indian designs: circles, curves, a swastika, simulated flowers, and a rooster. Leaning against the altar were four oil paintings: one the Virgin of Guadalupe; another the Showing of Christ at the Temple; the third, half hidden by the Virgin, the young St. John; and, finally, a small Infant of Prague. All were well done, although not in a good state of preservation. The nave was totally bare, with a dirt floor, but the roof was supported by handhewn beams themselves apparently buttressed by excellent handcarved corbels.

Nuestra Señora de los Dolores de Guacayebo

In 1725 the priest at Sisoguíchic, Juan Francisco Rexis, had just finished building a house in Guacayebo as well as a church which, while adequate, lacked adornment.[36] Whether the visita was ever supplied with those things necessary for the celebration of the sacrament simply doesn't appear, since the next report, in 1744, makes no mention at all of the church, but instead refers to Guacayebo as a new visita of Sisoguíchic[37]—a rather strange comment in view of its having been well established at least 20 years earlier. Neither Lizasoaín[38] nor Tamarón[39] says anything at all about the church, although both list the pueblo as a visita of Sisoguíchic.

While I have no way of knowing how long the Rexis church may have lasted after 1725, I very certainly know that it doesn't exist today. When we were at Guacayebo Viejo, portions of the walls of the old church were still visible, and there was still a cross, perhaps a grave marker, at about the middle of what once was the nave. But there was no other vestige of anything with any antiquity. A warehouse next door immediately to the south of the old church location appeared to have been occasionally used for religious purposes, or at least utilized as a combination church and meeting house, like many other church buildings throughout Tarahumara.

Guacayebo Viejo itself is in a lonesome Tarahumara valley, and the town is typically spread out over the entire area. To get there, go more or less due west from San Juanito, through the entirely separate town of Guacayebo Nuevo to the top of the sierra which lies to its west, and then south over a poor road to the valley of Guacayebo Viejo. At Guacayebo Nuevo there should be someone who can identify the turnoff.

But if you want to get to either of the two Guacayebos from San Juanito, don't ask directions for Guacayebo, but instead for Maguaríchic, a very interesting mining town, a good deal beyond Guacayebo Nuevo and on the same road. Maguaríchic is certainly not older than 1848, the date of the oldest bell hanging in front of the relatively modern church. The town itself is located deep in the sierra in a magnificent canyon heavily scarred by mining operations. For scenic purposes, Maguaríchic is well worth the trip.

La Asunción de Nuestra Señora de Bocoyna

Bocoyna,[40] located on the railroad northwest of Sisoguíchic about midway between San Juanito and Creel, was originally established as Echoguita, about four or five kilometers southwest of the present location. Finding the old town took us several years. Although thoroughly mestizo, Bocoyna is spread out in the Tarahumara fashion, with buildings scattered indiscriminately throughout a broad valley[41] and on both sides of the railroad and the small stream. The church of El Corazón de Jesús and most of the dwellings are somewhat north of the center of the valley, and the railroad station is at the southern end.

The first few times we were at Bocoyna we could find no one who confessed to any knowledge of Echoguita or who knew that Bocoyna had ever been moved. Ultimately, though, we got some directions and in October 1972, we located a road which crossed the arroyo just north of the railroad station, wound to the top of the sierra to the west and then plunged down southwest into another typical valley, substantially identical to that of Bocoyna except that it ran from west to east and had many fewer people. I believe we talked to all of them, but we located no ruins, foundations, walls, or other evidence of anything which had ever been a church building. Nor did we find any local tradition of the existence of a church, ancient or modern. But we did find one man who knew that Echoguita was older than Bocoyna and who thought the people had moved away because of inadequate water supply. Actually they had moved because of the substantially total destruction of the town in 1697.

The pueblo of La Asunción de Nuestra Señora de Echoguita was established sometime after 1676 by Antonio Oreña, the priest at Sisoguíchic.[42] In 1678 Ortiz reported that Oreña's activity had resulted in nine baptisms, but he said nothing about a church.[43] And there apparently wasn't one, because when Neumann first visited Echoguita on September 10, 1681, he said that "since as yet there was no Christian symbol in the valley, . . . [he] . . . had a large cross hastily made from the trunk of a tree, and caused it to be erected." In two days Neumann baptized 22, including two infants, and secured a promise from the Tarahumaras that they would build a church where he had placed the cross.[44]

Probably the Indians built no more than a jacal, but late in 1689 or early in 1690, Neumann began the construction of a fine church which was dedicated on August 15, 1693, the Feast of the Assumption of the Blessed Virgin. Fourteen Jesuit missionaries were present for the occasion, and there were three dedicatory Masses, by Neumann, Eymer and Verdier, in that order.[45]

The church, which must have been a very fine one, was destroyed. On June 21, 1697, at about mid-afternoon, "a great throng of rebels came down from the heights, descending by a rugged and seemingly impassable slope, and so entered the valley of Echoguita. The villagers were away, engaged in weeding their fields. . . . They then . . . battered open the doors of the church. . . . They climbed upon the altars, tore from their places the images of the Mother of God and of the Saints, rent them asunder, and cast the pieces into the river which flowed close by. They smashed the altars and the baptismal font, which was of carved stone; pillaged the sacristy; tore to ribbons six chasubles and all the other vestments, and scattered the fragments; beat the chalice against a rock, and broke it into three pieces; and lay sacrilegious hands upon everything else, destroying and ruining all. Finally, they kindled fires around the dwelling house and the church, and burned them to the ground. . . ."[46]

Writing many years later, Neumann referred to Echoguita as "Bocoyna, or Echoguita,"[47] but it's uncertain whether both names were used for the older settlement—in fact there's no way of being sure that when peace finally came to the sierra, Echoguita was moved across the mountain and renamed Bocoyna. It's just as possible that the people of Echoguita, who deserted the place at the time of the revolt,[48] returned to their old home and that Bocoyna was separately established, becoming more important only because the new church was built there rather than at Echoguita.[49]

In any event, a new church was under construction at Bocoyna in 1725,[50] and in both 1744 and 1761 the pueblo was reported as being in existence as Nuestra Señora de la Asunción.[51] While the name had changed by the 1970s, and repairs were needed, the church was impressive and, from a distance, rather splendid. The plain plastered façade, with an arched doorway, was esthetically marred by an electric fuse box embedded in the wall, and the superstructures above the façade badly needed repair and plaster.

Those superstructures deserve some mention. In the center, immediately above the door, was the butt end of what must once have been a vaulted ceiling, later merged into a pitched roof with shingles. On either side and at the corners were quadrilateral structures, each surmounted by a smaller pillared dome and a cross. If there were nothing else, the effect would not have been unpleasing. But the curved face of the central vault was surmounted by four masonry pillars surmounted by a second and smaller four-pillared dome-like canopy resembling a howdah. Both were probably originally intended to be campanarios, but they were without bells.

The unusual campanario at El Corazón de Jesús de Bocoyna
resembles a howdah. April 1970.

Inside there was a free-standing simulated marble altar, its face
decorated by four columns, in front of a sanctuary wall with ornamental columns, in a diagonal rope pattern. Some of the columns
ran from a succession of bas-relief arches to the floor, but those in
the center, obviously once terminating at a fixed altar, stopped
somewhat forlornly about four feet above the floor. There were two
tall columns, in the same diagonal rope pattern, in the middle of
the nave, which supported the folded plate ceiling of reinforced
concrete. Four more columns at the communion rail went to arches
under the ceiling, resulting in an arch and column system which
formed a sort of rood screen. The decorations were minimal, being
confined to one picture of the Virgin of Guadalupe, a good but
conventional statue and a small crucifix behind the altar.

Los Santos Cinco Señores de Cuzárare

Cuzárare[52] was a new visita of Sisoguíchic in 1744,[53] and the church of Los Santos Cinco Señores was probably built at about that time. By 1761 the name had been changed to Nuestra Señora de Bethlém[54] and since then both of the fine old names have given way to the more standard Nuestra Señora de Guadalupe.

Cuzárare has very little historical significance, but the church and its equipment are magnificent, and the place is reasonably accessible. An almost completely Tarahumara community,[55] Cuzárare is about a kilometer east of the main road which goes south from Creel. The turnoff is very nearly impossible to find, but that's not important to visitors who get to Creel by train and who stay at either the Hotel Nuevo in Creel, or, a good deal more luxuriously, at the Cabaña Cañón del Cobre, about 15 miles south of Creel and not more than three kilometers south of Cuzárare. Guided tours to Cuzárare are among the advertised attractions at both.

Creel, the metropolis of the area,[56] was named after Enrique C. Creel, who was governor of Chihuahua and vice president of the Kansas City, Mexico and Orient Railway Company (later the Chihuahua al Pacífico) when the railroad was pushed to this point in 1907 and the station and town were established. Creel is a splendid place to rest and resupply. Gasoline has always been available in quantity, and the stores well stocked. We have even found an excellent welding shop, which was able, in April 1972, to repair our front axle.

Father Luis Verplancken, the Jesuit whom I thought was Creel's greatest asset, was a whirlwind of energy: He built a magnificent church with some of the finest laminated beams I've ever seen; he established a children's hospital which has saved the lives of thousands of Tarahumara infants; he drove everywhere in his four-wheel drive Scout to serve the Indians in a vast area; and in between he still found time to take care of all kinds of civic betterment.

In April 1970, when we were first in the Cuzárare area, the rain was too heavy for photography and we didn't even drive to the church. But the next day we went back and I took pictures for many hours. The adobe church, inadequately plastered, was very large, very high, very wide, very long and beautifully simple. But it was

Since this picture was taken in April 1970, extensive repairs have closed the holes in the side and roof of Nuestra Señora de Guadalupe de Cuzárare.

in sad repair. The square bell tower which stood at the northwest corner in the 1940s[57] had fallen, carrying with it a good part of the pitched snow roof on the west side, some of the wall of the nave in front of the choir loft, and a bit of the ceiling. The accident exposed to the elements a perfectly magnificent collection of religious art.

Both then and the following April, when I took more pictures, each side of the nave at Cuzárare, from the choir loft to the transept crossing, had five very large and quite splendid oil paintings, all on canvas without frames. None was in good condition. The paint was cracking—snow and rain had taken their toll—but the pictures on the gospel side, with more protection from the elements, were in somewhat better shape. All of them were once very fine; four of the epistle side paintings (excepting only the one immediately below

The walls of the attractive sanctuary of Nuestra Señora de Guadalupe de Cuzárare display interesting examples of religious art. April 1970.

the break in the roof) and all on the gospel side were still quite recognizable: the Annunciation, the Circumcision of Christ, Christ Receiving the Tables of the Law from Moses, the Showing of Christ at the Temple, Mary and Elizabeth, No Room at the Inn, Adoration of the Magi, Adoration of the Shepherds, and Christ in the Temple Sitting and Disputing With the Doctors.

Cuzárare was in the classic cruciform style, with red firebrick columns providing added strength at the four corners of the crossing. The two subsidiary side chapels were empty, but the sanctuary in 1970 and 1971 was most unusual. Here were two more excellent oil paintings, both of the Savior and, with better protection from the elements, both in a much better state of preservation than those in the nave. Each was at the side of the five-sided sanctuary, and together they flanked two conventional pictures of the Virgin of Guadalupe, one only partly visible behind the altarpiece and another, draped in the colors of Mexico, on the altar itself behind a small crucifix and two small santos. Above the altar were emblazoned not the familiar Latin letters *JHS*, but, surmounting a palm branch of victory, the Greek capital letters *JHP*, for the word *Jerusalem*.

The choir loft of Cuzárare was old, and its beams were nicely carved. But interesting as was the loft, the pulpit was as well done as any I've seen in the sierra. It was on the epistle side of the nave, just short of the crossing, and consisted of a rather small platform with paneled wood sides, supported by a single carved post extending to the floor, with a sounding board above. An arched entrance in the wall led to spiral stairs which gave access from the transept. The effect was altogether pleasing.

In April 1972, we found that Cuzárare was being substantially rebuilt, with scaffolding and timbering on all sides and a bevy of workmen, not only reroofing the building in its entirety but pointing up the adobe and replacing the fallen bell tower with what promised to be a new and similarly built piece of masonry. When we drove up and saw the flurry of activity, we were concerned over the safety of the paintings, especially when we saw that the interior had been totally stripped. When we got to Creel, we were relieved to discover that Father Verplancken had all of the paintings in safekeeping and that he was searching for the best way to have them cleaned, restored where necessary and properly stretched and framed.

This then was Los Santos Cinco Señores de Cuzárare, one of the finest of the Spanish Jesuit churches in Tarahumara, and, because of relative accessibility, one of the very few which most tourists are likely to see. Fortunately the splendid building has been faithfully restored and rebuilt by the loving hands of skilled artisans. When I saw Father Verplancken at Sisoguíchic in May 1976, he told me that this work was at last finished, and that the splendid paintings were safely back on the walls. I was pleased, because the oils are a fitting memorial for Tomás Guadalajara, for Francisco María Pícolo, for José Neumann and for all the other Jesuits who strove so hard against such bitter odds to bring Christianity and European culture to a distant outpost of New Spain between 1611 and 1767.

Part III

Reference Material

Abbreviations

To conserve space, abbreviations have been used freely in the Biographical Directory and the Notes to the Chapters. If only one work by a particular author has been used as reference, that work is cited by the author's last name only. If more than one work by an author has been used, the author's name and the date of the specified work appear in the note. For frequently used works and works without authors, abbreviated titles have been cited. A list of these abbreviations appears below. Full entries for all works cited in the Notes and in the Biographical Directory are of course to be found in the Bibliography.

ABZ—Alegre, *Historia.*

Administrative Census of 1728—*Nominas de los Indios que contienen las misiones . . . . de la Compañía de Jesus.*

AGN, *Hist.*—Archivo General y Público de la Nación, *Historia*—México.

AGN, *Mis.*—Archivo General y Público de la Nación, *Misiones*—México.

AHH, *Temp.*—Archivo Histórico de Hacienda, *Temporalidades*—México.

AHSJ—Archivum Historicum Societatis Jesu—Rome.

Annua 1646 — *Letras Annuas de la Provincia* . . . . *Año de 1646.*

Annua 1667 — *Letras Annuas de la Provincia* . . . . *Año de 1667.*

APM—Archivo de la Provincia de México—México.

ARSJ—Archivum Romanum Societatis Jesu—Rome.

Arch., *Cárichic*—Archivo de la Iglesia, Cárichic.

Arch., *Guerrero* — Archivo de la Iglesia de la Purísima Concepción—Ciudad Guerrero.

Arch., *Parral*—Archivo Público, Parral.

Arch., *Sisoguíchic* — Archivo de la Iglesia — Sisoguíchic.

Bandelier—*Historical Documents.*

Burrus 1971—Salvatierra, *Selected Letters.*

Catálogo 1716-1720 — *Cathalogo de las Missiones de Esta Provincia de Cinaloa* . . . . *desde el Año de 1716 hasta el de 1720.*

Catálogo de Sonora—*Catálogo de los Partidos* . . . . *de Sonora por el año de 1658 (1685).*

Chihuahuenses—Almada, *Diccionario de Historia, Geografía y Biografía Chihuahuenses.*

Doc. Hist. Méx.—*Documentos para la Historia de México.*

EJMT—Dunne, *Early Jesuit Missions in Tarahumara.*

Estado de Norogáchic—*Estado de esta Visitación de Nuestra Señora del Pilar de Norógachic.*

Etimología—Almada, "Etimología de la Palabra Chihuahua."

González—González Rodríguez, Notes to Neumann, *Revoltes.*

Introduction—Christelow, Introduction to Neumann, *Letters* tr. by *Reynolds.*

Libro I—*Libro de Bautismos de Cárichic.*

Libro II—*Libro de Casamientos de Cárichic.*

Libro III—*Libro de Difuntos de Cárichic.*

Libro IV—*Libro de la Parroquia de Norogáchic.*

Libro V—*Libro de Bautismos de Papigóchic.*

Libro VI—*Libro de Bautismos de Santo Tomás.*

Libro VII—*Libro de Casamientos de Santo Tomás.*

Libro VIII—*Libro de Bautismos de Temeýchic.*

Libros I—*Libros Parroquiales de Cárichic.*

Libros II—*Libros Parroquiales de Santo Tomás.*

Lumholtz, *Bulletin* 1891—"Report on Explorations in Northern Mexico."

———— Nov. 1891—"Explorations in the Sierra Madre."

————, *Bulletin* 1894—"The American Cave Dwellers: The Tarahumaris of the Sierra Madre."

————, *Proceedings* 1894—"Cave Dwellers of the Sierra Madre."

———— July 1894—"Among the Tarahumaris—The American Cave Dwellers."

———— Sept. 1894—"Tarahumari Life and Customs."

———— Oct. 1894—"Tarahumari Dances and Plant Worship."

Misiones—Burrus, *Misiones Norteñas Mexicanos.*

Obra—Decorme, *La Obra de los Jesuitas Mexicanas.*

Pobladores—Almada, "Los Primeros Pobladores de Santa Eulalia y San Francisco de Cuéllar."

Resumen—Almada, *Resumen de Historia del Estado de Chihuahua.*

Robles — Notes to Tamarón y Romeral, *Demostracion.*

Roca — Paul Roca, *Paths of the Padres.*

Saravia, *Historia*—Saravia, *Apuntes para la Historia de la Nueva Vizcaya.*

S. J.—Societatis Jesu.

Biographical Directory

Note: Since most non-Spanish Jesuits working in New Spain before the expulsion either Hispanicized the spelling of their names or adopted more Iberian forms, Spanish spelling has been used for names in most of the following entries.

ABEÉ, JULIÁN FERNÁNDEZ. See FERNÁNDEZ.

AGUIRRE, SALVADOR MARTÍNEZ. See MARTÍNEZ.

ALAVEZ, LUIS, S. J., was born in Oaxaca in 1589, studied in Oaxaca and México and became a Jesuit in 1607. He seems to have gone to the Tepehuán mission field in that year, and was stationed with Juan del Valle at Zape on November 18, 1616, when both were killed at Mass. His body was recovered and taken to Guadiana for burial on March 7, 1617. Zambrano, III, 157–195; *EJMT*, 27–29; Saravia 1943, 60; ABZ, II, 275, n. 15; Bancroft, I, 323; Decorme, *Mártires*, 48, 49 and n. 3.

ALDERETE, FLORENCIO, S. J., was born in Tlalpujahua, Michoacán, in 1656. He joined the Society in 1671, studied grammar in Valladolid in 1678 and then commenced the study of theology in México. He came to Tarahumara in 1683 and spent 36 years in the area, serving at Cocomórachic until the 1690 revolt. After peace, he took over Mátachic and, except for a year in Cocomórachic, stayed until the 1697 rebellion. He sat the war out in Papigóchic, and was then assigned to Norogáchic. He acted as military chaplain, was rector from 1690 to 1696 and visitador from 1711 to 1714. He interrupted his service at Norogáchic to act as visitador to the Chínipas mission and to help out, briefly, at the mission of San Joaquín and Santa Ana. He died at Norogáchic on December 8, 1719. Neumann, *Historia*, 205, 321, n. 176; Neumann 1698; *Introduction,* 49; González, 40, n. 6, 45, n. 13, 61, n. 48, 62, n. 49, 87, n. 43, 89, n. 46, 116, n. 105, 157, n. 170, 184, n. 31; Olave; *Libro IV.*

ALTIMIRANO, GARCÍA LEGAZPI VELASCO Y.   See LEGAZPI.

ALVAREZ, LUCAS LUIS, S. J., was born in Veracruz on October 27, 1688, and became a Jesuit on September 18, 1706. He was ordained in 1714 and taught in the colleges at Oaxaca in 1718, Monterrey in 1719, and Puebla in 1721. He became ill in 1722 and went to Tarahumara at least by 1726, but returned to the south again to be rector of the college at Sinaloa in 1730. According to Andonaegui, he was at Papigóchic "some years" before January 1748, but his name does not appear in *Libro V,* which has no entry before July 1742. Alvarez is reported to have served as visitador in Chínipas in 1742, which suggests that his tour of duty at Papigóchic ended late in 1741 or early in the following year. In 1747 he was visitador general, and in 1751 he served as superior of the Sinaloa missions, stationed at the Villa de Sinaloa. He was still at Sinaloa, as rector, in 1775. He died in Sinaloa in 1760. He was also a poet, having produced, in hexameter, *La Angelomaquia y La Josefina*. Dunne 1957, 70; *Obra*, I, 155, II, 244; *Misiones*, 93, 97; *Libro IV;* Zambrano-Gutiérrez, XV, 128–129.

ANDONAEGUI, ROQUE, S. J., was born in México on January 4, 1707, and became a Jesuit on October 23, 1723. He took his first orders in 1724 and taught grammar in Guadalajara in 1730. He reached the northern mission field at least by September 13, 1741, when his signature first appears in the register at Temeýchic. Andonaegui was accused of spending much time drinking and gambling in Cusihuiriáchic, where it was alleged he built and at mission expense furnished a fine house for his mistress, a daughter of the Góngora family. It was charged that she bore him three children, two sons and a daughter, and that his relationship with her was open and notorious, particularly because when visiting her overnight, he left his horse tied in front of the house.

The visitador Lorenzo Gera recommended his removal, but he was defended by Francisco Glandorff. Gera offered him a transfer to Sonora, and when Father Roque didn't accept, Gera ordered him to Durango to await trial. Andonaegui refused to leave Temeýchic, but the next visitador, Juan Manuel Hierro, issued a peremptory order that he deliver over the partido, and his last entry in the Temeýchic register is dated June 7, 1747. After Roque left, it was discovered that he and the mission were heavily in debt, not only for supplies and materials used in the partial construction of the church, but for goods which he had sent to California to barter for pearls. The accused priest tarried for a time in Cusi and Chihuahua, but reached Durango in October, stoutly denying any guilt. He had the support not only of Glandorff but also of Marcos Sánchez de Tagle, the vicar and ecclesiastical judge at Cusi, and his assistant, Francisco Zárate. The details and results of the disciplinary proceeding are recorded in nothing I have seen. In 1749 he was in Oaxaca, remaining there until at least 1761, but he was at San Andrés in México in 1764. At the expulsion Andonaegui was at the college in Valladolid, from whence he was transported to Spain. He died in prison at Puerto de Santa María on July 24, 1768. Zelis, 6–7, 121, 145; Andonaegui June 1744; Andonaegui Dec. 1744; Andonaegui Sept. 1747; Andonaegui Oct. 1747; Andonaegui 1748; Gera May 1747; Gera Oct. 25, 1747; Glandorff July 1747; González Noboa June 1747; González Noboa July 1747; Gutiérrez Ruiz; Hierro June 1747; Hierro Aug. 23, 1747; Hierro Aug. 30, 1747; Hierro Nov. 1747; Osorio 1747; Padilla; Palma; Sánchez, *Carta a Escobar;* Sánchez, *Carta al Provincial;* Téllez; Zárate; *Libro VIII;* Zambrano-Gutiérrez, XV, 141–142.

ARAGÓN, JUAN ANTONIO, S. J., born in 1685 in Durango, entered the Order in 1703, was in the mission field by 1711, was stationed at Santa María de las Cuevas in 1723, and in 1731 was in charge of Los Cinco Señores, later Nasas, a Tepehuán mission. The visitador in that year reported that Aragón was more inclined to favor the

Biographical Directory 237

Spaniards than the Indians, owed $400 and because of his laziness would probably be more heavily in debt. He died at Tepehuanes on January 27, 1737. González, 201, n. 65; *Obra*, II, 79; Zambrano-Gutiérrez, XV, 164.

ARETZAMOVSKY, ANTONIO, S. J. I don't believe such a person existed, but conclude, from the information in Chapter 8, note 26, that Braun 1765 wrote Aretzamovsky when he meant Strzanowski.

ARIAS IBARRA, ANTONIO, S. J., is one-third of a biographical jigsaw puzzle. There were three Jesuits in New Spain named Antonio Arias, and everyone since has done some mixing up. The first, and the one least likely to be confused with either of the others, was born about 1561, wrote learned works on theological subjects, and died in México in 1603. Zambrano, III, 494–512. The second Antonio Arius was born in Santa Ana, Guatemala, on July 26, 1660, and entered the Society in 1677. He finished his studies in 1689 and was sent to the Sonora missions. He arrived the following year and was assigned by Eusebio Francisco Kino to Tubutama, building its first church and gathering 500 Pimas to greet Kino and the visitador, Juan María Salvatierra, when they arrived on Epiphany, 1691. Arias left in 1693 and three years later became the first rector of the new seminary of San Gerónimo at Puebla. In 1703 he was assigned to the Philippines, where he was still active in 1708. *Obra*, II, 382, and n. 11, 384; Roca, 103; Bolton, 262; ABZ, IV, 176, and n. 34; Kino, I, 116; Zambrano-Gutiérrez, XV, 182.

Antonio Arias Ibarra was born in México in 1676 and entered the Society in 1694. After finishing his studies he went to Tarahumara and was rector of the partido of San Joaquín y Santa Ana by 1708, possibly as early as 1707. In 1716 he founded Chinarras, and even though he became visitador of Tarahumara in 1717 and assisted in the establishment of the college in Chihuahua, he remained in charge of Santa Ana until 1721. In the latter year he went to Nayarit in response to the provincial's instructions of the year before, founding at least three mission pueblos and serving as visitador for a term beginning in 1723. He returned to Tarahumara before 1727 and was at Santo Tomás until April of that year, when he dropped out of sight. He died on March 28, 1732 in Nayarit. *Chihuahuenses*, 158; Guenduláin, 23; *Obra*, I, 111; II, 311, 549,

550–555, 552; González, 184, n. 31, 195, n. 53, 200, n. 60; Arias Dec. 4, 1718; Arias Dec. 21, 1718; *Libro VI;* ABZ, IV, 255, and n. 6, 287, 288, 292; Zambrano-Gutiérrez, XV, 182–183.

ARMAS, JOSÉ, S. J., was born in Querétaro in 1679, and entered the Order twenty years later. He taught in the seminary at Guadalajara in 1708 and went to Tarahumara in 1714. Where he was stationed from 1714 to 1723 is uncertain, but it was not (as suggested by Gutiérrez) at the colegio in Chihuahua, where classes didn't begin until 1720. By 1725 he had left Chihuahua for Bacerac, in Sonora, and a year later he was transferred to Nacámeri. In 1727 he went to Batuc, where he died on February 2, 1731. ABZ, IV, 321, n. 3; Zambrano-Gutiérrez, XV, 187–188.

ARTEAGA, FRANCISCO, S. J., was born in Guatemala about 1648 and entered the Society in 1663. In 1677 he was assigned to Nonoava, where he stayed until 1684. He was rector of the college of Pátzcuaro in 1687, of Guatemala in 1690, of Tepotzotlán in 1693 and of Espíritu Santo in Puebla in 1699. He served as provincial of New Spain from 1699 until 1702 and during his tenure founded the seminary of San Ignacio in Puebla. From 1708 until his death on April 2, 1715, he lived at the college of San Andrés in México. In the summer after his death, he is said to have appeared to Juan María Salvatierra in a vision. Ydiáquez 1744; ABZ, IV, 152, and n. 12, 175, 234–235; *Obra,* I, 106–107.

ARTEAGA, MANUEL GUTIÉRREZ.   See GUTIÉRREZ.

BADILLO, FRANCISCO MARÍA, S. J., was born in Palencia, Spain, on October 12, 1719, and became a Jesuit on September 11, 1741. He was sent to California in 1752 and served at Santiago de los Coras from March 1, 1753, until February 1762, when, as a result of serious conflicts with Spanish miners who were, he believed, attempting to enslave the Indians, he was transferred to the mainland, presumably directly to Coyáchic. Deported to Spain and then to Italy, he died at Bologna on January 10, 1783. *Chihuahuenses,* 202, 556; Zelis, 42–43, 135, 162; *Misiones,* 102; Dunne 1937, 14; *Destierro; Obra,* I, 466, II, 512 and n. 10, 543 and n. 1.

BALLEZA, MARIANO, a secular priest, was born in Valladolid (now Morelia). He studied for the priesthood at the seminary in that city and was vicar of the parish of Dolores when Father Miguel Hidalgo Costilla, his immediate superior, issued the famous *grito* which called for revolution against Spain. Balleza enlisted in the revolutionary army, serving as lieutenant general. Captured and sentenced to death in Durango, he was executed at San Juan de Dios on July 17, 1812. *Chihuahuenses,* 59; *Diccionario Porrúa,* 169.

BALTHASAR, JUAN ANTONIO, S.J., was born on April 10, 1697, in Luzern and became a Jesuit on October 27, 1712, in the province of Venice. In 1719 he went to México, studying at the Colegio Máximo before ordination in 1722. Two years after ordination he was the missionary at San Andrés and Topia, in Nueva Vizcaya, and from 1736 until 1744 he served as rector of the Colegio de San Gregorio de México. In the latter year he was appointed visitador general, a post he relinquished in 1747 to become rector of the Colegio Máximo. He succeeded Andrés García as provincial on August 31, 1750, and in that capacity reported to Rome that in 60 years the Jesuit missionaries in New Spain had misappropriated a million and a half pesos, charges which were later disproved by the official report of Licenciado Martín Arámburu, the royal fisc between 1789 and 1794. Balthasar's term as provincial expired on August 31, 1753, and in 1755 he began a three-year term as rector of the Colegio de San Andrés de México and an indefinite term as procurador de misiones. He still occupied the latter position at his death in México on April 23, 1763. ABZ, IV, 15*, 314, n. 30; Dunne 1957, 33, 37, 38–39, 41, 43; *Libro IV;* Zambrano-Gutiérrez, XV, 227–281.

BAÑUELOS, FRANCISCO, S.J., was in charge of the Tepehuán partido of Santa Catalina in 1678, was administrator of the Jesuit haciendas at Parral in 1689, and in 1694 was rector of the college at San Luis Potosí. At least by 1708 he was back in the mission field, somewhere in Tarahumara Antigua. In 1723 he was visitador of those missions, but was stationed at Las Bocas. He died not long thereafter. Ortiz, 313; González, 184, n. 31, 201, n. 65; *Obra,* II, 77; Zambrano-Gutiérrez, XV, 281.

BARLI, JUAN BAUTISTA, S.J., an Italian, was at Cajuríchic in 1692, but by January 1693 was in Guadalajara. Later in the same year he went to Pimería Alta, where he took charge of Imuris and Cocóspera. He died at Cucurpe on January 3, 1694, and was buried in that church. González, 62, n. 49; ABZ, IV, 108–109, n. 22; *Obra,* II, 382, n. 11; Bolton, 270.

BARRAZA, JUAN, was described by a contemporary as the Spanish captain of whom the Indians were more afraid than any other. In 1623 he was in command of the presidio of Tepehuanes, and seven years later was assigned by Governor Hipólito Velasco to accompany Father Juan Heredía on an entrada which penetrated as far as Nonoava. He was assigned to Parral after the mines were discovered, serving as alcalde mayor. Not long thereafter he was appointed to command the presidio at Cerro Gordo, from which he took part in numerous punitive expeditions. In 1644 he successfully pacified the Tobosos, driving them as far as Río Bravo. When the Tarahumara disturbances began in 1648, he took the field from Cerro Gordo with 40 soldiers and engaged a much larger native force near Cárichic. In January 1649, he was joined in the field by the new governor, Diego Guajardo Fajardo, with 40 soldiers and 300 Indian auxiliaries. After three months of fighting, the Tarahumaras asked for peace, bringing in the heads of four of their leaders.

Barraza is said to have crossed Río Papigóchic and penetrated far into the sierra, showing a "demoniac spirit of vengeance." He is credited, undoubtedly with more enthusiasm than accuracy, with having destroyed 300 Indian settlements and burned 4,000 fanegas of corn.

By June 1650, when the frontier again erupted, he had been promoted to general. Again he took the field, this time chasing the Tarahumaras to an inaccessible peñol, where 6,000 Indians were attacked by Barraza's forces, augmented by soldiers from Parral under the command of Captain Manuel García Morales, and by a force under Governor Guajardo. There was no clear-cut victory, but the Indians retired from the peñol at night, García and the governor returned to the south, and Barraza "remained to ravage the country and harass the fugitive rebels" until peace, largely the result of exhaustion, was finally restored. *Introduction,* 19; Pascual 1651, 187, 193; Jordán, 75, 78–79; Bancroft, I, 333–334, 348, 349, 354–358; Saravia 1954, III, 277; *Obra*, II, 254, 271; González, 9, n. 4; Zepeda, 133; *Chihuahuenses,* 63.

BARRERA, DIEGO FELIPE JOSÉ, S.J., was born in Puebla on July 28, 1726, and joined the Society on February 29, 1744. In 1755 he was at Maicoba, but two years later he was in charge of Cumuripa, in Sonora. In July 1759, he baptized at Papigóchic, but not long thereafter, and certainly by 1761, he took over Santa María Suamca, in Pimería Alta. He was still at Suamca at the expulsion, which must mean that he was visiting when he baptized in Papigóchic in July and August 1764. Imprisoned for ten years in Spain, he died in a convent in Córdoba on March 2, 1782. *Misiones,* 98; *Libro V;* Roca, 369, n. 32; Zelis, 6–7, 134, 147; *Obra*, II, 429, n. 11; Pradeau, *Expulsión,* 130, 131.

BARRIONUEVO, FERNANDO, S.J., was born in Aguilar, in Andalucía, in 1627, entered the Society in 1642, and completed his studies after he reached México in 1645. He was assigned to the Sinaloa missions in 1661 or perhaps as early as 1659. In 1662 he was stationed at Huásabas, in Sonora, from which he also served Yécora and Oputo. He was transferred to Tarahumara and in September 1673, attended a strategy session at Parral, thereafter going north with Father Juan Gamboa to reopen Tarahumara Alta. With Gamboa in the winter of 1673–74, he began the work of establishing San Bernabé and reestablishing Papigóchic, but his health broke early in 1674 and he returned to Satevó, where he apparently remained until 1680 or 1681. In the latter year he was vice rector of the college at Durango, in 1683 he was at Veracruz, and in 1684 he was rector at Puebla. He died at Querétaro on July 8, 1686. *Chihuahuenses,* 64, 214, 481; *EJMT,* 98, 101, 104; *Introduction,* 29–30; Christelow 1939, 427; Jordán, 115; Bancroft, I, 363; *Obra,* II, 284, and n. 2; González, 22, n. 1; ABZ, III, 315, n. 4; Roca, 220, 404, n. 51; Zambrano, IV, 36–41.

BASALDÚA, JOSÉ, S.J., was in charge of Guazápares, Témoris and Valle Umbroso at least by 1716, but early in 1723 he was transferred to the college in Chihuahua. He served briefly in Norogáchic before June 1728. González, 201, n. 66; *Catálogo 1716–1720;* ABZ, IV, 321, n. 3; *Libro IV.*

BASILIO, GIACOMO ANTONIO, S.J., was born in Bari, Italy, in 1609; he entered the Society in 1630 and then came to New Spain in 1642. He was at the college in Tepotzotlán for five years, then served in the college of San Gregorio in México and as a visiting missionary at Indian posts in the Archdiocese of México. When word of the martyrdom of Cornelio Beudín reached the capital, Basilio asked to take his place. He apparently reached Papigóchic in the summer of 1651, rebuilding the church and working at outlying visitas. When the third revolt erupted on March 2, 1652, Basilio was at Temeýchic, but he promptly returned to Papigóchic and, with his servant from San Miguel de las Bocas, was killed the following day. As was the case with Beudín (see p. 243) he was hung from an arm of the cross before the burning church. Eight months after his death, his body was recovered and buried temporarily in Villa Aguilar, in the coffin with his predecessor. In 1653 both priests were reinterred in San Felipe. Zambrano, IV, 75–89; Pérez 1896, II, 550–552; *EJMT,* 69–70, 72–74; Neumann, *Historia,* 148, 150; *Introduction,* 22–23; Christelow 1939, 427; Pascual 1651, 197–198, 200; Jordán, 80–82; Saravia 1943, 103–105; Saravia 1954, III, 319–320, 323–324; Bancroft, I, 358; *Obra,* II, 271, n. 21, 272–274; Decorme, *Mártires,* 73–75; González, 12, n. 12, 13, n. 16.

BENAVIDES, MARTÍN, S.J., was born in Villanueva del Arzobispo, in the province of Jaén, Spain, about 1665 and became a Jesuit in 1683. He was at the Casa Profesa in México by 1692, and may have gone to the Chínipas mission as early as 1693. It seems more likely that he didn't get to the north until 1696, but it is certain that he served at various Chínipas locations until 1720. When the 1697 revolt erupted, he was in charge of the pueblos of Moris and Batopilillas, whose churches were burned by the rebels. After the final victory at Guadalupe in September, Benavides prepared the Indian captives for execution, and all died Christians. Beginning in 1698, he extended his work to the east and around the turn of the century crossed the barranca and baptized among the Pámachi and Sámachi. Benavides served at one time as rector of the Chínipas mission and was visitador from 1717 to 1720, his service being marked by the February 9, 1718, order which resulted in the official founding of Guaguevo, Pámachic and Guaguáchic in April and May of that year. From 1720 until 1723 he served as visitador of Tarahumara Antigua, and then left the area to become rector of the college at San Luis Potosí, where he died on March 30, 1724. Neumann 1698; Bannon, 31; Pennington 1963, 11; *Obra*, II, 234, 235, 241, n. 31; González, 112, n. 98, 205, n. 73; Rezawal 1797; *Thirteen Reports;* ABZ, IV, 132, n. 26; Almada 1937, 87.

BEUDÍN, CORNELIO, S.J., a Belgian, was born in Gravelines, France, November 25, 1615, became a Jesuit on April 3, 1635; and was ordained in 1645. Assigned to New Spain, he changed his surname to Godínez and joined a group of Jesuits which left Cádiz with the procurador, Andrés Pérez de Rivas, on July 13, 1647, arriving in Veracruz on September 20 of that year. From México he was sent north, reaching San Miguel de las Bocas in December 1647, or February 1648. He was briefly at Satevó with Vigilio Máez, but was soon at San Felipe de Jesús, studying Rarámuri and assisting José Pascual. The following year, when Governor Guajardo established Villa Aguilar, Pascual, as the superior, assigned Beudín to serve the Tarahumaras at nearby Papigóchic as well as the soldiers at the presidio. The Belgian built the church of La Purísima Concepción, a short distance from the garrison, and said his first Mass by the fall of 1649. About May 15, 1650, he gave the last rites to a child, who then died. The hechizeros blamed the death on the sacrament, and on June 4, 1650, the Tarahumaras revolted, killing Father Beudín and a soldier who served as his companion and protector. Both men were riddled with arrows, the soldier was decapitated, and each body was lashed to an arm of the cross in front of the burning church. Soldiers from the presidio recovered the bodies the next day and buried them near the presidial chapel at Villa Aguilar. Two years later, after the martyrdom of Father Giacomo Basilio, the bodies of both priests were put in the same coffin at Papigóchic, but both were moved to San Felipe in 1653. Zambrano, VII, 174–199; Pérez 1896, II, 544–549; *EJMT*, 47, 55, 61, 64–66; Neumann, *Historia,* 148–149; *Introduction,* 21–22; Pascual 1651, 180, 186, 190; Jordán, 77–78; Saravia 1943, 99–102; Saravia 1954, III, 307, 315–316, 319; Bancroft, I, 348,

353, 355–356; *Obra*, II, 268–271; González, 11, n. 10, 12, n. 12, 13, n. 14, n. 16.

Unfortunately Father Dunne was confused as to the time of Beudín's arrival in Tarahumara, since in *EJMT*, 47, he puts him there shortly after Figueroa and Pascual (who arrived in 1639) and (on the basis of a letter in AGN, *Mis.*, tomo 25, fol. 399) has him reporting that his mission was progressing satisfactorily in May 1646. González, 11, n. 10, suggests that since Beudín was still in Europe in 1646, Dunne misread the location from which the letter was sent. But González didn't see the letter. Written in Latin and dated May 18, 1646, it doesn't say where it was written but mentions Father Vigilio Máez, thus making it certain that Beudín's pen slipped and he wrote 1646 for 1648.

BOSQUE, FRANCISCO, S.J., was ordained on February 15, 1705, in Puebla, and in 1708 was briefly in Tutuaca. In both 1719 and 1723 he was at Satevó. González, 184, n. 31, 201, n. 65; Zambrano-Gutiérrez, XV, 346.

BRAUN, BARTOLOMÉ, S.J., was born in Montebourg, France, on June 27, 1718, and became a Jesuit in 1736. He came to Tarahumara in 1750 and served briefly at Tutuaca and Yepáchic before 1751, when he went to Yoquivo and stayed at least until 1755, and probably until 1758. In the latter year he went to Temósachic, where he remained until the expulsion, serving as superior of Tarahumara Alta in 1761. He died at sea on December 5, 1767. *EJMT*, 208, 226, 232, 234; Dunne 1937, 14, 18; Lizasoaín, *Noticia*, 21; *Chihuahuenses*, 74, 202; Zelis, 8, 9, 139, 147; Braun 1765; *Misiones*, 94, 98, 102; *Destierro; Obra*, II, 303. Bancroft, I, 599, n. 24, says Braun was at Guaguáchic in 1751, but it seems doubtful.

CALDERÓN, FELIPE, S.J., was born in México in 1685 and joined the Society of Jesus in 1704. He was ordained in 1715 and four years later went to the Jesuit residence and college under construction in Chihuahua. I have found no record of how long he stayed, but by 1723 he was at Baburigame and in both 1730 and 1737 he was still in Tarahumara Antigua. By 1744 Calderón was at Santa María de las Cuevas, which he had probably taken over after the death of

Balthasar de la Peña the preceding year. He was still there in 1748 but left before 1751. His *Report* was written from Santa María, probably in 1744. Calderón; *Misiones*, 91, 95; González, 201, n. 65; Zambrano-Gutiérrez, XV, 376.

CALDERÓN, JOSÉ, S.J., was born in Comayagua, Nicaragua, on August 8, 1691, and became a Jesuit on July 31, 1718. He was ordained in 1725 and by 1730 was at San Francisco Javier in Sonora. He baptized at Santo Tomás on February 22 in a year which is not stated but must have been 1730. His signature is on the same page as that of Benito Crespo, bishop of Durango from 1723 until 1734, and he may well have accompanied the bishop to the north. The date of Crespo's visit to Santo Tomás is unstated, but he was at Temeýchic on February 11, 1730. In 1744 Calderón was at Las Bocas and four years later he was at the Durango college. Thereafter he served at the colleges in Puebla and Zacatecas and when the expulsion order came, he was an invalid at the Colegio del Espíritu Santo de Puebla. He died in Veracruz on August 18, 1767. *Libro VI; Libro VIII;* Zelis, 10–11, 114, 148.

CALVO, JUAN, S.J., was at Yepómera as a temporary replacement for Juan Bautista Haller in 1692. González, 62, n. 49. He should not be confused with the Juan Calvo who was at Choix in Sinaloa from 1611 until 1620. *Obra*, II, ix, 191.

CARRAL, ANTONIO DE SAN JOSÉ.   See SAN JOSÉ.

CARTA, AGUSTÍN, S.J., was born in Serramanna, Sardinia, on May 31, 1698, and entered the Order on his eighteenth birthday. He went to New Spain in 1733 and in 1737 was at the residencia in Guanajuato. In 1744 he became secretary to the provincial and two years later was appointed rector of the college at Querétaro. Father Carta was visitador general in 1751, and served as rector of the Colegio Máximo de México from the conclusion of his tour of duty to his election as provincial in January 1755. From 1760 to the expulsion he was at the Casa Profesa in México. From there he was taken to Veracruz, where he died on August 8, 1767. ABZ, IV, 15*, 442, n. 1; Zelis, 12–13, 107, 148; *Libro IV*; Zambrano-Gutiérrez, XV, 430–452.

CASTAÑEDA, MARCOS FERNÁNDEZ.   See FERNÁNDEZ.

CASTILLO, MIGUEL, S.J., was born in México on August 2, 1707, and after studying medicine entered the Society in 1726. He was ordained in 1733, taught at Valladolid (Morelia) in 1737, at Parral from 1744 until 1748, at Tepotzotlán, at the Casa Profesa and, after 1751, at the Colegio Máximo in México, where he was stationed at the expulsion. He died in Veracruz on December 12, 1767. ABZ, IV, 407, n. 43; *Obra*, I, 283, 285; Zelis, 12, 148; Zambrano-Gutiérrez, XV, 468–469.

CASTILLO, RODRIGO, S.J., was born in Puebla in 1621 and entered the Society in 1638. He studied and taught in the college at Valladolid until 1651, when he went north, first to San Luis de la Paz and then to Las Bocas. In June 1667, when he was returning with a party of Spaniards and Indians to Las Bocas from Tizonazo, a rebel band of Tobosos attacked, killed and mutilated all the priest's companions, and carried him into the mountains. After serious emotional and physical suffering, he was released, but died on August 15, 1668. Zambrano, V, 25–33; ABZ, III, 226 and n. 18, 289–291; Saravia 1954, 335; *Introduction*, 25, 27; Figueroa 1668, 226–227; Pascual 1651, 206; Bancroft, I, 360, 362.

CELADA, FRANCISCO, S.J., was born in Alcalá de Henares, Spain, on July 14, 1648, joined the Order in 1665 and came to México in the same year. He studied humanities and rhetoric at Tepotzotlán from 1667 until 1669 and taught in the seminary of San Ildefonso in 1671. He was ordained in 1673 and sent to Conicari on Río Mayo, serving until the following year when he came across the sierra to take charge of San Francisco Borja. He was visitador of the Tarahumara missions during the term ending in April 1690, when, his place as visitor having been taken by Francisco María Pícolo, he was named rector of the college at Durango. He either didn't serve or delayed the beginning of his service until February 1691, when he was still at Borja. In 1692 he became rector of the college at Querétaro, remaining until 1696, when he returned to San Francisco Borja. He died there on January 28, 1707. *Introduction*, 88, n. 145; *Obra*, II, 285, 302, 305–306; González, 54, n. 34, 61, n. 48, 62, n. 49, 76, n. 20, 184, n. 31, 492, n. 22; ABZ, IV, 82, n. 36, 210, n. 21; Zambrano-Gutiérrez, XV, 481.

CEPEDA, NICOLÁS. See ZEPEDA.

CISNEROS, BERNARDO, S.J., was born in Carrión de los Condes, Spain, in 1582, and entered the Society in 1599. He came to New Spain in 1605, completed his studies in 1609 and went to the mission field the following year. He was stationed first at Papasquiaro, but served throughout the Tepehuán area before he and Diego Orozco died in the Tepehuán revolt on November 18, 1616. His body was not identified in the ruins at Papasquiaro. Zambrano, V, 183–225; Saravia 1943, 54–55; ABZ, II, 274, n. 12; Decorme, *Mártires,* 46, 48, 49 and n. 2; *EJMT,* 27–29; *Chihuahuenses,* 101; Bancroft, I, 323.

CONDARCO, CRISTÓBAL, S.J., became a Jesuit on April 20, 1681, and was at Huejotitlán in 1692. By 1708 he was in Oaxaca, at the colegio, and eleven years later his name was on the register at the college at Veracruz. González, 62, n. 49; Zambrano-Gutiérrez, XV, 507.

CONTRERAS, DIEGO RUIZ. See RUIZ.

COPART, JUAN BAUTISTA, S.J., said to have been a Belgian, was born in Tourcoing, France, in 1643, and entered the Society in 1662. He was to have been assigned to Guazápares in 1678 but went instead, probably in the following year, to Papigóchic. In the early fall of 1681 he heard rumors of a threatened revolt and fled to San Francisco Borja, but returned before long. In 1684 he was assigned as the third Jesuit (with Eusebio Kino and Matías Goñi) on the ill-fated California venture of Admiral Isidro Atondo y Antillón. He arrived on the peninsula on August 10, 1684, wrote a grammar of the Edú or Monquí tongue, and returned to the mainland in December, bringing three Indian boys as exhibits to promote help for the mission. The abandonment of the venture in August 1685, was said to have been such a shock that he lost his reason and had not recovered as late as 1702. From 1694 until 1708 he was at the Colegio Máximo or various haciendas operated by the college, and was living at a ranch near México when Salvatierra called on him to borrow his grammar before leaving for California. In 1708 he was at the college in Tepotzotlán, where he died on June 2, 1711. *EJMT,* 155, 157; Dunne 1952, 33–34, 43; Neumann

1682; *Introduction,* 38, 39, 47; Bannon, 27; Ortiz, 391; ABZ, IV, 14, n. 52, 56, n. 7, 56–57, 73, 134, n. 32; Bolton, 167, 168, 173, 231; Kino, 45, 49, n. 34; *Obra*, II, 478, n. 2; Zambrano-Gutiérrez, XV, 512.

CÓRDOVA, JUAN FERNÁNDEZ.   See FERNÁNDEZ.

CORRO, ILDEFONSO, S.J., was born in Córdoba, Veracruz, on April 22, 1732, and entered the Order in 1746. He was in charge of Norogáchic by 1762 but in 1765 was transferred to Sisoguíchic, from which he was expelled. He died at Veracruz on November 15, 1767, four days before the Jesuit prisoners sailed for Havana. Lizasoaín, *Noticia*, 24; *Chihuahuenses*, 122; Zelis, 14, 15, 135, 148; Braun 1765; *Misiones*, 102; *Destierro*; Zambrano-Gutiérrez, XV, 518.

COSÍO, DOMINGO, S.J., was born in Lombardy on August 30, 1710, joined the Society on April 30, 1728, and was ordained on November 3, 1737. He was promptly sent to Sinaloa and then Sonora, serving in 1741 at Aconchi and Guásabas, Sonora. In 1742 he was sent back to México by the visitador, but before long was permitted to return to the mission field. Soon after taking charge of Papigóchic in February 1746, he bought a nearby ranch, Estancia de Tezcatzi, and became so harsh with the Indians that the cabecera was nearly deserted. Juan Manuel Hierro, the visitador, grew progressively more apoplectic as he sought Cosío's removal throughout 1747, but the ranching priest didn't leave until September 1748. In 1751 he was at the college in Celaya, and four years later went to Espíritu Santo de Puebla. In 1764 he was transferred to the college at Valladolid, where he was arrested at the expulsion. He died in Rome on July 20, 1789. *EJMT*, 212; Zelis, 14–15, 100, 122, 149; *Misiones*, 91; Hierro June 1747; Hierro Aug. 23, 1747; Hierro Aug. 30, 1747; Hierro, Nov. 1747; *Libro V,* Zambrano-Gutiérrez, XV, 522–523.

CRÉSCOLI, DOMINGO, S.J., was born in Napoli in 1644 and became a Jesuit in 1664. He came to New Spain in 1687 and to Tarahumara either in 1688 with Jorge Hostinsky and Guillermo Illing or in

1690 with Juan Verdier. In either case it is certain that Créscoli was at Papigóchic in 1690 and that when peace was restored he had gone to the Colegio del Espíritu Santo in Puebla. In January 1706, he was assigned to work under Eusebio Kino in Sonora, and put in charge of Caborca, but by 1708 he had returned to Puebla and been replaced by Luis Velarde. He died on January 21, 1715, in Puebla. González, 40, n. 5, n. 6, 62, n. 49; *Obra*, II, 412, 413; Bolton, 534, n. 1, 538; Kino, II, 159; Roca, 118; Donohue 1957, 122, n. 17; Zambrano-Gutiérrez, XV, 527–528.

CUÉLLAR, LOPE, was the captain of the Royal Infantry Regiment whom the viceroy commissioned to execute, in Nueva Vizcaya, the order expelling the Jesuits. On June 26, 1767, he arrested the priests at the college in Parral, sending them to Zacatecas. Four days later he arrived at Chihuahua, where he arrested the four Jesuits who were at the college, sent Lieutenant Diego Becerril to arrest the Jesuits in the province of Chínipas, and after a short time proceeded to gather in the other priests in Tarahumara Alta. He took an inventory of the goods and possessions of the Jesuits in the colleges and missions and delivered the churches to the Franciscans. In January 1771, he received orders to rejoin his regiment in México, and in 1775 was promoted to lieutenant colonel and assigned to the Regiment of the Asturias. He died in México on March 9, 1775. *Destierro; Obra*, I, 465–466; *Resumen*, 117; *Chihuahuenses*, 127. Both Dunne 1937, 13, and *Destierro* refer to Cuéllar as governor of the province. José Carlos Agüero was governor of Nueva Vizcaya when Cuéllar arrived, and José Fayni served from 1768 until 1776. However, by appointment of Agüero, Cuéllar was military governor of Tarahumara Alta, Tarahumara Baja and of Tepehuana. *Chihuahuenses*, 18, 127, 202.

CUERVO, PEDRO, S.J., was born in México on March 15, 1735, became a Jesuit on January 21, 1757, and was ordained on October 7, 1764. He reached Nonoava, his only mission post, just in time to be expelled. He died at Cádiz on September 5, 1800, a victim of yellow fever, which struck him down just when Carlos IV gave him permission to return to New Spain. *Chihuahuenses*, 128; Zelis, 14–15, 100, 135, 149; *Misiones, 103*.

DE FRANCOS Y FERNÁNDEZ FRANCO, JUAN PARDIÑAS VILLAR. See PARDIÑAS.

DE LA OZADA, JOSÉ ZAMORA.   See ZAMORA.

DE LA PALMA, BLAS.   See PALMA.

DE LA PEÑA, BALTHASAR.   See PEÑA.

DUQUE, FELIPE, S.J., was at Las Bocas before 1662, but the dates of his service are vague. Castillo 1662 says he died of the plague and was one of three priests buried in the church. The date of his death is not given by Castillo, but a reference in Zambrano, VI, 347, indicates that he was alive in 1658. *Chihuahuenses*, 174, is certainly wrong in saying he was killed by the Tobosos in 1654, when on his way from Las Bocas to Parral.

DUQUESNEY, JUAN BAUTISTA, S.J., was born in Lille, France, in 1685, entered the order in 1705, and came to the Chínipas missions about 1719. In 1723 he was at Santa Ana, where he built a new church, but he had gone to Cerocahui by 1726, taking charge after Jacobo Doye left four years later. In 1734 he was briefly at Chínipas, returning to Cerocahui when Gabriel Urrutía was assigned to take his place. In addition to Santa Ana, he built churches in Cerocahui, Churo and Guapalaina and from Cerocahui intermittently served Guazápares, Tubares and Satevó. He served the Chínipas mission area as rector in 1729 and as visitador beginning in 1730, and was visitador of the Sinaloa missions for a term beginning in 1736. In 1741 he was assigned to Sonora, serving first in Arivechi, then moving in 1744 to Baviácora. In 1746 he was at Batuc and on May 5, 1748, he died at Banámichi. When Father Duquesney was at Cerocahui the visitador described him as very lovable, deeply religious, a great spirit, beloved of the Indians, hardworking, prudent, generous, and with a great heart. Miqueo; *Obra*, II, 239, 240, 241, 243, 244; Dunne 1957, 106; González, 201, n. 66; Almada 1937, 175; Zambrano-Gutiérrez, XV, 555–556.

EL HACHERO.   See TEPÓRACA.

ELIZACOECHEA, MARTÍN, was born in Azpilcueta, in Navarra, Spain, in 1679. A professor at Alcalá, he came to New Spain to be successively canon, archdeacon, and then dean of the cathedral in México. He was named bishop of Cuba, then, on September 6, 1736, became bishop of Durango. He visited Pimería Alta in 1737, and toured his diocese in 1740 and 1742. On March 8, 1745, he became bishop of Michoacán, and thereafter established at Valladolid, the see city, the church of Santa Rosa and the Colegio de Santa Rosa de Santa María, which he endowed. He died in Valladolid on November 19, 1756. Bancroft, I, 594; González, 129, n. 128; ABZ, IV, 9*, 10*, *Chihuahuenses,* 186; *Obra,* II, 428, n. 9; *Diccionario Porrúa*, 538; *Libro VIII; Libro V.*

ESCALANTE, PEDRO, S.J., was at San Felipe de Jesús by 1665, where, in 1666, he assisted in a miraculous cure. In 1673 he was transferred to San Miguel de las Bocas and was still there in 1678. Figueroa 1668; Ortiz, 316; *Introduction,* 29; *EJMT,* 95.

ESCALONA, JOSÉ GABRIEL, S.J., was born on March 18, 1700, in Puebla, became a Jesuit in 1716, and was ordained in 1726. In 1729 he took charge of Teópare in Sonora, and set about to build its church. The next year he moved to San Francisco Borja in Sonora, where he stayed until October 1743, when he was at Santa Ana de los Varohíos, in Chínipas. By the following June he was at Sisoguíchic, but before 1748 he had gone back to Santa Ana. In 1750 he moved to Camoa, in Sonora, where he probably stayed until 1757. Escalona; *Misiones,* 90, 94; *Obra,* II, 245; Almada 1937, 175; Roca, 289, 294, 336, 416, n. 3; Bancroft, I, 544, n. 49; Cañas, 621; Zambrano-Gutiérrez, XV, 567–568.

ESPADAS, JOSÉ IGNACIO, S.J., was born in Puebla on April 20, 1733, and entered the Society on February 22, 1750. He was at the Chihuahua residencia in 1761, as prefect of the congregation, but was at Santo Tomás by September or October 1762. By 1764 he had gone to the seminary in Durango, where he remained until the expulsion. He died in Bologna on February 23, 1799. *Chihuahuenses,* 196, 202; Zelis, 16–17, 100, 150; *Libro VI;* Zambrano-Gutiérrez, XV, 583.

ESTRADA, IGNACIO JAVIER, S.J., born in Parras, Coahuila, about 1673, became a Jesuit in 1688, and went to Tarahumara in 1699. In 1708 he was at Temeýchic and in January and February 1718, he was working with Antonio Arias and Francisco Navarrete in the construction of the college at Chihuahua. By 1719 he had returned to Temeýchic, where he served until his death late in June 1741. Andonaegui Dec. 1744; Palma; *Obra,* I, 111; González, 162, n. 181, 184, n. 31, 201, n. 65; ABZ, IV, 255, and n. 7; *Libro VIII;* Zambrano-Gutiérrez, XV, 593–594.

ESTRADA, NICOLÁS, S.J., was born in México about 1594, and entered the Society in 1611. About 1620 he went to the Tepehuán-Tarahumara country and spent some time at San Pablo. In 1625 he was at Indé but by 1626 was in Durango as superior of the Tepehuán mission. In 1630 he was transferred to Las Bocas, but by 1632 was rector of the college at Zacatecas. Two years later he was at the college at Pátzcuaro, and in 1637 or 1638 he was rector at Guadalajara. In 1648 he was rector of the Novitiate of Santa Ana in México, and in 1650 or 1651 he became rector of the Colegio del Espíritu Santo in Puebla, where he died early in 1652. Zambrano, VI, 529–563; Bandelier, II, 155; *Obra*, II, 253; *EJMT*, 33, 35, 37; ABZ, II, 434, n. 17.

ESTRADA, PEDRO, S.J., came to Satevó in 1727 and was still there ten years later. *Obra*, II, 281. Almada 1937, 175, is confused between the two towns named Satevó when he puts him in the Chínipas area after 1734.

EVÍA VALDEZ, FRANCISCO DIEGO, a native of Oviedo, Spain, and a Benedictine, was appointed the third bishop of Durango on May 17, 1639, and took possession of the see in January 1640. He spent most of his time in Parral and worked hard to expel the Franciscans and Jesuits from their mission stations. When the Toboso revolt threatened the Río Florido settlements, he ordered the Jesuits removed and the missions secularized, but he was overruled. He then sought to secularize the Franciscan establishments at Allende, Atotonilco and San Francisco de Conchos and the Jesuit partido of Huejotitlán, provoking a violent quarrel with Governor Diego Guajardo. Claiming that he did so to protect the bishop from possible harm, the governor put him under house arrest, and the bishop in turn excommunicated the governor. The Audiencia of Guadalajara ruled against the bishop, but he appealed to the Council of the Indies, which sustained the judgment in 1649. Undaunted, Evía tried again in 1650 and 1652, starting an inquiry which was finally settled (in favor of the missionaries) in 1665. But one result of the appeal to Sevilla was the bishop's transfer on November 15, 1655, to the Diocese of Oaxaca, where he served until his death on December 6, 1656. ABZ, III, 9*, 10*; *Chihuahuenses,* 198; Bancroft, I, 305, 338, 351, 360–361; *Obra*, II, 272.

EYMER, VENCESLAO, S.J., was born on November 5, 1661, in Melnik, in what became Czechoslovakia, joined the Society in 1678, and was ordained in 1690. He reached New Spain in 1692, going first to Ocoroni, Sinaloa. He was promptly sent to Tarahumara, serving at Arisiáchic, Tomóchic, and, after October 1695, Papigóchic. From 1699 until 1702 he was the Tarahumara visitador and in 1708 he served as rector. He died in Papigóchic on September 2, 1709. Neumann, *Historia*, 140, 150, 261, 279, 314, n. 126; Neumann July 1693; Neumann Sept. 1693; González, 14, n. 17, 62, n. 49, 70, n. 12, 162, n. 181, 184–185, n. 32; Fernández Retana 1700; Zambrano-Gutiérrez, XV, 600–601.

FAJARDO, DIEGO GUAJARDO. See GUAJARDO.

FERNÁNDEZ, JUAN FRANCISCO, S.J., came to Temeýchic in 1685 and was evidently exceptionally well loved, since Roque Andonaegui said in 1744 that his "memory is still as green among the Spaniards and Tarahumaras of the Real de Cusihuiriáchic and its vicinity. . . as if even now he were setting them an example with his virtues." He was reported to be in poor health as early as 1690, but didn't leave Temeýchic until 1699. He died at Malinalco, in what is now the state of México, on December 21, 1708. Andonaegui Dec. 1744; Neumann 1690; González, 154, n. 166, 157, n. 170.

FERNÁNDEZ, LUIS, S.J., was born in 1659 at Copandoro, near Morelia, and became a Jesuit in 1677. In 1690 he was at Huejotitlán, but by 1695 he was in Durango, attached to the staff of the bishop. Two years later he was again at work as a missionary, this time in Sonora, at Aconchi. He is said to have died in 1703, but the date and place are both unknown. Luis Fernández; Zambrano-Gutiérrez, XV, 612–613.

FERNÁNDEZ ABEÉ, JULIÁN ISIDRO, S.J., was born in Cusihuiriáchic on June 3, 1702, and joined the Society on June 2, 1720. He studied theology at the Colegio de San Pedro y San Pablo de México and was ordained on September 8, 1731. He served at Santiago Papasquiaro in 1734, was still among the Tepehuanes in 1737, and was in Chínipas before coming to Cárichic at the end of 1741 or the beginning of 1742. In July 1744, he wrote a history of Cárichic, and in 1747, was reported as being heavily in debt. Sometime after August 19, 1748, he was transferred to Navojoa in Sonora, and in the following year he was at Belén and Huírivis, both on the delta of Río Yaqui. In 1755 he was at Vaca, in Sinaloa, but in 1756 he was assigned to the Jesuit residence at Parras, where he remained until the expulsion. He died on July 15, 1769, at Puerto de Santa María, Spain. *Chihuahuenses*, 7, 202; Fernández Abeé; Zelis, 4–5, 130, 145; Hierro Aug. 30, 1747; *Misiones*, 91, 94, 97; González, xlvi; Almada 1937, 175; *Libros I;* Zambrano-Gutiérrez, XV, 36–37.

FERNÁNDEZ CASTAÑEDA, MARCOS ANTONIO, a general, was named the first alcalde of Cusihuiriáchic on January 13, 1688. He was still serving during the 1690 revolt, in which he participated with a force of soldiers from Cusi. When General Fernández Retana, his military superior, was inspecting Tarahumara late in 1691 to determine if the Jesuits could safely return, Fernández Castañeda, accompanied by Luis María Pineli of Yécora, was making a similar inspection of the Sonora frontier. *Chihuahuenses*, 130; González, 48, n. 19, n. 20, 62, n. 49.

FERNÁNDEZ CÓRDOVA, JUAN, was born at La Rambla, Córdoba, Spain, in 1653. He distinguished himself in the wars in Flanders and in Spain and on May 7, 1702, was appointed governor of Nueva Vizcaya, taking possession early the following year. He visited substantially the whole of the province, intervened to end a conflict in the Urique mines, provided economic assistance to the missions of Nabugame and Baburigame, and gave 1,200 pesos annually to the

Hospital de San Juan de Dios in Durango. He served until August 1708. *Chihuahuenses*, 204; *Resumen*, 88.

FERNÁNDEZ FRANCO, JUAN PARDIÑAS VILLAR DE FRANCOS Y. See PARDIÑAS.

FERNÁNDEZ MORALES, JUAN, a Spanish general, was in charge of the troops at Parral in 1652 and, with General Juan Barraza of Cerro Gordo, was ordered to Villa Aguilar. He led an unsuccessful assault on rebel Tarahumaras on a peñol and later, after several days of successive counterattacks from the Tarahumaras, was caught with his troops in an ambush from which Barraza was barely able to rescue him. Jordán, 78; *EJMT*, 66–68; and Bancroft, I, 356–357. The general should not be confused with the Juan Fernández Morales who was appointed the third *comandante* of Sonora sometime between 1644 and 1650, nor with the more famous General Juan Fernández Carrión, who led troops from Parral against the Tarahumaras in 1648. The Sonora Fernández is mentioned in Bancroft, I, 233, while Fernández Carrión is the subject of a full biography in *Chihuahuenses*, 204.

FERNÁNDEZ RETANA, JUAN, was born about 1650 in Manclares de Gamboa, Alava, Spain, and reached Nueva Vizcaya by 1675 and Parral at least by 1678. In 1684 he successfully led troops against the Conchos and Julimes, and in the following year established and, as *propietario perpetuo*, took command of the presidio of San Francisco de Conchos, east of Parral. On April 11, 1690, now a general, he was named commander of all the Spanish forces against the Tarahumaras and four days later arrived at Papigóchic to take charge. After the fighting stopped in the fall, he made a three-month tour of inspection of the whole of Tarahumara Alta, so as to be sure it was safe for the Jesuits to return to the north. Between wars he took the side of the Indians in a dispute with the miners at Cusihuiriáchic, and while he was contemporaneously referred to as the protector of the Tarahumaras, the more accurate title, apparently conferred by the Jesuits, was "perpetual protector of the [Jesuit] Province of Tarahumara."

During the 1697 revolt, he used his knowledge of the country to track down the rebels in the barrancas, burning their cornfields and chasing them as far as Guazápares and perhaps as far as Río

Chínipas. In April 1699, the viceroy, José Sarmiento Valladares, received accounts of the revolt and set in motion an audiencia in which the governor, Gabriel Castillo (who had died the preceding August), and General Fernández were accused of killing 61 Tarahumaras without following the prescribed judicial forms. At the December 1699 trial in Parral, five Jesuits testified in person and seven others sent in sworn statements, all in support of the general. On February 22, 1700, both Fernández and the deceased governor were finally acquitted.

In January 1708, while still in command of the presidio at San Francisco de Conchos, Fernández was named alcalde mayor of Santa Eulalia. He visited the newly reopened mines and ordered the construction, as a cabecera for the area, of what became Chihuahua at the junction of Río Chuvíscar and Río Sacramento. The following month, on February 24, 1708, he died of apoplexy at his presidio. Always a friend of the Jesuits, he was buried in the church of the college in Parral. Neumann, *Historia*, 259–260; Neumann, *Revoltes*, 160 (Latin), 161 (French); Jordán, 119; Bandelier, II, 461; *Obra*, II, 95–96, n. 63, 300–301; González, 46, n. 15, 62, n. 49, 158, n. 173, n. 174, 159, n. 175, 160, n. 177, 161, n. 178, n. 179; *Chihuahuenses*, 41, 205; Almada 1942, 3.

FERRER, NICOLÁS, S.J., was born in Acámbaro, Guanajuato, in 1645, and joined the Order in 1662. By 1678 he was in Papigóchic but, in bad health, he was transferred before the year was out to San Martín de Atotonilco. He died in Nabugame on July 12, 1679. Ortiz, 324, 417; Neumann, *Historia*, 158; González, 25, n. 9, n. 10.

FIGUEROA, GERÓNIMO, S.J., was at least part Indian. He was born in México in 1604, or in Toluca in 1606, and joined the Society in Tepotzotlán about 1621. He came to the Tepehuán mission in 1632 and in 1638 was in Durango. In 1639, when he was assigned to Tarahumara, he was in charge of Santa Catalina de los Tepehuanes. He and José Pascual arrived in Parral in June 1639, and he went north to found San Felipe de Jesús on Río Conchos, where he stayed until relieved, later in the summer, by Pascual. He then went southwest to establish San Gerónimo de Huejotitlán, serving there and at the reestablished San Pablo Balleza at least until 1673 or perhaps until 1679. He was superior of the Tarahumara Baja mission from his arrival in 1639 until he was succeeded ten years later by Father Pascual. In 1641 he may have gone to Sinaloa and Sonora as visitador and late in the summer may have returned from Sonora in the company of Captain Pedro Perea of the Spanish garrison at Sinaloa. It seems certain that in October of that year, after Perea had been appointed the first governor of Sonora, Figueroa went with him downstream along Río Papigóchic, and across the sierra to the new capital of San Juan Bautista. Figueroa was again superior in 1652, and served until about 1668. In 1674, or perhaps as late as 1678 or 1679, he returned to México. He died in the Casa Profesa on March 25, 1683. He wrote grammars and vocabularies for both Tepehuán and Rarámuri, as well as catechisms and confessions in both languages. Zambrano, VI, 672–694; *EJMT*, 45–47, 55, 60–61, 79, 89; *Chihuahuenses*, 209; Roca, 190, 399, n. 18; Figueroa 1662, 217; Figueroa 1668, 226; Pascual 1651, 206; *Introduction*, 12–14, 25, 29, 83, n. 100; Christelow 1939, 427; Bancroft, I, 346, 360, 361; Saravia 1954, III, 277–278, 325, n. 2, 332–333; *Obra*, II, 258–266, 277–278, and n. 26, 284, 312; González, 9, n. 3; ABZ, II, 466, n. 43; *Diccionario Porrúa*, 588.

FLORES DE LA TORRE, MANUEL, S.J., was born in Aguascalientes on January 28, 1727, and entered the Order on August 14, 1758. Rector of the Chihuahua college at the expulsion, he was sent to Spain and then to Rome, where he died on January 23, 1797. *Chihuahuenses*, 210; Zelis, 16–17, 100, 151; *Obra*, I, 113, 465.

FONT, JUAN, S.J., was baptized on August 20, 1574, in Tarrasa, Catalonia. He entered the Society of Jesus in 1593 and went to New Spain in 1599. By 1600 he was at Guadiana (now Durango) studying the Tepehuán language. Shortly thereafter he began work in the Tepehuán area, serving at Santiago Papasquiaro, Santa Catalina, Zape and Indé. In 1607 he went north to the Valle de San Pablo, met with about 800 Tarahumaras and returned to his headquarters at Zape. The following year he went to Guadiana to get permission from the governor to open a Tarahumara mission, but he didn't go north again until late 1610 or early 1611, when he went farther inland and induced several hundred Tarahumaras to come south to settle at the town (now Balleza) he established at Valle de San Pablo. On November 19, 1616, while he and Gerónimo Moranta, who had joined him at San Pablo in 1614, were on their way to a festival in Zape, the two priests were killed in the general Tepehuán revolt, which took the lives of eight Jesuits and hundreds of others. His body was recovered and buried in the Jesuit church in Guadiana on March 7, 1617. Ildefonso Roca, 4–6, 15; *EJMT*, 14–30; Burrus, 1956, 13; Zambrano, VII, 37–77; *Chihuahuenses*, 210; Jordán, 53–58; Saravia 1943, 61–63; Saravia 1954, III, 269; Bancroft, I, 124–125, 319, n. 31, 323, 333; *Obra,* II, 249, 253; Decorme, *Mártires,* 48, 49 and n. 5; ABZ, II, 276, n. 17.

FORONDA, DIEGO ORTIZ.   See ORTIZ.

FRANCO, JUAN PARDIÑAS VILLAR DE FRANCOS Y FERNÁNDEZ. See PARDIÑAS.

FRANCO, LÁZARO, S.J., was born on October 27, 1712, in Celaya, Guanajuato, and joined the Order on March 17, 1733. He was a professor of grammar, first at the college of Oaxaca in 1737 and then at the colegio in Parral in 1744. By 1748 he had abandoned formal teaching and was a missionary at Santa Apolonia near Piaxtla. Three years later, still a missionary, he was back among the Tarahumaras, in charge of San Pablo. In 1755 he was at Cárichic, but thereafter he is lost from view. ABZ, IV, 407, n. 43; *Misiones*, 91, 95, 98; Bancroft, I, 598, n. 24; Rinaldini; Zambrano-Gutiérrez, XV, 626–627.

FRANCOS Y FERNÁNDEZ FRANCO, JUAN PARDIÑAS VILLAR DE. See PARDIÑAS.

FREJOMIL, JOSÉ, S.J., was born at Querétaro on December 18, 1736, joined the Society on December 2, 1754, and may have served at the college in Parral. At the expulsion he was at Campeche, from which he was shipped to Spain. Sometime before the extinction of the Order on August 16, 1773, he was secularized at Ajaccio, Corsica. When the Society was reestablished by Pius VII in December 1814, Frejomil was at Pesaro, Italy. He died in 1821 or 1822 in Genoa. *Chihuahuenses*, 202, 211; Zelis, 18, 19, 93, 131; Zambrano-Gutiérrez, XV, 629–630.

GALLARATI, CONSTANCIO, S.J., was born about 1690 in Milano, Italy, and entered the Society in 1713. He came to the Chihuahua college as rector in mid-1725, and operated it successfully until his death. Troubled by evil spirits, Gallarati successfully exorcised the demons and died at his post on August 12, 1739, "in the repute of sanctity." ABZ, IV, 321, n. 3, 321–322; *Obra*, I, 111–112; *EJMT*, 210.

GAMBOA, JUAN MANUEL, S.J., was born in Valladolid, Spain, about 1644, entered the Order in 1662, and studied in México. He was assigned variously as a missionary and in colleges at Guadalajara and México. Transferred to Tarahumara, he attended a September 1673 strategy meeting at Parral, then on November 1 went north with Fernando Barrionuevo. With his companion, he founded Coyáchic and Cusihuiriáchic, which he made his headquarters. He may also have founded Santa Ana, southeast of Borja, as the first headquarters of the Misión de San Joaquín y Santa Ana. By the summer of 1675 he was sick, and on August 14 was replaced by Tomás Guadalajara. Gamboa returned to Parras, but was rector of the Querétaro college in 1686 when his friend Barrionuevo died. By 1708 he had been transferred to the college of San Gregorio, in México, and by the time of his death, on March 13, 1721, he was at the college of San Andrés in the same city. *EJMT*, 98, 101, 104–106; *Chihuahuenses*, 49, 64, 214, 235, 481; Guadalajara 1676; *Introduction*, 29–30; Jordán, 115; Bancroft, I, 363, 366; *Obra*, II, 284–285; González, 22, n. 1; ABZ, III, 315, n. 5; Gamboa; Zambrano-Gutiérrez, XV, 644.

GARCÍA, ANDRÉS XAVIER, S.J., was born in Beturia, Extremadura, on December 3, 1686, and joined the Society on January 27, 1705. He went to New Spain two years later and after being attached to the Colegio de San Gregorio de México, was succesively rector of the colleges of Espíritu Santo in Puebla, San Gregorio in México, San Andrés in México, and San Ildefonso in Puebla. In 1733 he was named procurador to Rome for the provincial congregation, in 1736 visitador general, and he served as provincial from March 1747, to August 31, 1750. In 1751 he became superior of the Casa Profesa in México, where he remained for ten years, when he went to his original post, the college of San Gregorio, where he died in 1764. ABZ, IV, 15*, 361, n. 14; *Libro IV*; Zambrano-Gutiérrez, XV, 650–657.

GARCÍA, ANTONIO, S.J., was at Santo Tomás on December 19 in a year which appears to have been either 1733 or 1734. *Libro VI.*

GARCÍA SALCEDO, JOSÉ, a native of Pamplona, was appointed governor of Nueva Vizcaya on June 14, 1670, but did not take office (from Bartolomé Estrada Ramírez) until March 1, 1671. He called and presided over a grand strategy meeting of priests, settlers and the military at Parral on September 30, 1673, and served with distinction until he was succeeded, on April 9, 1676, by Martín Rebollar Cueva. Charges of misconduct were brought by Captain Luis Valdez, but when they were not proven, Valdez was fined and, unable to pay the fine, imprisoned for five years at Acapulco. García died in Spain in 1686. Bancroft, I, 338; *Introduction*, 29; *Obra*, II, 284; González, 23, n. 5; *Resumen*, 73–74.

GARCÍA VALDEZ, JOSÉ, a secular priest, had been curate at Cusihuiriáchic when, early in 1709, he arrived in Chihuahua to serve at the city's first church. *Resumen*, 92.

GARFIAS, BERNARDO, S.J.,was born in El Rosario, Durango, in 1675. Having entered the Order in 1693, he was ordained ten years later on December 25. He was working in the Chínipas area as early as 1708. Between 1716 and 1720 he was rector of Santa Inés de Chínipas and was still there in 1723, when he was visitador. In 1725 he was named rector of the colegio in Chihuahua, but he didn't accept the office, instead remaining in the mission field. He was at Santo Tomás in June and September 1732. He died on April 10, 1736, somewhere in Tarahumara Alta. González, 184, n. 31, 201, n. 66; *Catálogo 1716–1720;* ABZ, IV, 492; *Libro VI;* Zambrano-Gutiérrez, XV, 665-666.

GASPAR, BERNARDO, S.J., does not appear in any record I have found except the *Administrative Census of 1728*, to which he reported the population of Santo Tomás on June 13, 1728.

GERA, LORENZO, S.J., was born in Italy on April 5, 1693, became a Jesuit in 1711, studied in México, was ordained in 1721, and came to Baburigame about 1723. He apparently took over Tónachic about 1731, and became visitador by 1744. In May 1747, he was in charge of Norogáchic, and while he was still there as late as 1751, he was succeeded by José Yáñez soon thereafter. Andonaegui Dec. 1744; Gera May 1747; Gera Oct. 18, 1747; Gera Oct. 25, 1747; *Misiones,* 91, 94; Rinaldini; *Obra*, II, 241–242; González, 201, n. 65; Zambrano-Gutiérrez, XV, 672.

GIRÓN, LUIS TÉLLEZ. See TÉLLEZ.

GLANDORFF, FRANCISCO HERMANO, S.J., was born in Osterkappeln, near Osnabrück, Germany, October 29, 1687, and became a Jesuit on May 21, 1708. He came to México in 1717 and finished his studies at the Colegio de San Pedro y San Pablo. Assigned to Tarahumara, he went first to Cárichic to work with José Neumann and learn Rarámuri. At Cárichic from March 1721, until February 1722, he was then assigned to Tomóchic, where he worked until his death on August 9, 1763. From Tomóchic he served a wide area which included not only the visitas of that post but also frequently Tutuaca, Yepáchic, Moris, Maicoba, Jicamórachic, Batopilillas and Babarocos. Because of a hernia or because he could not learn to mount a horse, or both, Glandorff walked from Veracruz to México, and from there to Tarahumara, but in the sierra he outran the natives and went continually from Tomóchic to Tutuaca to Moris to Maicoba and back without equipment or supplies. According to *EJMT*, 206, Glandorff "achieved fame of holiness, and, among the Indians, legendary repute for prowess in the wilds, for endurance, and fleetness of foot." He was buried at Tomóchic, but after the expulsion, the Franciscans removed his body to their college at Zacatecas. He was later reinterred by the Jesuits in México. *EJMT*, 207; *Chihuahuenses*, 223; Neumann 1723; Glandorff June 1747; Hierro June 1747; Guenduláin, 32; *Misiones*, 14, n. 15, 91, 94, 98; Terrazas; *Obra*, II, 239, 302, 308–310; González, xlvii; ABZ, IV, 445, n. 21; *Libro I;* Braun 1764.

GODÍNEZ, CORNELIO. See BEUDÍN.

GONZÁLEZ, CLAUDIO ANTONIO, S.J., was born on July 6, 1736, at Aguascalientes, and entered the Society on January 5, 1758. His first post was apparently as master of grammar at the college in Chihuahua, but in October 1766, he took over Chinarras. Still stationed at Chinarras, he happened to be visiting at the college on the following June 30, and was therefore arrested with the faculty. He died in Bologna on October 17, 1787. *Chihuahuenses*, 201, 231; Zelis, 20–21, 101, 135, 152, *Misiones*, 103; *Obra*, I, 465, II, 311.

GONZÁLEZ, JUAN MANUEL, S.J., was born in Compostela, Nayarit, on August 28, 1734, and became a Jesuit on January 5, 1759. Tomóchic, where he was located at the expulsion, was probably his first mission post. He sailed from Veracruz on November 19, 1767, and on December 3, 1767, was the first of the Jesuits to die at sea. *Chihuahuenses*, 232; Zelis, 20–21, 135, 152; *Misiones*, 102; *Destierro*.

GRISONI, NICOLÁS, S.J., born in Naples in 1648, became a Jesuit in 1672 and came to New Spain 20 years later. He went immediately to Mátachic, where he stayed only a year. He was then transferred to the colegio in Parral, where he couldn't have stayed past 1703, when he was appointed visitador for an unstated area. In 1707 he was at Macoyahui, Sonora. González, 62, n. 49; Zambrano-Gutiérrez, XV, 717.

GUADALAJARA, TOMÁS, S.J., born in Puebla in 1648, joined the Society on December 17, 1667. Late in 1673, he made a brief visit to Juan Gamboa and José Tardá in Tarahumara, then returned south until the summer of 1675, when he replaced Gamboa permanently. From then until 1685, alone and with Tardá, he crisscrossed Tarahumara Alta, building churches, baptizing and founding or reestablishing towns, including Cárichic, Papigóchic, Mátachic, Temeýchic, Yepómera, San Francisco Borja, Pachera, Coyáchic, Temósachic, Tutuaca, Napabéchic, Papajíchic, Nonoava, Cocomórachic, Yepáchic and many others. In 1678, when his headquarters were at Mátachic, he went with the visitador, Ortiz, to Sahuaripa in Sonora, founding Teópare on the way. In 1684 he became ill and was transferred to Parral, where he established the college, the first school in what is now Chihuahua. From late in 1690 until 1720, he was principally at Huejotitlán, from which he served from 1696 until 1699 as rector of Tarahumara Baja and made an excursion in 1708 to found Nabugame and Baburigame, on the Tepehuán-Tarahumara border. He was an accomplished linguist, and is reported to have preached a sermon at Mátachic in 1681 in Spanish, Rarámuri and Tepehuán and to have written grammars in Rarámuri, Tepehuán and Guazápar. He died at Huejotitlán on January 6, 1720. *EJMT*, 101, 106–107, 116, 130, 153, 163, 200; Dunne 1941, 272–287; *Chihuahuenses*, 88, 123, 235, 244, 326, 385, 482, 520, 544, 571; *Resumen*, 81, 97; Neumann, *Historia*, 157; Neumann 1682; Fernández Abeé; Ydiáquez 1744; Guadalajara 1676; Guadalajara 1677; Guadalajara 1684; Jordán, 115, 117; *Obra*, II, 234, 235, 285, 287–293, 302, 307, 312, n. 27; González, xlii, 22, n. 1, n. 3, 49, n. 23, 115, n. 102; ABZ, III, 327–331.

GUAJARDO FAJARDO, DIEGO, a native of Castilla, was a Knight of the Order of Santiago. He served as governor and captain general of the Philippines from 1644 until September 13, 1648, when he was named governor and captain general of Nueva Vizcaya. He assumed office on November 4, 1648, taking over from Luis Valdez, and in January 1649, took the field against the Tarahumaras. In April, largely because of hunger, the Indians sued for peace, but Guajardo demanded and got the heads of the leaders. After founding Villa Aguilar (now Ciudad Guerrero), he retired to Parral, but again led troops against the Tarahumaras in 1650. When rebellion flared in 1652 he was in the field against the Tobosos, but went promptly to the sierra to engage the enemy. Again his troops were finally successful, and he hanged Tepóraca, the native leader. When Bishop Evía moved to secularize the Franciscan missions around Allende and the southern Jesuit establishments, the governor took the side of the Orders, put the bishop under house arrest, and was himself excommunicated. While the two Orders finally prevailed, the dispute resulted in the bishop's transfer to the Diocese of Oaxaca and in the governor being relieved on March 7, 1653. He returned to the Philippines as governor and remained there until 1658. In that year he died at sea on his way to Acapulco. *Resumen*, 63; *Chihuahuenses*, 198, 238; *Introduction*, 19–20, 22; Pascual 1651, 189–190, 195; Jordán, 76; Bancroft, I, 354–355, 357–360; Bandelier, II, 465, n. 68; González, 10, n. 7, 15, n. 19.

GUENDULÁIN, JUAN, S.J., was born in Oaxaca about 1681, became a Jesuit in 1696, and was ordained on February 15, 1705. Guenduláin taught philosophy in the colleges at Oaxaca and México in 1708 and 1709 and was rector of the college of San Ignacio de Puebla in 1713. He was successively at the Colegio de San Ildefonso in Puebla, the college at Zacateas and visitador of the colleges of Parras and Monterrey before being appointed, in 1724, visitador general of the northern missions. In this capacity he made an inspection of Tarahumara, concluding his report at Cócorit, Sonora, on December 22, 1725. In November 1726, he was elected one of three procuradores, and in 1727 was rector at the college of Veracruz. Three years later he held the same post at Oaxaca, and in 1731 was transferred to the college at Tepotzotlán. In 1733 he was named first procurador to Rome and three years later returned from Europe. He became rector of the College of San Andrés in México in 1737, but a year later went in the same capacity to the Colegio del Espíritu Santo in Puebla. By the time of his death on July 31, 1748, he had moved to the Colegio de San Ildefonso in the same city. ABZ, IV, 326, and n. 24, 545, n. 1, 548, n. 1; Guenduláin, 33; Zambrano-Gutiérrez, XV, 721–722.

GUERRA, VICENTE, S.J., was born in Lagos, Jalisco, on November 27, 1723, and became a Jesuit on August 15, 1744. At the expulsion he was at the college in Parral. After his arrest he was taken to Spain and then to Italy, dying in Bologna on August 6, 1783. Zelis, 20, 21, 152; *Chihuahuenses*, 202, 243.

GUERRERO VILLASECA, JOSÉ MIGUEL, S.J., was born in Toluca about 1670, joined the Jesuits in 1687, and was at Santo Tomás briefly in 1690. When peace was restored he was assigned to San Pablo Guarizame, Topia, but sometime betwen 1696 and 1701 was sent to Nácori Chico, in Sonora. In the latter year he called for the military to punish witches who were killing people in Nácori and Bacadéhuachi. He served in the area until 1709. On June 2, 1737, during a severe epidemic, he died in the Colegio del Espíritu Santo, Puebla. González, 63, n. 49; ABZ, IV, 382–383, and n. 24; Roca, 229; Manje, 171.

GUEVARA, JOSÉ SÁNCHEZ.   See SÁNCHEZ.

GUTIÉRREZ, BERNABÉ FRANCISCO, S.J., was born about 1639 in Villa Carrillo, in the province of Jaén, Spain, and came to New Spain in 1665. In 1676 he was rector of the Jesuit college at

Durango and served as visitador general of the Jesuit missions. In November 1680, he was elected procurador of New Spain and two years later was named procurador to Rome and Madrid. He apparently did not return to México until 1687. *EJMT*, 123; ABZ, IV, 12 and n. 42, 33, 520, n. 3, 524, n. 15.

GUTIÉRREZ, PEDRO, O.F.M., from Zacatecas, was killed on November 17, 1616, at Atotonilco, a victim of the Tepehuán revolt. He was buried at Santiago Papasquiaro. *EJMT*, 28; *Chihuahuenses*, 247; Saravia 1943, 51.

GUTIÉRREZ ARTEAGA, MANUEL, S.J., surfaces from obscurity only long enough to be at Huejotitlán in 1678. Ortiz, 321; Bancroft, I, 368; *Obra*, II, 280.

HALLER, JUAN BAUTISTA, S.J., an Austrian, was born in Bohemia about 1658 and became a Jesuit in 1674. He sailed from Cádiz on July 1, 1678, and reached Tarahumara early in 1692. He didn't stay, but went to Yamoriba, of the mission of San Andrés de Topia. He returned in the same year and took over Yepómera, where he built a fine church and house. At the 1697 revolt he escaped to the safety of Villa Aguilar, returning after the peace to find his church destroyed. He rebuilt, serving from 1699 until 1702 as rector. By 1708 he had gone south and, in poor health, was at the College of San Pedro y San Pablo in México. It was reported that in 1714 he was again sick and died a short time later. Neumann, *Historia*, 197, 206–207, 257, 312–313, n. 114; Neumann July 1693; Neumann Sept. 1693; Neumann 1698; González, 62, n. 49, 88–89, n. 45, n. 46.

HAUGA, JUAN FRANCISCO, S.J., was born in San Sebastián, Spain, on May 5, 1716, entered the Order in 1735 and by 1748 was stationed at San Pablo. By 1751 he had been transferred to San Miguel de las Bocas, where he stayed until secularization in 1753. Where he was then sent doesn't appear, but in 1765 he was put in charge of Nonoava. Before the expulsion he had been transferred to Cárichic. He died in Bologna on February 15, 1795. Zelis, 22, 135, 153; *Misiones*, 91, 95, 102; Braun 1765.

HEREDÍA, JUAN, S.J., was born in Guadiana about 1597, entered the Society in 1615, taught grammar and rhetoric at the Colegio del

Espíritu Santo in Puebla, studied philosophy at the Colegio Máximo in México, and was ordained in 1624. In 1626 he was stationed at San Luis de la Paz, Guanajuato, but soon thereafter was sent north to Río Florido. In 1630 he and Captain Juan Barraza made an excursion to Río Conchos and returned with 400 Tarahumaras, thus officially founding San Gabriel de las Bocas. He stayed only briefly in the area, and by 1632 was in Durango. Four years later he was rector of the college at San Luis Potosí, and in 1647 he was at Guadalajara. By 1667 he was in México, and in 1675 there is a record of his service as rector of the seminary of San Gregorio in the capital. The date of his death is not known. Zambrano, VII, 513–522; ABZ, II, 412 and n. 11, 465; *EJMT*, 37; *Chihuahuenses*, 248; Saravia 1954, III, 277; *Introduction*, 11; Christelow 1939, 427; Bancroft, I, 333–334; *Obra*, II, 254; González, 9, n.4.

HERMOSILLO, GONZALO DE, O.S.A., was born in México, entered the Order of San Agustín, and was a professor of theology at La Real y Pontificia Universidad in México. By a bull of October 11, 1620, Pope Paul V carved the new Diocese of Durango out of the jurisdiction of Guadalajara and appointed Hermosillo its first bishop on the following day. He took possession of the see by proxy on December 12, 1620, and in person on March 9, 1621. While on an episcopal visitation, he died on January 28, 1631, at the Villa de Sinaloa. His remains were later removed to Durango. Bancroft, I, 307, 308; González, 128, n. 128; *Chihuahuenses*, 249; ABZ, II, 9*, 431, n. 7, n. 8; Cuevas, III, 553. The correct spelling of his name may have been Hermosilla. It so appears in *Chihuahuenses* and González, while Bancroft and Cuevas use the "o" ending. On the other hand, ABZ is undecided, using both.

HERRERA, ANTONIO IGNACIO, S.J., was born in the province of Valencia, Spain, in 1651, and became a Jesuit in 1666. In 1675 he studied metaphysics in México, where he was ordained in 1678. His first post was San Pablo in the Sierra de Piaxtla, but he was assigned to Tarahumara in 1684. He may have gone to Santa Cruz in that year, but I have found no record showing him there before 1692. He served as visitador for Tarahumara Antigua from 1708 until 1711 and from 1720 until early in 1723 was superior of the *residencia* at Chihuahua. On July 28, 1732, he died at Santa Cruz, which by then was called Padre Herrera in his honor. González, 62, n. 49, 184, n. 31, 187, n. 40, 201, n. 65; Herrera; Moreno; *Chihuahuenses*, 469.

HIDALGO, JOSÉ ANTONIO, S.J., is reported to have been born in Querétaro on April 13, 1734, which would mean that he was a 17-year-old missionary at Coyáchic in 1751. More surprising, he is said not to have joined the Society until February 1, 1762. At the expulsion he was at the college in Durango. He died in Bologna on May 8, 1781. *Chihuahuenses*, 202, 252; Zelis, 22–23, 101, 153; *Misiones*, 95; Rinaldini.

HIERRO, JUAN MANUEL DEL, S.J., was born on July 8, 1678, in México, became a Jesuit on March 31, 1696, and was ordained on February 15, 1705. He began his service in Tarahumara three years later, his first post being Yepómera, where he stayed at least until 1723, probably moving the cabecera to Temósachic in that or the following year. He served as rector in 1723 and in 1751 and was visitador in 1725, in 1728, in 1737, in 1747 (when he was somewhat disabled from a fall) and in 1755. In 1732 Father Hierro tried the city briefly—he spent a year as rector of the colegio in Parral. However, he left the north permanently in 1758, when he was retired to the college in Durango. He was still there in 1764, but evidently died before the expulsion. Gera Oct. 18, 1747; Hierro Aug. 30, 1747; Hierro Nov. 1747; Téllez; *Misiones*, 91, 94, 98; Rinaldini; González, xlvii, 184, n. 31, 201, n. 65; *Administrative Census of 1728;* Zambrano-Gutiérrez, XV, 757–758.

HITL, ANTONIO LUIS, S.J., was born at Pomeistl, in what is now Czechoslovakia, on June 1, 1732, and joined the Society on May 18, 1754. By 1761 he was at Sisoguíchic, where he learned to speak Rarámuri. By September 20, 1764, he had been transferred to Temeýchic, from which he was expelled. From Spain he was permitted to return to his homeland, where he died on an unrecorded date. *EJMT*, 226; Lizasoaín, *Noticia*, 23; Zelis, 22–23, 90, 135; *Chihuahuenses*, 202, 302; Braun 1765; *Misiones*, 102; *Libro VIII*.

HOSTINSKY, JORGE STANISLAS, S.J., was born at Valasské Klobouky, Moravia, in 1654 and became a Jesuit in 1669. He reached México in September 1687, and was in Tarahumara by the following year. Until the 1690 revolt, he was at Tomóchic, from which he escaped just ahead of its destruction. Late in 1692 or early in 1693 he went across the sierra to take charge of San Ignacio in Pimería Alta, and on April 26, 1693, preached the sermon at the dedication of Eusebio Francisco Kino's first church, Dolores. Before the year was out Hostinsky returned to Tarahumara, first going to Santo Tomás and then to Tomóchic and Arisiáchic. When the 1697 rebels attacked Tomóchic, Hostinsky was at Arisiáchic and escaped to Villa Aguilar. After peace he continued to take care of Tomóchic as well as Sisoguíchic and other churches in the sierra, but most of the time he lived in Santo Tomás. In 1706 he was briefly at Chínipas, as a temporary replacement for Guillermo Illing. He died in Papigóchic on November 16, 1726, leaving six unpublished volumes of history and poetry. Neumann, *Historia*, 104–105, 170, 173, 203–204, 207, 286, 291, 315, n. 129, 318, n. 157, 320, n. 173; Neumann Sept. 1693; Neumann 1698; Hostinsky 1725; Hostinsky 1726; González, 5, n. 13, 40, n. 5, 41, n. 6, 62, n. 49, 70–71, n. 12, 85, n. 38, 89, n. 46, 169, n. 9, 193, n. 47, 201, n. 65; *Obra*, I, 155, II, 234, 382, n. 11, 386; Roca, 58; Bolton, 270.

IBARRA, ANTONIO ARIAS. See ARIAS.

IBARRA, FRANCISCO, a Basque, was born in 1538, a nephew of one of the founders of Zacatecas and a son-in-law of Antonio Mendoza, New Spain's first viceroy. In 1554, aged only 16, he led an expedition into the sierra, locating a number of rich silver mines. In 1562 he was named governor of the newly organized province of Nueva Vizcaya and founded Guadiana, its capital. Three years later, with 60 soldiers, he explored northwestern Sonora, crossed the sierra at Carretas, went south to the Papigóchic, and then followed the river back to Sonora. He died at Pánuco, Sinaloa, in 1575. *Diccionario Porrúa*, 785; Lister, 15–20.

ILLING, GUILLERMO, S.J., was born in 1648 and joined the Order in 1664 in the Province of Bohemia. In July 1687, he sailed from

Cádiz, and in 1688 was assigned to Cajuríchic, from which he was obliged to flee in the April 1690 revolt. By 1692 he was at Loreto, north of Chínipas, but he returned to the east and Norogáchic by 1697. When the revolt reached Norogáchic, he fled a second time, returning to the area of Chínipas and serving in Guadalupe, where he succeeded Francisco María Pícolo. In the final battle at Guadalupe in 1698, he distinguished himself by walking onto the battlefield in surplice and stole and holding his crucifix high in the face of the enemy charge. About 1700 he succeeded Nicolás Prado at Chínipas and was himself succeeded in 1706 by Jorge Hostinsky. He remained in the Chínipas area until he died in 1712, probably in Loreto. *EJMT*, 167, 168, 185, 197; Neumann, *Historia*, 173, 227, 241; Neumann 1698; *Introduction*, 87, n. 141a, 48, 49; *Obra*, II, 234, and n. 18, 301; González, 4, n. 11, 40, n. 5, 41, n. 6, 62, n. 49, 89, n. 45, 154, n. 166, 184, n. 31, 185, n. 34.

IRANZO, JOSÉ, S.J., was born in Pitarque, in the province of Teruel, Spain, on July 12, 1734, and entered the Society in 1754. His only mission post was Guaguáchic, where he succeeded Antonio Strzanowski in 1765. Arrested at the expulsion, he died at sea on December 2, 1767, thirteen days after embarkation from Veracruz. *Chihuahuenses*, 202, 282; Zelis, 22–23, 135, 153; Braun 1765; *Misiones*, 103; *Destierro*; *Obra*, II, 303, n. 16.

LANDA, JUAN ANTONIO FRANCISCO, S.J., a native of New Spain, served in Tarahumara from 1706 until 1747. He was attached to the partido of San Joaquín y Santa Ana as early as 1708, and at least from 1723 until 1728 (and probably for quite a few years earlier and later) he was rector of the misión. While stationed at Borja and visiting at Cárichic, he saved the life of José Neumann by grasping a spear which a native was about to throw. In 1734 he was in charge of Cerocahui, but he returned to Borja probably in 1736. He died there in 1747. González, xlvii, 184, n. 311, 201, n. 65; Fernández Abeé; *Administrative Census of 1728*; Almada 1937, 175.

LA OZADA, JOSÉ ZAMORA DE.   See ZAMORA.

LA PUENTE, JUAN LARREA Y.   See LARREA.

LARIOS, MARTÍN, S.J., was in Zape in 1622. In 1623 he was probably in San Miguel de las Bocas, which he may have established with Tarahumara settlers from Valle de San Pablo. He was at Guanaceví in 1625. Zambrano, VIII, 319–324; Dunne, 1944, 174; *EJMT*, 35–36; Bandelier, II, 131, 157; González, 9, n. 4.

LARIS, CRISTÓBAL, S.J., is recorded only at Huejotitlán in 1723. González, 201, n. 65. He should not be confused with Cristóbal Lauria, S.J., an Italian who was in Nayarit from 1723 until 1727 or later. By 1730 Lauria was at Sahuaripa, in Sonora, but in 1749 he was deposed as rector by the visitador, Carlos Rojas, and assigned to Guazápares. His friend Francisco Glandorff protested violently. *EJMT*, 211; ABZ, IV, 307; *Obra*, II, 310, 552, 555, n. 5; Roca, 273–274, 414, n. 16; *Misiones*, 89; Glandorff 1749; Pradeau, *Expulsión*, 164, n. 53, 214, 220.

LARREA Y LA PUENTE, JUAN BAUTISTA, son of a rich merchant of México, Knight of the Order of Santiago, general of artillery, and maestre de campo, was named governor and captain general of Nueva Vizcaya at the end of 1697, to succeed General Gabriel Castillo, who surrendered the office in April 1698. In September 1698, Larrea was said to have gone to the Tarahumara revolt area, visiting Cárichic, Papigóchic and other points, and he is reported to have made a similar trip in the fall of 1700. It is certain, however, that in February 1701 he met in Papigóchic with General Fernández Retana and other commanders. A final Tarahumara visit is reported early in 1703, just before he was succeeded as governor by Colonel Juan Fernández Córdova. *Obra*, II, 301; González, 142, n. 148; Larrea Jan. 1701; Larrea Feb. 1701; *Chihuahuenses*, 307; *Resumen*, 87, 88.

LEGAZPI VELASCO Y ALTIMIRANO, GARCÍA, of the family of the Counts of Santiago, was born in México and served as alcalde mayor of Puebla before he took holy orders. As a priest he was curate in San Luis Potosí and canon, treasurer and archdeacon of the cathedral of México. The eighth bishop of Durango, Manuel Herrera, died in January 1689, and while Legazpi was named to succeed him on December 12, 1689, he didn't take possession of the see until December 22, 1692. He undertook the erection of the cathedral of

Durango and in 1697 visited Cusihuiriáchic and Cárichic, confirming 2,000 Indians. He was named bishop of Valladolid on March 5, 1700, but didn't begin his service there until August 8, 1701. On January 14, 1704, he surrendered the see, having been named bishop of Puebla, which he governed from October 5, 1704, until his death on March 7, 1705. Bancroft, I, 339; *Obra*, II, 300–301; González, 119, n. 109; Neumann, *Revoltes*, 128 (Latin), 129 (French); ABZ, IV, 9*, 10*, 11*; *Chihuahuenses*, 307.

LILÍN, DIEGO, S.J., was born at Seste, Sardinia, in 1666, entered the Society in 1685, studied Latin and Greek at Iglesias, Sardinia, and began his study of philosophy at Sassari, also in Sardinia. He went to México in 1692 or 1693, studying at the Colegio de San Pedro y San Pablo in México and at the Colegio de San Ildefonso in Puebla before his ordination in 1697. He took charge of Mátachic in 1699, and also administered Cocomórachic for two years. In 1705 he went to the college at Valladolid (Morelia), serving as rector until 1708. He left Valladolid for Durango in 1720, and was rector of the college until 1726. He died at Durango on July 15, 1729. Neumann, *Historia*, 257; González, 155, n. 168, 162, n. 181.

LIZARRALDE, DOMINGO, S.J., was at Satevó in 1692 and served as visitador of the missions of Tarahumara Antigua and of Tepehuana. In 1708 he was still serving in Tarahumara Antigua. González, 62, n. 49, 184, n. 31.

LIZASOAÍN, TOMÁS IGNACIO, S.J., was born in Pamplona on April 8, 1717, and became a Jesuit in 1744. He landed at Veracruz on August 25, 1750, and early in 1751 gathered 100 families and founded San José de Guaymas, northeast of the present Sonora city. During the Pima revolt of the following year, the Seris burned the church and house and killed nine of the faithful. The mission was abandoned and Lizasoaín retired first to Belén and then, by 1755, to Bácum, which was his headquarters until 1764. Appointed visitador general in 1761, he was the first Jesuit visitor in the north to be given authority to confirm. In Tarahumara Alta he confirmed 5,888 Indians and, in the course of his two-year visitation, confirmed a total of 18,431. He went to Rome in 1764, but returned to become rector of the Colegio de San Gregorio in México, where he was serving at the expulsion. Transported to Spain and then to Italy, he was elected, in 1772, the last Jesuit provincial of New Spain. He died in Bologna on January 12, 1789. *EJMT*, 221, 225, 226; *Misiones*, 94, 97; Zelis, 24–25, 154; Lizasoaín, *Informe*, 685; *Obra*, I, xvi, 433, II, 457; Roca, 287, n.52; Donohue 1957, 250, 254, 270; Donohue 1969, 127, 135.

LOMAS, JOSÉ, S.J., was born in Zacatecas in 1576 and entered the Society in 1592. In 1606 he was assigned to Atotonilco, where he stayed until 1618, when he moved north to Papasquiaro. He visited San Pablo and traveled north, perhaps beyond Río Conchos, and is said to have introduced poultry to the Tarahumaras. In 1625 he was at Guanaceví. He died at Valladolid (now Morelia) in 1634. Zambrano, VIII, 623–636; ABZ, II, 156, n. 12; *EJMT*, 32, 35; *Chihuahuenses*, 311; *Introduction*, 11; Bancroft, I, 329, n. 44; Bandelier, II, 157; *Obra*, II, 253.

LOYA, JOSÉ JOAQUÍN, a *bachiller de las artes* and secular priest, was named *cura teniente, vicario* and *juez eclesiástico* for Valle de Olivos in 1753 and, then in middle age, was assigned not only Olivos but also Santa Cruz, San Pablo and Huejotitlán. *Testimonio*, 28, 29, 117.

LOYOLA, PEDRO IGNACIO, S.J., was born Ignace Vah in Brussels about 1648 and joined the Order in 1663. He served in the Misión de San Joaquín y Santa Ana at one time, founded Norogáchic and possibly also Humariza, was visitador in 1692, and served Norogáchic at least from 1690 to 1696. Thereafter he was successively in charge of the colleges at Durango and Guatemala, then secretary of the province, in charge of the novitiate of San Andrés, then at Espíritu Santo in Puebla and finally at the Colegio Máximo in México. In November 1713, he was named procurador but was unable to sail for Rome until early March 1715. His ship was wrecked and he died at sea on July 31, 1715, but word didn't reach México until November of that year and meanwhile, on October 14, 1715, he had been elected provincial. On November 21, 1715, he was officially replaced by Gaspar Rodero. *Chihuahuenses*, 364; Ydiáquez 1744; *Introduction*, 44; Neumann 1690; *Obra*, II, 306, 307; González, 40, n. 6, 62, n. 49; ABZ, IV,15*, 229, 230, 233, n. 35, 235.

MÁEZ, VIGILIO, S.J., was born in Dunkerque, France, in 1611 and entered the Society in 1633. He took charge of Satevó at its founding in 1640 and built its first church. When the revolt broke out in 1648 he was ordered by the military to abandon his post for the safety of San Felipe, but in January 1649 he joined Captain Juan Barraza in the field as military chaplain. He presumably returned to San Felipe rather than Satevó after the brief peace of late 1649 and early 1650, but was again with the troops in the summer of 1650, following the uprising at Papigóchic in which Cornelio Beudín was killed. Later during that campaign he traded places for a time with José Pascual, returning to San Felipe while Pascual went with the soldiers. He was back in Satevó in 1652 and escaped just ahead of the attack by the rebel Tepóraca. When peace was finally restored the following year, Máez returned to his post, where he found the church and house burned, most of the village destroyed and the Indians largely dispersed into the hills and caves. He induced the faithful to return and rebuilt the church and house. In 1664 he was appointed visitador general, and in June 1673 was elected to succeed Andrés Cobián as provincial. Bedfast and paralyzed, he could not serve. He died in México on January 3, 1675. *EJMT*, 56, 66, 79; *Introduction*, 12–13, 19, 22, 25; Pascual 1651, 186, 189, 193, 195, 206; Jordán, 79, 83; Saravia 1954, III, 307, 316, 325, n. 2, 331; *Obra*, II, 262; ABZ, III, 12*, 38, n. 34, 358, IV, 235; Zambrano, IX, 66–81. I have picked what I think is a logical course through the confused reports of Máez's later years. ABZ, III, 12*, shows him elected provincial on February 28, 1675, two months after his death; the same volume, 38, n. 34, has him elected on June 4, 1663, to succeed Cobián, who is there said to have died on June 2, 1663. However, the list at 12* shows that Cobián began his service on April 25, 1671. *Obra*, I, xvi, says that Cobián was succeeded as provincial by Manuel Arteaga on June 2, 1673. I conclude that the February 28, 1675, date is wholly erroneous and that both of the June 1663 dates should read 1673. I also conclude that *Obra*, II, 266, is wrong in showing Máez still at Satevó in 1674.

MANCUSO, LUIS, S.J., was born in Palermo, Sicily, about 1662, and became a Jesuit in 1680. He arrived in New Spain with Agustín Campos by 1688, went to Tarahumara in 1689, and was assigned to

San Francisco Borja in 1692. I haven't found the date of his transfer to Santa María de las Cuevas, but it was certainly after 1696. In 1714 and 1717 he served as visitador and was instrumental in the establishment of the college in Chihuahua. In 1723 he was rector of the Colegio Máximo in México but returned to his post at Santa María, where he died on November 28, 1728. Calderón; *Obra*, I, 111; II, 306; González, 62, n. 49, 184, n. 31; *Catálogo, 1716–1720; Administrative Census of 1728;* ABZ, IV, 254–255, and n. 3; Almada 1952, 136.

MARTÍNEZ AGUIRRE, SALVADOR, S.J. Bishop Martínez was born at Arandos, Jalisco, on November 25, 1897, joined the Society of Jesus on July 30, 1913, was assigned to the Misión de la Tarahumara on September 15, 1923, and was ordained on July 28, 1929. The first vicar apostolic at the Misión, he was consecrated Bishop of Arca (in Armenia) on September 9, 1954, serving until June 16, 1973, when he retired to act as parish priest at Chínipas.

MARTINI, PEDRO ANTONIO, S.J., was born about 1687 and went to Norogáchic in 1719. He left about 1727 for Chínipas, from which he also took care of Santa Ana de los Varohíos. In the spring of 1731 he was briefly at Cárichic, helping out José Neumann, then in his 83rd year, but he soon returned to Chínipas and was moved to Santa Ana on a full-time basis in or after 1737. Very heavy and inclined to be lazy and slow, he was not loved by the Indians. Martini; *Obra*, II, 239 and n. 28, 244, n. 34; González, 201, n. 65; Almada 1937, 175; *Libro III*.

MATEU, JAIME, S.J., was born in Lérida, Spain, on October 3, 1734, and entered the Society 20 years later. He took charge of Tónachic sometime before 1765 and was there at the expulsion. He died in Rome on March 15 or May 15, 1790. *Chihuahuenses*, 202, 327; Zelis, 28–29, 135, 155; Braun 1765; *Misiones*, 103; *Obra*, II, 466.

MEDRANO, FRANCISCO JAVIER, S.J., lived from 1643 until 1713, but the details are few. In 1685 he was stationed at Las Bocas, was still there in 1692, but by 1699 he was the superior at the colegio in Parral. Neira; Medrano 1690; Medrano 1699; Banda; González, 62, n. 49; Zambrano, IX, 325.

MENDÍVIL, LORENZO, S.J., was at Chinarras in 1723, and in 1726 was living at Satevó, near Batopilas, from which he served Cerocahui. By 1731 he had left Satevó, and in 1739 is reported to have been suddenly expelled and to have died. González, 201, n. 65; Mendívil; *Obra*, II, 241 and n. 30.

MERINO, LUCAS JOSÉ ATANASIO, S.J., was born in Spain on October 23, 1712, became a Jesuit on November 21, 1728, and went to Nueva Vizcaya in 1740. He served in the partido of Coyáchic, is said to have been rector of the college of Chihuahua, and was at Papigóchic in February and March 1743. In 1747 he was still in the Tarahumara area, although he is reported in 1748 as having been both at Pasaje, a Tepehuán mission, and at Onapa in Sonora. In 1751 he was briefly at the Jesuit residence in Parras before going to Yécora, where he probably served until succeeded in 1754 by José Wazet. He then apparently went to Tesia in Sonora and later in the same year took over Navojoa, which he served until the expulsion. He died at Ixtlán, Nayarit, on September 2, 1768. Pradeau, *Expulsión*, 174–175; *Obra*, I, 409, 480; *Libro V*; Roca, 415, n. 60; Almada 1937, 175; Téllez; *Misiones*, 90, 94; Rinaldini; Zelis, 28–29, 155.

MESA, ALONSO, O.F.M., was in charge of Namiquipa, on Río Santa María in the plains north of Papigóchic, at least from 1675 to 1677, when he and Tomás Guadalajara engaged in a dispute as to the jurisdictional boundary between the area assigned to the Franciscans and that reserved for the Jesuits. Guadalajara 1677.

MIER, XAVIER FÉLIX, S.J., baptized in Papigóchic in January 1746, when he was probably serving Sisoguíchic. He had certainly succeeded José Escalona at that post by 1747, was there in 1748, and probably stayed until Martín Vallarta came in 1751. *Misiones*, 91; Andonaegui Sept. 1747; Glandorff Feb. 1747; *Libro V*.

MIQUEO, JOSÉ MARÍA, S.J., was at one time rector of Guadalupe and was in charge of Pámachic at least by 1744 and through the summer of 1748. By the fall of 1748 he had taken over Temeýchic from Bernardo Treviño and was visitador of Tarahumara, serving again as visitador when Ignacio Lizasoaín came to the area. An explorer of note, he wrote an account of his 1759 expedition to the barranca. He stayed at Temeýchic until June 1764, and presumably died in that or the following month. Lizasoaín, *Noticia*, 22; Miqueo; Glandorff, *Memoria; Misiones*, 17, n. 25, 91, 98; Rinaldini; *Libro VIII*.

MONSALVE SAAVEDRA, LUIS, became governor of Nueva Vizcaya in 1633, and almost immediately moved his headquarters to Parral. He promptly became embroiled in a dispute with *Oidor* Juan González Manjárrez, whom he imprisoned in 1638. The Audiencia de Guadalajara intervened, sending *Oidor* Alonso González Villalba to investigate. The latter deposed Monsalve and named Hurtado Mendoza as governor in his place, but the viceroy did not approve, and designated Francisco Bravo Serna as governor. Monsalve was put in the custody of the Audiencia and died in jail, presumably at Guadalajara. Bancroft, I, 306; Tamarón, 127; *Chihuahuenses*, 342.

MONTAÑO, JOSÉ, S.J.,was at Santo Tomás from December 1761 until June 1762. *Libros II*.

MONTEJANO, JACOBO RAMÍREZ.   See RAMÍREZ.

MORALES, JUAN DE DIOS, S.J., was in Tarahumara, probably at Mátachic, by 1708, or possibly as early as 1705. In the summer of 1715 he helped out at Cárichic, but was certainly back at Mátachic by 1723. He began the construction of a church during his Mátachic service. Téllez; González, 184, n. 31, 201, n. 65; *Libros I*.

MORALES, JUAN FERNÁNDEZ.   See FERNÁNDEZ.

MORANTA, GERÓNIMO, S.J., a kinsman of Ignacio Loyola, was born in Mallorca about 1575, entered the Society in 1595, and came to New Spain in 1605. In that or the following year he went north to work among the Tepehuán, where he stayed until he joined Juan Font at San Pablo in 1614. He was killed with Font when they were on their way to Zape on November 19, 1616, and was buried in the Jesuit church in Guadiana on March 7, 1617. Zambrano, X, 369–405; *EJMT*, 23, 28–30; Jordán, 56, 58; Saravia 1943, 61; Bancroft, I, 323; Dunne 1944, 148; ABZ, II, 276, n. 18; Decorme, *Mártires*, 48, 49, 50, n. 6.

MORENO, CRISTÓBAL, S.J., was at Santa Cruz in 1748 and 1751. He probably went to Tutuaca in 1753, and he was certainly there by 1755. It seems likely he stayed at Tutuaca until his death, which probably occurred shortly before the expulsion. *Misiones*, 90, 94, 95, 98; Rinaldini; Bancroft, I, 597, n. 23, 598, n. 24; Lizasoaín, *Noticia*, 20.

MURILLO, DIONISIO, S.J., was stationed at Papigóchic by July 1742, and served into January of the following year. He may have gone directly to Chinarras, of which he was certainly in charge by 1748. He remained at least until 1755. *Misiones*, 91, 95, 98; *Libro V*.

NARVÁEZ, CRISTÓBAL, was a captain in 1645, when Governor Luis Valdez put him in charge of troops guarding the settlements east of Parral against the Conchos. By 1652 he was in command of the presidio of Santa Catalina and had the care of the Tarahumara Baja missions west and north of Parral. He had gained the loyalty of the Indians of San Felipe, Huejotitlán and Las Bocas, and they were of substantial assistance against the forces of Tepóraca. When he defeated the rebel Tarahumaras in the last major engagement of the 1652 revolt, he took many prisoners, but released most of them to return to the barrancas to tell those still hiding that further resistance was fruitless. When large numbers came out to surrender, he made the delivery of Tepóraca the final condition of peace, and thus procured the betrayal of the Tarahumara leader. Jordán, 83; *EJMT*, 78; *Obra*, II, 277; ABZ, III, 42, 225 and n. 16; Almada 1937, 49, 52.

NAVARRETE, FRANCISCO ANTONIO, S.J., was born in Baeza, in the province of Jaén, Spain, about 1685, and joined the Society in México in 1708. He was stationed at San Francisco Borja in 1717 when, with Luis Mancuso, Antonio Arias and Ignacio Estrada, he was instrumental in the establishment of the Colegio de Nuestra Señora de Loreto in San Felipe el Real de Chihuahua. With Estrada and Arias, he chose the site for the college, a site now occupied by the Palacio del Gobierno and during the Revolution used as the prison in which Father Miguel Hidalgo y Costilla was executed on July 30, 1811. Navarrete laid the cornerstone on February 2, 1718, and became the first rector, serving the school in various capacities until 1737, when he was transferred to the college at Querétaro. The author of a descriptive poem, *Aqueducto de Querétaro,* published in 1739, he died in Querétaro on August 7, 1749. *EJMT*, 199; *Obra*, I, 111, 156; ABZ, IV, 255, and n. 4, 321, n. 3; *Chihuahuenses,* 104, 253; Barri, 85.

NEUMANN, JOSÉ, S.J., was born in Brussels on August 5, 1648, the child of a Belgian mother and an Austrian father in the service of Archduke Leopold Wilhelm, who had been named governor of Pays-Bas (Belgium) in 1647. The Neumann family returned with the archduke to Vienna in May 1656. By 1663, Neumann lived with his family on Olomouc, the capital of Moravia, and it was from here that he entered the Society on September 24, at the Bohemian Novitiate in Brno. From October 1665 to the following September he taught Latin in Prague, and spent the next three years studying mathematics and philosophy at the College of St. Clement in that city. For three years after September 1669, he taught Latin grammar and other subjects at Brno, and in the fall of 1672 began the study of theology at Olomouc. He was ordained in December 1675, completed his studies the following June, and apparently taught at Brno until he was accepted as a missionary. He left Prague on April 11, 1678, and, with eighteen other Jesuits including Eusebio Francisco Kino and Juan María Ratkay, sailed from Genoa for Spain on June 12. Neumann and Ratkay left Cádiz without Kino on July 11, 1680, landed at Veracruz on September 15 and, from México, started north to Tarahumara on November 18. They reached Coyáchic on February 1, 1681, and were assigned by José Tardá, the superior, Ratkay to Yepómera and Neumann to Sisoguíchic. Neumann served at Sisoguíchic, building churches there and at Echoguita, from March 7, 1681, until June 21, 1697, when he was forced to abandon his post for the comparative safety of Cárichic. After peace he stayed at Cárichic until his death on May 1, 1732. He served four terms as superior of the Rectorado de San Joaquín y Santa Ana and was thrice visitador of Tarahumara Alta, for a total of nine years. He is best known for his *Historia Seditionum*. With Ratkay he is buried under the floor of the Cárichic church, on the gospel side of the altar. *EJMT*, 138–140, 175, 182, 197; Bolton,

41, n. 1; Neumann, *Historia,* 140, 142, 166, 167, 221; Neumann 1681; Neumann Sept. 1693; Neumann 1698; Fernández Abeé; *Introduction,* 4; Christelow 1939, 424–426, 428, 440; *Obra,* II, 301, 308; González, xxxi–xxxv, xxxviii–xxxix, xli–xlii, xlvii, 2, n. 4, n. 5, 34, n. 33, n. 37, 103, n. 75.

NORIEGA OVIEDO ORDÓÑEZ DE MIER, PEDRO, S.J., was born in 1654 at Carreña, in the province of Asturias, Spain, and became a Jesuit in México in 1678. Nine years later he was assigned to Nonoava, where, except for two years in Guazápares and Tubares between 1690 and 1692, he stayed until his death on January 20, 1704. From 1699 until 1702 he served as rector of the partido of San Joaquín y Santa Ana. Neumann 1690; Bannon, 31; *Obra,* II, 234; González, 40, n. 6, 61, n. 48, 62, n. 49, 114–115, n. 102, 157, n. 170, 184, n. 31; ABZ, IV, 98, n. 14; *Chihuahuenses,* 364.

NORTIER, JUAN, S.J., was born in Flesinga, Holland, on February 22, 1726, and entered the Society on October 16, 1751. In charge of Tutuaca and Yepáchic at the expulsion, he was permitted to leave Spain and return to his homeland. *Chihuahuenses,* 202, 364; Zelis, 30–31, 90, 135; *Misiones,* 102.

NÚÑEZ, JUAN ANTONIO, S.J., first appears in a 1738 visitation report, when he had been for three months in charge of San Ignacio, a Cora settlement of Nayarit. By 1748 he was at Satevó, and was serving as superior of the missions, a post he still held in 1751. *Obra,* II, 557; *Misiones,* 90, 95; Rinaldini. Almada 1937, 175, is mistaken in putting Núñez at the Satevó near Batopilas on some date after 1734.

OÑATE, JUAN DE, was born about 1549, the son of Cristóbal Oñate, who had come to New Spain with Cortés. In 1595 he received a contract to colonize New Mexico, with the titles of governor, captain general and adelantado. With troops, settlers and Franciscans, he left Santa Bárbara on January 21, 1598, and reached Río Bravo (Río Grande) on April 20. After reconnoitering, the party established the first New Mexico capital on July 11 at San Juan, on the Río Grande, moving shortly to San Gabriel, near the junction of Río Chama, which remained the capital until the found-ing of Santa Fé in 1610. Oñate did extensive exploration, to the north and east into Kansas in 1601 and down the Colorado to the Gulf of California in 1605. In 1607 he resigned as governor and returned to the south to face the investigation and charges which were the usual fate of Spanish conquistadores. He was exonerated by 1624, and died in that year or in 1628. Hammond and Rey, I, 6–38; *Webster's Biographical Dictionary,* 1122.

ORDAZ, MANUEL, S.J., was born in Spain in 1660 and entered the Society in 1684. In 1692 he left for New Spain and by the following year was stationed at the Casa Profesa in México. From 1695 to 1720 he was in the Chínipas mission field, probably first at Guazá-pares, but he used Cerocahui as his base perhaps as early as 1696 and certainly after 1697. He began in 1696 to work among the Tubares and around Urique, and in December 1697, founded Cuiteco. When the 1697 revolt was at its height, he left the protection of the Spanish troops in the area, and, accompanied by three domestics, sought out the rebels to ask their surrender. He and his companions were seized and two of them were clubbed to death at his feet, the third escaping. Firmly clutching his crucifix while he prayed, Ordaz was unharmed and ultimately released. By 1699 he had probably established the pueblos of Tubares and Satevó (the one near Batopilas) and in that or the following year may well have crossed the barranca to baptize in the area of Sámachic. Ordaz was superior of the Chínipas mission from 1708 to 1711 and was visitor from 1714 to 1717. In 1720 he was transferred to the Villa de Sinaloa, serving also as visitador until 1723, when he became rector of the college at Valladolid. From 1726 until his death on June 22, 1738, he was at the Casa Profesa in México. *EJMT*, 183, 201; Neumann, *Historia*, 233, 291; *Introduction*, 49a; Bannon, 31; Pennington 1963, 11; *Obra*, II, 234, 241; González, 112, n. 98, 125, n. 119, 160, n. 176, 204, n. 70, 205, n. 73; *Catálogo, 1716–1720;* ABZ, IV, 491.

OREÑA, ANTONIO, S.J., was born in Santander about 1647 and reached México in 1665. His studies complete, he brought Christi-anity to Sisoguíchic in 1676. By 1678, when he left for Bácum, in Sonora, he had also founded Echoguita (now Bocoyna) and had baptized and taught on the western slope in Cuiteco. He died in Sonora between 1684 and 1686. Escalona; *Chihuahuenses*, 159, 503; Ortiz, 324, 332, 377; *Obra*, II, 229, 293; González, 25, n. 9, n. 11; Roca, 322, 422.

OROZCO, DIEGO, S.J., was born in Plasencia, in Extremadura, Spain, in 1587 or 1588, became a Jesuit in 1602 and went to New Spain in 1605. Until 1614 he studied in México, and then taught in Puebla and Oaxaca. In 1616 he became a missionary to the Tepehuán, and when the revolt broke, he was in charge of Santiago Papasquiaro. With Bernardo Cisneros and other Spaniards, he was besieged in the church, but came out with the other Europeans under a flag of truce and a promise of safety. Both priests and all but six of the others were killed on November 18, 1616. His body was not recovered. ABZ, II, 273, n. 11; *Chihuahuenses*, 380; Dunne 1944, 127–130; *EJMT*, 27–29; Bancroft, I, 323; Saravia 1943, 55–56; Zambrano, X, 612–627; Decorme, *Mártires*, 46, 48, 49, n. 1.

ORTEGA, MIGUEL, S.J., was at Coyáchic at least by February 1690, and he was still there in 1692. In 1708 he served as visitador of the mission of San Joaquín y Santa Ana, and died at Cárichic in 1712. González, 40, n. 6, 61, n. 48, 62, n. 49, 181, n. 23, 184, n. 31. Calling him Arteaga, Neumann 1690 suggested he ran Coyáchic more like a country estate than a mission.

ORTIZ FORONDA, DIEGO JUAN, S.J., was born in Guadalupe, Extremadura, in 1655, and joined the Society in 1674. He came to New Spain two years later with Manuel Sánchez, and by 1678 was teaching at the college in Veracruz. In 1681 he was at the San Luis Potosí college and three years later went to Tarahumara as a missionary. He spent three years at Tagírachic, a visita of Cárichic, and was transferred in 1687 to Parral, where he served as procurador of the college which Tomás Guadalajara had just established. Ortiz returned to the north before 1690 and was at Yepómera when the Tarahumaras revolted in that year. With two Spaniards, Lt. Juan Urías and Francisco Fontes, he was killed on an uncertain date, perhaps as early as March 29 (González, 42, n. 10), but not later than April 11 (Saravia 1943, 110). When Governor Juan Isidro Pardiñas arrived in Yepómera, he gathered up the bones of the three Europeans and on June 16, 1690, Tomás Guadalajara, rector of the colegio at Parral, and the visitador, Francisco María Pícolo, of Cárichic, saw to their burial in a single grave near the altar of the burned church. *EJMT*, 169; *Chihuahuenses,* 384; Neumann, *Historia*, 172, 175–176; Bannon, 23; González, 42, n. 10, 49, n. 23; ABZ, IV, 97, n. 10; Zambrano, X, 659–665.

ORTIZ ZAPATA, JUAN, S.J., is properly called Ortiz, but he has been almost universally referred to as Zapata. He was born in Zacatecas in 1620, became a Jesuit in 1638, and by 1644 was in charge of the Tepehuán mission of Santa Catalina. In 1677 he was named visitador general. By 1681 he was rector at San Luis Potosí, and from 1684 until 1687 he was at the Colegio Máximo in México. He is said to have died there on September 14, 1689, but there is a suggestion that he was alive in January of the following year. Bancroft, I, 345; Zambrano, X, 675–680; ABZ, III, 268, IV, 26, n. 37; *Diccionario Porrúa*, 1154. *Obra*, II, 292, asserts that in 1677, when he was named visitador general, Ortiz was in Tarahumara as an assistant at San Francisco Borja, from which he had founded one of its visitas, Saguárichic. The report seems highly questionable.

OSORIO, DIEGO, S.J., was born in Ribadeo, in Galicia, Spain, about 1608, and entered the Society in 1630. He took over the Tizonazo settlement on its establishment in 1639 and stayed until the Toboso revolt of 1645. After he returned to the south, he was rector of the college of San Jerónimo at Puebla in 1650, and of the college at Querétaro in 1653. He left the latter post to become procurador of the province. In 1657 he resigned as procurador because of his health, asking to be sent back to the mission field. Instead, in 1658 he was named rector of the college of San Ildefonso at Puebla and served at least until 1659. In 1662 he was at the college in Valladolid. ABZ, III, 39, n. 36, 39–40; *Obra*, II, 264; Zambrano, X, 694–698. Zambrano, X, 697, follows Pradeau, *Noticias,* in ascribing to Diego Osorio a letter from Mátape in Sonora, dated February 24, 1690. Pradeau must be confused with José Osorio S.J., whom Zambrano, X, 699, puts at Mátape from 1685 until his death on June 22, 1691.

OSORIO, FRANCISCO, S.J., was probably a native of México. He went to California in 1725 and stayed for two years, but at least from August 1738 to May 1739 he was in charge of Cárichic. He evidently remained in the area, since he baptized at Temeýchic in July 1741, but I can't place him definitely until May 26, 1743, when he was at Papigóchic. There, he found the parish books to be in error and complained that the pages were not numbered (they still weren't in 1971). He stayed at Papigóchic until February 1746, when he probably went to Coyáchic, where by the following year he was so deep in debt that the visitador was about to replace him. That summer he suffered a disabling stroke but was still in residence in 1748. Osorio 1744; Osorio 1747; Hierro Aug. 30, 1747; Hierro Nov. 1747; *Misiones,* 91; *Obra* II, 544; *Libro III; Libro V; Libro VIII.*

OZADA, JOSÉ ZAMORA DE LA.   See ZAMORA.

PALACIOS, RAFAEL, S.J., was born on August 5, 1733, at Huejotzingo, Puebla, and joined the Jesuits in 1750. He was in charge of Chinarras from 1759 until December, 1762, when he went to Santo Tomás. Arrested there, he was transported to Spain and died in Barcelona on June 23, 1801. *Chihuahuenses,* 392; Zelis, 32–33, 103, 135, 158; *Misiones,* 102; *Libro VI.*

PALMA, BLAS DE LA, S.J., was at Santo Tomás from April, 1727, until August 1762, and served as rector of Tarahumara Alta shortly after 1747. *EJMT,* 212; Lizasoaín, *Noticia,* 21; Palma; *Misiones,* 91, 94, 98; Rinaldini; *Libro VI.*

PARDIÑAS VILLAR DE FRANCOS Y FERNÁNDEZ FRANCO, JUAN ISIDRO, Knight of the Order of Santiago, had been governor of the province of Puebla from 1684 until August 16, 1687, when he became governor of Nueva Vizcaya, having bought the position for 35,000 pesos. He blamed the 1690 Tarahumara revolt on Jesuit persecution of the Indians and sought their removal, but Father José Neumann crossed the sierra and made a fast trip through Chínipas and Sinaloa to México, where he succeeded in getting the viceroy to direct that the Jesuits should be restored to their churches and protected by armed guards until peace should be fully secured.

Pardiñas served as governor until March 30, 1693, but in 1703 he was exiled from New Spain for engaging in contraband trade. He died in 1726. Bancroft, I, 581; *Obra*, II, 299; González, 46, n. 14; *Chihuahuenses,* 395; Bandelier, II, 48, 49, 52.

PARDO, SEBASTIÁN, S.J., was the first priest to be stationed permanently at Santa María de las Cuevas, but in less than a year he went to Tizonazo and was lost to view. Calderón; González, 62, n. 49.

PASCUAL, JOSÉ, S.J., was born in Valencia about 1609, entered the Society in 1626, and had just finished his studies and been ordained when he was sent to Tarahumara in 1639. He and Gerónimo Figueroa arrived in Parral in June, but Pascual was sent south to Las Bocas to learn Rarámuri. On August 15, 1639, he joined Figueroa at San Felipe de Jesús, of which he was intermittently in charge until after 1673. In 1648 or 1649 he became superior of the Tarahumara missions, and served until about 1652. In the summer of 1650, after the martyrdom of Cornelio Beudín at Papigóchic, he accompanied Governor Guajardo and his troops in their campaign against the Tarahumaras.

Late in 1650 and in 1651, Diego Evía, Bishop of Durango, citing the constant dangers from the Tarahumaras, renewed his attempt to secularize the missions, and to replace both Franciscans and Jesuits with secular clergy. Pascual vigorously defended the missionary position, and on February 7, 1652, the Real Audiencia at Guadalajara ruled in favor of the two Orders and against Bishop Evía. The next year the bishop renewed the attack, claiming that the Jesuits overworked the Indians and trafficked in corn and cattle to their own profit and at the expense of the Tarahumaras. The bishop was transferred to Oaxaca, but an inquiry was begun and dragged on interminably. The Jesuit defense was finally concluded on July 12, 1664, when Pascual sent from Parral his *Respuesta* on behalf of the Society. The Audiencia again ruled for the missionaries on February 7, 1665. Father Pascual apparently was transferred to Las Bocas in 1667 and served until 1673, when he was back at San Felipe. On some date thereafter he became rector of the college at Guadalajara, where he died on April 25, 1676. In addition to his defenses of the Jesuits, he wrote a Rarámuri dictionary (unpublished) and numerous reports including the *Noticias*, an account of the midcentury revolts. Zambrano, XI, 111–151; ABZ, II, 466, n.

44; *EJMT*, 45, 47, 55, 61, 68, 80; *Chihuahuenses*, 397; Pascual 1651, 179, 187, 206; Pascual 1664; *Carta de la Real Audiencia; Introduction,* 12, 13, 25, 29; Christelow 1939, 427; Bancroft, I, 346, 354–355, 359–361; Saravia 1954, III, 278, 317, 324; *Obra,* II, 258–260, 266, 268–269, 272, 277, 284, 312; González, 9, n. 5.

PASTRANA, JOSÉ LUIS, S.J., was born in Puebla on February 29, 1716, became a Jesuit at 16, and served in the province of Piaxtla, at San Pablo in 1748 and Yamoriba in 1751. When he came to the college at Parral is not clear, but by 1761 he had served long enough to have rebuilt the church after a fire. He was arrested at Parral on June 26, 1767, transported to Spain and then to Italy, and died in Bologna on January 17, 1780. *Chihuahuenses*, 202, 398; Zelis, 32–33, 157; *Misiones*, 91, 95; *Obra*, I, 96, 465.

PEÑA, BALTHASAR DE LA, S.J., born in New Spain, was assigned to Santo Tomás in 1695. When the 1697 revolt broke, he escaped to the safety of the presidio at Villa Aguilar, and from there went to Parral. He was sent first to Parras, but in 1723 returned to Tarahumara and was stationed at Satevó. From late in 1728 or early in 1729, he was at Santa María de las Cuevas, serving as rector from 1734 to 1737. He died at Santa María in 1743. Neumann, *Historia*, 196, 207; Neumann 1698; Calderón; *Introduction,* 49; Peña; *Obra*, II, 281; González, 70–71, n. 12, 89, n. 46, 154, n. 166.

PEÑA, SALVADOR IGNACIO DE LA, S.J., was born at Compostela, Nayarit, on February 1, 1719, and became a Jesuit on December 31, 1739. He was a missionary among the Seris until 1750, when he took over Cucurpe in Sonora, where he served until late in 1763. In 1766 he came to Chihuahua to serve the college, where he was arrested and from which he was deported. He died at Ferrara, Italy, on October 18, 1775. *Chihuahuenses*, 500; Zelis, 32–33, 103, 157; *Obra*, I, 113; Roca, 132.

PEREIRA, JOSÉ, S.J., was born on July 30, 1735, at San Vicente, Guatemala, and entered the Order on January 25, 1755. He taught grammar at the Colegio de Loreto in Chihuahua at the time of the expulsion, and after arriving in Spain was sent to Italy. He died on June 22, 1798, at Bologna. *Chihuahuenses*, 401; Zelis, 32–33, 103, 158; *Obra*, I, 113, 465.

Pícolo, Francisco María, S.J., was born in Palermo, Sicily, on March 25, 1654, studied grammar, literature, rhetoric and philosophy at the Jesuit college in Palermo, and joined the Order on November 1, 1673. He taught in colleges in Marsala and Malta from 1676 until 1680, when he returned to Palermo to study theology. After ordination he asked for a missionary post, went to Rome, then Naples and Cádiz and reached México by way of Guatemala in February 1684. Assigned to Cárichic, he began work on April 20, 1684, and served until 1697, his last entry in the *Libro de Difuntos* being October 13 of that year. He served as visitador of Tarahumara from 1690 until 1693, and built at Cárichic what Peter Masten Dunne called "the finest church in all the land."

In 1697 Juan María Salvatierra was organizing the second Jesuit assault on California and, when the provincial decided that Eusebio Kino should stay in Pimería, Pícolo, who had gone from Cárichic to Guadalupe in October, asked to take his place. He reached California on November 23, 1697, a month after Salvatierra. In California he founded San Javier de Biaundó in Viggé and San Juan Londó, was sent to the mainland on a begging trip toward the end of 1701 and in 1702 wrote his famous *Informe* regarding California, carrying it to Guadalajara and México, where he successfully sought aid for the Jesuit churches. In 1704 he took charge of the new mainland post of Guaymas, established as a supply station for the peninsula. From 1705 until 1709 he served as visitador of Sonora, returning to Santa Rosalía Mulegé, which he administered until 1718, when he was transferred to Loreto Conchó. He became superior of California in 1720, but had relinquished the office by 1726. On February 22, 1729, he died at Loreto in the arms of Father Nicolás Tamaral, thus ending what Father Dunne called "a heroic and a well-nigh perfect career." Neumann, *Historia*, 168, 256, 261, 262; Neumann 1698; *Obra*, II, 294, n. 8; González, 37, n. 48, 37, n. 49, 49, n. 22, 162, n. 182; ABZ, IV, 82, n. 36, 140, n. 11, 154, n. 166, 161, 162, 180 and n. 1, 182, 193, 260, 339, n. 26; Pícolo 1702, ed. Burrus, 2–13; Pícolo 1702, ed. Hammond, 27–28; *EJMT*, 197; Dunne 1952, 255; *Libro III*; Balthasar, 55–56; Burrus 1955, 66, 75.

Prado, Martín, S.J., was at San Pablo in 1673 and 1678, but otherwise is unknown. *EJMT*, 98; *Obra*, II, 280; ABZ, III, 315; Zambrano-Gutiérrez, XII, 41–43.

PRIETO, SEBASTIÁN, S.J., was at Cocomórachic until October 1748, when he took over Cárichic, serving through April 1749, when he traded places with Luis Angel Yáñez of Papigóchic. He stayed at Papigóchic until the end of June 1758, when it seems likely that he died. *Misiones*, 91, 94, 98; Rinaldini; *Libros I; Libro V.*

PROTO, PEDRO MARÍA, S.J., born at Milazzo, Sicily, in 1652, joined the Society in 1680 and reached México late in 1692. Assigned to Cocomórachic in 1693, he was rector of the area when the 1697 revolt occurred. He happened to be at Mátachic when the rebels attacked his church and house at Cocomórachic, and he therefore proceeded to Villa Aguilar, directing the other priests in the Papigóchic valley to join him. From September to November 1697, he helped out at Cárichic, but when peace was restored he took charge of Santo Tomás, serving there until 1701, when he was transferred to Yécora. Before his death at Yécora in 1730, he had built churches both there and in Maicoba. Neumann, *Historia*, 170, 198, 205–207, 257; Neumann 1698; Neumann 1723; *Introduction*, 49; Januske; *Obra*, II, 238, n. 24; González, 79, n. 27, 88, n. 44, 185, n. 32; Pineli; *Catálogo, 1716–1720;* ABZ, IV, 500; Roca, 300, 302, 417, n. 37; Cañas, 622. Fernández Abeé says Proto succeeded Francisco María Pícolo at Cárichic and was himself succeeded by José Neumann, but Fernández must have been misled by seeing a Proto signature on the Cárichic registers. A more careful examination would demonstrate that Proto was merely a visitor, since one page of *Libro III* shows, in succession, signatures of Neumann, Pícolo, Neumann, Proto and Neumann.

PUENTE, JUAN LARREA Y LA. See LARREA.

RAMÍREZ MONTEJANO, JACOBO, S.J., was rector of the Chihuahua college in 1747. *Pobladores*, 6.

RAMOS, FRANCISCO XAVIER, S.J., surfaces only at San Pablo in 1745. Ramos 1745.

RATKAY, JUAN MARÍA, S.J., an Hungarian baron, belonged to the family of the Counts of Ratkay. He was born on November 13, 1647, at Velik Tabor, Croatia, was a page at the court of Emperor Leopold I in Vienna, and entered the Society on November 13,

1664. He studied at the Jesuit seminary in Trencsén, Upper Hungary, and after ordination went to Genoa, where, with José Neumann, Eusebio Francisco Kino and others, he sailed for Spain on June 12, 1678. He spent two years in Sevilla, where he was assigned the name Arrasquín, learned Spanish and became proficient as a glassblower, cartwright, tinsmith, tailor, hempspinner, sackmaker and woodcarver.

Ratkay and Neumann sailed from Cádiz on July 11, 1680, went north late in November and reached Coyáchic on February 1, 1681. José Tardá, the superior, immediately assigned Ratkay to Yepómera, but the Hungarian baron was unable to stand the cold climate either there or in Tutuaca, to which he was transferred. Later in the year, and certainly before August 14, 1681, Bernardo Rolandegui was called to México from Cárichic, and Ratkay filled the vacancy, building, or rebuilding, a stone church and establishing four visitas. On March 20, 1683, he completed his *Account of the Tarahumara Missions,* to accompany which he drew a map of Tarahumara, described in Burrus 1967, I, 27, and reproduced as one of the 46 numbered maps comprising Vol. II of that work. Another copy of the Ratkay map is bound at the end of Father Burrus' 1962 edition of Pícolo's *Informe.* Ratkay died at Cárichic, unattended, on December 26, 1683, and while Neumann initially thought he had been poisoned, he was later satisfied that death was due to a heart attack. He is buried, with Neumann, under the floor of the Cárichic sanctuary, on the gospel side of the altar. *EJMT*, 138, 139, 140, 142, 163; Neumann, *Historia*, 167, 318, n. 151, n. 152, 168; Neumann 1681; Neumann 1682; Neumann 1686; *Introduction*, 47; *Obra*, II, 308 and n. 22; González, xxxviii, xxxix, xli, xliv, 34, n. 33, 34–35, n. 38, 37, n. 47; Zambrano, XII, 405–411; Gyula Tömördy, 41–43, 45.

RAUCH, BALTHASAR, S.J., a German, was born about 1683 and entered the Society in 1704. In 1720 he was at Sisoguíchic, but by June 1722, he had gone to Cárichic, apparently returning to Sisoguíchic in October of the same year. By 1725 he had built a fine new church at Sisoguíchic, as well as a good house, but two years later he went to Guazápares, and he was still there in 1731. He died on January 20, 1735, in the Chínipas area, and probably at Guazápares. He was reported in 1731 to be undertaking a biography of Neumann, but if it was ever completed it has not been found. Neumann, *Historia*, 291; Neumann, *Letters*, 305, n. 67; Guendulián, 31; *Obra*, II, 240; González, xxxl, lxii, n. 2, 201, n. 65; *Libro I*.

RETANA, JUAN FERNÁNDEZ.   See FERNÁNDEZ.

REXIS, JUAN FRANCISCO, S.J., should not be confused with the French Jesuit saint of the same name. In 1725 he served at Sisoguíchic and before that he had completed a church and house at Guacayebo. Bancroft, I, 599, n. 24; Guendulián, 31.

RICO, FELIPE, S.J., was at Zape in 1748 and came to Santa María de las Cuevas in 1751. He probably left in the following year. *Misiones*, 91, 95; Rinaldini; Bancroft, I, 598, n. 24.

RINALDINI, BENITO, S.J., was born in Brescia, Italy, on June 15, 1695, and entered the Society in 1712. In 1724 he went to Nabugame as its first missionary, but to escape the severe winters he stayed at Batayapa near Chinatú most of the time. In 1743 he completed a Tepehuán grammar, and late in the following year was transferred to Huejotitlán. He was still there in 1751, but ABZ, II, 355, n. 40, and Pennington 1969, 37, n. 29, are wrong in reporting his death between that year and 1755, an error undoubtedly resulting from the fact that his name is not in the 1755 list in *Misiones*, 96–99. Where he was in 1755 doesn't appear, but by 1759 he was at Coyáchic serving as visitador. Téllez; *Misiones*, 91, 95; Rinaldini; Bandelier, III, 500; *Obra*, II, 234, n. 19, 242, 243, and n. 32, 245, 310, n. 24; Almada 1937, 175.

RÍOS, FRANCISCO XAVIER DE LOS, S.J., baptized at Santo Tomás from March until June, 1762. *Libro VI*.

ROA, AGUSTÍN, S.J., was in Tarahumara as early as 1689 and at some point served under Tomás Guadalajara. In 1708 he was reported in Tarahumara Antigua and by 1723 was stationed at San Pablo, serving as rector. He wrote a Rarámuri dictionary, never published. *Obra*, II, 312, and n. 27; González, 44, n. 12, 184, n. 31, 201, n. 65.

ROBLEDO, JOSÉ, S.J., was on his way north to be rector at the Chihuahua college in September 1747, but I can find no other reference to him. Andonaegui Sept. 1747; Gera Oct. 25, 1747.

ROLANDEGUI, BERNARDO, S.J., a Basque, was born in Zaragoza, Spain, in 1648, and entered the Order in 1665. His first missionary post was Cárichic, which he took over in 1679. By January 1681, when José Neumann and Juan María Ratkay arrived in Tarahumara, he was in charge of San Bernabé, serving Cárichic and Coyáchic as visitas. In 1681, he was called to serve in the cathedral in México, returning the following year as visitador. He completed his visitation report in México on February 14, 1682, and went north again, to serve as superior of the Tarahumara missions from 1684 until 1687, when he became rector of the college at San Luis Potosí. In November 1689, he was named substitute procurador, and in 1690 he was rector of the college at Pátzcuaro. In 1696 he was given the same post at the college of San Ildefonso in Puebla, and in November, 1698, he was elected procurador. While he was in Spain he was chosen to succeed Juan María Salvatierra as provincial, a post he assumed on September 17, 1706. He died on November 3, 1707. *EJMT*, 142, 144; Neumann, *Historia*, 167; Fernández Abeé; *Introduction*, 38, 47; Neumann 1682; *Obra*, II, 294, and n. 8, n. 9, 307; Rolandegui, González, xli, 25, n. 11, 35, n. 40; ABZ, IV, 14*, 211, n. 25, 152, 175, 208–209.

ROMERAL, PEDRO TAMARÓN Y.   See TAMARÓN.

ROMERO, MANUEL, S.J., was in Cárichic between May and December 1738. *Libro III*.

RUANOVA, FELIPE, S.J., was born in Veracruz on May 9, 1716, and joined the Society on March 18, 1737. By 1750 he was in charge of Los Cinco Señores, a Tepehuán mission at Nazas, but in 1753 he was transferred to Sisoguíchic. On some date after 1755 and before 1761 he went to Mátachic, from which he was serving as visitador at the time of the expulsion. He died in Bologna on May 16, 1779. *EJMT*, 231; Dunne, 1937, 14; Lizasoaín, *Noticia*, 22; *Chihuahuenses*, 202, 472; Zelis, 38–39, 135, 159; Braun 1765; *Misiones*, 95, 98, 102; *Destierro*; Rinaldini.

RUIZ CONTRERAS, DIEGO, S.J., born about 1635 in Guatemala, was ordained in 1665. Except for brief service at Cárichic which may have begun a year or so before 1678 but did not extend beyond 1679, his work was entirely with the Indians in Tepotzotlán and Pátzcuaro. He died in México on June 16, 1683. Ortiz, 324, 329; *EJMT*, 131; Fernández Abeé; *Introduction*, 36; *Obra*, II, 293; González, 25, n. 9, n. 11; ABZ, IV, 29, n. 54.

SAAVEDRA, LUIS MONSALVE. See MONSALVE.

SAAVEDRA, YSIDRO IGNACIO, S.J., was born in Oaxaca on February 7, 1727, joined the Order on April 26, 1749, and first appears in the Papigóchic baptismal register in November 1758. His last entry was in July 1764, during which month he also served Temeýchic, temporarily without a priest. At the expulsion, he was at the Colegio de Zacatecas, from which he was deported, first to Spain, and then to Italy. He died in Bologna on October 13, 1772. Lizasoaín, *Noticia*, 22; Zelis, 38–39, 124, 160; *Libro V*; *Libro VIII*.

SACHI, NICOLÁS, S.J., was born in Napoli, Italy, on July 4, 1703, and joined the Society on October 9, 1720. He was successively at the Colegio de Loreto, at Chinarras, and, by 1748, at Tubares. In 1750 he was transferred to Cerocahui, where he built the church which, with reconstruction, has remained standing. In 1759, with José Miqueo of Temeýchic, he explored the Barranca del Cobre. He was still at Cerocahui at the expulsion and, with the other Chínipas Jesuits, was taken to Parral, and then to Zacatecas, by Lieutenant Diego Becerril, acting under orders of Captain Lope Cuéllar. He died on May 12, 1774, in Bologna. *Chihuahuenses*, 202, 437; Zelis, 38–39, 104, 133, 160; *Misiones*, 18, n.26, 90, 94, 98, 101; Rinaldini; Almada 1937, 175.

SALCEDO, JOSÉ GARCÍA. See GARCÍA.

SALVATIERRA, JUAN MARÍA, S.J., was born in Milano, Italy, on November 15, 1648, and joined the Society in 1668. He was ordained in 1675 and arrived in Veracruz on September 13, 1675. He concluded his studies in México and went to the Chínipas mission field in 1680. In 1690 he was appointed visitador of Pimería Alta, and in January 1693, became rector of the college at Guadalajara. Three years later he was appointed rector and master of novices at Tepotzotlán, and in February 1697, was authorized by the viceroy to take Christianity to California. He left immediately and was primarily responsible for the Jesuit establishments on the peninsula. From October 21, 1704, until September 17, 1706, he served as provincial of New Spain, but when his term was concluded, he returned to California, from which he was en route to México when he died in Guadalajara on July 18, 1717. Dunne, 1952, 38, 45, 135; ABZ, IV, 66, n. 57, 249–250, and n. 16; Almada 1952, 712–713; Venegas; Burrus 1971, 13–80; Dunne 1950, 31–50.

SÁNCHEZ, MANUEL, S.J., born in Machena, province of Sevilla, in December 1651, entered the Order in 1669. In 1676 he came to New Spain, in 1678 commenced the study of theology at the Colegio de San Pedro y San Pablo, México, and three years later was teaching grammar at the Colegio del Espíritu Santo in Puebla. In 1684 he went as a missionary to Sonora and by the following year was in charge of Yécora and Maicoba. In 1887 he was transferred to Tutuaca. When his Tarahumaras became restive in March 1690, he went to Sonora and appealed to the governor for help against the threatened revolt. Captain Manuel Clavero of San Nicolás returned with the priest and on April 11, 1690, probably near Yepáchic, they were ambushed and killed by a group of rebels led by two Pimas, Ignacio and José Tucubonabapa. Both bodies were later returned to Sonora and buried at Bacanora on November 20, 1690. *EJMT*, 168; *Chihuahuenses*, 489; Neumann, *Historia*, 172–173, 254; Bannon, 23; *Obra*, II, 298 and n. 12; Decorme, *Mártires*, 76; González, 44, n. 12; Roca, 299–300, 417; n. 38; ABZ, IV, 97 and n. 12; *Catálogo de Sonora*, 791.

SÁNCHEZ DE TAGLE, MARCOS ANDRÉS, who may have been a Jesuit, studied at the college of San Ildefonso in México and in July 1747 was vicar and ecclesiastical judge at Cusihuiriáchic. Sánchez, *Carta á Escobar;* Sánchez, *Carta al Provincial.*

SÁNCHEZ GUEVARA, JOSÉ, S.J., was born in Puebla about 1654 and came to Tarahumara in 1678, going briefly to Cusihuiriáchic and then to Temeýchic. He is said to have founded Píchachic in the same year, but he may have been transferred from Temeýchic to Sisoguíchic in 1679 and may have stayed at the latter post until early in 1681. He was certainly assigned to Huejotitlán in 1681, where he died two years later on Octover 22. *EJMT,* 131; Ortiz, 324; *Chihuahuenses,* 412; *Introduction,* 36, 38; González, 25, n. 9, n. 11; Zambrano, VII, 430, in reliance on Pradeau, *Relación.*

SANGUESA, JUAN, S.J., was born at Estella in Navarra in 1585, and became a Jesuit in 1605. He finished his studies in México and taught at the Jesuit colleges at Puebla and Tepotzotlán. After the Tepehuán revolt, he went to San Pablo with Nicolás Estrada and stayed for several months. By April 1622, he was in charge of Zape. He visited San Pablo a second time shortly after 1626 and again in 1630. He is probably identical to Julio Sangueza, whom *EJMT*, 36, puts at Indé and Guanaceví in 1623. In 1643, while rector of the college at Tepotzotlán, he was elected procurador. He died on June 23, 1645, at the Colegio Máximo in México. ABZ, III, 16 and n. 12; *EJMT*, 33, 37; *Obra*, I, 253; *Introduction*, 11; Bandelier, II, 131.

SAN JOSÉ CARRAL, ANTONIO DE, S.J., was at Papigóchic on January 30, 1746. *Libro V.*

SAN JUAN Y SANTA CRUZ, MANUEL, a native of Valle de Zopuerta, Vizcaya, Spain, was a Knight of the Order of Santiago. Named governor and captain general of Nueva Vizcaya, he took possession in 1714 and served for six years. He was instrumental in the establishment of the Jesuit college at Chihuahua, giving 40,000 pesos in exchange for the title of fundador. Upon his death on January 23, 1749, he was buried in the college chapel. *Chihuahuenses*, 486; *Obra*, I, 111, II, 311; González, 186, n. 38, 205, n. 73; Barri; Arias Dec. 4, 1718; San Juan.

SANTA CRUZ, FRANCISCO, S.J., appears only at Mátachic in 1755. *Misiones*, 98.

SANTA CRUZ, MANUEL SAN JUAN Y.   See SAN JUAN.

SANTARÉN, HERNANDO, S.J., was born in Huete, in the province of Cuenca, Spain, probably in 1557. He became a Jesuit in 1582, studied in Jesuit colleges in Huete and Belmonte, came to New Spain in 1588, and completed his studies in México in 1592. He served first in Puebla and then in Sinaloa. In 1599 he was assigned to the Acaxée country, founded the missions of Topia, and is said to have built more than 40 churches and baptized 50,000. On November 19, 1616, when he was on his way to join in a festival at Zape, he fell into the hands of rebel Tepehuanes at Yoracapa, near Tenerapa, about sixty miles south of Papasquiaro. His body was found months later and was buried at Guadiana with the other priests whose bodies were recovered after the Tepehuán revolt. Dunne, 1944, 132–133; *EJMT*, 29–30; ABZ, II, 276, n. 19; Saravia 1943, 63–66; *Chihuahuenses*, 495; Bancroft, I, 323–324, and n. 36; Decorme, *Mártires*, 52–53; McShane, 146–161; Gutiérrez Casillas, 1964, 14 f f.; Trueba, I, 84.

SARMIENTO, JUAN, S.J., was born in Tapijulapa, Tabasco, in 1634, joined the Order in 1653, went to Satevó in 1665 and stayed at least until 1678. After his missionary service he taught at the Colegio del Espíritu Santo in Puebla and then served as rector of the college at Oaxaca, where he died on October 18, 1700. *EJMT*, 95; *Introduction,* 28; Figueroa 1668, 229; Ortiz, 316; ABZ, III, 285, n. 9; *Diccionario Porrúa*, 1464. Pennington 1963, 18, n. 128, confuses the Jesuit Juan Sarmiento with Antonio de Oca Sarmiento, governor of Nueva Vizcaya from 1665 until 1670. (Bancroft, I, 337.) The basis of the confusion is the complaint in the Parral Archives (referred to by Pennington in his note) made by the priest at Satevó on February 21, 1667, entitled *Queja de los Indios del Pueblo de Satevó*, which is clearly addressed to Governor and Captain General Don Antonio de Oca y Sarmiento but which, at first blush, appears to have been signed *"su humilde capellan Juan Antonio de Oca y Sarmiento,"* whereas in fact it is signed *"su humilde capellan Juan,"* with the name of the addressee repeated at the foot of the instrument.

SIMOIS, LUIS, a native of Guimarães, Portugal, gave two houses on August 15, 1685, to start the Jesuit college at Parral, and the following February gave an additional 18,000 pesos to cover operating expenses. He died in Parral on March 7, 1728, and was buried in the college chapel. His brother José Simois became the patron of the college until his death in 1744. *Obra*, I, 95; *Chihuahuenses*, 503; *Resumen*, 81.

SOTO, BERNABÉ, S.J., was born in Chicuantla, New Spain, about 1629, and entered the Society in 1647. In 1659 he went to the Tepehuán country, serving in Tizonazo at least until 1667 and staying in the north until 1681, when he was named rector of the college at Veracruz. In May 1683, the French pirate Lorenzo Jácome attacked Veracruz, and Soto was held for ransom, beaten, and imprisoned for eight days. He was chosen as Jesuit provincial for New Spain in 1686 and served until 1689. He died at the Colegio Máximo in México on April 25, 1698. *Annua, 1667; Introduction*, 27; Figueroa 1668, 227; *Obra*, I, xvi, 89, 99, 347–348, II, 76, 279; ABZ, III, 268, 357, IV, 49, n. 17, 49–50.

SOTOMAYOR, ANDRÉS ANTONIO, S.J., was at Coyáchic in 1723 and was rector in 1728. González, 201, n. 65; *Administrative Census. of 1728*.

STEFFEL, MATEO, S.J., was born in Iglavia, Bohemia, on September 20, 1734, and joined the Society on October 27, 1754. He was assigned to the northern missions in 1755 and on the death of Francisco Glandorff in August 1763 succeeded him at Tomóchic. Sometime during the two years before June 1767, he was transferred to San Francisco Borja, where he was in charge on the date of the expulsion order. From Spain he was permitted to return to Germany, where, in 1773, he published his *Tarahumarisches Wörtebuch*. He died after 1781. *Chihuahuenses*, 202, 506; Zelis, 40–41, 90, 135; *Obra*, II, 304, n. 18, 312; Braun 1765.

STIGER, GASPAR, S.J., was born at Oberried, Switzerland, on October 20, 1695, became a Jesuit in 1725, and reached New Spain in 1729, traveling as far as Durango with three northern European Jesuits assigned to Pimería Alta: Juan Bautista Grazhoffer, Felipe von Brunegg Ségesser, and Ignacio Javier Keller. He was at Cárichic by November 12, 1731, and, after Neumann's death the following year, administered the partido alone, engaging in a dispute with Spaniards who encroached on the lands of his Indians near the visita of Pasigóchic. In 1733 he was transferred to Pimería Alta, serving very briefly at San Ignacio under Agustín Campos and then replacing Grazhoffer, who had died at Guévavi in May. Ségesser, who was at San Xavier del Bac, became ill and returned to the south, leaving Stiger in charge of both Guévavi and Bac until April 1736, when he replaced the ailing Campos at San Ignacio. He served San Ignacio until his death there in April 1762. During his long tenure he was instrumental in gathering up and sending the papers of Eusebio Kino to México. He also made a map of the area extending to Río Colorado, but it has not been found. Burrus 1967, I, 61–62; Dunne 1957, 54–55; González, xlvii, xlix; Stiger; *Libro III;* Roca, 360, n. 43; *Obra*, II, 422, 430, 474; Donohue 1960, 129; Bancroft, I, 524; Nentvig 1951, 112; Nentvig 1971, 155, n. 69; Dobyns, 6.

STRZANOWSKI, ANTONIO, S.J., was born in Moravia on January 12, 1728, and entered the Society in 1753. His first post was apparently Guaguáchic, where he worked from 1757 until he was transferred to Norogáchic in 1765. He was an expert in the native dialects, founded Sámachic, and built houses and churches there and in Guaguáchic, Guaguevo and Pámachic. He was in charge of Norogáchic at the expulsion, but after his transportation to Spain was permitted to return to his home province. *EJMT*, 231; Dunne 1937, 14; Lizasoaín, *Noticia*, 24; *Chihuahuenses*, 202, 506; Zelis, 40, 41, 90, 135; *Misiones*, 102; *Destierro*; Bancroft, I, 599, n. 24; *Obra*, I, 466, n. 2, II, 303, n. 16. The usual, but incorrect, spelling is *Sterkianowsky*. I am indebted for the correction to the Reverend Ernest J. Burrus, S.J., who has examined the missionary's original signature, dated April 13, 1768, at Puerto de Santa María, Spain.

SUGASTI, IGNACIO, S.J., was born about 1696 in Astigárraga, province of Guipúzcoa, Spain, and entered the Society in 1713. He was at the college in Parral for many years before 1744, when he was transferred to Durango. He died at the college there on May 4, 1747. ABZ, IV, 407 and n. 42.

TAGLE, MARCOS SÁNCHEZ DE.   See SÁNCHEZ.

TAMARÓN Y ROMERAL, PEDRO, the 16th Bishop of Durango, was born in Guardia, Archbishopric of Toledo, Spain, probably in 1695. He received his doctorate and became professor of canon law at the University of Santa Rosa in Caracas. Appointed to the episcopate, he took possession of the see of Durango on March 22, 1758, and served until December 21, 1768, when he died in Bamoa, Sinaloa. He was buried in the parish church in the Villa de Sinaloa. Tamarón, v-vi; González, 129, n. 128.

TÁPIZ, PEDRO, the 12th Bishop of Durango, was born in Burgos, Spain, about 1673. He had been 12 years abbot of the cathedral of Burgos and visitador of the diocese of Tarazona when he was named bishop in 1711. He took possession of the see on February 21, 1713, finished construction of the cathedral at Durango, and made a general visitation of the diocese from May 6, 1715, to February 16, 1716, covering a total of 1,116 leagues and confirming 58,475 persons. He was the first bishop to visit the Villa de Chihuahua, and on April 25, 1718, gave permission for the establishment of its college. He died on April 13, 1722, and three days later was named Bishop of Guadalajara. Bancroft, I, 594; González, 129, n. 128; *Chihuahuenses*, 513; *Obra*, I, 111; ABZ, IV, 9*, 255.

TARDÁ, JOSÉ, S.J., was born about 1645 at Marquisanes in Valencia, entered the Society in 1666, and completed his studies in México. He replaced Fernando Barrionuevo in Tarahumara in December 1673 or early in 1674, and worked with Juan Gamboa until the latter was replaced by Tomás Guadalajara in the summer of 1675. Soon thereafter Tardá and Guadalajara, on orders from the provincial, made an extensive reconnaisance downstream on the Papigóchic as far as Yepómera and into the sierra as far as Tutuaca, reporting on the whole of Tarahumara Alta in a long letter on February 2, 1676. Tardá made his headquarters at Cusihuiriáchic and Coyáchic at least until 1683, serving as rector from 1678 and as visitador and superior from 1681. In March 1683 he was at Las Bocas, learning the language of the Tobosos in preparation for a new assignment, but by 1684 he was rector at Pátzcuaro. In 1687 he became rector of the college at Oaxaca, and in 1690 was sent as procurador to Rome. He died at sea on August 5, 1690. *EJMT* 101,

104, 106–107, 131; Ortiz, 324; González, xvi, 22, n. 1, n. 2, 34, n. 36; Neumann, *Historia*, 157; Neumann 1681; Ratkay, 13; Guadalajara 1676; *Introduction*, 30, 31, 34, 37, 47–48; Jordán, 115, 117; Bancroft, I, 366; *Obra*, II, 284–285, 287–290, 293; ABZ, III, 323, n. 30.

TEJERÍA, DOMINGO, S.J., a brother rather than a priest, had charge in 1723 of the hacienda de Santo Domingo at Tabaloapa, near Santa Eulalia, which Governor San Juan had purchased for the college at Chihuahua. ABZ, IV, 321, n. 3.

TÉLLEZ GIRÓN, LUIS, S.J., appears in the parish records of Temeýchic from December 1735 through June 1736 probably as a temporary assistant to Ignacio Estrada before he took charge of Cerocahui as the successor to Juan Antonio Landa. When Landa died at San Francisco Borja in 1747, Téllez succeeded him there also, serving until 1756. He should not be confused with Juan Téllez Girón, missionary to Nayarit, who was born in Capula, New Spain, and died in Chiapa in 1737. Since it is highly likely that they were brothers, Luis was probably also a native of Capula. Andonaegui Sept. 1747; Téllez; *Misiones*, 91, 95, 98; *Testimonio*, 141; Rinaldini; ABZ, IV, 287, n. 29; Almada 1937, 175; *Libro VIII*.

TEPÓRACA, baptized Gabriel and known as Tepórame or El Hachero (The Woodcutter), has been called the greatest rebel figure of his race. He conceived and led the 1652 revolt, destroying first Villa Aguilar, then San Lorenzo and Satevó before moving on and devastating the Franciscan settlements of Santiago, Santa Isabel, San Gregorio, San Diego and San Bernardino. As though satiated with destruction, he then retired to the sierra. After the main Tarahumara force was defeated by Cristóbal Narváez and after the other leaders began drifting in to surrender, his own people delivered Tepóraca to General Sebastián Sosoaga at Tomóchic on February 27, 1653. Found guilty of treason by a summary court convened by Governor Guajardo at Tomóchic, he refused to confess or to accept the last rites of the Church and was hung on March 4, 1653. His former followers riddled his body with arrows, and it was not cut down, but left hanging. Jordán, 81–83, 85–86; Gómez, xi;

Chihuahuenses, 521–522; Almada 1937, 48–54; Bancroft, I, 356, 358, 360; Saravia 1954, III, 328; *Obra*, II, 273, n. 22, 277; ABZ, III, 225; *EJMT*, 78–79. The formal records of the court proceeding, the sentence and its execution are set forth in full in Almada 1937, 52–53; the sentence only is in *Chihuahuenses*, 521–522.

TEPÓRAME. See TEPÓRACA.

TEXEIRO, ANTONIO, S.J., was at Chinarras, perhaps as a temporary substitute for Dionisio Murillo, sometime during the first half of the decade of the 1750s. Benito Rinaldini, whose report is undated but, by internal evidence, was written during that period, shows the name "Dionisio Murillo" as the Chinarras entry, but it has been crossed out and "Antonio Texeiro" added, apparently in the same hand.

TORRE, MANUEL FLORES DE LA. See FLORES.

TOVAR, HERNANDO, S.J., was born in Culiacán in 1580 or 1581, and joined the Jesuits in 1598. He studied in Valladolid (now Morelia) and México, served in Parras and founded San Andrés, west of Durango. He was passing through Santa Catalina when the Tepehuán revolt broke on November 15, 1616, and he was killed the following day. His body was never found. ABZ, II, 272, n. 6; *Chihuahuenses*, 534; *EJMT*, 27, 29; Bancroft, I, 319, n. 31, 322, n. 34; Saravia 1943, 49–50; Decorme, *Mártires*, 41–44.

TREVIÑO, BERNARDO, S.J., was born about 1694 and came to the northern mission field about 1724. He stayed at Las Bocas, which may have been his first post, at least until 1731, when he was characterized by the visitador José Echeverría as wholly unfit for missionary work. On an uncertain date he was transferred to the college at Chihuahua, where he remained until June 1747, when he took over Temeýchic from Roque Andonaegui. In 1748 he was at Yécora but left by 1750 and was at Santa María de las Cuevas within a year or two thereafter. Palma; Andonaegui Sept. 1747; Téllez; *Misiones*, 91; Rinaldini; Aguirre; Roca, 300, 417, n. 41; *Obra*, II, 77; *Libro VIII*.

TRUJILLO, GASPAR, S.J., was said by Benito Rinaldini, writing about 1750, to have been at Parral. Trujillo was in Nayarit before 1721 and went to California in 1744, where he was in charge of Loreto, served as superior, and in 1748 took over Dolores. His health broken, he returned to the mainland the same year. Rinaldini; ABZ, IV, 278, n. 2; *Obra*, II, 530, 544, n. 4; Dunne 1952, 393, 397.

TRUJILLO, JOAQUÍN, S.J., was born at Fresnillo, Zacatecas, on April 29, 1726, and entered the Order in 1745. He may have gone to California in 1754. For an uncertain time, perhaps between 1751 and 1761, he was at Yepáchic, which he was said to have left in a deplorable state, both spiritual and temporal. By 1761 he was in charge of Tónachic, from which he was removed before June 1765. At the expulsion he was at Puebla. He died in Faenza, Italy, on February 21, 1775. Lizasoaín, *Noticia*, 25; Zelis, 42–43, 104, 161; Braun 1765; *Obra*, II, 544; *Chihuahuenses*, 74; *Misiones*, 94.

ULLOA, ANTONIO DEZA.   See DEZA.

VADILLO, FRANCISCO.   See BADILLO.

VAH, IGNACE.   See LOYOLA.

VALDÉS, FRANCISCO DÍAZ.   See DÍAZ.

VALDEZ, FRANCISCO EVÍA.   See EVÍA.

VALDEZ, JOSÉ GARCÍA.   See GARCÍA.

VALLADARES, DIEGO, S.J., was on the faculty of the college at Chihuahua on March 25, 1723. ABZ, IV, 321, n. 3.

VALLARTA, MARTÍN, S.J., was born in Puebla on August 16, 1711, and entered the Society on July 21, 1726. He came to Onavas, in Sonora, in 1745, but by 1750 he had gone to Yécora and in the following year was at Sisoguíchic. He probably stayed only until 1753, when Felipe Ruanova arrived, but it is certain that in February 1754 he was at Papigóchic, perhaps on his way to another post. At the expulsion he was on the staff of the Colegio del Espíritu Santo de Puebla. He died in Bologna on February 18, 1783. *Misiones*, 89, 94; Rinaldini; Almada 1937, 175; Roca, 261, 412, n. 112; *Chihuahuenses*, 472; *Libro V*; Zelis, 42–43, 114, 162.

VALLE, JUAN DEL, S.J., was born in Vitoria, in Vizcaya, Spain, in 1574 or 1576. He entered the Society in 1591 and came to New Spain in 1594. After completing his studies in México, he went to the Tepehuán country and was at one time superior of the Tepehuán mission. Along with Luis Alavez, 29 Spaniards, 70 Negro slaves and other servants, he was killed at Zape on November 18, 1616. He was buried at Guadiana with the other priests. Dunne 1944, 131; *EJMT*, 29–30; ABZ, II, 275, n. 16; Saravia 1943, 58–59; Pérez 1944, III, 225–232; Decorme, *Mártires*, 48, 49, 50, n. 5.

VARGAS, GREGORIO XAVIER, S.J., was born in Barajas, Spain, on May 9, 1724, and became a Jesuit on December 2, 1741. He was trained at the college of San Andrés in México and in 1756 went to San Francisco Borja. He was still there when the visitador Lizasoaín made his inspection (c. 1762), but probably sometime after June 1765, but before the expulsion he was transferred to México. Transported to Spain and then to Italy, he died in Bologna on March 8, 1801. Lizasoaín, *Noticia*, 26; Zelis, 44–45, 105, 162; Braun 1765. Och, 42, places him (with only the initials "G.B.") at "the first mission of Borgia" when he went through in 1756 on his way to Pimería Alta. Och's editor, Treutlein, 189, n. 30, credits Father Burrus with identifying "G.B." as Gregorio Vargas, and Treutlein may be correct in adding that Vargas was assigned to Satevó in the province of Chínipas on January 19, 1755. But he must certainly be wrong in identifying the Satevó which is hard by Batopilas as the place through which Och passed more than a year later and which he calls "the first mission of Borgia." Och went nowhere near Batopilas or the Chínipas province, but went from Parral north to Satevó, west to San Francisco Borja and thence northwest to Temeýchic, Tomóchic, Tepáchic, Tutuaca, Yepómera and Maicoba.

VARILLAS, GASPAR, S.J., was born about 1637 at Talavera la Real, in Badajoz, Spain, joined the Order about 1652, and arrived in México on October 15, 1678. He reached Temeýchic the following year, remaining until 1685. He stayed in the north at least until 1690, but by 1696 was chaplain of the haciendas of the Colegio del Espíritu Santo in Puebla. He was assigned to Pimería Alta at the end of 1697, reaching Dolores in January 1698. Eusebio Kino sent him to Caborca in June, but he left in July. He apparently remained in the area, visiting Caborca from time to time until 1701, when he was again permanently stationed at that place. He left before the fall of 1702, presumably returning to the south. Andonaegui Dec. 1744; ABZ, IV, 14, n. 52, 123–124, n. 25; Bolton, 331, n. 2, 379, 510, 511, n. 1, 512; Kino, I, 160–164, 174–175, 303–304, II, 251; Manje, 156; Roca, 118.

VASALDÚA, JOSÉ.   See BASALDÚA.

VEGA, JOSÉ HONORATO, S.J., was born in México on February 18, 1726, and joined the Society on June 28, 1748. He served as prefect of the college at Chihuahua, but in September 1764, was assigned to Papigóchic to succeed Ysidro Saavedra. He died in Tamara, Italy, on June 10, 1797. *Chihuahuenses*, 202, 560; Zelis, 44–45, 105, 135, 162; Braun 1765; *Misiones*, 102; *Libro V.*

VELASCO, FRANCISCO, S.J., was born in Castilla in 1656 and joined the Society in 1671. He finished his studies at the Colegio de San Pedro y San Pablo in México in 1681 and left the following year for Tarahumara. He may have gotten to Tutuaca in 1682, and was certainly there by 1684. By 1687 he had been transferred to Mátachic, where he served as rector until 1690. In the latter year he went to San Pablo, where he stayed at least until 1699. He died at Parral on January 18, 1701. González, 40, n. 6, 42, n. 10, 45, n. 13, 62, n. 49.

VELASCO Y ALTIMIRANO, GARCÍA LEGAZPI.   See LEGAZPI.

VERA, FRANCISCO, S.J., was at Tecoripa in Sonora by 1662, but he left sometime after 1674 and was in charge of Tizonazo by 1678. Ortiz, 312; ABZ, III, 354; Roca, 246, 408, n. 45.

VERDIER, JUAN CRISTÓBAL, S.J., obviously of French or Belgian ancestry, was born in 1662, joined the Society in the Bohemian province in 1680 and reached México in 1689. In 1690 he was assigned to Papigóchic, where, except for periods of temporary assistance at Nonoava and Cárichic, he stayed until October 1695, when he was transferred to Sonora. He died before 1708. *EJMT*, 175, 197; Neumann, *Historia*, 140, 170; Neumann Sept. 1693; González, 3, n. 9, 40, n. 5, 41, n. 6, 54, n. 34, 62, n. 49, 70–71, n. 12.

VILLANUEVA, JORGE, S.J., was born in Irapuato, Guanajuato, in 1684 and became a Jesuit in 1704. In 1708 he commenced the study of theology at the Colegio de San Pedro y San Pablo in México, and by 1714 he was in Tarahumara, assigned to the rectorate of Guadalupe. He served a year at Tutuaca, but not before 1717, apparently leaving for Sonora in bad health. Neumann, who was often uncharitable to Creoles, suggests in *Historia*, 287, that he may have "lacked the courage for the many arduous duties of apostolic service." In 1723 he left Sonora and from then until his death on September 17, 1744, was at the college in Valladolid. González, 195, n. 53, 196, n. 54.

VILLAR DE FRANCOS Y FERNÁNDEZ FRANCO, JUAN PARDIÑAS. See PARDIÑAS.

VILLAR, GABRIEL, S.J., was born in México about 1620, became a Jesuit in 1635, and went to San Pablo in 1647. Probably in the following year he transferred to Huejotitlán, trading places with Gerónimo Figueroa. Villar remained at Huejotitlán until his death on January 3, 1689, thus completing 42 years in Tarahumara. He served as rector of Tarahumara Antigua in 1653 and 1678. ABZ, III, 226, n. 17; *EJMT*, 136; Ortiz, 316; *Introduction*, 13; Pascual 1651, 206; Bancroft, I, 348; González, xlvii, 22.

VILLASECA, JOSÉ GUERRERO,   See GUERRERO.

VIVANCO, MANUEL, S.J., was born in Acajete, Puebla, on May 30, 1693, and entered the Society in 1710. He was assigned to the northern missions in 1720, and was at Tizonazo from 1745 on. After secularizaton he was sent to Nonoava, arriving at least by 1755. In March 1765, he was transferred to Papigóchic where, now in failing health, he was assisted by the younger José Vega. Two years later, at the expulsion, he had lost his sight. He started out with the others, but at Zacatecas was unable to continue. He was kept in Zacatecas a month, then moved to Querétaro and a little later to the Colegio del Espíritu Santo in Puebla, where he died on September 9, 1771. Lizasoaín, *Noticia*, 25; Vivanco; Zelis, 46–47, 90, 135, 162; Braun 1765; *Misiones*, 90, 95, 98, 102; Rinaldini; *Obra*, I, 468, and n. 3, II, 312; *Libro V.*

YÁÑEZ, JOSÉ, S.J., was born in Puebla on March 17, 1716, became a Jesuit in 1745, and served at Norogáchic in 1755. Before 1762 he returned to the Colegio de San Javier at Puebla, from which he was expelled. He died in Bologna, Italy, on February 2, 1801. Zelis, 46, 47 117, 163; *Misiones*, 98; Rinaldini.

YÁÑEZ, LUIS AGUSTÍN ANGEL, S.J., was born at Querétaro on October 7, 1719, and entered the Society on April 30, 1738. Before 1748 he was at Tutuaca, from which he also served Yepáchic. In September 1748, he took over Papigóchic, staying until the following February. By April 1749, he was at Cárichic but by 1755 he was in Coyáchic, where he probably served until 1759. In 1761 he was back at Cárichic, but by 1765 he was in failing health, and by the time of the expulsion he was being assisted by Juan Francisco Hauga. Deported to Spain and Italy, Yáñez died in Bologna on May 29, 1779. Lizasoaín, *Noticia*, 23; *Chihuahuenses*, 202, 570; Zelis, 46–47, 135, 163; Braun, 1765; *Misiones*, 91, 94, 98, 102; Rinaldini; Bancroft, I, 599, n. 24; *Libros I; Libro V.*

YDIÁQUEZ, ANTONIO, S.J., took over Norogáchic in December 1719, after the death of Florencio Alderete, but was replaced in February 1720. He probably then went to Nonoava, which he had certainly reached by 1723, and where he stayed at least until 1755. He served as superior in 1748 and helped out at Norogáchic for a time in both 1727 and 1728. *Libro IV;* Hierro June 1747; Ydiáquez 1725; Ydiáquez 1744; *Misiones*, 91, 94, 98; Rinaldini; González, 201, n. 65.

ZAMORA DE LA OZADA, JOSÉ, S.J., was born in Zacatecas on January 6, 1715, became a Jesuit on October 27, 1731, and baptized at Papigóchic during the spring of 1755 and the summer of 1758. Later he officiated at Santo Tomás in September 1762, and was there from April until June in 1766. At the expulsion he was stationed at the college in Celaya, Guanajuato. Permitted to remain in New Spain, he died in Puebla on June 17, 1772. *Libro VI*; *Libro V*; Zelis, 46–47, 90, 128, 163.

ZANNA, GASPAR, S.J., was born in Sassari, Sardinia, in 1673, and entered the Order at age 15. He reached México in 1693 and was ordained three years later. He served in Temeýchic from 1700 until the fall of 1701, when he returned to México because of an unsuccessful attempt by natives of Pachera to burn the Temeýchic church. He worked in México from 1702 until his death on February 13, 1740. González, 166, n. 1; Andonaegui Dec. 1744; Neumann, *Revoltes*, 166, 168, 170· (Latin), 167, 169, 171 (French); Fernández Retana 1701.

ZAPATA, JUAN ORTIZ. See ORTIZ.

ZÁRATE, FRANCISCO XAVIER, probably not a Jesuit, served as vice curate and assistant ecclesiastical judge at Cusihuiriáchic until May, 1747. Zárate; Palma.

ZELADA, FRANCISCO. See CELADA.

ZEPEDA, NICOLÁS, S.J., was born in Puebla about 1610. He apparently came north in 1638 or 1639, and was undoubtedly the founder of Tizonazo, of which he remained in charge until the Toboso revolt of 1644 and 1645, when he retired to Las Bocas and wrote his *Relación*, an account of the revolt.˙He blamed the uprising on the Spanish officials and the miners, whom he accused of exploiting the Indians and holding them in virtual slavery. When his brashness resulted in the bishop ordering him from his visita, he went to Indé and later to México, where he was rector of the college of Santa Ana in 1658. In 1663 he was again in Puebla. Zepeda, 130, 140, 143; Jordán, 74; *Obra*, II, 264; Bancroft, I, 348; *EJMT*, 84; Zambrano, V, 147–158; ABZ, III, 24 and n. 13. *Chihuahuenses*, 59, 469, 481, is certainly wrong in saying that, with José Pascual, Zepeda founded Felipe de Jesús in 1639 and Balleza and Santa Cruz (now Valle de Rosario) the next year.

Notes to the Chapters

Preface

1. *Rarámuri* is probably derived from *rárá* (foot), *júma* (to run) and *ri* (a particle). Pennington 1963, 1, n. 1; Hodge, II, 692; Gómez, 44.
2. As in Pennington 1963.
3. As does Hodge.
4. As does Lumholtz, July 1894, 31 ff.; Lumholtz, Sept. 1894, 296 ff.; Lumholtz, Oct. 1894, 438 ff.; Lumholtz, *Bulletin*, 1894, 299 ff. But Lumholtz 1902 uses *Tarahumare* throughout.
5. And at least one geographer. See Gajdusek, 15 ff.
6. Ortiz.
7. Tamarón.

Chapter 1. Geography

1. Pennington 1972, 1–2.
2. I know of no wholly adequate popular map of Tarahumara. Most are largely inaccurate, and all are incomplete. While not purporting to be complete nor intended as guides for automobile travel, the Operational Navigation Charts issued by the United States Air Force are quite accurate. Similarly, the maps of the American Geographical Society of New York, while now out of date, approach completeness as of their date of issue. Also excellent, although incomplete, are the 1:250,000 maps of the U.S. Army Map Service, issued under the caption *Estados Unidos Mexicanos*, Series F 501.
3. Comparison of the barrancas, and particularly of Barranca del Cobre, to the Grand Canyon is inevitable, but, as pointed out by Gajdusek, 17, unjust because they are so qualitatively different: "The cliff walls are in general less sheer, the colors more delicate, the vegetation more profuse. Moreover, the Sierra Tarahumara presents a system of canyons rather than a single canyon, all carved

by rivers much smaller than the Colorado, though in several places the barrancas are probably deeper than the Grand Canyon."

4. In October 1972, Charles J. Hitch, with whom I had visited Jesuit church sites in Sonora when we were students in Tucson, went with Paul Urbano and me to the sierra. Charlie has become an aficionado of the trees of California, and particularly the spectacular sugar pine of the Sierra Nevada. Between Cárichic and Sisoguíchic the jeep broke down, and while Paul and I were repairing it, Charlie found, on the high ridges, a number of specimens of sugar pine, returning to the car with two of the distinctive long cones. We spent the rest of the trip looking for sugar pines, and thought we saw a few on the ridges between Bocoyna and Creel. But before we got back to the border we lost the two cones, and in the United States Charlie and I found that our botanical friends simply didn't believe our story. The authorities agree with them. Martínez, 57–58, lists as the only pines in the state of Chihuahua, *Pinus Arizonica, Pinus ayacahuite brachyptera, Pinus cembroides, Pinus Chihuahuana, Pinus durangensis, Pinus durangensis quinquefoliata, Pinus leiophylla, Pinus Lumholtzii, Pinus Engelmanni, Pinus Engelmanni Blancoi, Pinus oocarpa,* and *Pinus reflexa.* Pennington 1963, 31, adds *Pinus ponderosa.* Neither lists *Pinus Lambertiana* (the sugar pine) as occurring in the sierra, and Martínez, 57, shows Baja California as the only area in all of Mexico in which it is found.

5. See Kerr, 19; Almada 1971, 1. The highly publicized line through the sierra is the final link in an international rail project which originated in 1900, with promotional overtones, as the Kansas City, Mexico and Orient Railway Company. Kerr, 57.

Chapter 2. The People

1. The precise boundaries of the ancient Tarahumara homeland are necessarily somewhat vague, but there is general agreement respecting the area I delineate. See Sauer 1934, particularly 58.

2. Pennington 1972, 1. Gómez, xiii, estimates 40,000 square kilometers.

3. Ortiz, 316–419.

4. Pennington 1963, 23–24.

5. Lumholtz July 1894, 31.

6. Bennett and Zingg, vii.

7. Plancarte, 101.

8. Plancarte, 17, 101–102. The 1945 count is consistent with the 46,000 reported by the Jesuits in 1920. See Ocampo, 100.

9. Pennington 1963, 24.

10. Rather than the term *Mexican*, I use *mestizo* for the non-Tarahumara population. Because all native-born persons are *ciudadanos,* or citizens, Tarahumaras are, and are entitled to be called Mexicans.

11. In an October 1972 letter to me, the Reverend Luis Verplancken, S.J., quotes a doctor who spent 11 years in the Jesuit hospital at Sisoguíchic as estimating that 80% of the newborn Tarahumara children die before age five. Father Verplancken reports a great fall in this mortality rate since he established a children's hospital and clinic in Creel, and similar improvement is undoubtedly found at Sisoguíchic and Norogáchic.

12. See, for example, Neumann Sept. 1693. There seems to be some evidence, probably questionable, that plagues and epidemics were less severe than

elsewhere because the Tarahumaras were rather quickly cured of at least some European diseases, such as syphilis. See Lumholtz 1902, I, 242.

13. Kennedy 1963, 630–640. The use of alcohol by the Tarahumaras has always been somewhat of a problem. The early Jesuits believed that tesguino contributed to apostasy, revolt and evil living, and did all they could to stamp out its use. See, for example, the account of the experience of Fathers Tardá and Guadalajara at Tutuaca in *EJMT*, 113–115. The civil and military authorities agreed, and sought to curb the liquor traffic. On January 18, 1718, Governor San Juan issued a decree prohibiting Spaniards, Negroes and mulattos from giving the Indians wine or other liquors in exchange for native produce. Spaniards who violated the order were subject to imprisonment, flogging and forced labor in the mines. San Juan 1718.

14. Lumholtz Sept. 1894, 297, tells of the Indians who ran from Guazá-pares to Chihuahua and back in five days, a distance of "nearly eight hundred miles." Unless calculated up and down, the estimate is grossly exaggerated. But since the Barranca del Cobre lies between the two towns, a pedometer would probably register well in excess of the Lumholtz figure. The tale is separately printed under another title in Lumholtz 1895, 92.

15. The *carrera de bola* was discussed in some detail in Lumholtz 1902, I, 282–294. Fried, V. 8, Pt. 2, 865–866, describes the races, differentiating between *dalahípu*, the men's race, and *dowérami*, the women's race, in which a wooden hoop and stick are used instead of a ball. The subject is also treated by Bennett and Zingg, 335–341, and by both Kennedy 1969, 17–42, and Pennington 1970, 15–40. Pennington, 16, differs with Fried, saying that *carrera de bola* is called *rarajípari*, a linguistic combination of *rará* (foot) and *pa* (throw). Pennington adds that while *rarajípari* resembles the tribal name of the Tarahumara, one should resist the temptation to equate the name of the game with that of the tribe and thus grant antiquity to kickball.

16. See Kirchhoff, 529–560, which includes Beals, 551–553, Sauer 1954, 553–556, and Kroeber 1954, 556–559.

17. Kroeber 1934, 16–17, divided the Uto-Aztecan language family into four groups: 1. Shoshonean, in which he included Hopi, Ute, Comanche, several southern California tongues, and related languages, all in the United States; 2. Pima-Tepehuán; 3. Cáhita-Opata-Tarahumar, in which he also included Jova, Concho, Varohío, Chínipa, Guasápar, Témori and, tentatively, the languages of other groups in physical proximity; and 4. Nahuatl or Mexicano. Because he was uncertain as to their proper classification, Kroeber assigned no position in his grouping to Cora, Huichol or Guachichil.

Earlier Brinton had classified all Uto-Aztecan languages except Shoshonean (the most northern) and Nahuatl (the most southern) as "Sonoran." In 1926, Mason, 183–196, rejected as misleading the term "Sonoran." Mason and Whorf place all the Uto-Aztecan languages except Shoshonean (which was outside the scope of their study) into four groups: 1. Taracahitian, with three branches: a. Tarahumar; b. Cáhitan, in which are placed Cáhita (with its dialects of Yaqui and Mayo), Varohío, Tehueco, Acaxee, and (perhaps) Nío; and c.Opatan, in which are placed Opata, Eudeve, Tubar, Concho and Jova; 2. Coran, including Cora, Huichol and Guachichil; 3. Nahuatlán; and 4. Piman, which they divide into two types: a. Tepecano and Tepehuán, and b. Upper and Lower Pima, Sobaípuri, Névome, and Pápago. With much vigor Whorf, 198, argues that "Piman...[is]...a group which is poles apart from the other Uto-Aztecan languages of Mexico" and "Taracahitian and Coran are more like Nahuatlán than they are like Piman."

18. There is a fairly substantial body of ethnological literature relating to the Tarahumaras, the earliest sources being Lumholtz 1902, I, and his eight earlier reports: Bulletin 1891, 386–402; Nov. 1891, 531–548; 1893, 64–65; Bulletin 1894; July 1894; Sept. 1894; Oct. 1894; and Proceedings 1894, 100–112. Subsequent ethnological studies, or at least works with ethnological overtones, are Bennett and Zingg, Cabeza de Vaca, Gómez, Plancarte, Pennington 1963, Pennington 1970, Pennington 1972, Kennedy 1963, Kennedy 1969, Kennedy 1970, Fried, and López, 207–233. Purely archæological studies of the culture which preceded the Tarahumaras in the area are limited to three papers in *American Antiquity* by Robert Ascher and Francis J. Clune, Jr., Dorris Clune, and Hugh Cutler.

19. Tellechea.

20. Hilton has written extensively. His principal works are those to which I refer in the text and others set forth in the bibliography.

21. Thord-Gray.

22. Brambila.

23. A most enlightening and useful study of the influence of the railroad on the Tarahumaras is Llaguno 1971.

24. Lumholtz 1902, I, 150. At 163, he has a drawing of a woman, "The Belle of the Cave," naked above the waist. Bennett and Zingg, 105 ff., describe women's clothing with no suggestion of nakedness, even partial.

25. Lumholtz 1902, I, 168, vigorously rejects any suggestion that the Tarahumaras are related to the ancient cliff-dwellers.

26. The Jesuits sent Father Luis Verplancken, now at Creel, to get an M.S. in agriculture from Louisiana State University so that he could teach the Tarahumaras crop rotation. He says the education hasn't helped to rotate any crops.

Chapter 3. History

1. The Society was founded by Iginio López de Recalde (Ignacio Loyola) in 1534 and was given formal recognition in September 1540, in the papal bull *Regimini Militantis Ecclesiae*. Fülöp-Miller, 65; Coulson, 231–232.

2. The name was changed in 1620. *Resumen*, 58.

3. González, 115, n. 102.

4. There had been some inadvertent exploration of the northern area by Francisco Ibarra, who, with 60 Spanish soldiers, went north from Culiacán along the west coast in 1565. They went inland and crossed the sierra at Carretas, came south to Paquimé (now Casas Grandes) and then southwest to Río Papigóchic, which they followed downstream to what is now Sonora. Lister, 15–20.

5. Santa Bárbara was founded in 1567, when the mines were discovered. Tamarón, 127, n. 24. *Chihuahuenses*, 492, says the mines were discovered and the town founded in 1564.

6. In addition to Fathers Font and Moranta, the martyred Jesuits were Hernando Tovar, Diego Orozco, Bernardo Cisneros, Luis Alavez, Juan del Valle and Hernando Santarén. The Franciscan was Pedro Gutiérrez, but I find no record of the name of the Dominican. Saravia 1943, 43 ff.; Dunne 1944, 126–134; Trueba, I, 58–95.

7. San José del Parral, now Hidalgo del Parral, dates from July 1631, when silver was discovered by Juan Rangel Biesma. Jordán, 65; Tamarón, 127, n. 23; *Resumen*, 56.

8. See Treutlein 1937, 104–123; Treutlein 1945, 219–242. Throughout the text and notes I have used the Hispanized spelling of transliterated or translated surnames, as well as the modern Spanish forms of Christian names. Almost all of the Jesuits, regardless of nationality, spelled their names in the Spanish manner, but, orthography not having settled down, the actual spellings, particularly of Christian names, varied tremendously.

9. In 1684 silver was found at Coyáchic, and the following year gold was discovered near Sisoguíchic. The year of the great silver strike at Cusihuiriáchic was 1687. *EJMT*, 166.

10. The priest had gone from his post in Tutuaca to Sonora for help and, with a captain from San Nicolás, was returning home when the ambush occurred and both were killed. In *EJMT*, 206, Father Dunne puts the ambush "A few miles . . . downstream . . ." from Papigóchic, but Neumann, *Historia*, 254, is certainly nearer the mark when he says Yepáchic is to be remembered for the martyrdom of Father Sánchez. The San Nicolás from which the priest and the captain were returning was almost certainly the Chihuahua real south of Moris near Agua Caliente in the municipio of Ocampo. A much less likely possibility is the Sonora settlement of the same name between Movas and Yécora. If the men came from Chihuahua, a logical route home could have been (and if they came from Sonora it must have been) through Yécora and Maicoba to Yepáchic and on to Tutuaca, and thus many leagues west and south of Río Papigóchic. That Father Sánchez went for help is the prevalent account—if this is accurate, then he would logically have gone to his old mission post of Yécora and the governor of Sonora would logically have assigned an officer from the San Nicolás in Sonora. But the Sonora settlement is today a ranch with no evidence of ever having been a real, while the Chihuahua place, although on no map, is still a mineral (see *Chihuahuenses*, 487). A version which seems more logical is given by Venegas, 131. Venegas sends Sánchez "to hold a revival during Lent in the camp of San Nicolás." He and Captain Clavero were returning home when they heard of an uprising of the Pimas of Maicoba and Moris, and betwen Yécora and Tutuaca (an area which certainly includes Yepáchic) they were attacked. This account clearly refers to the San Nicolás in Chihuahua and also permits a more logical route home through Ocampo, leaving Moris and Maicoba (which were in revolt) to the west. But it still wholly avoids Río Papigóchic.

11. Spicer, 35, may be simplifying somewhat when he blames the revolt on Fernández and the impaled heads: ". . . Retana's action now precipitated a general revolt. . . ."

12. For the story of the Tarahumara revolts and the general outline of pre-expulsion Jesuit activity in Tarahumara, I have replied primarily on Neumann, *Historia; EJMT; Resumen;* and Lister.

13. El Real de San Francisco de Cuéllar, later San Felipe el Real de Chihuahua, resulted from the discovery, in 1707, of a new vein of silver at Santa Eulalia, now called Aquiles Serdán and then sometimes called Santa Eulalia de Chiguagua. In January 1708, an alcaldía mayor was created, and General Juan Fernández Retana was named the first alcalde mayor. Before he died the following month, Fernández visited the mines and ordered the founding of a Cabecera de los Reales de Minas, at the junction of Río Sacramento and Río Chuvíscar. The order not having been carried out, the new governor, Antonio Deza Ulloa, went to the area and called a council on October 5, 1709, for the purpose of determining

what should be done. Opinion of the settlers was divided between Santa Eulalia itself and the river junction, but the governor thought the latter location, called "Chuvisca," was more convenient and therefore issued a decree on October 12, 1709, formally establishing El Real de San Francisco de Cuéllar. On October 1, 1718, the Real Audiencia in México authorized the erection of a villa with the new name San Felipe el Real de Chihuahua, and the order was confirmed by the Audiencia of Nueva Galicia on March 23, 1720. Almada 1942, 2–5; *Resumen,* 90; *Chihuahuenses*, 41, 136–138.

14. By the *breve Dominus ac Redemptor,* signed on July 21, 1773, and published on August 16 of the same year. Fülöp-Miller, 384; *The Popes,* 403.

15. The expulsion of the Society from Chihuahua is treated by Almada in *Resumen,* 115 ff., by Dunne in *EJMT,* 230 ff., and in Dunne 1937, 3–30. Contemporary accounts by expelled Jesuits include Ducrue, Och, and the anonymous *Destierro*, which was written either by Antonio Strzanowski, S.J., a native of Moravia, or by the Spaniard Jaime Mateu, S.J. In *EJMT,* 255, n. 3, and Dunne 1937, 13, n. 30, Father Dunne attributed *Destierro* to Strzanowski. However, in Burrus 1959, 454, n. 43, and in personal correspondence, Father Burrus argues in favor of the logic of Mateu's authorship, basing his belief in large part on the purity of the Spanish text and the tendency of the expelled Jesuits to conceal from official notice their authorship of controversial works. At the time of the expulsion, Strzanowski was the missionary at Norogáchic and Mateu was in charge of Tónachic. Two references in *Destierro* to Norogáchic as the residence of the author and one reference (in the third person) to the missionary at Tónachic make it difficult for me to side with Father Burrus. Rafael Zelis, S.J., began, and after his death, Pedro Márquez, S.J., completed, a *Catálogo* of all the Jesuits expelled from New Spain, which was later published in México in 1871. A reasonably complete treatment of the expulsion from New Spain is in *Obra,* I, 439–494. Documents of some collateral interest are collected in *Documentos sobre la Expulsión.*

16. On order of the viceroy, the Franciscan Colegio de Guadalupe in Zacatecas sent 15 priests to care for the churches of Tarahumara and Chínipas. Bancroft, I, 654. The 15 Franciscans took over 56 churches or church locations, divided into 16 cabeceras and 40 visitas: Nabugame as a cabecera with two visitas, Baburigame with seven, Tónachic with four, Norogáchic with two, Baquéachic with three, Guaguáchic with three; Cerocahui with two, Guazápares with two, Chínipas with four, Santa Ana with two, Batopilillas with one, Moris with one, Tutuaca with one, Tomóchic with three, Concepción de Tubares with one, and San Miguel de Tubares with two. *Descripcion Topografica*, 92–101. The *Descripcion* is undated, but Bancroft I, 30, says it was written about 1780. There is no published count of the secular clergy in Tarahumara Alta, but Spicer, 37, may be overlooking some dedicated priests when he says, "In the Upper Tarahumara country there was no regular clergy to continue the management of the missions. The Franciscans were without the resources or inclination to do so."

17. In April 1974, Father Benjamín Tapia, S.J., formerly the superior at Sisoguíchic and then in Chihuahua as procurador for the Misión de la Tarahumara, told me the missionary work was in the hands of 21 padres and 20 hermanos. The history of the Jesuits in Tarahumara since the restoration is set forth by Ocampo. Their activities throughout Mexico during the last century are recounted in Gutiérrez-Casillas, *Jesuitas en México.*

Chapter 4. San Miguel de Las Bocas

1. Which has been Hidalgo del Parral since August 20, 1833. *Chihuahuenses*, 252.

2. Jordán, 65.

3. Bandelier, III, 124.

4. Ratkay, 21.

5. Jordán, 394, n. 1.

6. Robles, 127, n. 23.

7. The uncertainty is the result of a peculiarity of the *IX Censo General de Población, 1970*, which gives no population figures for cities and towns, only for municipios (roughly equivalent to U.S. counties). *Diccionario Porrúa*, 742, gives 41,461 as the 1960 population of the city of Parral and 45,080 as the population of the municipio of the same name. *IX Censo 1970*, 17, gives 61,817 as the 1970 population of the municipio, composed of 122 localities.

8. Jordán, 69. A full-scale discussion of the Parral trade in Blacks is to be found in Mayer.

9. *EJMT*, 89, 94; *Obra*, I, 96.

10. *Obra*, I, 95.

11. Oliva.

12. Guadalajara 1684.

13. González, 22, n. 3.

14. González, 42, n. 10.

15. Tamarón, 124.

16. Zelis, 21, 33. Perhaps José Frejomil was also at Parral at the expulsion. *Chihuahuenses*, 202, 211, says so, as does *Obra*, I, 465. But Zelis, 131, shows Pastrana and Guerra as the only Jesuits at Parral in 1767 and lists Frejomil as being at Campeche on that date.

17. *EJMT*, 250, n. 2.

18. *Diccionario Porrúa*, 1124, shows a population of 1,000 for 1960, but, largely because of a suspicion of round figures, I think it is a low guess. The same source gives 12,917 as the 1960 population of the municipio, while *IX Censo 1970*, 18, assigns 15,168 people to the 70 localities in the municipio in 1970.

19. Saravia 1954, III, 335.

20. *EJMT*, 36.

21. González, 9, n. 4.

22. *EJMT*, 37; Castillo 1662.

23. *EJMT*, 37, has Díaz replaced in 1630 by Nicolás Estrada, S.J., but at 45 and 47 he has Díaz still at Las Bocas in 1639. *Introduction*, 18, has Díaz still at Las Bocas in 1646 and early 1648, and *Chihuahuenses*, 167, says he died there on September 25, 1648. There seems no particular reason to suppose that he was not in the area more or less continually from 1630 until his death.

24. González, 8, n. 5.

25. *EJMT*, 48, 85; Bancroft, I, 348; Zepeda, 143.

26. *EJMT*, 85.

27. Pascual 1651, 206.

28. Castillo 1662.

29. Castillo 1667.

30. Figueroa 1668, 226.

31. Castillo 1667; *EJMT*, 93; *Introduction*, 28. *EJMT*, 93, is four months early in placing Castillo's death "within a few hours" of the dedication of the church.

32. *Introduction*, 29.

33. Ortiz, 317.

34. Medrano 1699.

35. *Testimonio*, 81.

36. *EJMT*, 37.

37. Bancroft, I, 334, says Díaz founded San Gabriel, "of whose subsequent history nothing is known," and *Introduction*, 11, echoes: "What became of San Gabriel is unknown."

38. *Testimonio*, 88.

39. *EJMT*, 43.

40. Ortiz, 315, says Tizonazo in 1678 was part of the Tepehuán *misión* and that the language, strangely enough, was Ore. Hodge, II, 761, supports the language phenomenon by saying that after the Toboso revolt, the town was repopulated with Opatas from Ures in Sonora.

41. *EJMT*, 50.

42. Zepeda, 138.

43. *EJMT*, 84, says it was Zepeda.

44. *Annua* 1646.

45. Castillo 1667; Figueroa 1668; Bancroft, I, 345, 361.

46. *Testimonio*, 69.

Chapter 5. Huejotitlán

1. *Introduction*, 12. *Chihuahuenses*, 256, is wrong in ascribing the founding (in the same year) to José Pascual and Nicolás Zepeda.

2. Gómez, 259.

3. Ortiz, 321.

4. See Bible, St. John 19:20 and Ferguson, 150.

5. Ratkay, 48.

6. *EJMT*, 200, reports with poetic feeling: "...and today at that ancient spot the tombstone, the inscription worn with time, marks the sod where his bones have mouldered into dust."

7. *Testimonio*, 109.

8. *Chihuahuenses*, 378, says Valle de Olivos was founded by Jesuits in 1680 as San José de los Olivos.

9. *Testimonio*, 29.

10. *Testimonio*, 29; *Chihuahuenses*, 256.

11. Tamarón, 133.

12. Jordán, 394, n. 1.

13. Tamarón, 133.

14. *Testimonio*, 116.

15. Tamarón, 132.

16. Figueroa 1668.

17. *Introduction*, 28.

18. *Testimonio*, 115.

19. *Obra*, II, 276.

20. Ortiz, 321.

21. *Testimonio*, 115.

22. Tamarón, 132.

23. *Testimonio*, 116.

24. Ratkay, 48.

Chapter 6. Balleza

1. By legislative act, the name was changed to Balleza in 1830, in honor of Father Mariano Balleza. *Chihuahuenses*, 59.
2. Jordán, 259.
3. Ortiz, 319.
4. *Obra*, II, 253.
5. *Obra*, II, 254.
6. González, 129, n. 128.
7. *EJMT*, 37; *Introduction*, 11.
8. *Obra*, II, 260; *Introduction*, 12. *Chihuahuenses*, 59, is correct as to the year of reestablishment but wrong in ascribing the founding to José Pascual and Nicolás Zepeda.
9. *Introduction*, 13, says Villar took over San Pablo shortly after it was founded, but González, xlvii, puts him in Tarahumara only after 1647. In view of his age this seems more likely.
10. Figueroa 1668, 225.
11. *Introduction*, 29, says Prado was at San Pablo in 1673, but *Obra*, II, 266, reports Figueroa there in 1674 and, at 261, says he did not go south until 1679. The fact that Ortiz, 316, doesn't mention Figueroa in 1678 suggests that he had gone south by then, not, as stated by *EJMT*, 135, that he was dead.
12. Ortiz, 316.
13. González, 45, n. 13.
14. González, 184, n. 31, 201, n. 65.
15. *Misiones*, 91.
16. *Misiones*, 95; Rinaldini.
17. *Testimonio*, 121, 122.
18. The 1960 population was 1,229. Tamayo.
19. Figueroa 1668, 226.
20. Ortiz, 320.
21. *Testimonio*, 125.
22. Ramos 1745.
23. Tamarón, 133.
24. Figueroa 1662, 221.
25. Ortiz, 320.
26. *Testimonio*, 125.
27. *Introduction*, 35; Ramos 1745.
28. Hodge, I, 112, does not suggest a Tepehuán origin, but says Atotonilco is from the Nahuatl words *atl* (water) and *totonilli* (warm). He incorrectly locates San Juan in eastern Sinaloa.
29. Ortiz, 412.
30. Ortiz, 311.
31. In *Rarámuri*, the word means *piedra agujerada* or "pierced stone." Gómez, 148.
32. Ramos, *Report*.
33. *Obra*, II, 262.
34. *Testimonio*, 126.
35. In *Rarámuri:* "canyon between the landslides." Gómez, 147.
36. *Testimonio*, 126.
37. *Obra*, II, 262.
38. Ramos, *Report*.
39. Tamarón, 133.

Chapter 7. Tónachic

1. *Libro IV.*
2. Tamarón, 144.
3. *Libro IV.*
4. Although Pennington 1963, 2 and n. 6, by a casual reference implies that Guachóchic is referred to in Tamarón, 169–172.
5. *Descripción Topográfica*, 95.
6. Gómez, 43, says the word means "place of the herons," while Hodge, I, 508, renders it "blue herons."
7. *Chihuahuenses*, 235, gives a 1960 population of 2,612 for the pueblo and 8,053 for the municipio, while *IX Censo 1970*, 17, assigns 16,192 persons to the 88 localities in the municipio.
8. Braun 1765.
9. *Obra*, II, 242.
10. Braun 1765.
11. Lizasoaín, *Noticia*, 25.
12. *Descripción Topográfica*, 125–126.
13. Except for the rebuilding, the church in 1970 was substantially the same as shown in an undated photograph in Ocampo, 380.
14. The word *Tónachic* means "place of pillars." Gómez, 79; Hodge, II, 777.
15. Gómez, 79.
16. Tamarón, 143.
17. Hodge, II, 777.
18. Robles, 160, n. 27, says 414.
19. *Descripción Topográfica*, 95.
20. Which translates roughly as "hello," "how does it go with you?" and "goodbye."
21. Which fact was later confirmed by an examination of a picture of "un entierro tarahumar" in Ocampo, 378.
22. Braun wrote a letter from Nra. Sra. de Loreto de Yoquibo on September 11, 1751. *Libro IV.*
23. *Misiones*, 98.
24. *EJMT*, 226.
25. Braun 1765 tells the provincial, Francisco Ceballos, S.J., that the reassignment took place during the term of his predecessor. ABZ, IV, 15*, lists as the predecessor Pedro Reales, who served from early in 1760 to May 19, 1763.
26. Which means "the place with many little blue birds." Gómez, 148.
27. Lizasoaín, *Noticia*, 25; Tamarón, 144.
28. *Descripción Topográfica*, 25, puts Aboréachic four leagues north of Tónachic and, at 95, puts Tecabórachic nine leagues east of Tónachic. Both directions and both distances are certainly wrong.
29. Robles, 160, n. 28, couldn't locate any Tecabórachic anywhere, which helped me reach my conclusion.

Chapter 8. Norogáchic

1. Which means "place where much beer is drunk." Hodge, II, 201.
2. In 1752 Rochéachic was a ranchería which was considered part of the Norogáchic mission field. *Libro IV.* But no subsequent report suggests that the

ranchería was evangelized, and the present residents assure me there never was an old church in the place.

3. And by no means in ruins, as suggested by Gómez, facing 169, in a caption to pictures of four churches, including Papajíchic, which he labels Choguita.

4. Guenduláin.

5. The existence of Papajíchic as a Norogáchic visita with 126 families is reported in *Estado de Norogáchic*, an undated and unsigned manuscript. It seems probable that the visitador to whom reference is made in the manuscript is Antonio Herrera, S.J., who served Tarahumara Antigua as visitador from 1708 until 1711 (see González, 187, n. 40), which superficially suggests that *Estado de Norogáchic* may have been written about 1710. But so early a date is impossible, since the text refers, as visitas of Norogáchic, to Pámachic, Guaguáchic and Guaguevo, all three of which were established in 1718. *Acta de Fundación de Pámachic; Acta de Fundación de Guaguáchic; Acta de Fundación de Guaguevo*. Since Guenduláin says Papajíchic had 130 families in 1725, and since *Estado de Norogáchic* gives it 126, it thus seems not illogical to assign to the undated manuscript a date between 1720 and 1725.

6. Lizasoaín, *Noticia*, 24.

7. Tamarón, 144.

8. *Descripción Topográfica*, 95.

9. Tamarón, 144.

10. *Estado de Norogáchic*.

11. In 1744 Miqueo referred to Tetaguíchic as a Norogáchic visita in a context which argues against recent settlement.

12. Tamarón, 144. The larger population may have remained into this century, since a picture of the church in Gómez, facing 169, shows the building approximately in the condition in which we found it, but with almost 100 Tarahumaras standing in front, apparently in a formal ceremony of some sort.

13. Which means "where there are round hills." Gómez, 148. Or "where there is a rock in front." Hodge, II, 83.

14. *Chihuahuenses*, 364. Gómez, 95, is probably wrong when he puts the founding between 1640 and 1650.

15. *Libro IV*.

16. Neumann, *Historia*, 227.

17. Neumann 1698; *Obra*, II, 301.

18. *Introduction*, 49.

19. González, 43, n. 13; *Libro IV*.

20. *Libro IV*.

21. Martini.

22. *Libro IV*.

23. Gera, May 1747; *Misiones*, 94.

24. *Libro IV*. Before January 1752, Norogáchic had theoretical jurisdiction over a very large area, since *Libro IV* shows that it was in that month, on order of the visitador general, that Tónachic was split off, with (as dependencies) Mova, Tecabórachic, Guachóchic, Sípochic, Paguíchic, Temósachic and probably Yoquivo, leaving Norogáchic with jurisdiction over the pueblos of Pámachic, Guaguevo, Guaguáchic, Tetaguíchic and Papajíchic, as well as the rancherías of Rochéachic, Paquíranachic, Curachacáchic, Tajírachic, Saquéachic, Nanavaguáchic, Nagúchic, Pasigóchic and Ochacaláchic.

25. Braun 1765.

26. Antonio Aretzamovsky, S.J., and Antonio Strzanowski, S.J., are, I firmly believe, one and the same person. The only authority for the separate existence of Aretzamovsky is Braun 1765, who says that when he was transferred to Norogáchic in 1765, Aretzamovsky had worked for more than eight years at Guaguáchic, had founded a new town (certainly Sámachic) and had built churches and houses in the new settlement as well as in Guaguáchic, Pámachic and Guaguevo. *Obra*, II, 303, n. 16, attributes to Braun's very 1765 letter the information that Antonio Strzanowski was in charge of Guaguáchic between 1757 and 1765, that he founded a new town and that he built churches and houses in his four towns (Guaguáchic, Guaguevo, Pámachic and Sámachic). I can only conclude that Braun misspoke and Decorme knew it.

27. A potpourri of information, accounting, receipts and miscellaneous records, not all relating to Norogáchic, referred to in the notes as *Libro IV*.

28. *Descripción Topográfica*, 126.

29. Ocampo, 370, has a picture of the old church, which he labels "antes del incendio." Gómez, facing 169, and *Obra*, II, facing 302, also have similar (and older) pictures. The description in the text is based on these pictures. Gómez, 96, reported that in 1941 the church was in ruins, but that the secular priest (the area had not yet been assigned to the Jesuits) had plans for rebuilding.

30. Which means "caves among the rocks." Gómez, 148.

31. Lizasoaín, *Noticia*, 26.

32. Which Father Díaz said means "place of the lake."

33. *Estado de Norogáchic*.

34. Lizasoaín, *Noticia*, 24; Tamarón, 144.

35. *Descripción Topográfica*, 96.

Chapter 9. Guaguáchic

1. Currently called Samachique. The Rarámuri syllable *chic* is a regularly used locative which has now fallen into widespread disuse among most mestizos and many Tarahumaras. The result is either a dropped final *c*, as in Sisoguichi, Norogachi, Cárichi and Mátachi, to name a few, or a diminutive, as in Samachique, Paguichique, Guaguachique and Pamachique. I prefer the older *chic* form.

2. Braun 1765. Braun's actual reference is to Aretzamovsky, but as indicated in Chapter 8, note 26, I prefer to accept the statement in *Obra*, II, 303, n. 16, that the founder was Strzanowski. While the new pueblo is unnamed in Braun 1765, Lizasoaín, *Noticia*, 24–25, reports that the partido consisted of Guaguáchic as the cabecera and Pámachic, Guaguevo and Sámachic as visitas.

3. *Actas de Fundación*.

4. Pennington 1963, 11, seems to overstate the fact when he has Ordaz establish a mission (as distinct from doing itinerant preaching) among the Samachiqui about 1700. Pennington undoubtedly follows Neumann, *Historia*, 291, who refers (in 1724, not 1700) to "new reductions" by Ordaz "among the Sarichiquis." I rely for Strzanowski's later establishment of Sámachic on Braun 1765.

5. Pennington 1963, 11; *Obra*, II, 241, n. 31.

6. Gómez, 123.

7. *Acta de Fundación de Guaguáchic.*

8. Which Father Díaz said means *cerro agujerado*, or "hill with a hole in it."

9. González, 205, n. 73. Pennington 1963, 11, is undoubtedly early when he reports that Jacobo Doye established churches at Pámachic, Guaguáchic and Guaguevo in 1714.

10. Braun 1765; *Estado de Norogáchic.*

11. *Obra*, II, 303, n. 16. Bancroft, I, 599, n. 24, puts Bartolomé Braun at Guaguáchic in 1751, but it seems likely that Bancroft is wrong and that *Misiones*, 94, is correct in listing him at Yoquivo in that year.

12. Braun 1765; *Obra*, II, 303, n. 16.

13. So Father Díaz has written on a large poster at the church. His evidence for the precise dating is the date on the bell, dedicated to Sr. San Joseph, in the tower at Guaguáchic.

14. *Descripción Topográfica*, 125–126.

15. Lizasoaín, *Noticia*, 24.

16. Which means "place of a muddy meadow." Gómez, 148.

17. *EJMT*, 201.

18. *Estado de Norogáchic.*

19. Miqueo.

20. Tamarón, 143.

21. González, 204, n. 70, suggests Ordaz may have gotten to Pámachic as early as 1696, but it seems more likely that he didn't get beyond Tubares and Urique until well after peace was restored. There is certainly no accuracy to the assertion of *Obra*, II, 234, that Jacobo Doye had crossed the barranca to Pámachic by 1690, since Doye didn't sail for New Spain until 1712. González, 206, n. 74.

22. *Obra*, II, 241, n. 31, has Benavides crossing the barranca to baptize in the Sámachic area in 1698, but Pennington 1963, 11, is probably closer to the mark when he suggests the visit was shortly after 1700.

23. Neumann, *Historia*, 292.

24. *Acta de Fundación de Pámachic.*

25. Miqueo.

26. *Estado de Norogáchic.*

27. Miqueo.

28. *Misiones*, 91.

29. *Misiones*, 98.

30. *Obra*, II, 303, n. 16.

31. For Señor San José. The English spelling was commonly then used.

32. Almada, *Chínipas*, 73.

33. Miqueo.

34. González, 205, n. 73.

35. *Acta de Fundación de Guaguevo.*

36. *Estado de Norogáchic.*

37. Braun 1765.

38. Tamarón, 143.

Chapter 10. Chihuahua and Chinarras

1. *Chihuahuenses*, 41. As has been so often the case, Santa Eulalia has been renamed to honor a revolutionary. In this instance, by decree of December 28, 1932, the pueblo was named for Aquiles Serdán, killed by government forces on

November 18, 1910. Almada credits the pueblo of Aquiles Serdán, whose boundaries include an area locally called Chihuahua el Viejo, with 4,357 inhabitants.

2. Almada 1942, 2; *Chihuahuenses*, 363; Bancroft, I, 365.

3. Almada 1942, 2.

4. Almada 1942, 3.

5. Almada 1942, 3; *Resumen*, 90. In *Chihuahuenses*, 137, Almada suggests, undoubtedly correctly, that the "San Francisco" in the name was because of the Franciscan activity in the area, and particularly because José Zamora, O.F.M., was the first priest in the new real. But he has a curious contradiction regarding the rest of the name. In the same article, and also in *Resumen*, 92, he says, undoubtedly again correctly, that the "Cuéllar" was included to honor the viceroy, Francisco Fernández de la Cueva Enríquez, Duque de Alburquerque, Marqués de Cuéllar. But in "Etimología," 20, he is unable to account for the word and suggests the governor or one of the other officials may have come from the city of Cuéllar in Spain.

6. *Resumen*, 95. The creation of the villa was confirmed by the Audiencia of Nueva Galicia on March 24, 1720 (Almada 1942, 5), but Philip V had issued an order on December 19, 1719, which pointed out that while a viceroy had no power to create a villa, he would nevertheless not revoke the title. *Chihuahuenses*, 138.

7. The derivation of the word "Chihuahua" or "Chiguagua" is the subject of Dr. Almada's essay, "Etimología." Because the settlement was Spanish and not Tarahumara, he rejects four proposed derivations based on Rarámuri (including the interesting suggestion that Chiguagua uses the same syllables as, and is therefore identical in meaning to, Guaguáchic), and contends that Chihuahua is of Nahuatl origin and means "dry" or "arid."

8. González, 186, n. 36.

9. *Obra*, I, 110.

10. Tamarón, 152.

11. Lafora, 69.

12. Jordán, 394, n. 1.

13. *Chihuahuenses*, 135–136.

14. Unfortunately, I have no exact figure. *Chihuahuenses*, 139, gives 1960 population of 150,430 for the city proper and 186,089 for the municipio, while *IX Censo 1970*, 17, reports that 277,099 people lived in the 78 localities in the municipio in 1970.

15. The division was decreed in 1629 by Rodrigo Pacheco y Osorio, Marqués de Cerralvo, viceroy from 1624 until 1635. *EJMT*, 125.

16. *Resumen*, 92.

17. *Chihuahuenses*, 97.

18. Neumann, *Historia*, 333, n. 198; ABZ, IV, 254. Barri, 48, sets out the formal request which the governor sent to the viceroy from Parral on August 27, 1717, as well as, at 50, the license issued by the viceroy, Baltasar de Zúñiga, Guzmán Sotomayor y Mendoza, Marqués de Valero, who served from 1716 until 1722.

19. Neumann, *Historia*, 280.

20. *EJMT*, 199; ABZ, IV, 255; *Obra*, I, 111; *Chihuahuenses*, 104.

21. Jordán, 125.

22. González, 187, n. 40, is the only authority who assigns Herrera to the post, but it seems clear that he is correct. Neumann, who often studiously avoided naming the Jesuits to whom he referred in his writings, says in *Historia*,

281, that "A veteran missionary from Valencia undertook the management of the college." Neumann's editor, Christelow, at *Historia*, 324, n. 199, suggests the reference is to Francisco Celada, who "was a Valencian, and was certainly a veteran." But Neumann, *Historia*, 196, says Celada was a native of Toledo, and González, who is usually accurate, says, 76, n. 20, that Celada was born at Mondéjar, Alcalá de Henares. There is no doubt that the priest first in charge of the seminary was in fact Navarrete, whose place of birth is given in ABZ, IV, 255, n. 4, as Baeza, province of Jaén. Toledo is of course not in Valencia, but neither is Alcalá de Henares or Baeza. On the other hand, Neumann is not wrong. His reference is not to either Celada or Navarrete, but instead to Antonio Herrera, who was superior of the living quarters at the college from 1720 (the year classes began—see Jordán, 125) until 1723, who came to Tarahumara in 1684 (certainly a veteran) and who was born in the province of Valencia (González, 187, n. 40). As to titles, *EJMT*, 199, says Navarrete was "rector," while ABZ, IV, 321, n. 3, says that in March 1723, he was "superior," the term used by González, 187, n. 40, for Herrera, who, by ABZ's list, had left by March 1723. I suggest that between 1720 and March 1723, both Navarrette and Herrera were there, and that Herrera had particular charge of student discipline in the new school, an assumption consistent with the Latin original of Neumann's report ("aduente Collegii regimen veterano quodam missionario, patria Valentiniano"), Neumann, *Revoltes*, 186 (Latin), and with the French translation ("et c'est un ancien missionnaire, natif de Valencia, qui a pris en charge la discipline du collège"). Neumann, *Revoltes*, 187 (French).

23. ABZ, IV, 321; *Obra*, I, 111.
24. Tamarón, 153.
25. *Obra*, I, 112–113.
26. "Pobladores," after 10.
27. *Chihuahuenses*, 158. Almada also says that the governor's permission to the Jesuits was ratified by Philip V, but he doesn't give the date. In "Etimología," 21, he says that because Chinarras was outside the Tarahumara area, the governor's approval was required, but he says nothing about the king.
28. Guenduláin, 23.
29. *Catálogo 1716–1720*, 496.
30. Guenduláin, 23. Either Guenduláin is wrong in reporting that Arias was the only priest who had been stationed at Chinarras, or González, 201, n. 65, is wrong in reporting Mendívil as having been there in 1723.
31. *Chihuahuenses*, 392. *Obra*, II, 311, says Palacios was the third missionary to serve Chinarras, but this could be accurate only if the reports about Mendívil, Sachi and Texeiro are wrong.
32. Tamarón, 148. The bishop's editor, Vito Robles, suffers from overcertainty. At 162, n. 56, he says there is today no pueblo named Chinarras, but that the place can with certainty be identified as Aldama. Bancroft, I, 655, n. 37, is almost as guilty of conclusion-jumping when he says that Santa Ana "was probably merged in San Gerónimo."

Chapter 11. San Felipe

1. There is confusion among the commentators about the date of founding and the identity of the founder. *EJMT*, 45–46, is undoubtedly correct in saying that Pascual and Figueroa came to Parral early in June 1639, that Pascual went to

Las Bocas, and that Figueroa went north before the month was up to establish San Felipe. Figueroa left San Felipe to found Huejotitlán later in the summer when Pascual relieved him, and the date of Pascual's arrival may well have been August 15, 1639, as contended by *Obra*, II, 259. On the other hand, in *Chihuahuenses*, 397, Almada is certainly not accurate when he ignores Figueroa and says that San Felipe was founded on August 15, 1639, by Pascual and Nicolás Zepeda. But in *Introduction*, 12, Christelow is equally wrong when he says that Figueroa came north from Parral in November 1639, to found San Felipe.

    2. Figueroa 1668, 229.

    3. *Introduction*, 12.

    4. *Obra*, II, 258.

    5. Pascual 1651, 206.

    6. Saravia 1954, III, 332.

    7. Saravia 1954, III, 317.

    8. Pascual 1651, 206. Bancroft, I, 354, is confused when he says that Pascual, the priest at Huejotitlán, went to San Felipe for safety.

    9. *EJMT*, 55.

    10. Pascual 1651, 186.

    11. *EJMT*, 95; *Introduction*, 29.

    12. *Introduction*, 28.

    13. *Testimonio*, 103

    14. *Introduction,* 29; *Obra*, II, 284; *EJMT*, 98; *ABZ*, II, 466, n. 44.

    15. *Obra*, II, 280, n. 27.

    16. Neumann 1682.

    17. González, 62, n. 49.

    18. *Administrative Census of 1728.*

    19. *Chihuahuenses*, 469, says it was established by Pascual and Nicolás Zepeda and that they called it Santa Cruz de los Tarahumaras. The added identification on the name was occasionally used to distinguish the pueblo from Santa Cruz de los Tepehuanes, a visita of Tizonazo.

    20. *Chihuahuenses*, 469.

    21. *Obra*, II, 260, n. 10.

    22. *Obra*, II, 255.

    23. Robles, 135, n. 2.

    24. *Obra*, II, 260.

    25. Pascual 1651, 207.

    26. Ortiz, 318.

    27. Neumann 1682.

    28. González, 62, n. 49.

    29. González, 187, n. 40.

    30. *Obra*, II, 280, n. 27.

    31. *Testimonio*, 92.

    32. Tamayo.

    33. *Introduction*, 19.

    34. *Obra*, II, 260.

    35. Ortiz, 318.

    36. *Testimonio*, 105.

    37. Ortiz, 318.

    38. *Chihuahuenses*, 485, prefers San José del Sitio, to which he assigns a population of 333.

    39. *Administrative Census of 1728.*

40. Díaz Valdés.
41. *Testimonio*, 105.
42. Tamarón, 131.
43. *Obra*, II, map, 255.
44. Robles, 135, n. 4.
45. U.S. Army Map Service.

Chapter 12. Satevó

1. Named by decree of October 27, 1932, after General Angel Trías, 23rd governor of Chihuahua, who was born in 1809 and died on August 30, 1867. *Chihuahuenses*, 222, 538–540.
2. Founded in 1668. *Chihuahuenses*, 222.
3. *Chihuahuenses*, 292. Tamarón, 139, reported 40 Indian families and a total of 100 people. It hasn't grown much.
4. *Testimonio*, 136.
5. In 1934 the name was changed to Juan Mendoza. *Chihuahuenses*, 292.
6. *Obra*, II, 266.
7. Ortiz, 323.
8. *Testimonio*, 135–136.
9. *Chihuahuenses*, 496.
10. *Chihuahuenses*, 496.
11. *Introduction*, 12.
12. *Chihuahuenses*, 507. I find no actual record of the church construction, but it is clear that in their subsequent attacks on Satevó, the rebels burned the church and priest's house. *Obra*, II, 276–277; Saravia 1954, III, 331.
13. Pascual 1651, 186.
14. *Introduction*, 19.
15. Pascual 1651, 206; *Introduction*, 23.
16. Pascual 1651, 206.
17. Jordán, 83.
18. Saravia 1954, III, 331; *Obra*, II, 277.
19. Zambrano, IX, 75.
20. Ortiz, 322. Decorme must have read Ortiz too fast when he says, in *Obra*, II, 262, that the church which was destroyed in 1648 was not rebuilt until 1678.
21. *EJMT*, 101, 104.
22. ABZ, III, 315, n. 4.
23. *EJMT*, 217, has Lizarralde at Satevó "a few decades" before 1753.
24. Tápiz, 5.
25. *Obra*, II, 281.
26. *Misiones*, 90, 95.
27. *Testimonio*, 130.
28. *Chihuahuenses*, 496, says the roads to the west are only for horses.
29. Not a Jesuit mission pueblo, but nevertheless old and with an interesting church. *Chihuahuenses*, 234, says the settlement has been known since 1686, was originally called Puesto de Carretas, was later named San Nicolás de Carretas (the church is San Nicolás), and since July 1933 has borne the name Gran Morelos in honor of José María Morelos y Pavón.

30. *Chihuahuenses*, 173, says the name was changed to honor Dr. Domínguez, a senator who was assassinated October 7, 1913, by order of General Victoriano Huerta.

31. *Chihuahuenses*, 397.

32. *Chihuahuenses*, 173. *Testimonio*, 150, says San Lorenzo was founded by Balthasar de la Peña, a manifest impossibility.

33. *EJMT*, 76.

34. Jordán, 83.

35. Ortiz, 323.

36. *Administrative Census of 1728*.

37. Calderón.

38. *Testimonio*, 145, 149, 150.

39. Tamarón, 140.

40. *Chihuahuenses*, 173, says the population is 614, but Tamayo puts it at 962.

41. The population of Santa Rosalía exceeds 1,000. Robles, 159, n. 9, puts the figure at 1,069, while *Chihuahuenses*, 494, says 1,210.

42. Calderón.

43. *Testimonio*, 145, 149.

44. Ortiz, 323.

45. Calderón. Calderón says that the records at Santa María go back only to 1707, but that Mancuso said that the visita was established in 1692. Obviously, neither Mancuso nor Calderón had access to Ortiz.

46. Calderón; González, 62, n. 49.

47. ABZ, IV, 255, n. 3.

48. Calderón.

49. Calderón.

50. González, 154, n. 166.

51. Rinaldini.

52. *Testimonio*, 143. At 146 there is a notation that in the priest's house was a painting of Juan María Salvatierra. How did it get there? What has happened to it? What is its relationship to the painting by María Magdalena Medrano in the Museo Nacional in México, which is reproduced as a frontispiece in Venegas as well as in Burrus 1971?

53. *Chihuahuenses*, 493, puts it at 837.

54. *Administrative Census of 1728* shows 191 families and *Testimonio*, 143, reports 187 families.

Chapter 13. San Joaquín y Santa Ana

1. *EJMT*, 132, based on Ortiz, 325–327.

2. *Chihuahuenses*, 491.

3. The Rarámuri name has been in disuse for 300 years, and the spelling is most uncertain. Tagúrachic is the spelling in Lizasoaín, *Noticia*, 26, while Ortiz, 325, uses Tayegáchic (as well as the alternate Don Pedro). Ratkay uses Taguéachic; *Chihuahuenses*, 482, and Guenduláin, 29, both use Tehuacachi; while *EJMT*, 132, renders it Tayeguáchic.

4. *EJMT*, 47.

5. *Introduction*, 17.
6. Pascual 1651, 181.
7. Jordán, 75.
8. *EJMT*, 107; *Introduction*, 30; Guadalajara 1676. The lack of activity after 1648 is attested by Father Dunne's statement in *EJMT*, 105, that "About this same period [1674] San Francisco de Borja was founded...."
9. *Obra*, II, 306.
10. *Obra*, II, 292. I am very dubious.
11. Ortiz, 325.
12. Ratkay.
13. González, 62, n. 49.
14. González, xlvii.
15. Lizasoaín, *Noticia*, 26.
16. *Chihuahuenses*, 491.
17. Lizasoaín, *Noticia*, 26.
18. Ortiz, 325.
19. Guenduláin, 29.
20. Ortiz, 325.
21. Ortiz, 325.
22. *Administrative Census of 1728.*
23. Fernández Abeé.
24. Tamarón, 141.
25. *Chihuahuenses*, 491.
26. Ortiz, 325.
27. Guenduláin, 29.
28. Lizasoaín, *Noticia*, 26.
29. Ortiz, 326.
30. Guenduláin, 29.
31. González, 178–179, n. 21.
32. *Obra*, II, 292, says Ortiz founded Saguárachic before he left Borja in 1677, but I doubt he was ever in either place, except as *visitador*.
33. Ortiz, 325. *EJMT*, 132, is more expansive in the translation, rendering it "...one of the finest churches in all Tarahumara."
34. Guenduláin, 29.
35. *Report on Borja.*
36. Tamarón, 142. Robles, 159, n. 16, incorrectly identifies the pueblo as a ranch called Sohuárachic, with 31 people. *Chihuahuenses*, 504, says that Sohuárachic is near Bocoyna. At 474 Almada correctly locates Saguárachic.

Chapter 14. Nonoava

1. The word *Nonoava* is said to mean *lugar residencia del Padre,* the place of residence of the priest. Gómez, 148. To the same general effect is Robles, 159, n. 17, who cites Ponce de León, II, 30, and who shows "padre" as the equivalent of the Rarámuri word *onó*. Hodge, II, 81, and Lumholtz 1902, I, 223, give the word from which the name is derived as *nonó*, meaning "father." Thord-Gray, 311 and 690, says *onó* or *nonó* is the word for "father" and, at 949, *pari* is the word for "priest." Since the name Nonoava was in common use 150 years before Arteaga, the first priest, came to live there, and since Rarámuri (as do Spanish and English) has words for both "father" and "priest," the reference must be to a

natural father rather than to a father-in-God. Thus, Gómez is probably wrong in capitalizing Padre.

2. *Obra*, II, 262.

3. Robles, 159, n. 17, says 1,476 meters.

4. González, 115, n. 102.

5. Saravia 1954, III, 277.

6. Ydiáquez 1744, says Guadalajara was there in 1675, while González, 115, n. 102, says both priests were there the following year. In the text of Guadalajara 1676, Nonoava is not mentioned, but in a postscript Guadalajara and Tardá say that when they got to Parral they found up to 18 *Judíos Tarahumares* from Nonoava asking for baptism and that priests be sent to their town.

7. Gutiérrez 1676.

8. Ydiáquez 1744.

9. Ortiz, 327–328.

10. Neumann 1690; González, 115, n. 102.

11. Neumann, *Historia*, 227–228.

12. *Libro IV*.

13. *Misiones*, 98.

14. González, xlvii, 22, n. 3, says no Jesuit exceeded José Neumann in length of Tarahumara service, and that only six (Neumann, Juan Manuel del Hierro, Tomás Guadalajara, Gabriel Villar, Juan Antonio Landa, and Francisco Hermano Glandorff) served 40 or more years. As nearly as I can tell, there were eight Jesuits who served that long in Tarahumara or, if combined time in Tepehuana and Tarahumara is counted, a total of nine: Francisco Díaz Valdés, whose 73 years of reported service between 1673 and 1746 are truly incredible; Neumann, who spanned 51 years between 1681 and 1732; Hierro, who served 50 years (1708 to 1758); Antonio Ignacio Herrera, with 48 years between 1684 and 1732; Manuel Vivanco, with 47 years of combined Tepehuana-Tarahumara service between 1720 and 1767; Guadalajara, with 45 years (1675 to 1720); Villar, with 42 years (1647–1689); Landa, who served from 1706 until 1747, for 41 years; and Glandorff, 41 years between 1722 and 1763.

15. Guenduláin, 30.

16. Lizasoaín, *Noticia*, 25.

17. *Obra*, II, after 302.

18. The spelling is worth a passing comment. The mountain and the Benedictine monastery in Catalonia are both called *Montserrat,* as is the Leeward Island of that name. But the other colonial uses of the word, for a peak north of Bogotá and for an island in the Sea of Cortés, follow the Nonoava spelling of *Monserrate. National Geographic Atlas*, 269–270.

19. *Misiones*, 98.

20. Lizasoaín, *Noticia*, 25.

21. Braun 1765.

22. Spicer, 41; Ocampo, 77.

23. Ocampo, 78.

24. The word is from *Húmashi*, meaning "to run." Hodge, I, 578.

25. *Chihuahuenses*, 258.

26. Ortiz, 328. González, 115, n. 102, misunderstands Ortiz when he says that the visitador reported that Humariza in 1678 had 91 Christian families with 322 persons. The figures are Ortiz's census for the entire partido.

27. Ydiáquez 1744.

28. González, 115, n. 102.

29. *Estado de Norogáchic.*
30. *Chihuahuenses*, 258.
31. Guenduláin, 30.
32. Ydiáquez 1744.
33. Tamarón, 142.
34. Robles, 159, n. 8.
35. Guenduláin, 30.
36. Ortiz, 328.
37. Ydiáquez 1744.
38. *Estado de Norogáchic.*
39. Guenduláin, 30.
40. Coulson, 250.
41. *Chihuahuenses*, 482.

15. Cusihuiriáchic

1. Which means *lugar de palo parado* (Gómez, 148), or "where the upright pole is" (Hodge, I, 373).
2. La Bufa de Cusihuiriáchic, the peak, rises to 7,918 feet, while the pueblo is said to be at an altitude of 6,275 feet. Kimball, 1.
3. At one time Paul and I almost agreed with Bancroft, I, 363, n. 46, who concluded that there is "no apparent possibility of fixing the exact" location of Cusi.
4. The 1788 population was 10,750. Jordán, 394, n. 1.
5. *Chihuahuenses*, 130. It may be worse now. *Chihuahuenses*, 129, reports 9,244 people in the municipio in 1960, but ten years later *IX Censo 1970*, 17, gives the figure for the 85 localities in the municipio as 8,768.
6. *EJMT*, 104.
7. Ortiz, 334.
8. *Chihuahuenses*, 130.
9. Neumann, *Historia*, 171.
10. Located on January 12, 1690. *Chihuahuenses*, 549. Between 1687 and 1689 there had been more than 400 men at Cusi who were skilled in the use of arms, but so many went to Urique in 1690 that there remained only a hundred or so. González, 41, n. 7.
11. Neumann, *Historia*, 173.
12. Neumann, *Historia*, 184. But the ubiquitous and highly professional Juan Fernández Retana characterized the citizen-soldiers as worthless. González, 60, n. 48.
13. Neumann, *Historia*, 210.
14. Neumann, *Historia*, 229.
15. Rezawal 1698.
16. *Obra*, II, 302.
17. *Estado de Norogáchic.*
18. Guenduláin, 24.
19. *Administrative Census of 1728.*
20. Tamarón, 141.
21. Jordán, 394, n. 1.
22. "From the discovery of the mines...up to 1778, their registered production was 35,000,000 dollars....On this amount...the tax of one-fifth

(*quinto*) was paid to the crown of Spain; and it is justifiable to suppose that about as much more was clandestinely produced. From the same record it appears that, during the middle of the 17th century, eight separate workings produced an aggregate of 5,000 to 6,000 marcs of silver annually.... From 1783 to 1806, the number of workings was increased to 27, and the acknowledged annual production had mounted to 18,000 marcs ($168,200)....[Thus]...$44,021,500...[is]... the total reported production of these mines from first to the last. By applying the accepted rule for estimating the *actual* production ... the approximate total [actual production] of $60,000,000 to $90,000,000 [is reached]." Kimball, 1-2.

    23. Kimball, 2.

    24. Called, as were some of its predecessors, Santa Rosa rather than San Bernabé.

    25. Coyáchic really isn't all that hard to find, but, as with Cusi, Bancroft, I, 363, n. 46, thought there was "no apparent possibility" of fixing its location.

    26. Jordán, 90, 115.

    27. Ortiz, 334–335.

    28. *EJMT*, 142; Neumann 1681; González, xli.

    29. *EJMT*, 166.

    30. Neumann, *Historia*, 171.

    31. Neumann 1690.

    32. *Estado de Norogáchic.*

    33. Guenduláin, 24.

    34. Bandelier, III, 500.

    35. Dunne 137, 14.

    36. *Chihuahuenses*, 123.

    37. *Chihuahuenses*, 126.

    38. *Chihuahuenses*, 331.

    39. Robles, 159, n.12.

    40. Guadalajara 1676.

    41. Ortiz, 335. *Obra*, II, 288, is clearly confused in reporting that Tardá built a church here early in November, 1675.

    42. Guenduláin, 24.

    43. Jordán, 90; *EJMT*, 104.

    44. Ortiz, 334–335.

    45. Guenduláin, 24.

    46. Lizasoaín, *Noticia*, 26. Tamarón, 140–141, gives the same report.

    47. *Chihuahuenses*, 481.

16. Temeýchic

    1. Which means "storage place for bread." Och, 189, n. 31.

    2. *EJMT*, 64–65.

    3. *Introduction*, 22.

    4. "...la pequeña iglesia que en este puesto años ha hizo el venerable padre Antonio Basilio...." Ortiz, 333.

    5. Christelow 1939, 427.

    6. *EJMT*, 70.

    7. Guadalajara 1676.

8. Ortiz, 333.
9. Andonaegui Dec. 1744.
10. Andonaegui Dec. 1744.
11. *EJMT*, 189–190; Neumann, *Revoltes*, 166, 168, 170 (Latin), 167, 169, 171 (French).
12. Zambrano-Gutiérrez, XV, 593; Andonaegui Dec. 1744; González, 201, n. 65.
13. Guenduláin, 27.
14. Andonaegui 1748.
15. Téllez. But the claim of completion is disputed by another contemporary, who reported that Father Roque built only "a large part of the walls," leaving the rest unfinished. Hierro Aug. 30, 1747.
16. Palma.
17. *Libro VIII*.
18. The modern population is only 528. *Chihuahuenses*, 235.
19. Of about 738 persons. *Chihuahuenses*, 388.
20. Andonaegui Dec. 1744 calls them Río Píchachic and Río Temeýchic, but it's customary not only for river names to change in two centuries but also for rivers to be named, successively, after each community through which they pass. However, Hodge, II, 183, is on the wrong side of the Continental Divide when he says Pachera is at the extreme headwaters of the north branch of Río Nonoava.
21. *EJMT*, 112.
22. *Chihuahuenses*, 388.
23. Ortiz, 333.
24. Neumann 1698.
25. Neumann, *Revoltes*, 166, 168, 170 (Latin), 167, 169, 171 (French); *EJMT*, 190–191. Strangely, Dunne—who seemed to know all about Pachera at 112 and 131—reported the incident as one occurring at Pozera, which he did not otherwise identify.
26. *EJMT*, 112.
27. Ortiz, 333.
28. Guenduláin.
29. Andonaegui Dec. 1744.
30. Tamarón, 145.
31. Robles, 161, n. 39.
32. *Chihuahuenses*, 412.
33. Ortiz, 333.
34. Andonaegui Dec. 1744.
35. *Chihuahuenses*, 412.
36. Tamarón, 146.
37. *Chihuahuenses*, 142, puts the figure at 158.
38. Personal correspondence of the Reverend Carlos Díaz Infante, S.J., June 1972. Father Dunne undoubtedly had this Jesuit in mind when he said, in *EJMT*, 8, that the Jesuits were working in the mid-twentieth century at Cárichic, Sisoguíchic and Píchachic, although his more precise listing, at 239, n. 3, does not mention Píchachic, and shows only Norogáchic, Cerocahui, Narárachic, Sisoguíchic, Chinatú and Guadalupe y Calvo. In June 1974, padres and brothers of the Jesuit Misión de la Tarahumara were at work in Sisoguíchic, Cárichic, San Juanito, Creel, Norogáchic, Guachóchic, Batopilas, Cerocahui, Chínipas, Chinatú and Guadalupe y Calvo.

Chapter 17. Papigóchic

1. Named in honor of General Vicente Guerrero on April 11, 1859. *Chihuahuenses*, 244.

2. Which means *donde habitan pájaros de pico largo*, or "where the long-beaked birds live." Gómez, 148. See, to the same effect, *Obra*, II, 268. But Hodge, II, 201, is more imaginative with "snipe town."

3. *Alzamiento*, 177–178; Pascual 1651, 190; *EJMT*, 60–61; Jordán, 76; Saravia 1954, III, 311; Bancroft, I, 355.

4. Robles, 162, n. 46.

5. The founding garrison, a corporal and 30 men, were given supplies for eight months. *EJMT*, 60–61.

6. The response to the first appeal for colonists was disappointing. Only four Parral families volunteered to go to the new town. Jordán, 76; *Introduction*, 20.

7. Pascual 1651, 190; Jordán, 77.

8. *Introduction*, 22; Neumann, *Historia*, 149–150; Pascual 1651, 191; *EJMT*, 64–69.

9. Jordán, 80.

10. *EJMT*, 69–70; Jordán, 80.

11. *EJMT*, 72–74; Pascual 1651, 200; Jordán, 81–83; *Introduction*, 23. In his *Historia*, 150, Father Neumann combines the 1650 and the 1652 revolts and has Beudín and Basilio killed, along with the rest of the European population, in the same uprising, Beudín at La Purísima and Basilio at the presidial chapel. He also recounts that 40 years later Basilio's bones were found in the ruins and buried by Father Venceslao Eymer at La Purísima, where they are "piously preserved to this day." In fact Basilio's body was recovered eight months after his death and put in the coffin which held Beudín's remains. In 1653 both martyrs were removed to San Felipe. González, 13, n. 16.

12. Jordán, 83.

13. *EJMT*, 80. But the abandonment was not permanent, and Spicer, 32, is wide of the mark when he says that after peace "the Spaniards were again in control of the area, but their plan for a town in the heart of Tarahumara country was permanently given up. Villa de Aguilar was not resettled and the mission of Papigochic was abandoned."

14. *EJMT*, 96–100.

15. *EJMT*, 101.

16. *EJMT*, 106, 109, 112; Guadalajara 1676.

17. Gutiérrez 1676.

18. *EJMT*, 100, says four rather than six, but it doesn't name them. González, 25, n. 9, gives the names of the six, but inadvertently refers to José Sánchez Guevara as Sánchez de Arteaga.

19. Ortiz, 336, 337.

20. *Introduction*, 88, n. 152, says 1683 because Christelow mistakenly thought Copart went to California with Kino, Goñi and Atondo.

21. González, 62, n. 49.

22. González, 185, n. 32.

23. Neumann, *Historia*, 193–194.

24. Neumann, *Revoltes*, 182 (Latin), 183 (French); *EJMT*, 195.

25. Guenduláin, 27.

26. He was at Papigóchic "some years" before 1748. Andonaegui 1748. But he does not appear in *Libro V*, which begins in July 1742.

27. *Libro V.*
28. *Libro V.*
29. Osorio 1744.
30. His last entry in *Libro V* is February 25, 1746.
31. *Libro V.*
32. Hierro Aug. 23, 1747.
33. *Libro V.*
34. *Libro I.*
35. Lizasoaín, *Noticia*, 22.
36. *Libro V.*
37. Vivanco was still in Nonoava in 1761. Lizasoaín, *Noticia*, 25. *Chihuahuenses*, 568, is thus in error in reporting that he went to Papigóchic when Tizonazo was secularized in 1753. He first appears on the Papigóchic register on March 17, 1765. *Libro V*. Braun 1765 says he had considered sending Juan Francisco Hauga to help the failing Vivanco, but that both the Papigóchic Indians and Father Vivanco preferred Vega. Since Vega got there six months before Vivanco, Braun must mean that he had considered sending Hauga to replace Vega.
38. Bancroft, I, 657, n. 38.
39. *Chihuahuenses*, 244, credits it with 2,717 people.
40. My conclusion flies in the face of Father Dunne's comment in *EJMT*, 203, that the old church "has entirely disappeared."
41. Ortiz, 336.
42. Guenduláin. By 1766 the name had been slightly changed, apparently temporarily, to San Ygnacio de Loyola. *Libro V.*
43. *Chihuahuenses*, 388, assigns a population of 423.
44. Ortiz, 337.
45. Guenduláin.
46. Osorio 1744.
47. Tamarón, 147.
48. Lizasoaín, *Noticia*, 22.
49. *Obra*, II, 313, n. 29.
50. Bancroft, I, 599, n. 24.
51. *Chihuahuenses*, 533.
52. Guenduláin, 27.
53. Tamarón, 147.
54. Ortiz, 337.
55. *Introduction*, 44, says that by 1697 Santo Tomás had become a cabecera, but in giving the missionary assignments made after the Jesuits were permitted to return to their posts in January 1692, González, 63, n. 49, says that Guerrero, who had been at Santo Tomás, now went to another assignment. Obviously, Guerrero could only have been at Santo Tomás before the revolt began in April 1690.
56. González, 71, n. 12. Neumann, who almost never called his fellow Jesuits by name, referred to Peña in *Historia*, 196, as the priest stationed at the mission dedicated to St. Thomas the Apostle, and Guenduláin, 26, fell into the same error with respect to the patron saint. St. Thomas of Villanova, archbishop of Valencia, died in 1555 and was canonized in 1658. Coulson, 434–435.
57. Neumann, *Historia*, 257.
58. *EJMT*, 188; Neumann, *Historia*, 257.

59. González, 88, n. 44.
60. González, 201, n. 65.
61. Lizasoaín, *Noticia*, 21.
62. *Libro VI; Libro VII; Libro II.*
63. *Chihuahuenses*, 202, 392.

Chapter 18. Mátachic

1. Which is said to mean "place of the dark lizards." Robles, 162, n. 53, citing Ponce de León, 33.
2. With a population somewhere between 147 (Robles, 162, n. 53) and 1,045 (*Chihuahuenses*, 517).
3. Guadalajara 1677.
4. Ortiz, 338–340.
5. *Obra*, II, 301.
6. Guenduláin, 26. I can find support for this assertion neither in the records nor in logic.
7. Tamarón, 148.
8. Lizasoaín, *Noticia*, 22.
9. Which means "place of the *metate*." Gómez, 148.
10. Guadalajara 1676.
11. Ortiz, 324, 338–339.
12. Neumann, *Historia*, 173.
13. Neumann 1698.
14. Neumann, *Historia*, 257.
15. González, 155, n. 168.
16. Téllez.
17. Guenduláin, 26.
18. Lizasoaín, *Noticia*, 22.
19. Dunne 1937, 14.
20. *EJMT*, facing 128.
21. *EJMT*, 203.
22. Which means *subió por un pino*. Robles, 162, n. 51, in reliance on Ponce de León, 25. Since the pueblo is well below the pine country, the suggestion seems dubious.
23. In 1960, it had 472 people. *Chihuahuenses*, 103.
24. Ortiz, 339–340.
25. *Introduction*, 44, says that by 1696 Cocomórachic was independent of Mátachic and had been established as a separate cabecera. But González, 40, n. 6, says that Alderete, by then the rector, was at Cocomórachic in 1690. The same author, 45, n. 13, says he was a missionary in Tarahumara from 1683 until his death in 1719. Since nothing suggests that he served before 1690 at a place other than Cocomórachic, I have concluded he was probably first assigned there in 1683.
26. Neumann, *Historia*, 173.
27. González, 88, n. 44.
28. Neumann, *Historia*, 194.
29. *Chihuahuenses*, 103.
30. Neumann, *Historia*, 202. In Neumann 1698, he increased the number of executed prisoners to 40.

31. Neumann, *Historia*, 257.
32. Guenduláin, 26. The visitador referred to the Cocomórachic church as Nuestra Señora de Aranzazú, but I believe he was confused about the name. Lizasoaín, *Noticia*, 20, correctly lists Cajuríchic as Nuestra Señora de Aranzazú y Cahulitzi.
33. *Misiones*, 91.
34. *Misiones*, 94.
35. Tamarón, 147; Lizasoaín, *Noticia*, 21.
36. Which means "place of the rock pile." Robles, 162, n. 54 (Ponce de León, 33). Hodge, II, 727, says the word is a corruption of *Remosachic*, meaning "stone heap."
37. Guadalajara 1677.
38. Ortiz, 338–339.
39. Neumann, *Historia*, 172.
40. *EJMT*, 168.
41. *Chihuahuenses*, 520, says the original name was San Francisco Javier, but since Ortiz, 338, called it San Miguel, I'm dubious.
42. Guenduláin, 25. With slight editing, the translation is from *EJMT*, 202, where, undoubtedly because he read the report too fast, Father Dunne said the description refers to the church at Yepómera.
43. Hodge, II, 727.

Chapter 19. Yepómera

1. Which means *llano arriba*, or "high plain." Robles, 162, n. 55 (Ponce de León, 34). Or, to adopt the more descriptive language of Guenduláin, 25, "está mas adentro en la falda de la sierra, donde termina el llano, lo cual significa Yepomera en la lengua taraumara," which can be roughly translated "it is more within the slope of the sierra, where the plain ends, which is what Yepómera means in the Tarahumara language."
2. Rinaldini.
3. Pennington 1963, 6, n. 38.
4. Guadalajara 1677.
5. Yet none of the old references suggests that Yepómera was otherwise than on a tributary. Guadalajara 1677; Ortiz, 339.
6. Guadalajara 1677.
7. The bell is marked "Año de 1737 Señor San Joseph." The fact that Yepómera was called San Gabriel and later San Nicolás Obispo, but never San José, is of no significance. Bells came from anywhere and weren't necessarily marked with the name of the church where they were first (or ever) hung.
8. *EJMT*, facing 128. The picture shows a campanario above the doorway with the three bells, the middle (and largest) of which looks remarkably like the bell on the rack in front of the church we saw under construction. Father Dunne gave no picture credits, and the photo is undated. Presumably he saw the church before 1948 and presumably the interior looked enough like the description of the Temósachic church in Guenduláin, 25, to lead him into confusing the descriptions and saying, after quoting Guenduláin, "And so it stood in the mid-twentieth century dominating the little village and looking down the arroyo which winds south to the Papigochic." *EJMT*, 202.
9. Guadalajara 1676.

10. In Guadalajara 1677, he reported to the Jesuit provincial that the Tarahumaras of Yepómera didn't like the Franciscans because, in the name of charity but nevertheless by force, they took their chickens, sheep, corn and other goods.

11. *EJMT*, 124 ff; *Obra*, II, 293, n. 6; ABZ, IV, 20–22.

12. *EJMT*, 127.

13. Ortiz, 339.

14. González, 34, n. 37; Ratkay.

15. Neumann, *Historia*, 172.

16. *EJMT*, 168.

17. González, 49, n. 23.

18. Neumann July 1693.

19. *EJMT*, 180, 184, 187.

20. Neumann, *Historia*, 257.

21. Jordán, 119.

22. González, 201, n. 65.

23. Guenduláin, 25.

24. *Chihuahuenses*, 571.

25. Neumann, *Historia*, 198–200.

26. Ortiz, 343.

27. Neumann, *Historia*, 172.

28. *EJMT*, 134.

29. Ortiz, 343.

30. Neumann, *Historia*, 172.

31. *Obra*, II, 297. At n. 11, Father Decorme suggests that Ortiz was in fact killed at Nahuárachic.

Chapter 20. Tutuaca

1. Ortiz, 340, called it San Evangelista de Tosónachic, but *EJMT*, 133, in reporting on the Ortiz *Relación*, refers to San Juan de Tosónachic. Undoubtedly the completely correct title was San Juan Evangelista.

2. Ortiz, 340.

3. *Chihuahuenses*, 534, says it has a population of 621.

4. Guadalajara 1676. In commenting on their trip, Jordán, 117, says "Tutuaca es la región virgen. Ni los blancos, ni Dios, ni el mismo Diablo han pisado antes este terreno montañoso y cubierto de bosques. Guadalajara y Tardá son los primeros," or, roughly translated, "Tutuaca is virgin territory. Neither whites, nor God, nor the Devil himself has tread before on this mountainous and forest-covered terrain. Guadalajara and Tardá are the first."

5. Guadalajara 1676 reports the Indians of Tutuaca as being about half Tarahumara and half Tepehuán. Undoubtedly the authors meant Pima, a conclusion which is buttressed by the reference, later in the same letter, to the Tepehuana de Sonora.

6. Guadalajara 1676; *Obra*, II, 290.

7. Gutiérrez 1676.

8. Ortiz, 340; *EJMT*, 133; *Introduction*, 37.

9. González, 34, n. 37. In the text I ignore the possibility that Ratkay served at another post between Tutuaca and Cárichic. At 35, n. 38, González says his posts (after Yepómera) were Tutuaca, San Xavier and Cárichic. The only San

Xavier in the area was Mogúriachic, which seems highly unlikely, particularly since the place doesn't appear in the reports until long after Ratkay's death.

10. González, 45, n. 13, 44, n. 12.

11. Neumann, *Historia*, 438.

12. Neumann, *Historia*, 185.

13. The view I express is not unanimous, but is that of Neumann, *Revoltes*, 62 (Latin), 63 (French), and González, who at 63, n. 51, charges *EJMT*, 171, with error in reporting that after 1690 "Tutuaca remained without a padre for two years."

14. Neumann, *Historia*, 257.

15. *Obra*, II, 301.

16. Zambrano-Gutiérrez, XV, 346; González, 193, n. 47.

17. Neumann 1723.

18. *Misiones*, 91; *Chihuahuenses*, 570.

19. *Libro III*.

20. *Chihuahuenses*, 74.

21. *Misiones*, 94.

22. *Misiones*, 98.

23. Lizasoaín, *Noticia*, 20.

24. With perhaps 500 people. *Chihuahuenses*, 544, says 448.

25. Tamarón, 174, called it El Arcángel San Miguel.

26. Gómez has a fine picture, facing 252, in the caption of which he reports the height at 311 meters, or 1,020.702 feet.

27. From *yepá* (snow) and *chic* (place). Hodge, II, 997.

28. Ortiz, 340. The simple translation "rough road" is not nearly strong enough.

29. Ortiz, 341.

30. Neumann, *Historia*, 254.

31. Trujillo could not have been there earlier than 1751, since for the year before, Bartolomé Braun served both Tutuaca and Yepáchic. *Chihuahuenses*, 74; *Misiones*, 94. By 1761, he was at Tónachic. Lizasoaín, *Noticia*, 25.

32. Braun 1765.

33. Lizasoaín, *Noticia*, 20.

34. Ferguson, 152.

35. Ortiz, 340–341.

Chapter 21. Tomóchic

1. *EJMT*, 206.

2. González, 5, n. 13.

3. González, 4, n. 11.

4. González, 185, n. 32.

5. Guenduláin, 32.

6. González, 85, n. 38.

7. *Libro I*.

8. Guenduláin, 32. St. Aloysius Gonzaga was not canonized until 1726, the year after the report. *Britannica*, IV, 626.

9. *Administrative Census of 1728*.

10. Glandorff 1730, quoted in part in *Obra*, II, 303.

11. Glandorff 1752. *EJMT*, 210, makes the 1752 report sound as though it were contained in the shorter 1730 statement and mistakenly reads the church list: Glandorff "had early built five churches, one in each of five pueblos which he named... Santa María Immaculata, San Miguel, San José, San Luis de Gonzaga and Santa María Dei Para Aranzassassana!" An examination of a photostat of the 1752 letter readily shows that the word *Aranzazú* is closely followed by the word *afanes*, and that whoever made the typescript in the Bancroft Library (which is obviously all that Father Dunne saw) hastily assumed that they were one word, rendering the original as transcribed in *EJMT*. But it is nevertheless strange, because Father Dunne must have known of the appearance of the Virgin at Aranzazú, a very small town in the Spanish province of Vizcaya. Additionally, he certainly had available Braun 1764, 27, which recounts Father Glandorff's conversions attributed to La Santísima Virgen de Aranzazú.

12. Which means either "place of gold," Neumann Sept. 1693, or "winterhouse." Och, 189, n. 31.

13. Neumann July 1693.

14. Jordán, 76.

15. Jordán, 76.

16. Jordán, 86; Saravia 1954, III, 328.

17. Neumann, *Historia*, 173.

18. *Introduction*, 48.

19. González, 70, n. 12.

20. Neumann, *Historia*, 203–204, 208, 228.

21. *EJMT*, 188.

22. Neumann, *Historia*, 258.

23. *Report on Tomotzi, 1744*.

24. Guenduláin, 32.

25. On August 9, 1763. ABZ, IV, 445, n. 21.

26. Lizasoaín, *Noticia*, 20.

27. Braun 1765.

28. *Misiones*, 102.

29. *Chihuahuenses*, 530–533; *Resumen*, 349–353. The rebellion was sympathetically treated by one of the federal soldiers, the novelist Heriberto Frías, in his *Tomóchic*, México, 1968.

30. González, 185, n. 32.

31. González, 71, n. 12.

32. Which means one-eyed, or blind in one eye.

33. *Obra*, II, 300, and n. 14.

34. Neumann, *Historia*, 204–205; Neumann 1698.

35. González, 4, n. 11.

36. Neumann, *Historia*, 173.

37. Neumann, *Revoltes*, 62 (Latin), 63 (French); Neumann, *Historia*, 185; González, 157, n. 170; *EJMT*, 171.

38. *EJMT*, 188; Neumann, *Historia*, 258.

39. *Obra*, II, 303; *EJMT*, 210.

40. *The Gospel According to Saint John*, King James Version, 6:9.

41. Guenduláin, 32.

42. Tamarón, 146.

43. Robles, 161, n. 45.

44. González, 85, n. 38.

45. Tamarón, 146.

Chapter 22. Cárichic

1. Which means "where houses are built." Gómez, 147.

2. In Guadalajara 1676, Fathers Guadalajara and Tardá report that one of them (and they don't say which) went alone to Guerucárichic. *EJMT*, 109–110, says the lone priest was Guadalajara, as does *Obra*, II, 288, but neither gives any reason for the selection. Jordán, 116, says both priests were there, which is clearly contradicted by their letter. *Chihuahuenses*, 64, says the pueblo was founded by Fernando Barrionuevo and Juan Gamboa in November 1673, but the assertion is difficult to accept.

3. Guadalajara 1676.

4. Gutiérrez 1676.

5. Ortiz, 329.

6. González, 25, n. 11.

7. ABZ, IV, 14*.

8. Christelow 1939, 430; Neumann 1682.

9. Neumann, *Historia*, 168.

10. Who reached Cárichic by April 20, 1684. González, 37, n. 48.

11. Neumann 1690.

12. Neumann, *Historia*, 261–262. I have taken liberties with Father Neumann's text in that I have used the Spanish instead of the Italian form for Father Pícolo's name.

13. *EJMT*, 197. But note the unfortunate, and obviously accidental, attribution of Pícolo's church to Neumann in Dunne 1957, 54.

14. Guenduláin, 28.

15. González, xlvii, in reliance on the statement of P. Benjamín Tapia, S.J., upon whom, as well as P. Valente Herrera, S.J., I also rely.

16. *EJMT*, 203, is clearly over-enthusiastic in saying that the church "stands perfectly intact."

17. I rely on a picture in Ocampo, after 370.

18. There is no tower in the picture in *EJMT*, 112.

19. González, 3, n. 9.

20. Neumann, *Historia*, 221, says that on the night of June 21, 1697, he went to Cárichic, but he doesn't appear in *Libro I* until September 15, 1697. On the other hand, González, xlii, says he was at Cárichic after February 25, 1698, and, at 163, n. 184, after February 27, 1698. It is true of course that Neumann traveled about as visitador until his term was up in 1699, but *EJMT*, 189, is certainly mistaken in suggesting that he didn't take up residence at Cárichic until that year.

21. *Libro III*.

22. *Libro III*. *EJMT*, 189, is inaccurate in reporting that "just prior to the trouble of 1697 Pícolo had gone off to the newly organized missions of Lower California," and while the dating (1698) in *Introduction*, 47, is perhaps closer to the fact, Christelow's assignment of a reason for Pícolo's leaving is equally questionable: "discouragement caused by the revolt of 1697 drove him to California."

23. Neumann, *Historia*, 236. Neumann adds that the bishop was the "first to bring the sacrament of confirmation to this nation of the Tarahumaras," a statement which, as González, 129, n. 128, points out, omits to take into account Gonzalo Hermosillo, the first bishop of Durango, who confirmed at San Pablo in 1624. Neumann doesn't identify the seven Jesuits, but in *Historia*, 228, he says he and two other Jesuits (presumably Pícolo and Proto) spent the early

months of the war at Cárichic. I cannot be certain of the date of the bishop's visit, but if it was before Pícolo left, only five visiting priests came with him.

24. Neumann, *Historia*, 262.
25. González, 184, n. 31.
26. *Libro III*.
27. *Libro I*.
28. *Libro I*; Terrazas, 376, n. 1. *Obra*, II, 308, says Glandorff came in 1723 and stayed a year.
29. *Libro I*.
30. *Libro I*.
31. *Libro III*.
32. González, xlvii.
33. Dunne 1957, 54.
34. *Libro III*.
35. *Libro III*.
36. Osorio 1744.
37. *Libro III*.
38. González, 129, n. 128.
39. *Misiones*, 91.
40. The last entry by Fernández is August 19, 1748, in *Libro II*. The first Prieto entry is October 23 in the same volume.
41. The last Prieto entry in *Libro I* is April, 1749, which is the month of the first Yáñez signature in *Libro III*.
42. *Misiones*, 98.
43. Lizasoaín, *Noticia*, 23.
44. Braun 1765.
45. *Misiones*, 102.
46. Zelis, 153, 163.
47. Robles, 160, n. 33, says at an altitude of 2,190 meters, or 7,187 feet.
48. P. Carlos Díaz Infante, S.J., told me the word in Rarámuri is *Rajírachic* and that it means *lugar del fuego*, or "place of fire."
49. *EJMT*, 112.
50. *Chihuahuenses*, 511, says Tagírachic was founded in 1677 by Luis Contreras and, except for the fumble on the name, the statement is probably accurate.
51. Ortiz, 330.
52. ABZ, IV, 97, n. 10, and Zambrano, X, 660, say that in 1684 Ortiz Foronda went to Beato Luis Gonzaga in Tarahumara, and González, 42, n. 10, says he was the procurador of the college in Parral in 1687. Tagírachic is not mentioned, but the only other Tarahumara churches dedicated to Aloysius Gonzaga, those in Peguáchic and Tecabórachic, were established after 1726, when he was canonized.
53. Pícolo 1690.
54. Neumann, *Historia*, 262. Neumann doesn't name the visitas in which he built, but these are the only logical choices.
55. Guenduláin, 29.
56. Tamarón, 145.
57. Ortiz, 330.
58. Neumann, *Historia*, 262. González, xliv, refers to its *élégance*.
59. Fernández Abeé.
60. Fernández Abeé.
61. Ortiz, 330.

62. Ratkay.
63. Neumann, *Historia*, 262.
64. Guenduláin, 29.
65. Lizasoaín, *Noticia*, 25.
66. *Descripción Topográfica*, 95—96.
67. Fernández Abeé.
68. Which means "place of bamboo reeds." Hodge, I, 130. In correspondence, P. Carlos Díaz Infante, S.J., is probably more accurate in saying *lugar de juncos* ("rushes"), bamboo being unlikely in the area.
69. *Descripción Topográfica*, 125.
70. *Descripción Topográfica*, 95—96.
71. Except for the new roof, today's building is substantially the same as that shown in the undated photograph in *Obra*, II, after 288.
72. Tamarón, 145.
73. Lizasoaín, *Noticia*, 25.
74. *Descripción Topográfica*, 96, 129.

Chapter 23. Sisoguíchic

1. Which means *lugar de saetas* ("place of arrows or darts"). Gómez, 148.
2. Ocampo, 353.
3. Ocampo, 348—349.
4. The new bishop is the author of *La personalidad jurídica del indio y el III Concilio Provincial Mexicano (1585)*, México, 1963.
5. *Chihuahuenses*, 503.
6. *Obra*, II, 293, says Oreña had built a chapel and house by 1677.
7. Ortiz, 331.
8. González, 25, n. 11.
9. Zambrano, VII, 430, in reliance on Pradeau, *Relación*.
10. The account in Neumann 1682 seems much more probable: "Five years earlier, our brethren had attempted to establish a mission there. They began the construction of a church...[the]...mission was abandoned about three years ago, for there was no missionary to carry on the work which had been begun."
11. Neumann 1682.
12. Neumann 1682.
13. Neumann 1686.
14. Neumann 1690.
15. Neumann, *Historia*, 211.
16. Neumann Sept. 1693.
17. Neumann, *Historia*, 221.
18. Neumann, *Historia*, 219—225.
19. González, lxii, n. 2. Rauch couldn't have gotten to Sisoguíchic many years before 1720, since he didn't join the Society until 1704, when he was about 21.
20. Guenduláin, 31; Neumann, *Letters*, 305, n. 67. *EJMT*, 189, was confused when he reported: "Neumann now set himself to rebuild what had been destroyed, for though residing at Cárichic and having charge of that partido, he did not relinquish the spiritual administration of Sisoguíchic. At Sisoguíchic, at Echoguita, and at one of the visitas of Cárichic he began to rebuild the churches. In three years the three were completed." There can be no real doubt that the

three churches Neumann built were in Cárichic's three visitas—Tagírachic, Pasigóchic and Bacaburiáchic. Neumann, *Historia*, 262.

21. *Chihuahuenses*, 472.
22. *EJMT*, 226.
23. Lizasoaín, *Noticia*, 23.
24. Braun 1765.
25. According to P. Luis Verplancken, S.J.
26. Ocampo, after 370.
27. Neumann 1681.
28. Neumann 1682.
29. Neumann 1682. González, xlii, is probably overenthusiastic when he calls it a Neumann visita.
30. Escalona.
31. Lizasoaín, *Noticia*, 25.
32. Braun 1765.
33. *Descripción Topográfica*, 96.
34. Pennington 1963, 12, says Narárachic is the site of a legendary battle between the Tarahumaras and the Apaches. The Apaches are said to have penetrated south to this point and to have taken refuge in the numerous caves. The Tarahumaras burned pine torches at the entrances and the Apaches came out weeping—hence the name for Narárachic, "the place where they cried." Gómez, 148, calls it *lugar donde lloraron*, and Hodge, II, 28, "place of tears."
35. *EJMT*, 128.
36. Guenduláin, 31.
37. Escalona.
38. Lizasoaín, *Noticia*, 24.
39. Tamarón, 143.
40. Which means *lugar de pinos* (place of pines). Gómez, 147. Or, more imaginatively, Hodge, I, 158, says "turpentine," on the theory that the place name comes from the *Rarámuri* words *Ocó* ("pine") and *Ina* ("drips").
41. Bocoyna's valley is at an altitude of 2,222 meters, or 7,293 feet. Robles, 160, n. 20. *Chihuahuenses*, 71, puts the population at 492.
42. *Chihuahuenses*, 159.
43. Ortiz, 331.
44. Neumann 1682.
45. González, 95, n. 60, gives the construction and dedication dates, but calls the church Desponsación de Nuestra Señora con San Joseph. In *Historia*, 211, Neumann forgetfully gives the year of dedication as 1696, but in Neumann Sept. 1693 he describes and correctly dates the ceremony.
46. Neumann, *Historia*, 216–217. Neumann completed his *Historia* in 1724, but in Neumann 1698 (the year after it happened) he described the pillage not very much differently. The Reynolds translation in Neumann, *Letters*, 128–129, is "They overturned the altars; tore and cut to pieces the nine beautiful pictures of the saints and the Mother of God; hurled the other pictures to the floor, and pierced them with their weapons; took all the sacred vessels from the sacristy; ripped apart the priestly vestments and divided them among themselves; broke the chalices; dashed to pieces the bronze and the silver-plated candlesticks, and distributed the fragments among their band; tore asunder the missals and the other sacred books; and, in short, left not one thing whole, not even the baptismal font of stone; for this, too, they hacked to pieces with their axes. Then they heaped together tables, chests, benches, beams, logs, and everything else that

would burn, and set fire to the church and to the missionary's house which adjoined it, and they both were consumed together."

47. Neumann, *Historia*, 211.

48. Christelow 1939, 440.

49. *Chihuahuenses*, 159, says Echoguita was repopulated in 1702, and, on 71, that Bocoyna was founded in the same year, with the name Nuestra Señora de Guadalupe de Bocoyna.

50. Guenduláin, 31. Father Dunne was mistaken in *EJMT*, 189, in saying that Neumann rebuilt the church at Echoguita.

51. Escalona; Lizasoaín, *Noticia*, 24.

52. The older form is *Usárare*, which means *donde abundan las águilas* (where there are many eagles). Gómez, 148. Or, more simply, *Usárare* is from *Usáka*, which means "eagle." Hodge, I, 377.

53. Escalona.

54. Lizasoaín, *Noticia*, 24.

55. Of 300 *habitantes*. Robles, 160, n. 21.

56. *Chihuahuenses*, 124, puts the population at 1,500 and the altitude at 2,358 meters, or 7,739 feet.

57. Gómez, photo, facing 169.

Bibliography

NOTE: Names and locations of the various archives have been abbreviated in this bibliography. For additional archival information see the Abbreviations. The alphabetical arrangement, not only of the Bibliography, but also of the Index, follows the Spanish rather than the English style: CH, LL and Ñ are considered separate letters which occur respectively after C, L and N. For documentary materials, original idiosyncratic spellings have been used.

ABEÉ, JULIÁN ISIDRO FERNÁNDEZ, S.J.   See FERNÁNDEZ ABEÉ.

Acta de Fundación de San José Pámachi, April 24, 1718, in *Archivo General de las Indias,* Sevilla, Audiencia de Guadalajara, 109: ff 8r–9r.

Acta de Fundación de San Luis de Guagueibo, May 8, 1718, in *Archivo General de las Indias,* Sevilla, Audiencia de Guadalajara, 109: ff 8r–9r.

Acta de Fundación de Santa María de el Pópolo Guaguachiqui, April 28, 1718, in *Archivo General de las Indias,* Sevilla, Audiencia de Guadalajara, 109: ff 8r–9r.

AGUIRRE, JOSÉ.
   Report. Pueblo de San Miguel de las Bocas, 19 de mayo de 1729. In Arch., *Parral.*

ALEGRE, FRANCISCO JAVIER, S.J.
   Historia de la Provincia de la Compañía de Jesús de Nueva España. Ed. Ernest J. Burrus, S.J., and Felix Zubillaga, S.J. Institutum Historicum S.J., Rome, 4 vols., tomo I, 1956; tomo II, 1958; tomo III, 1959; tomo IV, 1960.

ALESSIO ROBLES, VITO.   See LAFORA , *Relación* and TAMARÓN Y ROMERAL.

ALMADA, FRANCISCO R.
   Apuntes Históricos de la Región de Chínipas. Talleres Linotipográficos del Estado de Chihuahua, Chihuahua, 1937.

[341]

ALMADA, FRANCISCO R.
Diccionario de Historia, Geografía y Biografía Chihuahuenses. Universidad de Chihuahua, Departamento de Investigaciones Sociales, Sección de Historia, Impresora de Juárez, S.A., Ciudad Juárez, Segunda Edición, 1968.

————. *Diccionario de Historia, Geografía y Biografía Sonorenses.* Chihuahua, n.d.

————. *El Ferrocarril de Chihuahua al Pacífico.* Editorial Libros de México, S.A., México, 1970.

————. "Etimología de la Palabra Chihuahua," *Boletín de la Sociedad Chihuahuense de Estudios Históricos,* tomo 1, núm. 1, Chihuahua, 1942, pp. 20–24.

————. "La Fundación de la Ciudad de Chihuahua," *Boletín de la Sociedad Chihuahuense de Estudios Históricos,* tomo 1, núm. 1, Chihuahua, 1942, pp. 1–5.

————. "Los Primeros Pobladores de Santa Eulalia y San Francisco de Cuéllar," *Boletín de la Sociedad Chihuahuense de Estudios Históricos,* tomo 1, núm. 1, Chihuahua, 1942, pp. 6–9.

————. *Resumen de Historia del Estado de Chihuahua.* Libros Mexicanos, México, 1955.

Alzamiento de los Indios Taraumares y su Asiento, año de 1646 (1649). In *Doc. Hist. Méx.,* 4a ser., III, pp. 172–178.

ANDONAEGUI, ROQUE, S.J.
Carta al P. Provl. Andrés Xavier Garzía, Durango, Henero 29 de 1748, in AGN, *Hist.,* tomo 333.

————. *Carta al P. Provl. Andrés Xavier Garzía,* Valle de San Bartholomé, Septiembre 27 de 1747, in AGN, *Hist.,* tomo 333.

————. *Carta al P. Provincial Andrés Xavier Garzía,* Durango, 6 de (October), 1747, in AGN, *Hist.,* tomo 333.

————. *Report, al R. P. Visitador Lorenzo Gera,* Thameychic, December, 1744, in Bolton (Maggs) Collection, Bancroft Library, Univ. of California, Berkeley.

————. *Report, Mission de San Joseph de Tameichi,* June 21, 1744, in Bolton (Maggs) Collection, Bancroft Library, University of California, Berkeley.

ARIAS, ANTONIO, S.J.
Carta al Sr. General y Capitán General Don Manuel San Juan de Santa Cruz, Parral, December 4, 1718, in Arch., *Parral.*

————. *Carta al Gobernador Capitán General, Don Manuel San Juan de Santa Cruz,* San Francisco de Cuéllar, December 21, 1718, in Arch., *Parral.*

ASCHER, ROBERT and CLUNE, FRANCIS J., Jr.
"Waterfall Cave, Southern Chihuahua, Mexico," *American Antiquity,* Vol. 26, No. 2, 1960, pp. 270–274.

BALTHASAR, JUAN ANTONIO, S.J.
Carta del P. Provincial Juan Antonio Balthassar, en que dà noticia de la exemplar vida, religiosas virtudes, y apostolicos trabajos del fervoroso Misionero el Venerable P. Francisco Maria Picolo. n.p. México, December 23, 1752.

BANCROFT, HUBERT HOWE.
History of the North Mexican States and Texas. 2 vols., Vol. I, A. L. Bancroft & Company, San Francisco, 1884; Vol. II, The History Company, San Francisco, 1889.

BANDA LARREA, LUIS.
Order, el Real de Minas de San Joseph del Parral en 14 de Marzo de 1699, in Arch., *Parral.*

BANDELIER, ADOLPH F.A. and FANNY R. BANDELIER. See *Historical Documents.*

BANNON, JOHN FRANCIS, S.J.
"The Conquest of the Chínipas," *Mid-America,* Vol. 21 (New Series, Vol. 10), No. 1, 1939, pp. 3–31.

BARRI, LEÓN, JR.
"Documentos Sobre la Fundación del Colegio de los Jesuitas en Chihuahua," *Boletín de la Sociedad Chihuahuense de Estudios Históricos,* tomo 2, núm. 2, pp. 48–51, núm. 3, pp. 82–86; núm. 4, pp. 125–127, 151.

BEALS, RALPH L. See KIRCHOFF, "Gatherers and Farmers."

BENNETT, WENDELL C. and ZINGG, ROBERT M.
The Tarahumara, An Indian Tribe of Northern Mexico. The University of Chicago Press, Chicago, 1935.

BEUDÍN, CORNELIO, S.J.
Letter, May 18, 1646, in AGN, *Mis.,* tomo 25, fol. 399.

BIANCHI, JOSÉ VERGARA, S.J. See BRAMBILA.

BOLTON, HERBERT EUGENE.
Rim of Christendom, A Biography of Eusebio Francisco Kino, Pacific Coast Pioneer, The MacMillan Company, New York, 1936.

————. See NEUMANN, *Letters.*

BRAMBILA, DAVID, S.J., with VERGARA BIANCHI, JOSÉ, S.J.
Gramática Rarámuri. Editorial Buena Prensa, México, 1953.

BRAUN, BARTOLOMÉ, S.J.
Carta del P. Bartholomé Braun, Visitador de la Provincia Tarahumara a los PP. Superiores de Esta Provincia de Nueva España sobre la Apostolica Vida, virtudes, y Santa Muerte del P. Francisco Hermano Glandorff. Colegio de San Ildefonso de México, año de 1764.

————. *Carta al Mi Amantisimo Padre Provincial Francisco Zevallos.* Temotzatzu, Junio 17 de 1765, in AHH, *Temp.,* leg. 17, ex. 57.

BRINTON, D. G.
The American Race. D. McKay, Philadelphia, 1891.

BURRUS, ERNEST J., S.J.
"Francesco María Piccolo (1654–1729), Pioneer of Lower California in the Light of Roman Archives," *Hispanic American Historical Review,* Vol. 35, February, 1955, pp. 61–76.

————. *La Obra Cartográfica de la Provincia Mexicana de la Compañía de Jesús (1567–1967).* Ediciones José Porrúa Turanzas, Madrid, 2 vols., 1967.

————. *Misiones Norteñas Mexicanas de la Compañía de Jesús, 1751–1757.* Antigua Librería Robredo de José Porrúa e Hijos, México, 1963.

BURRUS, ERNEST J., S.J.
"Pioneer Jesuit Apostles among the Indians of New Spain (1572–1604): Ignatian Principles Put into Practice," *Institutum Historicum S.I.,* Vol. XXV, Rome, 1956, pp. 574–597, renum. in reprint as pp. 3–26.

———. "Research Opportunities in Italian Archives and Manuscript Collections for Students of Hispanic American History," *Hispanic American Historical Review,* August, 1959, p. 428–463.

———. See ALEGRE, *Historia*, DUCRUE, PÍCOLO, and SALVATIERRA.

CABEZA DE VACA, F.
Apuntes Sobre la Vida de los Tarahumaras. Sisoguíchic, Chihuahua, 1940; ed. Vargas Rea, Biblioteca Aportación Histórica, México, 1943.

CALDERÓN, FELIPE, S.J.
Report, from Santa María de las Cuevas, n.d. but c. 1720, in *Papeles Relativos a los Jesuitas en Baja California y Otras Regiones Septentrionales de la Nueva España, 1686–1793.* Bolton (Maggs) Collection, Bancroft Library, University of California, Berkeley.

CAÑAS, CRISTÓBAL, S.J.
Estado de la Provincia de Sonora, con el catálogo de sus pueblos, iglesias, padres misioneros, número de almas capaces de administracion, lenguas diversas que en ella se hablan y leguas en que se dilata; con una breve descripcion de la Sonora jesuítica, segun se halla por el mes de Julio de este año de 1730, escrito por un padre misionero de la provincia de la Compañía de Jesus de Nueva-España, in *Doc. Hist. Méx.,* 3a ser., pp. 617–625.

CARLSON, PAUL. See HILTON and CARLSON.

Carta de la Real Audiencia, Guadalajara, February 7, 1665. In AHH, *Temp.,* leg. 27, ex. 30.

CASILLAS, JOSÉ GUTIÉRREZ, S.J.   See GUTIÉRREZ CASILLAS.

CASTILLO, RODRIGO, S.J.
Annua, 1662, San Miguel de las Bocas, in AGN, *Mis.,* tomo 26, núm. 85.

———. *Annua, 1667,* in AGN, *Mis.,* tomo 26, núm. 90.

Catalogo de los Partidos Contenidos en los Rectorados de las Misiones de Sonora por el año de 1658 (1685), in *Doc. Hist. Méx.,* 3a ser., pp. 790–794.

Cathalogo de las Missiones de Esta Provincia de Cinaloa, Divididas en Tres Rectorados; Collegio de Cinaloa, Rectorado de N.P.S. Ygnacio y Santa Ynes de la Sierra de Chinipas, que se haze desde el Año de 1716, hasta el de 1720. In ARSJ, *Mexicana*, 18, fol. 20–21v, and in ABZ, Vol. IV, pp. 491–518.

(IX) Censo General de Población. 1970. Secretaria de Industria y Comercio, Dirección General de Estadística, México, 1972.

CLUNE, DORRIS.
"Textiles and Matting from Waterfall Cave, Chihuahua," *American Antiquity,* Vol. 26, No. 2, 1960, pp. 274–277.

CLUNE, FRANCIS J., JR. See ASCHER.

COULSON, JOHN. See *The Saints: A Concise Biographical Dictionary.*

CUEVAS, MARIANO, S.J.
Historia de la Iglesia en México. Editorial Patria, México, 5 vols., vols. 1–4, 1946; vol. 5, 1947.

CUTLER, HUGH.
"Cultivated Plant Remains from Waterfall Cave, Chihuahua," *American Antiquity*, Vol. 26, No. 2, 1960, pp. 277–279.

CZIGÁNY, LÓRÁNT. See TÖMÖRDY.

CHRISTELOW, ALLAN.
"Father Joseph Neumann, Jesuit Missionary to the Tarahumares," *The Hispanic American Historical Review*, Vol. XIX, No. 4, November 1939, pp. 423–442.

_____. *Introduction* to José Neumann, S.J., *Letters*, col. by Herbert Eugene Bolton, tr. Marion L. Reynolds, typescript, 1936, in Herbert E. Bolton Papers, Bancroft Library, University of California, Berkeley.

DECORME, GERARDO, S.J.
La Obra de los Jesuitas Mexicanos Durante la Epoca Colonial 1572–1767 (Compendio Histórico). José Porrúa & Hijos, México, 2 vols., 1941.

_____. *Mártires jesuitas de la Provincia de México.* Talleres Linotipográficos VERA, Guadalajara, 1957.

Descripción Topográfica de las Misiones de Propaganda Fide de Nuestra Señora de Guadalupe de Zacatecas la Sierra Madre. In *Doc. Hist. Méx.*, 4a ser., IV, pp. 92–131.

Destierro de Misioneros de la America Septentrional Española. Por Dn. A. S. Olim Misionero de Norogachic en la Provincia de la Tarahumara Alta. Dividido en dos partes. MS., National Library, Rome.

DÍAZ VALDÉS, FRANCISCO, S.J.
Report, n.d., in Bolton (Maggs) Collection, Bancroft Library, University of California, Berkeley.

Diccionario Porrúa de Historia, Biografía y Geografía de México. Editorial Porrúa, México, 1965.

DOBYNS, HENRY F.
Pioneering Christians Among the Perishing Indians of Tucson. Editorial Estudios Andinos, Lima, Peru, 1962.

Documentos para la Historia de México. México, 20 vols., 4 series, 1853–1857.

Documentos sobre la Expulsión de los Jesuítas y Ocupación de sus Temporalidades en Nueva España (1772–1783). Intro. by Victor Rico González. Universidad Nacional Autónoma de México, Instituto de Historia. Editorial Jus, México, 1949.

DONOHUE, JOHN AUGUSTINE, S.J.
After Kino, Jesuit Missions in Northwestern New Spain, 1711–1767. Jesuit Historical Institute, Rome, 1969.

_____. *Jesuit Missions in Northwestern New Spain, 1711–1767.* Typescript dissertation for Ph.D., University of California, Berkeley, 1957.

_____. "The Unlucky Jesuit Mission of Bac, 1732–1767," *Arizona and the West*, Vol. 2, No. 2, Summer, 1960, pp. 127–139.

DONOVAN, FRANK. See KERR.

DUCRUE, BENNO, S.J.
Ducrue's Account of the Expulsion of the Jesuits from Lower California (1767–1769). An Annotated English Translation of Benno Ducrue's *Relatio Expulsionis*. Tr. & ed. Ernest J. Burrus, S.J., Jesuit Historical Institute, Rome, 1967.

DUNNE, PETER MASTEN, S.J.
   Black Robes in Lower California. University of California Press, Berkeley and
   Los Angeles, 1952.
————. *Early Jesuit Missions in Tarahumara*. University of California Press,
   Berkeley and Los Angeles, 1948.
————. "The Expulsion of the Jesuits from New Spain, 1767," *Mid-America*,
   January 1937, Vol. 19 (New Series, Vol. 8), No. 1, pp. 3–30.
————. *Juan Antonio Balthasar—Padre Visitador to the Sonora Frontier, 1744–
   1745: Two Original Reports*. Arizona Pioneers' Historical Society, Tucson,
   1957.
————. *Pioneer Jesuits in Northern Mexico*. University of California Press,
   Berkeley and Los Angeles, 1944.
————. "Pioneer Jesuit Missionaries on the Central Plateau of New Spain,"
   Greater America, Essays in Honor of Herbert Eugene Bolton, University of
   California Press, Berkeley and Los Angeles, 1945, pp. 163–180.
————. "Salvatierra's Legacy to Lower California," *The Americas*, Vol. VII, No.
   1, July, 1950, pp. 31–50.
————. "Tomás de Guadalajara, Missionary of the Tarahumares," *Mid-America*,
   October 1941, Vol. 23 (New Series, Vol. 12), pp. 272–287.
Encyclopaedia Britannica. 15th Ed., 30 vols. Encyclopaedia Britannica, Inc.,
   Chicago, 1974.
ESCALONA, JOSÉ, S.J.
   Report, June 7, 1744, in Bolton (Maggs) Collection, Bancroft Library, Uni-
   versity of California, Berkeley.
*Estado de esta Visitación de Nuestra Señora del Pilar de Norogáchic hasta la presente
   visita del P. Visitador General Joseph de Herrera*. MS., n.d., in W. B. Stevens
   Collection, No. 684, University of Texas Library, Latin American Collec-
   tion, Austin.
FERGUSON, GEORGE.
   Signs & Symbols in Christian Art. Oxford University Press, New York, 1961.
FERNÁNDEZ, LUIS, S.J.
   *Padrón de las Personas de Confesión, que tiene este Partido de San Gerónimo
   Guexotitlán, Año de 1690*, in AHH, *Temp*., leg. 279, ex. 113.
FERNÁNDEZ ABEÉ, JULIÁN ISIDRO, S.J.
   *Razón de la Fundación y Progresos que ha venido esta Misión de Jesús Cárichic desde
   el día 8 de Noviembre del año de 1675*. Cárichic, July 8, 1744, in Bol-
   ton (Maggs) Collection, Bancroft Library, University of California,
   Berkeley.
FERNÁNDEZ RETANA, JUAN.
   Auto hecho en la visita del Pueblo de Papigóchic, en 1 de Diciembre del año 1700,
   in Arch., *Parral*.
————. *Report, En el Pueblo de Papigóchic, en cuatro días del mes de Enero de 1701
   años*, in Arch., *Parral*.
FIGUEROA, GERÓNIMO, S.J.
   *Puntos de Anua de estos Diez Años que he Asistido en este Partido de San Pablo, de
   la Misión de Taraumares y Tepeaunes (de unas y otras hay), desde el Año de
   1652 Hasta este de 1662 Sumariamente lo que ha pasado cuanto a lo Es-
   piritual*, in Doc. Hist. Méx., 4a ser., III, pp. 217–222.

_____. *Puntos de Anua de esta Misión de Taraumares de la Compañía de Jesús de estos Años Proximos Pasados, Hecha a Catorce de Noviembre de 1668,* in *Doc. Hist. Méx.,* 4a ser., III, p. 223–230.

FLINT, F. S. See FÜLÖP-MILLER.

FRÍAS, HERIBERTO.
Tomóchic. Editorial Porrúa, S.A., México, 1968.

FRIED, JACOB.
"The Tarahumara," *Handbook of Middle American Indians,* Vol. 8, Ethnology, Pt. 2, University of Texas Press, Austin, 1969, pp. 846–870.

FÜLÖP-MILLER, RENÉ.
The Power and Secret of the Jesuits. Tr. F. S. Flint and D. F. Tait, George Braziller, Inc., New York, 1956.

GAJDUSEK, D. CARLETON.
"The Sierra Tarahumara," *Geographical Review,* Vol. 43, No. 1, January 1953, pp. 15–38.

GAMBOA, JUAN MANUEL, S.J.
Carta de edificación a la muerte del P. Fernando de Barrionuevo. Querétaro, July 8, 1686, in APM, and in Zambrano, Vol. IV, pp. 39–40.

GERA, LORENZO, S.J.
Carta a mi amo P. Roque de Andonaegui. Norogachi, Mayo 30 de 1747, in AGN, *Hist.,* tomo 333.

_____. *Carta a mi Padre Andrés Xavier Garzía de la Compañía de Jesus, Provincial de esta Provincia de Nueva España.* Norogatzi, Octubre 18 de 1747, in AGN, *Hist.,* tomo 333.

_____. *Carta a mi amo Padre Provincial Andres Xavier Garzia.* Norogachi, Octubre 25 de 1747, in AGN, *Hist.,* tomo 333.

GIRÓN, LUIS TÉLLEZ, S.J. See TÉLLEZ GIRÓN.

GLANDORFF, FRANCISCO HERMANO, S.J.
Carta Annua Missionis Tohomochensio. August 16, 1730. In AGN, *Hist.,* tomo 308, pp. 862–865.

_____. *Carta al mi amadisso Padre Vr Lorenzo Gera.* Tutuaca, Feb. 2 de 1747. In AGN, *Hist.,* tomo 333, p. 390.

_____. *Carta al mi amantisso Padre Vr Lorenzo Gera.* Tomotzí, Junio 12 de 1747. In AGN, *Hist.,* tomo 333, pp. 388–389.

_____. *Carta al mi amantisso Padre Provincial Andres Xavier de García,* Tomotzi, July 6 de 1747. In AGN, *Hist.,* tomo 333, pp. 399–401.

_____. *Carta a mi amantisimo Padre Provincial Andres Xavier García.* Tomobis, 15 de 7b, de 1749. In AGN, *Hist.,* tomo 333, pp. 212–213.

_____. *Letter to Very Reverend Father Sixtus Hesselmeier,* Tomotzi, June 18, 1752. Original (Latin) is Jesuitica No. 283, *Bavarian Haupstaatarchiv,* Munich; typescript in Bolton Collection, Bancroft Library, University of California, Berkeley.

_____. *Memoria,* n.d., signed by José María Miqueo, S.J., in AHH, *Temp.,* leg. 321, ex. 35.

GÓMEZ GONZÁLEZ, FILIBERTO.
Rarámuri, Mi Diario Tarahumara. Talleres Tipográficos de Excelsior, México, 1948.

GONZÁLEZ, VICTOR RICO. See *Documentos sobre la Expulsión.*

GONZÁLEZ NOBOA, DOMINGO ANTONIO.
  Carta al Señor Don Gabriel Gutiérrez de Riba. Villa, June 22, 1747, in AGN, *Hist.*, tomo 333.

———. *Carta al Señor Don Gabriel Gutiérrez de Ruia.* Villa, July 3, 1747, in AGN, *Hist.*, tomo 333.

GONZÁLEZ, RODRÍGUEZ, LUIS, S.J.
  Introduction and notes to *Revoltes des Indiens Tarahumaras (1626–1724)* by José Neumann, S.J. Typescript dissertation, Univ. of Paris, 1962.

GUADALAJARA, TOMÁS, S.J.
  Carta al mi Padre Provincial. Triunfo de los Angeles, Julio 20 de 1677 años. In AGN, *Mis.*, tomo 26.

———. *Informe del Padre Tomás de Guadalajara al Padre provincial Bernardo Pardo.* San Joseph de Parral, diziembre 4 de 1684 años. In ARSJ, *Mexicana*, and in ABZ, Vol. IV, pp. 463–465.

GUADALAJARA, TOMÁS, S.J., and TARDÁ, JOSÉ, S.J.
  Carta, October 14, 1675, in Bolton Collection, Bancroft Library, University of California, Berkeley.

———. *Carta de los Padres Joseph Tardá y Tomás de Guadalaxara, Missioneros de la nación Tarahumara escrita al Padre Francisco Ximenes Provincial de la Compañía de Jhs de la Provincia de la Nueva España; su fecha de dos de febrero de 1676.* In AGN, *Mis.*, tomo 26.

GUENDULÁIN, JUAN, S.J.
  Carta del Padre San Juan de Guenduláin al Provincial Gaspar Roder. Cocorim, Diciembre 22 de 1725. In *Doc. Hist. Méx.*, 4a ser., IV, pp. 22–23.

GUITÉRAS, EUSEBIO. See NENTVIG, *Rudo Ensayo.*

GUTIÉRREZ, BERNABÉ FRANCISCO, S.J.
  Carta escrita por el Padre Bernave Francisco Gutiérrez, Visitador de las Missiones de la Compañia de Jhs al Padre Francisco Ximenez Provencial de la Provencia de la Nueva España de dicha Compañia fecha de 28 de Abril de 1676. In AGN, *Mis.*, tomo 26.

GUTIÉRREZ CASILLAS, JOSÉ, S.J.
  Jesuitas en México durante el Siglo XIX. Editorial Porrúa, S.A., México, 1972.

———. *Santarén, Conquistador Pacífico.* Editorial Jus, S.A., México, 1964.

———. See ZAMBRANO and GUTIÉRREZ CASILLAS.

GUTIÉRREZ RUIZ, GABRIEL.
  Carta al M. R. Padre Blas de la Palma. San Ygnacio, Julio 12 de 1747. In AGN, *Hist.*, tomo 333.

HACKETT, CHARLES WILSON. See *Historical Documents.*

HAMMOND, GEORGE P. See PÍCOLO, *Informe on the New Province.*

HAMMOND, GEORGE P. and REY, AGAPITO.
  Don Juan de Oñate, Colonizer of New Mexico, 1595–1628. Coronado Cuarto Centennial Publications, 1540–1940, The University of New Mexico Press, Albuquerque, 2 vols., 1953.

Handbook of American Indians North of Mexico. Ed. Frederick Webb Hodge, Pageant Books, New York, 2 vols., 1959.

HERRERA, ANTONIO, S.J.
Carta al Sr. Gobernador Don Juan Fernández de Retana, Santa Cruz, Noviembre 19 de 1700. In Arch., *Parral.*

HIERRO, JUAN MANUEL DEL, S.J.
Carta a Mi Padre Provincial Andrex Xavier García. S. Xavier de Temotzaziki, Junio 29 de 1747. In AGN, *Hist.,* tomo 333.

————. *Carta a Mi Padre Provincial Andrés Xavier García.* S. Xavier de Temotzaziki, Agosto 23 de 1747. In AGN, *Hist.,* tomo 333.

————. *Carta a Mi Padre Provincial Andrex Xavier García.* S. Francisco Xavier de Temotzaziki, Agosto 30 de 1747. In AGN, *Hist.,* tomo 333.

————. *Carta a Mi Padre Provincial Andrex Xavier Garcia.* S. Xavier de Temotzatziki, Nov. 8 de 1747. In AGN, *Hist.,* tomo 333.

HILTON, KENNETH S.
El Nuevo Testamento de Nuestro Señor Jesucristo. La Biblioteca Mexicana del Hogar, México, 1972.

————. *Los Evangelios y los Hechos de los Apóstoles.* Sociedad Bíblica de México, México, 1969.

————. *Vocabulario Tarahumara.* Instituto Lingüístico de Verano, México, 1959.

HILTON, KENNETH S. and PAUL CARLSON.
Rarámuri Nahuajíhuara. Wycliffe Bible Translators, Santa Ana, California, 1962.

HILTON, KENNETH S. and MARTHA HILTON.
Alfabeto Tarahumara. Wycliffe Bible Translators, Santa Ana, California, 1948.

————. *Rarámuri Orisúami.* Wycliffe Bible Translators, Santa Ana, California, 1950.

————. *Rarámuri Oseríame.* Wycliffe Bible Translators, Santa Ana, California, 1948.

Historical Documents relating to New Mexico, Nueva Vizcaya, and Approaches Thereto, to 1773. Col. by Adolph F. A. and Fanny R. Bandelier; ed. with intro. and anno. by Charles Wilson Hackett. Carnegie Institution of Washington, Washington, D.C., 3 vols., Vol. I, 1923; Vol. II, 1926; Vol. III, 1937.

HODGE, FREDERICK WEBB. See *Handbook of American Indians.*

HOSTINSKY, JORGE, S.J.
Memoria, April 21, 1725, in AHH, *Temp.,* leg. 321, ex. 50.

————. *Memoria, March 20, 1726,* in AHH, *Temp.,* leg. 282, ex. 24.

JANUSKE, DANIEL, S.J.
Breve Informe del Estado Presente en Que Se Hallan las Missiones de esta Provincia, c. 1723, in AHH, *Temp.,* leg. 278, ex. 2.

JOHN, ERIC. See *The Popes.*

JORDÁN, FERNANDO.
Crónica de un País Bárbaro. Talleres de B. Costa-Amic, Editor, México, 1967.

KARNS, HARRY J. See MANJE.

KENNEDY, JOHN G.
Inápuchi, una Comunidad Tarahumara Gentil. Instituto Indigenista Interamericano, México, 1970.

KENNEDY, JOHN G.
"La carrera de bola tarahumara y su significación," *América Indígena,* Vol. XXIX, No. 1, January, 1969, pp. 17–42.

———. "Tesguino Complex: The Role of Beer in Tarahumara Culture," *American Anthropologist,* Vol. 65, No. 3, June 1963, pp. 620–640.

KERR, JOHN LEEDS, with FRANK DONOVAN.
Destination Topolobampo, The Kansas City, Mexico & Orient Railway. Golden West Books, San Marino, California, 1968.

KIMBALL, J. P.
The Silver Mines of Cusihuiriáchic, Chihuahua, México. E. V. Armstrong & Co., Printers, New York, *circa* 1860.

KINNAIRD, LAWRENCE. See LAFORA, *The Frontiers of New Spain.*

KINO, EUSEBIO FRANCISCO, S.J.
Kino's Historical Memoir of Pimería Alta, A Contemporary Account of the Beginnings of California, Sonora, and Arizona. Tr., Ed. and Annot. Herbert Eugene Bolton. University of California Press, Berkeley and Los Angeles, 1948, two volumes in one.

KIRCHOFF, PAUL, with Comments by Ralph L. Beals, A. L. Kroeber and Carl O. Sauer.
"Gatherers and Farmers in the Greater Southwest: A Problem in Classification," *American Anthropologist,* Vol. 56, No. 4, 1954, pp. 529–560.

KROEBER, A. L.
Uto-Aztecan Languages of Mexico. University of California Press, Berkeley, and Cambridge University Press, London, 1934.

———. See KIRCHOFF.

LAFORA, NICOLÁS DE.
Relación del Viaje que Hizo a los Presidios Internos Situados en la Frontera de la América Septentrional Perteneciente al Rey de España. Ed., bib. & anot. Vito Alessio Robles, Editorial Pedro Robredo, México, 1939.

———. *The Frontiers of New Spain, Nicolás de Lafora's Description, 1766–1768.* Tr. and ed. Lawrence Kinnaird, The Quivira Society, Berkeley. The University of New Mexico Printing Plant, Albuquerque, 1958.

LARREA, LUIS BANDA. See BANDA LARREA.

LARREA Y LA PUENTE, JUAN BAUTISTA.
Auto. En el Real de San Joseph del Parral, 25 días del mes de Enero de 1701 años, in Arch., *Parral.*

———. *Auto con Junta de Capitanes.* En el pueblo de Papigochic de la Tarahumara, a catorce días del mes de Febrero de 1701 años, in Arch., *Parral.*

LEÓN, JOSÉ M. PONCE DE. See PONCE DE LEÓN.

Letras Annuas de la Provincia de la Compañía de Jesús en México, Año de 1646, in AGN, *Mis,* tomo 26.

Letras Annuas de la Provincia de la Compañía de Jesús en México. Año de 1667, in AGN, *Mis,* tomo 26.

Libro de Bautismos de Cárichic. In *Archivo de la Iglesia,* Cárichic.

Libro de Bautismos de Papigóchic. In *Archivo de la Purísima Concepción,* Ciudad Guerrero.

Libro de Bautismos de Santo Tomás. In *Archivo de la Purísima Concepción,* Ciudad Guerrero.

Libro de Bautismos de Temeýchic. In *Archivo de la Purísima Concepción,* Ciudad Guerrero.

Libro de Casamientos de Cárichic. In *Archivo de la Iglesia,* Cárichic.

Libro de Casamientos de Santo Tomás. In *Archivo de la Purísima Concepción,* Ciudad Guerrero.

Libro de Difuntos de Cárichic. In *Archivo de la Iglesia,* Cárichic.

Libro de la Parroquia de Norogáchic. In *Archivo de la Misión,* Sisoguíchic.

Libros Parroquiales de Cárichic. In *Archivo de la Iglesia,* Cárichic.

Libros Parroquiales de Santo Tomás. In *Archivo de la Purísima Concepción,* Ciudad Guerrero.

LISTER, FLORENCE C. and ROBERT H. LISTER.
Chihuahua, Storehouse of Storms. The University of New Mexico Press, Albuquerque, 1966.

LIZASOAÍN, TOMÁS IGNACIO, S.J.
Informe del Padre Lizasaoín sobre las Provincias de Sonora y Nueva Vizcaya. Doc. Hist. Méx., 3a ser., 1856, pp. 683–702.

————. *Noticia de la visita general de P. Ignacio Lizasoaín, Visitador General de las Missiones de esta Prov. de Nueva España q. comenzó día quatro de Abril de 1761 ans. y se concluyo a finis de Henero de 1763 con algunas notas y addiciones q. pueden servir pa. el conocimiento de estas Missiones y Provincias de ellas.* W. B. Stevens Collection, University of Texas Library, Austin.

LÓPEZ, RAÚL A.
"Tarahumara Ritual Aesthetic Manifestations," *The Kiva,* Vol. 37, No. 4, Summer 1972, pp. 207–223, Tucson.

LORESÓN, DIEGO PADILLA. See PADILLA LORESÓN.

LUMHOLTZ, CARL.
"Among the Tarahumaris—The American Cave-Dwellers," *Scribner's,* Vol. XVI, July 1894, pp. 31–48.

————. "Cave-Dwellers of the Sierra Madre," *Proceedings of the International Congress of Anthropology,* Chicago, 1894, pp. 100–112.

————. "Explorations in the Sierra Madre," *Scribner's,* Vol. X, No. 5, November, 1891, pp. 531–548.

————. "Mr. Carl Lumholtz in Northern Mexico," *Bulletin of the American Geographical Society,* 1893, pp. 64–65.

————. "Report on Explorations in Northern Mexico," *Bulletin of the American Geographical Society,* 1891, pp. 386–402.

————. "Tarahumari Dances and Plant Worship," *Scribner's,* Vol. XVI, No. 4, October 1894, pp. 438–456.

————. "Tarahumari Life and Customs," *Scribner's,* Vol. XVI, September 1894, pp. 296–311.

————. "Tarahumari Runners," *American Anthropologist,* Vol. VIII, January 1895, p. 92.

————. "The American Cave-Dwellers: The Tarahumaris of the Sierra Madre," *Bulletin of the American Geographical Society,* Vol. XXVI, No. 3, 1894, pp. 299–325.

————. *Unknown Mexico, A Record of Five Years' Exploration Among the Tribes of the Western Sierra Madre; in the Tierra Caliente of Tepic and Jalisco; and Among the Tarascos of Michoacan.* Charles Scribner's Sons, New York, 2 vols., 1902.

LLAGUNO, JOSÉ A., S.J.
La personalidad jurídica del indio y el III Concilio Provincial Mexicano (1585).
Editorial Porrúa, S. A., México, 1963.

LLAGUNO, RODRIGO J., S.J.
Change in the Tarahumara Family: The Influence of the Railroad. Typescript
thesis for M.A., Louisiana State University, June 1971.

MCSHANE, CATHERINE MARY, R.S.C.J.
"Hernando de Santarén, S.J., Pioneer and Diplomat, 1565–1616," *Greater
America, Essays in Honor of Herbert Eugene Bolton,* University of Califor-
nia Press, Berkeley and Los Angeles, 1945, pp. 145–161.

MANJE, JUAN MATEO.
Luz de Tierra Incógnita. Tr. Harry J. Karns, Arizona Silhouettes, Tucson,
1954.

MÁRQUEZ, PEDRO. See ZELIS.

MARTÍNEZ, MAXIMINO.
Los Pinos Mexicanos, Ediciones Botas, México, 1948.

MARTINI, PEDRO ANTONIO, S.J.
Carta al Mi Padre Procurador Antonio Garcia, Norogachic, Abril 17 de 1725,
in AHH, *Temp.,* leg. 321, ex. 41.

MASON, J. ALDEN.
"The Classification of the Sonoran Languages," with an Appendix by B. L.
Whorf, *Essays in Anthropology in Honor of Alfred Louis Kroeber,* Univer-
sity of California Press, Berkeley and Los Angeles, 1936.

MAYER, VINCENT, JR.
The Black on New Spain's Northern Frontier: San José de Parral 1631 to 1641,
Occasional Papers of the Center of Southwest Studies, Fort Lewis Col-
lege, Durango, Colo., November 1974.

MEDRANO, FRANCISCO JAVIER, S.J.
*Memoria de lo que tiene en lo temporal esta Missión de las Bocas de la Nación
Tarahumara,* in AHH, *Temp.,* leg. 279, ex. 69.

———. *Petition, Al Gobernador y Capitán General,* in Arch., *Parral.*

MENDÍVIL, LORENZO, S.J.
Carta y Memoria a Mi Padre Procurador Joseph Ferrer, Satebó, Mayo 18 de
1726, in AHH, *Temp.,* leg. 282, ex. 83.

MIQUEO, JOSÉ, S.J.
Report, October 28, 1744, to Lorenzo Gera, S.J., in Bolton (Maggs) Collection, Bancroft Library, University of California, Berkeley.

MORENO, ILDEFONSO MIGUEL.
Bando en el Pueblo de San Filipe, in treinta y un días del mes de Julio de Mil
Setecientos veintinueve años, in Arch., *Parral.*

National Geographic Atlas of the World. National Geographic Society, Washington,
D. C., 1970.

NEIRA QUIROGA, JOSÉ.
Autos y Vistas de Ellos. En el Real de Minas de San Joseph del Parral, seis de
Junio de mil seiscientos ochenta y cinco años. In Arch., *Parral.*

NENTVIG, JUAN, S.J.
Descripción Geográfica de Sonora. Ed., Intro., Notas, Apend. y Index Germán
Viveros. Publicaciones del Archivo General de la Nación, México,
1971.

————. *Rudo Ensayo, Tentativa de una Prevencional Descripcion Geographica de la Provincia de Sonora, Sus Terminos y Confines; ó mejor, Coleccion de Materiales para Hacerla Quien lo Supiere Mejor.* Ed. Buckingham Smith, San Augustin de la Florida, Munsell, Printer, Albany, 1863. Tr. Eusebio Guitéras and pub. as Vol. V, No. 2, Records of the American Catholic Historical Society of Philadelphia, Philadelphia, June 1894; republished by Arizona Silhouettes, Tucson, 1951.

NEUMANN, JOSÉ, S.J.
Historia Seditionum quas Adversus Societatis Jesu Missionarios, eorumq. Auxiliares Moverunt Nationes Indicae ac Potissimum Tarahumara in America Septentrionali, Regnoque Nova Cantabriae, jam Toto ad fidem Catholicam propemodum redacto, Auctore P. Josepho Neymanno Ejusdem Societatis Jesu in Partibus Tarahumarorum Missionario. Typis Univers. Carolo-Ferd. Soc. Jesu, ad S. Clem., Prague 1724. Tr. (Eng.) Marion L. Reynolds, typescript, n.d., in Herbert E. Bolton Papers, Bancroft Library, University of California, Berkeley.

————. *Letters* col. by Herbert Eugene Bolton, tr. Marion L. Reynolds, ed. with intro. by Allan Christelow, typescript, 1936, in Herbert E. Bolton Papers, Bancroft Library, University of California, Berkeley.

————. Letter, January 15, 1681. Copies in *Archives of Moravia*, Brno, MS, No. 557, VI, fol. 37, and in Bolton Collection, Bancroft Library, University of California, Berkeley. (Letter No. I of NEUMANN, *Letters.*).

————. Letter, February 20, 1682. Copies in Strahov Monastery of the Praemonstratensian Order, Prague, DH IV.5, in private Library of Dr. E. Lange, Broumov, Bohemia KIA 30, MS. 410, and in Bolton Collection, Bancroft Library, University of California, Berkeley. (Letter No. II of NEUMANN, *Letters.*)

————. Letter, July 29, 1686. Copies in Praha, Hradni archiv 419, in Stocklein, No. 32, and in Bolton Collection, Bancroft Library, University of California, Berkeley. (Letter No. III of NEUMANN, *Letters.*)

————. Letter, February 4, 1690. Copies in AGN, *Mis.,* tomo 26, núm. 120, and in Bolton Collection, Bancroft Library, University of California, Berkeley. (Letter No. IV of NEUMANN, *Letters.*)

————. Letter, July 6, 1693. Copies in *Archives of Moravia*, Brünn, MS., No. 550, Vol. VI, fol. 19; and in Bolton Collection, Bancroft Library, University of California, Berkeley. (Letter No. VI of NEUMANN, *Letters.*)

————. Letter, September 15, 1693. Copies in *Bavarian Haupstaatarchiv*, Munich, Jesuitica No. 283, and in Bolton Collection, Bancroft Library, University of California, Berkeley. (Letter No. V of NEUMANN, *Letters.*)

————. Letter, April 23, 1698. Copies in *Austrian Staatsarchiv*, Jesuitica, no. 294, and in Bolton Collection, Bancroft Library, University of California, Berkeley. (Letter No. VII of NEUMANN, *Letters.*)

————. Letter, May 30, 1723. Copies in Arch., *Parral*, and in Bolton Collection, Bancroft Library, University of California, Berkeley. (Unindexed letter in NEUMANN, *Letters.*)

————. *Revoltes des Indiens Tarahumars (1626–1724).* Latin text, tr. (Fr.), intro. and notes by Luis González Rodríguez, S.J. Typescript dissertation for Ph.D., Paris, 1962.

Noboa, Domingo Antonio González. See González Noboa.

Nominas de los Indios que contienen las misiones que administran los Reverendos Padres de la Compañía de Jesús. — Remitido al Gobernador Barrutia. In Arch., *Parral.*

Ocampo, Manuel, S.J.
  Historia de la Misión de la Tarahumara (1900–1965). Editorial Jus, S. A., México, 1966.

Och, Joseph, S.J.
  Missionary in Sonora, the Travel Reports of Joseph Och, S.J., 1755–1767. Tr. and annot. Theodore E. Treutlein, California Historical Society, San Francisco, 1965.

Olave, José.
  Report. En el Pueblo de Norogachis, March 21, 1719, in Arch., *Parral.*

Oliva, Juan Paulo, S.J.
  Respuesta de N.M.R.P. Juan Paulo Oliva, Prepósito General de la Compañía de Jesús, a Varios Postulados, que le Propuso el P. Juan de Monrroy, Procurador de la Provincia de México, Roma, Diziembre 31, 1677. In ARSJ, Congregatio 79, fols. 155–158. Also in ABZ, Vol. III, pp. 407–409.

Ortiz Zapata, Juan, S.J.
  Relación de las misiones que la Compañía de Jesús tiene en el reino y provincia de la Nueva Vizcaya en la Nueva España, hecha el año de 1678 con ocasion de visita general de ellas, que por orden del padre provincial Tomás Altamirano, hizo el padre visitador Juan Ortiz Zapata de la misma Compañía. In *Doc. Hist. Méx.*, 4a ser., III, pp. 301–419.

Osorio, Francisco, S.J.
  Carta a Mi Padre Visitador Juan Manuel de Hierro. Coyachi, Junio 19 de 1747. In AGN, *Hist.*, tomo 333.

———. *Report.* Misión de Papigóchic, 1744, in Bolton (Maggs) Collection, Bancroft Library, University of California, Berkeley.

Padilla Loresón, Diego.
  Carta al M. Reverendo Padre Roque Andonagui. Cusigiárichi, Junio 15 de 1747. In AGN, *Hist.*, tomo 333.

Palma, Blas de la, S.J.
  Carta a Mi am. Padre Provincial Andres Xavier García. Sto. Thomas, Octubre 28 de 1747. In AGN, *Hist.*, tomo 333.

Pascual, José, S.J.
  Noticias de las Misiones Sacadas de la Anua del Padre José Pascual, Año de 1651, in *Doc. Hist. Méx.*, 4a ser., III, pp. 179–209.

———. *Respuesta del Padre Rector Joseph Pasqual a la peticion de el Promotor Fiscal de el Señor Obispo,* Parral, Julio 12 de 64. In AHH, *Temp.*, leg. 325, ex. 56.

Pennington, Campbell W.
  "La carrera de bola entre los tarahumaras de México. Un problema de difusión." Tr. Demetrio Sodi. *América Indígena*, Vol. XXX, No. 1, January, 1970, pp. 15–40.

———. *The Tarahumar of Mexico, Their Environment and Material Culture.* University of Utah Press, Salt Lake City, 1963.

———. *The Tarahumara.* MS. prepared for *Handbook of North American Indians,* Smithsonian Institution, Washington, D. C., 1972.

_____. *The Tepehuán of Chihuahua, Their Material Culture*. University of Utah Press, Salt Lake City, 1969.

PEÑA, BALTHASAR DE LA, S.J.
   Memoir, April 12, 1727, in AHH, *Temp.*, leg. 321, ex. 37.

PÉREZ DE RIVAS, ANDRÉS, S.J.
   Crónica y Historia Religiosa de la Provincia de la Compañía de Jesús de México en Nueva España, Fundación de sus Colegios y Casas, Ministerios que en ellos se exercitan y frutos gloriosos que con el favor de la Divina gracia se han cogido, y Varones insignes que trabajando con fervores santos en esta Viña del Señor pasaron á gozar el premio de sus santas obras á la gloria: unos derramando su sangre por la predicación del santo Evangelio, y otros exercitando los Ministerios que el Instituto de la Compañía de Jesús profesa, hasta el año de 1654. Imprenta del Sagrado Corazón de Jesús, México, 2 vols., 1896.

_____. *Historia de los Triunfos de Nuestra Santa Fe entre Gentes las más Bárbaras y fieras del Nuevo Orbe; conseguidos por los soldados de la Milicia de la Compañía de JESUS en las Misiones de la Provincia de Nueva España.* Alonso de Paredes Junto a los Estudios de la Compañía. Madrid, 1645. Reprinted Editorial Layac, México. 3 vols. 1944.

_____. *My Life Among the Savage Nations of New Spain.* Tr. and condensed Tomás Antonio Robertson, The Ward Ritchie Press, Los Angeles, 1968.

PÍCOLO, FRANCISCO MARÍA, S.J.
   Informe del Estado de la Nueva Cristiandad de California 1702 y Otros Documentos. Ed. & notes Ernest J. Burrus, S.J., Ediciones José Porrúa Turanzas, Madrid, 1962.

_____. *Informe on the New Province of California, 1702.* Tr., ed. George P. Hammond, Dawson's Book Shop, Los Angeles, 1967.

_____. *Nomina de los hijos Tarahumares Baptizados que al presente administra el Padre Francisco Maria Picolo su Ministro.* Pueblo de Jesus Carichic, 4 de Diciembre de 1690. In AHH, *Temp.*, leg. 279, ex. 64.

PINELI, LUIS MARÍA, S.J.
   Carta, August 23, 1698, in Arch., *Parral.*

PLANCARTE, FRANCISCO M.
   El Problema Indígena Tarahumara. Ediciones del Instituto Nacional Indigenista, México, 1954.

PONCE DE LEÓN, JOSÉ M.
   "Nombres Geográficos de Origen Tarahumara usados en Chihuahua," *Anales del Museo Nacional*, tomo II, México, 1924.

The Popes, A Concise Biographical History. Ed. Eric John. Hawthorn Books, New York, 1964.

PRADEAU, ALBERTO FRANCISCO.
   La Expulsión de los Jesuitas de las Provincias de Sonora, Ostimuri y Sinaloa en 1767. José Porrúa & Hijos, México, 1959.

_____. *Relación de los Jesuitas en el Noroeste de Nueva España.* MS., cited in Zambrano, Vol. VII, p. 430.

_____. *Noticias sobre Jesuitas en el Noroeste de Nueva España.* MS., cited in Zambrano, Vol. X, p. 697.

QUIROGA, JOSÉ NEIRA. See NEIRA QUIROGA.

RAMOS, FRANCISCO XAVIER, S.J.
   Report on San Pablo, 1745, in Bolton Collection, Bancroft Library, University of California, Berkeley.

RATKAY, JUAN MARÍA, S.J.
   An Account of the Tarahumara Missions, and a Description of the Tribe of the Tarahumaras and of their Country. Cárichic, March 20, 1683. Tr. Marion L. Reynolds. Bolton Papers, Bancroft Library, University of California, Berkeley.

   Report on San Francisco de Borja, 1744. In Bolton (Maggs) Collection, Bancroft Library, University of California, Berkeley.

   Report on Tomotzi, 1744. In Bolton (Maggs) Collection, Bancroft Library, University of California, Berkeley.

RETANA, JUAN FERNÁNDEZ. See FERNÁNDEZ RETANA.

REY, AGAPITO. See HAMMOND and REY.

REYNOLDS, MARION L. See NEUMANN, *Historia.*

————. See NEUMANN, *Letters.*

————. See RATKAY.

REZAWAL, ANDRÉS.
   Carta. Pueblo de Moris, 23 de Diciembre de 1698 años. In Arch., *Parral.*
   ————. *Carta al Amigo y señor mío.* n.p. n.d. In Arch., *Parral.*

RICO GONZÁLEZ, VICTOR. See *Documentos sobre la Expulsión.*

RINALDINI, BENITO, S.J.
   Relación de la Fundación, Aumento, y Estado Presente de Estas dos Missiones de Navogame y Baburigame, MS., W. B. Stevens Collection, No. 1771, University of Texas Library, Austin.

RIVAS, ANDRÉS PÉREZ DE, S.J. See PÉREZ DE RIVAS.

ROBERTSON, TOMÁS A. See PÉREZ DE RIVAS, *My Life.*

ROBLES, VITO ALESSIO. See LAFORA, *Relación.*

————. See TAMARÓN Y ROMERAL.

ROCA, ILDEFONSO, S.J.
   El Mártir P. Juan Font de la Compañía de Jesús. Librería Religiosa, Barcelona, 1924.

ROCA, PAUL M.
   Paths of the Padres Through Sonora, An Illustrated History & Guide to its Spanish Churches. Arizona Pioneers' Historical Society, Tucson, 1967.

RODRÍGUEZ, LUIS GONZÁLEZ, S.J. See GONZÁLEZ RODRÍQUEZ.

ROLANDEGUI, BERNARDO, S.J.
   Carta a Mi Padre provincial Benardo Pardo. México, 14 de Febrero de 1682 años. In ARSJ, *Mexicana*, 8. f. 314v and in ABZ, Vol. IV, pp. 466–472.

ROMERAL, PEDRO TAMARÓN Y. See TAMARÓN Y ROMERAL.

RUIZ, GABRIEL GUTIÉRREZ. See GUTIÉRREZ RUIZ.

The Saints, A Concise Biographical Dictionary. Ed. John Coulson, Hawthorn Books, New York, 1960.

SALVATIERRA, JUAN MARÍA, S.J.
   Selected Letters about Lower California. Tr., annot. & intro. Ernest J. Burrus, S.J. Dawson's Book Shop, Los Angeles, 1971.

SÁNCHEZ DE TAGLE, MARCOS ANDRÉS, S.J.
Carta a Mi Padre Provincial Andrés García. Cusiguriáchici, Julio 30 de 1747 años. In AGN, *Hist.*, tomo 333.

————. *Carta a Mi Padre Misionero Christobal Llamas de Escobar.* Santa Rosa de Cusiguriachi, Julio 30 de 1747 años. In AGN, *Hist.*, tomo 333.

SAN JUAN Y SANTA CRUZ, MANUEL.
Decree. Parral. January 18, 1718. In Arch., *Parral.*

————. *Order.* Real de Batopilas, February 16, 1719. In Arch., *Parral.*

SARAVIA, ATANASIO G.
Apuntes para la Historia de la Nueva Vizcaya, Tomo III, Las Sublevaciones. Manuel Porrua, S.A., México, 1954.

————. *Los Misioneros Muertos en el Norte de Nueva España.* Ediciones Botas, México. 1943.

SARMIENTO, JUAN, S.J.
Queja de los Indios del Pueblo de Satevó contra Valerio Cortez del Rey por Usurpación de Propriedades. Satevó, Febrero, veintiuno de mil seiscientos sesenta y siete años. In Arch., *Parral.*

SAUER, CARL O.
The Distribution of Aboriginal Tribes and Languages in Northwestern Mexico. University of California Press, Berkeley, 1934.

————. See KIRCHOFF.

SMITH, BUCKINGHAM. See NENTVIG, *Rudo Ensayo.*

SODI, DEMETRIO. See PENNINGTON, "La carrera de bola."

SPICER, EDWARD H.
Cycles of Conquest, The Impact of Spain, Mexico, and the United States on the Indians of the Southwest, 1533–1960. The University of Arizona Press, Tucson, 1962.

STIGER, GASPAR, S.J.
Declaración. Carichiquei, Mayo 31 del año de 1732. In Arch., *Parral.*

TAGLE, MARCOS ANDRÉS SÁNCHEZ DE, S.J. See SÁNCHEZ DE TAGLE.

TAIT, D. F. See FÜLÖP-MILLER.

TAMARÓN Y ROMERAL, PEDRO.
Demostración del Vastísimo Obispado de la Nueva Vizcaya–1765, Durango, Sinaloa, Sonora, Arizona, Nuevo Mexico, Chihuahua y Porciones de Texas, Coahuila y Zacatecas. Intro., biblio. & notes Vito Alessio Robles, José Porrúa e Hijos, México, 1937.

TAMAYO, JORGE L.
Carta general del Estado de Chihuahua, Librería Patria, México, n.d.

TÁPIZ, PEDRO.
Report of Visitation, February 15, 1715, to February 6, 1716, in *Archivo General de las Indias,* Sevilla, Audiencia de Guadalajara, 67-5-15.

TARDÁ, JOSÉ, S.J. See GUADALAJARA and TARDÁ.

TELLECHEA, MIGUEL, O.F.M.
Compendio Gramática para la Inteligencia del Idioma Tarahumara. Imprenta de la Federación en Palacio, México, 1826.

TÉLLEZ GIRÓN, LUIS, S.J.
Carta a Mi Padre Provincial Andrez Xavier García. San Borja, Agosto 16 de 1747. In AGN, *Hist.*, tomo 333.

358   Bibliography

TERRAZAS, SILVESTRE.
"El Gran Sabio y Santo Padre Glandorf en Chihuahua," *Boletín de la Sociedad Chihuahuense de Estudios Históricos*, Vol. II, July, 1940, pp. 375–377; December, 1940, pp. 408–411.

Testimonio Authentico sobre la entrega de las once Misiones de la Tepehuana y Tarahumara, hecha por la Sagrada Compañía de Jesús á la Sagrada Mitra De Durango Reyno de la Nueva Vizcaya. Vino con Carta de el Virrey de 9 de Marzo de 1755. In *Archivo General de las Indias*, Sevilla, Audiencia de Guadalajara, 67-4-2.

Thirteen Reports, Declarations and Certificates, dated September 24, 1967, through September 27, 1697, relating to the execution of eight Indian prisoners at Guadalupe. In Arch., *Parral*.

THORD-GRAY, I.
Tarahumara-English, English-Tarahumara Dictionary and an Introduction to Tarahumara Grammar. University of Miami Press, Coral Gables, Florida, 1955.

TÖMÖRDY, GYULA.
"Baron Josef Rátkay in the Land of the Tarahumar—Incas in 1682," *Hungarian Historical Review*, Vol. I, No. 2, February, 1970, pp. 40–47, tr. Lóránt Czigány.

TREUTLEIN, THEODORE EDWARD.
"Jesuit Travel to New Spain (1678–1756)," *Mid-America*, Vol. 19, (New Series Vol. 8), No. 2, April, 1937, pp. 104–123.

————. "Non-Spanish Jesuits in Spain's American Colonies," *Greater America, Essays in Honor of Herbert Eugene Bolton*, University of California Press, Berkeley and Los Angeles, 1945, pp. 219–242.

————. See OCH.

TRUEBA, ALFONSO.
Cabalgata Heroica, Misioneros Jesuitas en el Noroeste. Editorial Jus, S.A. México, 2 vols., 1961.

U. S. Army Map Service
Estados Unidos Mexicanos 1:250,000, Series F501, NG 13-1.

VALDÉS, FRANCISCO DÍAZ, S.J. See DÍAZ VALDÉS.

VARGAS REA. See CABEZA DE VACA.

VENEGAS, MIGUEL, S.J.
Juan María de Salvatierra of the Company of Jesus; Missionary in the Province of New Spain, and Apostolic Conqueror of the Californias. Tr., ed. & annot. Marguerite Eyer Wilbur, The Arthur H. Clark Company, Cleveland, 1929.

VERGARA BIANCHI, JOSÉ, S.J. See BRAMBILA.

VIVANCO, MANUEL, S.J.
Report, April 18, 1745, in Bolton (Maggs) Collection, Bancroft Library, University of California, Berkeley.

VIVEROS, GERVÁN. See NENTVIG, *Descripción*.

Webster's Biographical Dictionary. G. & C. Merriam Company, Springfield, Massachusetts, 1972.

WHORF, B. L. See MASON.

WILBUR, MARGUERITE EYER. See VENEGAS.

YDIÁQUEZ, ANTONIO, S.J.
Memoria. Nonohaba, Abril 15 de 1725. In AHH, *Temp.*, leg. 321, ex. 51.
————. *Report*. Nonoava, c. 1744. In *Papeles Relativos a los Jesuitas en Baja California y Otras Regiones Septentrionales de la Nueva España 1686–1793*, in Bolton (Maggs) Collection, Bancroft Library, University of California, Berkeley.

XAVIER RAMOS, FRANCISCO, S.J. See RAMOS.

ZAMBRANO, FRANCISCO, S.J.
Diccionario Bio-Bibliográfico de la Compañía de Jesús en México, tomo I, 1961; tomo II, 1962; Editorial Jus, S.A., México; tomo III, 1963, Buena Prensa, México; tomos IV & V, 1965; tomo VI, 1966; tomo VII, 1967; tomo VIII, 1968; tomo IX, 1969; tomo X, 1970; tomo XI, 1972, Editorial Jus, S.A., México.

ZAMBRANO, FRANCISCO, S.J., and GUTIÉRREZ CASILLAS, JOSÉ, S.J.
Diccionario Bio-Bibliográfico de la Compañía de Jesús en México. tomo XII, 1973; tomo XIII, 1974; tomo XIV, 1975; tomos XV & XVI, 1977, Editorial Tradición, S.A., México.

ZAPATA, JUAN ORTIZ. See ORTIZ ZAPATA.

ZÁRATE, FRANCISCO XAVIER, S.J.
Carta al Mui R. P. Provincial Andres Garcia. Cusiguariachic, Julio 28 de 1747 años. In AGN, *Hist.*, tomo 333.

ZELIS, RAFAEL, S.J., and MÁRQUEZ, PEDRO, S.J.
Catálogo de los Sugetos de la Compañía de Jesús que Formaran la Província de México el día del Arresto,25 de Junio de 1767. Imprenta de I. Escalante y Cia., México, 1871.

ZEPEDA, NICOLÁS, S.J.
Relación de lo sucedido en este reino de la Vizcaya desde el año de 1644 hasta el de 45 acerca de los alzamientos, daños, robos, hurtos muertes y lugares despoblados de que se sacó un traslado para remitir al padre Francisco Calderon, provincial de la provincia de México de la Compañía de Jesús. Y para que conste en todo tiempo como se le dió cuenta de todo como á superior, queda este original en esta mision de Taraumara, siendo superior de ella el padre Nicolás de Zepeda el cual despachó á México á 29 de Abril de este presente año de 1645. In *Doc. Hist. Méx.*, 4a ser., III, pp. 130–171.

ZINGG, ROBERT M. See BENNETT.

ZUBILLAGA, FELIX, S.J. See ALEGRE.

Index